Inside Nuclear South Asia

Inside Nuclear South Asia

Edited by Scott D. Sagan

STANFORD SECURITY STUDIES
An Imprint of Stanford University Press
Stanford, California

Stanford University Press
Stanford, California

Printed in the United States of America on acid-free, archival-quality paper

Library of Congress Cataloging-in-Publication Data

Inside nuclear South Asia / edited by Scott D. Sagan.
   p. cm.
  Includes bibliographical references and index.
  ISBN 978-0-8047-6238-0 (cloth : alk. paper) — ISBN 978-0-8047-6239-7 (pbk. : alk. paper)
  1. Nuclear weapons—South Asia. 2. South Asia—Military policy. 3. South Asia—Politics
and government. I. Sagan, Scott Douglas.
  UA832.7.I518 2009
  355.02'170954—dc22

2009010153

Typeset by Bruce Lundquist in 10/15 Minion

Special discounts for bulk quantities of Stanford Security Studies are available to
corporations, professional associations, and other organizations. For details and discount
information, contact the special sales department of Stanford University Press.
Tel: (650) 736-1783, Fax: (650) 736-1784

CONTENTS

ILLUSTRATIONS

Tables

Figures

ACKNOWLEDGMENTS

I HAVE MANY PEOPLE TO THANK, in addition to my contributing authors, for their important roles in producing *Inside Nuclear South Asia*. First, and foremost, I must thank my colleagues at Stanford's Center for International Security and Cooperation (CISAC) for maintaining such a stimulating intellectual environment and for providing opportunities to present my own work, and the research of the other contributing authors, in the social science seminars at Stanford. Siegfried Hecker, Christopher Chyba, and Lynn Eden have shared directing responsibilities with me at CISAC during the years that this book was written, and I thank them for enabling me to focus, for at least some portion of my time, on my own research and writing. Second, I thank Rupal Mehta, Josh Weddle, Kate Hadley, Oriana Mastro, Michael Orgil, Natasha Pereira-Kamath, and David Robbins for their excellent research assistance. Third, I want to thank the Strategic Studies Institute at the U.S. Army War College and the Carnegie Corporation of New York for providing funds to support a conference in which many of the authors were able to try out their ideas and receive feedback from each other. Fourth, I want to thank my many colleagues and friends in India and Pakistan, from whom I have learned so much over the years and who have maintained a constant spirit of intellectual cooperation even when we disagreed about the effects of nuclear weapons on South Asian security. I especially want to express my gratitude to V. R. Raghavan and K. Shankar Bajpai for hosting me at many seminars at the Delhi Policy Group and to Jehangir Karamat for arranging my meetings in Lahore and Islamabad.

Finally, I thank my wife, Sujitpan Bao Lamsam, and my children, Benjamin, Charlotte, and Samuel, for accepting that I will occasionally fly off to distant parts of the world to conduct research and have been, even more often, distracted at home by the books and papers I am reading about nuclear proliferation. I hope that my children will someday inherit a safer and more just world. If my scholarly work and that of my coauthors contribute, even in a small way, toward those lofty goals, I trust that my children will feel that my time away from them has been well spent.

Scott D. Sagan

Inside Nuclear South Asia

INTRODUCTION
Inside Nuclear South Asia

Scott D. Sagan

THERE IS AN OLD SAYING IN WASHINGTON THAT "politics ends at the water's edge." The sentiment behind this aphorism—that foreign policy and security policy should be bipartisan—has always been more of an ambition than a reality. But the saying is certainly accurate when describing both popular and scholarly knowledge of other countries' foreign and defense policy: our understanding of domestic politics too often ends at the water's edge. Policy makers and scholars find it easy to understand how conflicting domestic political interests and bureaucratic infighting can influence major foreign policy decisions—even decisions involving crucial national security issues like nuclear weapons policies—in their own countries. American analysts, for example, find it quite natural to focus on differences between Democratic and Republican administrations, and their ability to control shifting majorities in Congress, when examining support for national missile defense programs or to examine differences between the position of the secretary of state and the secretary of defense, and who has the president's ear, when explaining the U.S. stance in an international arms control negotiation. Yet when these same analysts focus on similar national security issues in other countries, they too often simply assume that decisions are made by a unitary rational actor and that objective national security interests, not competing domestic political parties or parochial bureaucratic interests, are the key determinant of policy choice.

Studies of nuclear weapons proliferation are particularly vulnerable to this kind of analytic bias. Sensitive policy decisions inside countries seeking to develop nuclear weapons are typically made in a highly secretive manner within tightly compartmentalized government decision-making bodies.

1

Crucial documents, which might be available for scholarly review in other issue areas, are usually kept highly classified in the nuclear weapons arena. In addition, politicians who might be willing to discuss or even brag about the local interests behind their positions regarding a trade bill or new environmental legislation ironically have domestic political incentives to deny that domestic politics influence crucial national security decisions. It is considered far more legitimate and patriotic for leaders to take positions on nuclear weapons issues strictly based on the national interest, at least as they envision it. In political science, scholars who assume that states behave in a highly rational manner, responding to vital international security interests in an anarchical world, are called "realists" or "neorealists." Politicians in all nuclear countries have political motives for speaking like realists, stressing the necessity of responding to adversaries' threats in justifying their nuclear weapons policies to foreign or domestic audiences, rather than acknowledging that they have been influenced by domestic politics or other parochial concerns.[1] All politics are local, U.S. Congressman Tip O'Neill famously said. But all politics concerning national security issues are *not* supposed to be local; they are supposed to be designed solely to serve the national interest.

India and Pakistan tested nuclear weapons in May 1998. Despite the passage of time and the emerging evidence of the complex process by which the governments in New Delhi and Islamabad develop their nuclear weapons policies, it is still common for scholars and journalists—especially, though not exclusively, in the United States—to anthropomorphize the Indian and Pakistani states when explaining their governments' nuclear policies. "India believes in a no-first-use policy," or "New Delhi feels threatened by the growth in China's nuclear arsenal," it is claimed. "Pakistan understood that it had to respond in kind to India's nuclear tests," or "Islamabad thinks it can maintain a minimal deterrence posture," analysts will argue. The chapters in this book demonstrate that such thinking grossly understates both the diversity of opinion on nuclear weapons issues and the complexity of the decision-making process that exists inside both South Asian nuclear powers. Ignoring such domestic complexities, however, can lead to faulty analysis and poor predictions about what policies are likely to be chosen by the governments in New Delhi and Islamabad. The U.S. government and most scholars, for example, were taken by surprise when the Indian government ordered the nuclear tests in 1998, when Pakistani soldiers crossed into Indian-controlled Kashmir in 1999, and when parts of the Pakistani government, under the leadership of senior nuclear laboratory official A. Q. Khan, were caught leading a global nuclear technology smuggling network in 2003.[2]

This book provides both new insights into the domestic politics and organizational interests behind specific nuclear policy choices in South Asia and a sustained critique of excessively narrow realist views of nuclear proliferation in general. Realists in political science argue that states will acquire nuclear weapons only if such an arsenal is absolutely necessary to counter an international threat to vital security interests. They also maintain that mutual possession of nuclear weapons by two rival states is likely to produce stable nuclear deterrence.[3]

The authors of this volume demonstrate that neither of these predictions has been accurate inside nuclear South Asia and that an understanding of domestic actors and their interests is necessary to understand both the causes and consequences of nuclear proliferation. International threats to India were not greater in 1998, for example, when the Bharatiya Janata Party (BJP) chose to test nuclear weapons, in contrast to the decision made by the Congress Party and coalition government leaders to refrain from nuclear testing during their time in power in the 1980s and 1990s. The Pakistani military, to give another example, has maintained virtually complete and independent control over Pakistan's nuclear arsenal, shunning the input of civilian leaders throughout the past decade. It is therefore not surprising that common military biases can be seen to have influenced Pakistani crisis behavior, its development of its nuclear arsenal, and the doctrine that guides the potential use of nuclear weapons in war.

This volume also explains the important puzzle about why the advent of nuclear capabilities between the two South Asian rivals has not led to a stable nuclear peace. The importance of this phenomenon must not be minimized. Indeed, the Kargil War of 1999 contradicts two of the most widely held theories in modern political science: the democratic peace theory and the nuclear peace theory. Regarding the democratic peace, Jack S. Levy has argued that "the absence of war between democracies comes as close to anything we have as an empirical law in International Relations."[4] The absence of war between nuclear weapons powers has also been granted the status of an empirical law of political science. "There is no more ironclad law in international relations theory than this," Devin Hagerty has written; "nuclear states do not fight wars with each other."[5] Yet the Kargil War is a clear exception to both these purported "empirical laws." In the literature assessing the democratic peace theory, scholars use a measure of +7 on the Polity IV data set (on a scale of +10 and −10) as the cutoff point for characterizing a state as a democracy.[6] In the spring of 1999, India had a polity score of +9, and Pakistan had a polity score of +7,[7] yet they went to war in the Kashmiri mountains above the town of Kargil. With respect to the nuclear peace theory, scholars use a minimum of 1,000 battle deaths as the cutoff point in determining whether a conflict is best characterized as a low-level dispute or an actual war. The Kargil conflict resulted in an estimated 1,174 fatalities, thus making it a war by widely accepted social science standards.[8]

Why did nuclear proliferation not lead to nuclear peace in South Asia? This volume explains why domestic political incentives, common military biases and organizational pathologies, and state-supported terrorist incidents have produced a series of military crises and one war between India and Pakistan despite (and in some cases *because of*) their acquisition of nuclear weapons. Some of these events reflect the intent of lower-level government officials or military officers; others are better described as inadvertent outcomes of internal politics and poor civil-military decision making.

In short, to understand India and Pakistan's nuclear past and predict their nuclear future, it is necessary to get "inside nuclear South Asia" and examine the domestic political interests, power relations, and bureaucratic processes that contribute to policy choices. The authors of this book seek to do precisely that. They may use different analytic methods and may reach different conclusions about specific nuclear decisions made in South Asia, but they share a common analytic assumption: domestic politics, civil-military relations, and bureaucratic decision-making processes matter greatly in both Indian and Pakistani nuclear weapons policy. *Inside Nuclear South Asia* thus lifts the curtain behind which governments in New Delhi and Islamabad made decisions about whether to test and develop nuclear weapons, how to use nuclear weapons if necessary, and how to engage in strategic competition in military crises since 1998. The first part of the book focuses on the causes of proliferation. The second part examines the consequences of nuclear proliferation in South Asia.

TESTING, TESTING: THEORIES AND WEAPONS IN SOUTH ASIA

In Chapter 1, "The BJP and the Bomb," Kanti Bajpai argues that India would not have tested nuclear weapons in May 1998 had the BJP not come to power in New Delhi as the head of a coalition government. In contrast to policies pursued by previous Indian governments led by the Congress Party, the political culture and Hindu nationalist ideology of the BJP encouraged its leaders to pursue an operational nuclear arsenal and Prime Minister Atal Behari Vajpayee's need to consolidate his power in the BJP-led coalition government required that he order nuclear weapons tests immediately upon taking over the reins of government in New Delhi. Bajpai explicitly criticizes the 1998 claims of the Indian government and the sympathetic analyses of many realist scholars—that the Indian government was compelled to test nuclear weapons because of increasing security threats from China and Pakistan and because of the looming threat of a global Comprehensive Test Ban Treaty (CTBT)—through a comparative analysis, noting that Congress-led governments faced similar structural incentives to conduct nuclear weapons tests yet refrained from doing so. He traces in detail the ideological vision of the BJP that encouraged Vajpayee to favor a more aggressive pursuit of an operational nuclear arsenal and notes that the brevity of his earlier tenure in office, a sixteen-day stint as prime minister in a highly unstable coalition government in 1996, further encouraged Vajpayee to test quickly, without consulting coalition partners or Indian military authorities. The "politics of political survival," Bajpai argues, dictated that Vajpayee would order the scientists to conduct multiple test explosions in the Rajasthan desert. The Pakistani missile tests that occurred right after the BJP election victory did not cause Vajpayee's decision but were rather (in a phrase attributed to Brajesh Mishra, later Vajpayee's national security advisor) "a good enough excuse to go ahead with the nuclear tests."

Bajpai's detailed tracing of the history of Indian nuclear decision making notes that the U.S. economic sanctions in response to the Indian test, in contrast to their intended effect, actually helped Vajpayee project the image of a leader who made tough decisions for the sake of national security, against the opposition of foreign powers, and made it more difficult for domestic opposition to form, with Indian public opinion following the "rally-round-the-flag" effect after the tests. The result was that Vajpayee's more assertive nuclear weapons policy created what Bajpai calls a "Teflon surface" for the BJP: Vajpayee remained popular, and the BJP stayed in power until the 2004 elections despite a series of clear foreign policy failures, including the Kargil War of 1999, the rise in terrorist attacks inside India, and New Delhi's backing down, without Pakistan conceding to its central demands, in the 2001–2002 crisis with Pakistan. "The BJP played politics with the bomb," Bajpai concludes, predicting that further tests and growth of India's nuclear arsenal will be much more likely in the future if the BJP comes back into office in India. Bajpai's predictions will be tested if the BJP or a BJP-led coalition comes to power in future Indian elections.

Karthika Sasikumar and Christopher Way contribute an important chapter that situates the proliferation decisions of India and Pakistan within the broader global pattern of decisions made by many states considering whether or not to develop nuclear weapons. Chapter 2, "Testing Theories of Proliferation in South Asia," builds upon Way's earlier quantitative analysis of the technological, security, and domestic political variables that correlate with decisions to start nuclear weapons programs and successfully acquire the bomb by all potential nuclear powers.[9] Sasikumar and Way find that neither India nor Pakistan is an exception to the general rule that states that face severe military threats to their national security, *and* lack a "nuclear umbrella" defense pact with a nuclear-armed power, are significantly more likely to seek their own nuclear arsenal than are similar states not facing such external threats to their security. Indeed, they perform a kind of counterfactual quantitative analysis, holding other variables constant while changing the security threats and alliance with a nuclear power variables, and produce results that suggest that neither India nor Pakistan would have been likely to develop nuclear weapons had they not faced severe threats from each other and, in the case of India, from China, or had either New Delhi or Islamabad maintained reliable alliances with the existing nuclear powers. This finding generally supports the logic of realist theories that predict proliferation based on the severity of the security threats a state faces in its region.

Yet Sasikumar and Way also argue that Pakistan and India are quite unusual proliferants in other important ways. First, Pakistan both started its program and successfully developed nuclear weapons when it was economically weaker and technologically less advanced than is the norm for nuclear weapons states. The authors speculate that the phenomenon of less developed states successfully getting the bomb may be more likely in the future because of the growth of illicit nuclear technology smuggling networks, such as the "proliferation ring" run by A. Q. Khan in Pakistan.[10] Second, India appears not to have been subject to the general law that increasing trade openness reduces a state's incentive to develop nuclear weapons. Sasikumar and Way theorize that increased openness to international trade, which reduced the likelihood of nuclear proliferation in most states, did not do so in India because its effects were offset by the related increases in economic growth, making it easier for the government in New Delhi to afford spending its limited resources on nuclear programs in the 1980s and 1990s. This phenomenon, too, may bode poorly for the prospects for global nonproliferation in the future.

Third, with respect to domestic politics, Sasikumar and Way find no significant relationship between increases in democracy in India and Pakistan (where democratic institutions have repeatedly risen and fallen in strength) and opposition to their nuclear weapons development programs. Although some theorists have maintained that democratic institutions can be a constraint on a government's interest and ability to use its limited resources for nuclear weapons programs, Sasikumar and Way's statistical analysis of India and Pakistan suggests the opposite: "[T]here is a mild positive effect of democracy on nuclear propensity" in South Asia. Still, they recognize that democracies and nondemocracies alike may have domestic actors—especially in some military organizations and in some laboratories—who strongly favor developing nuclear weapons. Future studies should therefore not focus on the effects of democracy and regime type on nuclear weapons acquisition. Sasikumar and Way conclude that instead, "when it comes to nuclear proliferation, approaches that further unpack the state and examine the autonomy and influence of the military and scientific establishments are more promising."

Chapter 3, Itty Abraham's "Contra-Proliferation: Interpreting the Meanings of India's Nuclear Tests in 1974 and 1998," is both a powerful critique of the assumptions and approaches used by American scholars of nuclear proliferation in general and an original reinterpretation of the history of the Indian nuclear program. Abraham's critique begins by noting that most U.S. scholarship on current nuclear weapons issues—indeed, even the term "nuclear proliferation"—focuses on determining when and why a government decides to develop a nuclear weapons program, with the explicit goal being to promote nuclear nonproliferation. He argues that this focus, which he labels "the discourse of control," distorts reality much of the time, both because nascent nuclear programs may serve multiple purposes within a government and because different individuals, bureaucracies, or nongovernment actors may have different reasons for supporting specific nuclear programs. Instead, Abraham argues, scholars should adopt a "nuclear developmentalism" framework that focuses on how different actors view the role of nuclear energy programs in providing increased legitimacy for the state, especially (though not exclusively) in a postcolonial state.

This analytic framework enables Abraham to differentiate between the "opacity" of reasons behind a government's nuclear program (is the government pursuing civilian nuclear power only, or is it secretly pursuing nuclear weapons?) and "ambivalence" of the purpose of early nuclear programs (actors hold different and indecisive views about the goals, which are fluid and subject to change over time). The "discourse of control" in much of the nuclear proliferation literature, Abraham argues, also diverts attention from the failure of the existing nuclear weapons states to "work in good faith" to eliminate their own nuclear weapons arsenals under Article VI of the Nuclear Non-Proliferation Treaty (NPT). Finally, it focuses too much attention on the "failures" of nonproliferation, states that have developed nuclear weapons or threaten to do so, and not on the "successes" of nonproliferation, especially states that started nuclear weapons programs but chose to abandon them afterward.[11]

Abraham shows how the early Indian nuclear program was neither a secret nuclear weapons program nor a purely civilian nuclear energy program; it was inherently flexible in its meaning, with the potential to become either kind of nuclear program and thus appealing to many more actors inside India than might otherwise have been the case. Nuclear power was an important symbol of Indian independence, demonstrating to Indian leaders, the Indian public, and the outside world alike that the new state could develop the most modern and sophisticated technology possible in an independent manner. Little did it matter, Abraham demonstrates, that the so-called indigenous Indian nuclear power program was in reality highly influenced, indeed often directly dependent upon, technology developed elsewhere. Other countries' nuclear programs—those of France, China, Pakistan, and Israel—were similarly advertised as being home-grown technologies, when in fact their success was highly dependent on official or clandestine nuclear cooperation. The perception of nuclear independence mattered more, politically speaking, than the reality of the complex global network of scientists and engineers. In each case, an international nuclear development system was labeled as a national program to make it appear more prestigious and legitimate to domestic audiences.

Abraham's subtle analysis encourages us to see India's 1974 peaceful nuclear explosion (PNE) test not as a secret weapons test, as in the common interpretation, but as a demonstration of India's nuclear potential. India's decades-long restraint in developing an operational nuclear arsenal after 1974 was due less to technological constraints than to a deeper strategic ambivalence among Indian leaders and prolonged domestic political disagreement about appropriate next steps.[12] New Delhi's 1998 nuclear weapons tests, under this interpretation, were not a case of India "coming out of the nuclear closet," as is often stated, but represented the Indian leadership and public accepting a new identity, as members of a normal nuclear weapons state, like other nuclear powers, rather than being an exceptional, ambiguous, and ambivalent "nuclear-capable" state. Abraham therefore concludes with a note of deep pessimism about the prospect of Indian nuclear disarmament in the future: "If Indian independence was defined in relation to nuclear 'developmentalism,' then giving up the nuclear program becomes equivalent to giving up the project of a sovereign Indian state." In short, democracy and disarmament may not be compatible under conditions in which nuclear weaponry is seen as an intrinsic part of modernity and independence.

THE CONSEQUENCES OF NUCLEAR WEAPONS IN SOUTH ASIA

The second part of this volume focuses on how nuclear weapons have influenced India and Pakistan, and the relations between the two states, since the May 1998 nuclear tests. Vipin Narang analyzes the history and future prospects for arms races in South Asia in Chapter 4, "Pride and Prejudice and Prithvis: Strategic Weapons Behavior in South Asia." Narang argues that existing studies of the causes of India's and Pakistan's decisions to test nuclear weapons in 1998 are inevitably inconclusive because with limited evidence and only one case of the behavior in question, a number of plausible explanations cannot be effectively ruled out. Rather than throw up his hands and give up in the effort to assess causes of proliferation and predict the future, however, Narang takes a novel, indirect approach to the problem, examining the pattern of missile testing. Because there have been dozens of nuclear-capable missile tests in South Asia over the past two decades, in contrast to the single case of the 1998 nuclear weapons tests, this focus provides more data to discern patterns of interaction and potential causes of future weapons development in South Asia.

Narang presents a new database in his chapter—examining all the strategic missile tests conducted by both India and Pakistan between 1988 and 2008—and codes each of the eighty-three missile tests as having been launched in response to a rival's threatening behavior (a security explanation), for direct electoral benefits (a domestic politics explanation), or for prestige motives (a norms-based explanation). Importantly, Narang looks both at the timing of missile tests, seeking correlations with threats to national security (such as a rival's missile tests), and the public justification of the missile tests, seeking insights into government officials' views on the main causes for their policy decisions.

His research leads to two important insights about politics and behavior inside nuclear South Asia. First, the evidence suggests that Pakistan is indeed primarily responding to security concerns when it tests nuclear-capable missiles, a conclusion based on both the timing of its tests, usually launched in response to an Indian test, and the way that the government in Islamabad (and the military leadership in Rawalpindi) explains its decisions. Second, and in contrast, Indian missile tests do not appear to be highly correlated either to Pakistani missile developments or to Chinese strategic missile tests. Whereas Pakistani missile test patterns do not differ regardless of whether a civilian-led or military-controlled government is in power, in India the leadership of the government in power matters significantly. Distinct patterns are discernible based on whether the BJP or the Congress Party controls the reins of power in New Delhi. BJP governments develop and test new nuclear-capable missile systems largely to promote what Narang (following Jacques Hymans) calls "oppositional nationalism," a desire for military and technological superiority over Pakistan to promote the prestige and influence of the BJP.[13] Congress-led governments have a much more moderate policy objective, seeking prestige through developing an Indian missile program that is seen as independent and successful, without tying it to Pakistani or Chinese developments.

These findings about missile programs in South Asia lead to predictions about the future prospects of nuclear weapons testing, further missile testing, and even ballistic missile defense deployments. As Narang puts it, "[T]he South Asian arms race and the general risk of regional escalation are critically tied to the domestic political configuration in New Delhi." In short, Narang's analysis leads to the prediction that the BJP, if it comes back into office, is much more likely than a Congress Party–led coalition to initiate a new round of nuclear weapons tests and start more missile procurement programs, military developments that will encourage Pakistan to respond in kind.

Chapter 5 by S. Paul Kapur, "Revisionist Ambitions, Conventional Capabilities, and Nuclear Instability: Why Nuclear South Asia Is Not Like Cold War Europe," argues that the possibility of war between India and Pakistan remains high despite an understanding in both Islamabad and New Delhi that escalation to nuclear weapons use could be catastrophically costly. Indeed, Kapur maintains that a conventional war remains likely in the region precisely because Pakistani leaders believe that Indian (and American) officials estimate that nuclear war would be so costly.

Many scholars have attributed ongoing violence in South Asia to a phenomenon known as the stability/instability paradox.[14] According to this theory, which was developed in the 1960s by U.S. scholars who feared a Soviet attack on NATO Europe, mutual possession of nuclear weapons by two states in conflict lowers the probability that either side would deliberately escalate to the nuclear exchange. If the Soviet leaders believed that they could, in Paul Nitze's phrase, "deter our deterrent," it would encourage them to initiate a conventional war against the NATO alliance.[15]

Kapur argues that this form of a stability/instability paradox does *not* explain ongoing South Asian conflict, especially the 1999 Kargil War. The Kargil War was initiated by the Pakistani government, which sent Northern Light Infantry troops into Indian-held territory in Kashmir in the winter of 1999. But it was not the Pakistani leaders' perception that the nuclear balance was stable that led them to engage in this act of conventional or subconventional aggression against India in Kashmir. Instead, as Kapur shows, the Kargil invasion was inspired by their belief that nuclear escalation was actually likely, if India responded by using its conventional superiority to cross the Line of Control (LOC) in Kashmir or the international border. The Pakistani leadership, or more correctly, the subset of leaders who made the actual decision to send Pakistani military units across the LOC, believed that fear of nuclear escalation would both inhibit the Indian government from ordering conventional retaliation in kind and lead the U.S. government to intervene to stop any limited war from escalating further.[16]

This phenomenon is quite different, however, from the stability/instability paradox feared in Cold War Europe, in which the stronger conventional power (the USSR and the Warsaw Pact) was expected to use its achievement of nuclear parity with the United States as a counter to the U.S. nuclear first-use threats that were designed to prevent an attack on NATO. In the South Asian case, it is the weaker conventional power (Pakistan) that has territorial ambitions (to unite Kashmir under Pakistani rule) and has used its nuclear weapons as a shield behind which to engage in conventional military aggression against its neighbor. Kapur concludes with a pessimistic appraisal of the prospects for peace. Indeed, what could be called an "instability/instability paradox" exists in South Asia, with nuclear danger facilitating, rather than impeding, lower-level conflict in the region.

In Chapter 6, "The Evolution of Pakistani and Indian Nuclear Doctrine," I broaden the analytic lens to examine the evolution of ideas in Islamabad and New Delhi about how to use nuclear weapons threats and potential nuclear war fighting or retaliation options in South Asia. The chapter examines in detail how the Indian and Pakistani governments (and the Pakistani military establishment in Rawalpindi) have incorporated nuclear weapons into their military doctrines and war plans. This is a subject about which relatively little has been written in the past, primarily because of the lack of firm sources about such plans and doctrines. Emerging evidence, however, now permits a more thorough analysis to be conducted. Although both governments use the same label to describe their nuclear doctrine in public—claiming that they follow a "minimum credible deterrence" doctrine—the evidence presented in the chapter demonstrates both that Pakistani and Indian doctrines are very different from one another and that neither government now follows a genuine "minimum deterrent" policy under which the state develops only a small number of nuclear weapons, aims them exclusively at its adversary's urban industrial areas, and threatens to use them only in retaliation after another state's nuclear attack against the homeland.

The evidence presented in Chapter 6 suggests that Pakistani nuclear doctrine is strongly influenced by the autonomy of the Pakistani military and its ability to make nuclear war plans and operational decisions on its own, with little input from civilians inside or outside the government who might be a check on military biases. Although Pakistan has a nuclear first-use doctrine, as realism would predict, the military leadership has apparently developed plans for using its weapons more quickly and under a wide variety of scenarios, not just under conditions of "last resort" in a conventional war. Moreover, common military biases that favor massive uses of force if needed and that entrust the operational control of weaponry to the military commanders in the field appear to exist in Pakistan. I find little evidence, however, that the Islamic beliefs of Pakistani military officers have influenced their doctrinal preferences or attitudes toward nuclear weapons use.

The chapter presents an analysis of how different perceptions of nuclear weapons influenced Pakistani and Indian crisis behavior and military operations during both the Kargil conflict in 1999 and the 2001–2002 crisis over terrorist attacks in New Delhi and Kashmir. Civilian and military leaders in both countries held contrasting, and often conflicting, views on the effects of nuclear weapons threats on the adversary. In India in 2002, for example, senior military officers made direct nuclear threats, for the first time, that were not authorized by political leaders in New Delhi. Military leaders in Pakistan, however, had much more autonomy and control over military operations and doctrine than was the case in India, leading the Pakistani military to engage in highly provocative conventional operations and risky nuclear threats.

The chapter also demonstrates that Indian nuclear doctrine has moved significantly away from its traditional "no-first-use" policy of the 1990s. Although the Indian government claims that it continues to follow a no-first-use and minimum credible deterrence doctrine, official statements issued in 2003 demonstrate that the government now holds open the option of using nuclear weapons first against any state that has used chemical or biological weapons and also that it conceives of nuclear weapons as providing a shield behind which it could use conventional superiority against Pakistan and "deter the Pakistani nuclear deterrent." The history of the 2001–2002 crisis and the Indian reactions to the 2003 U.S. invasion of Iraq also highlight the possibility of further doctrinal changes in New Delhi, with civilian strategists and military officers discussing preemption as a legitimate military option for the first time. The evidence suggests, moreover, that the Indian government's movement away from no-first-use doctrine was strongly influenced by its perceptions of developments in U.S. nuclear doctrine under the George W. Bush administration.

IN LIEU OF LESSONS: PREDICTIONS AND PUZZLES

Traditional realist studies of regional or global nuclear weapons proliferation issues focus on shifts in military balances, especially new nuclear weapons states, and how they may change individual governments' assessments of their security options. Such realists are generally pessimistic about the long-term prospects for stopping the spread of nuclear weapons, arguing that, in the face of international anarchy and emerging nuclear threats, any rational government will eventually acquire the most powerful weaponry available. Kenneth Waltz, for example, envisions a world of fifteen to eighteen nuclear weapons states emerging in the future: "Countries have to take care of their own security. If countries feel insecure and believe that nuclear weapons make them more secure, America's policy of opposing the spread of nuclear weapons will not prevail."[17] Yet Waltz, like many other realist scholars, is optimistic about the consequences of proliferation, maintaining that stable deterrence is easy to produce even with small numbers of nuclear weapons: "The likelihood of war decreases as deterrent and defensive capabilities increase. Nuclear weapons make wars hard to start. . . . Because they do, the gradual spread of nuclear weapons is more to be welcomed than feared."[18]

In contrast, "liberal" or "neo-institutionalist" international relations scholars tend to be nonproliferation optimists and nuclear deterrence pessimists. In fact, these two predictions are logically related, with analysts believing that government leaders in non-nuclear-weapon states will clearly understand that mutual nuclear deterrence will be difficult to maintain and will therefore prefer to remain within mutual arms control constraint regimes, such as the NPT.[19] William Potter and Gaukar Mukhatzhanova summarize the resulting optimistic vision of the nuclear future: "[P]ast predictions of rapid proliferation have proved faulty . . . [and] the current alarm over impeding proliferation doom is largely without merit."[20]

In contrast to both of these schools of thought, the contributing authors to *Inside Nuclear South Asia* have emphasized the importance of shifts in the power of domestic political coalitions and the role of parochial interests inside government bureaucracies and military organizations in determining both the nuclear weapons acquisition and testing decisions and the subsequent crisis behavior and weapons procurement and doctrines of the Indian and Pakistani governments. Although New Delhi and Islamabad have not engaged in direct warfare since 1999, and have avoided serious military crises since 2002, this particular "innen-politik" approach leads, unfortunately, to doubly pessimistic predictions both about the stability of nuclear deterrence in South Asia and about the prospects for nuclear proliferation elsewhere around the globe. This introduction therefore ends by highlighting the particular sources of pessimism that emerge from the analysis in this book and identifying remaining puzzles about regional and global proliferation that should be the subject of further empirical research.

THE PERMANENT PERILS OF PROLIFERATION IN SOUTH ASIA

The chapters in this volume lead to three major reasons to be pessimistic about the long-term prospects for maintaining nuclear peace in South Asia. First, war and the threat of war serve an important function in producing political settlements in international politics because governments that lose wars or are overthrown by them, or those that fear such outcomes, have strong reasons to curb their geopolitical ambitions and make lasting political compromises. This has not happened in South Asia, however, in large part because Pakistani leaders believe that they are protected from all-out war by Pakistan's nuclear arsenal, leaving open the option of using conventional military forces or irregular forces to conduct offensive campaigns or destabilize the rival government in India. Pervez Musharraf, for example, when he was chief of army staff after the 1998 nuclear tests, proclaimed that "since World War II, no nation has ever exercised its nuclear option. Conventional weapons continue to be the actual tools of war even in the nuclear era."[21] Pakistani military officers, moreover, have both a national security interest and parochial organizational incentives to maintain an active insurgency in Indian-held Kashmir because the insurgency ties down large numbers of Indian armed forces that might otherwise be used in a potential conflict with Pakistan and because the continued tension with India justifies the political prominence and budgets of the Pakistan Army.[22]

The structural and organizational problems in Pakistan, which are highlighted in Chapters 5 and 6 of this book, are unfortunately likely to remain, regardless of who is in power in Islamabad. The return of civilian rule to Pakistan in 2008, with the resignation of President Pervez Musharraf, may be welcomed for many reasons with respect to the political rights and economic well-being of the Pakistani people, but there is little historical evidence to suggest that civilian control of the reins of government will lead the Pakistani government to abandon its support for the Kashmiri insurgency. Nor is there reason to believe that the Pakistani military will give up its central autonomy in decision making about the size, posture, and operational doctrine of Pakistani nuclear weapons. Indeed, granting the Pakistani military a high degree of autonomy over military policy is one traditional method used by civilian leaders in Islamabad to reduce the risks of a military coup against them.

A second, and related, continuing nuclear danger in South Asia is the risk that a Pakistani nuclear weapon could fall into the hands of terrorists and be used against the government of Pakistan, or against India, or against the United States. This is a continuing concern because of the difficulty of combating the "insider threat" in a highly volatile country like Pakistan, in which, through corruption or ideological affinity, a military officer or guard with nuclear command and control or physical security responsibility might help the Taliban, or al Qaeda or its Pakistani affiliates, acquire a nuclear weapon.

The Pakistani military is acutely aware of the need for tight command and control over its nuclear arsenal, of course, and the U.S. government has reportedly spent approximately $100 million since 2001 to help the Pakistani military protect its weapons from terrorists.[23] Yet there is a permanent risk of nuclear terrorism emerging from Pakistan because of what can be called the "vulnerability/invulnerability paradox": If the posture and operational deployments of the Pakistani nuclear arsenal are designed to maximize protection against terrorist theft or seizure, the arsenal will be vulnerable to an Indian or U.S. military attack; if the posture and deployments are designed to maximize protection against an Indian or U.S. military attack, however, Pakistani nuclear weapons will be more vulnerable to a terrorist seizure or theft. This paradox is played out in the operational decisions made in peacetime and in crisis by the Pakistani military. In order to reduce the danger of weapons being seized by a terrorist organization or its sympathizers, the Pakistani military reportedly keeps its weapons in a not fully assembled status, off alert, and not mated to their delivery vehicles during peacetime. In a crisis, however, the Pakistani military has strong incentives to alert its arsenal and move the missiles, bombers, and nuclear weapons away from their peacetime bases, where they would be vulnerable to an Indian (or an American) military attack, into more secret, but less secure, positions in the countryside. This military alert and dispersal operation would make Pakistani weapons less vulnerable to an Indian or U.S. military attack but more vulnerable to a terrorist seizure, either independently or through help from a sympathetic insider.[24] The Indian government's movement away from its traditional no-first-use doctrine has encouraged the Pakistani military to contemplate earlier dispersal of its arsenal in crises. The resulting risks can be reduced but not eliminated. Indeed, one discomforting probability estimate was given by then president Pervez Musharraf in May 2003. When asked to provide a "confidence rating" from 1–100 on the likelihood that a Pakistani nuclear weapon could be protected against falling "into unfriendly hands," Musharraf answered: "I would certainly give it over 90. I am very sure of it."[25]

Third, understanding the ideological proclivities and domestic electoral incentives for the BJP to engage in provocative military actions, which were highlighted in both Kanti Bajai's chapter and Vipin Narang's analysis, leads to a pessimistic assessment of the future ability of India and Pakistan to constrain the risk of a nuclear arms race on the subcontinent. If the governments in Islamabad and New Delhi were driven purely by national security concerns, it might be possible to reach arms control agreements that provide mutual and verifiable constraints on the future deployments of nuclear weapons, missiles, or ballistic missile defenses. Yet if future Indian nuclear decisions— such as ordering new tests or development of new missile systems—are based on ideological beliefs in "oppositional nationalism" or electoral incentives to pander to the popularity of displays of nuclear weapons strength among the Indian mass public, then a mutual constraint regime is likely to break down.

In short, the enduring rivalry between India and Pakistan and their mutual possession of nuclear arsenals are a dangerous mix.[26] Different governments in Islamabad and New Delhi may well be better than others in managing their emerging nuclear rivalry. But the analysis in this volume demonstrates that the nuclear dangers are persistent and will not be eliminated in South Asia short of an agreement for nuclear disarmament. That point naturally leads to a final set of insights from the South Asian experience for understanding the prospects for global nuclear weapons proliferation.

OUTSIDE NUCLEAR SOUTH ASIA:
THE RISKS OF GLOBAL PROLIFERATION

This study of the history of nuclear weapons decision making in India and Pakistan also highlights three issues that can help us understand the future risks of nuclear proliferation elsewhere in the world. First, it should lead scholars and policy makers alike to be more skeptical of claims that new nu- clear states will all behave alike, cautiously using their nuclear arsenal only to maintain the status quo, under the logic of mutual deterrence, and carefully controlling their nuclear technology, materials, and actual weapons to pre- vent them from spreading further to other states or terrorist organizations. It is sometimes assumed, for example, that if the United States was able to cope with the Soviet Union and the People's Republic of China developing nuclear weapons during the Cold War, through mutual deterrence, surely it can do so again when new hostile nuclear powers, such as the Islamic Republic of Iran, emerge in the future. "I believe we have the power to deter Iran," retired U.S. Army General John Abizaid has argued: "Let's face it, we lived with a nuclear Soviet Union, we've lived with a nuclear China, and we're living with (other) nuclear powers as well."[27]

If Iran is permitted to develop nuclear weapons in the coming decade, how- ever, its behavior will more likely resemble that of Pakistan than China or the Soviet Union, because of both the Iranian regime's ambitions and its inter- nal characteristics. A nuclear-armed Iran would be highly dangerous because of President Mahmoud Ahmadinejad's hostile anti-Israeli statements and

Holocaust-denial rhetoric and because leaders in Tehran continue to hold revolutionary ambitions against their conservative (and Sunni) Muslim neighbors, provide support for Hezbollah and other terrorist organizations, and are unlikely to maintain centralized control over all nuclear weapons or materials in the future. Indeed, there are good reasons to fear that central political authorities in Tehran could not completely control the details of nuclear operations by the Islamic Revolutionary Guards Corps (IRGC) or their ties to external terrorist organizations, even if they wanted to. The IRGC recruits militant, young, "true believers" to join their ranks, subjects them to ideological indoctrination but not psychological stability testing, and—as the International Atomic Energy Agency (IAEA) discovered when it inspected Iran's centrifuge facilities in 2003—gives such IRGC units responsibility for physical security over nuclear materials production sites. Finally, Iran's nuclear facilities, like its chemical weapons programs, are apparently under the ostensible control of the same organization that manages Tehran's contacts with foreign terrorist clients. In short, the fragile control and aggressive stance of nuclear Pakistan are likely to be repeated if Iran obtains nuclear weapons in the future.[28]

Second, the spread of democracy in the future is not likely to reduce the likelihood of the spread of nuclear weapons. Indeed, Sasikumar and Way found a slight positive correlation between the growth of democracy in India and Pakistan and the development of nuclear weapons capabilities, a relationship that has also been found in broader quantitative studies of global nuclear proliferation.[29] Broad public support for the development, testing, and growth of nuclear arsenals in both India and Pakistan, moreover, should provide a cautionary note about the prospects for both nuclear proliferation and nuclear disarmament in the future. It is likely, for example, that the spread of democracy in Egypt and Saudi Arabia would make it more difficult, not less, for new governments in Cairo and Riyadh to ignore populist and nationalist calls for acquiring their own nuclear weapons.[30] It is also worth noting that once a state has developed nuclear weapons, democracy does not necessarily encourage nuclear disarmament. Indeed, only one autocratic government (South Africa), and no democratic state, has ever disarmed itself by destroying a nuclear arsenal once it was fully developed.[31]

A third puzzle emerges when looking at the future prospects for nuclear weapons proliferation through the lens of the South Asian nuclear experience. Will the further spread of civilian nuclear power capabilities around the globe make nuclear weapons proliferation more or less likely in the future?

In many ways, this is the $64,000 question (and also the 64,000 rial question for Iran or the 64,000 pound question for Egypt) for the long-term prospects for nuclear weapons nonproliferation. The experience of India is not reassuring in this respect, since its nuclear energy establishment increasingly turned toward support for nuclear weapons acquisition in the 1970s, in part because the bomb option provided justification for their programs and even an increased budget despite the difficulties experienced in the production of civilian nuclear power. Will this Indian experience prove to be an exception to the rule or a warning about the risks of the spread of nuclear power? In this respect, the spread of nuclear reactors (and especially of uranium-enrichment and plutonium-reprocessing capabilities) is likely to bring more and more governments closer to having the complex technical capability to build nuclear weapons in the future. The South Asian nuclear experience suggests that new states' incentives to cross over the nuclear divide, however, will be influenced not just by international arms control regimes or regional military balances but also by the even more complex interplay of shifting coalitions of domestic political actors and their interests.

NOTES

1. On the realist bias in national security discourse concerning nuclear weapons, see Scott D. Sagan, "Realist Perspectives on Ethical Norms and Weapons of Mass Destruction," in Sohail H. Hashmi and Steve P. Lee, eds., *Ethics and Weapons of Mass Destruction* (Cambridge: Cambridge University Press, 2004), 78–79; and Nina Tannenwald, "Stigmatizing the Bomb: Origins of the Nuclear Taboo," *International Security*, vol. 29, no. 4 (Spring 2005), 5–49.

2. On surprise about the nuclear tests and the A. Q. Khan network, see George Perkovich, *India's Nuclear Bomb: The Impact of Global Proliferation* (Berkeley: University of California Press, 1999), 404–443; Strobe Talbott, *Engaging India: Diplomacy, Democracy, and the Bomb* (Washington, DC: Brookings Institution Press, 2004), 48–50, 154–160; Gordon Corera, *Shopping for Bombs: Nuclear Proliferation, Global Insecurity, and the Rise and Fall of the A. Q. Khan Network* (New York: Oxford University Press, 2006); and Douglas Franz and Catherine Collins, *The Nuclear Jihadist* (New York: Twelve, 2007).

3. See especially T. V. Paul, *Power Versus Prudence: Why Nations Forgo Nuclear Weapons* (Montreal: McGill-Queens University Press, 2000); Scott D. Sagan, "Why Do States Build Nuclear Weapons? Three Models in Search of a Bomb," *International Security*, vol. 21, no. 3 (Winter 1996–1997), 54–86; and Kenneth N. Waltz, "More May Be Better," in Scott D. Sagan and Kenneth N. Waltz, *The Spread of Nuclear Weapons: A Debate Renewed* (New York: W. W. Norton, 2003), 3–45.

4. Jack S. Levy, "Domestic Politics and War," in Robert I. Rotberg and Theodore K. Rabb, eds., *The Origins and Prevention of Major War* (Cambridge: Cambridge University Press, 1989), 88.

5. Devin T. Hagerty, *The Consequences of Nuclear Proliferation* (Cambridge, MA: MIT Press, 1998), 184.

6. Bruce Russett and John Oneal, *Triangulating Peace: Democracy, Interdependence, and International Organizations* (New York: W. W. Norton, 2001), 48.

7. Monty G. Marshall and Keith Jaggers, "Polity IV Project: Political Regime Characteristics and Transitions, 1800–2002," typescript (College Park: University of Maryland, 2002). Also see Russett and Oneal, *Triangulating Peace*, 47–48.

8. *From Surprise to Reckoning: The Kargil Review Committee Report* (New Delhi: Sage Publications, 2000), 22–23, 98.

9. Sonali Singh and Christopher R. Way, "The Correlates of Nuclear Proliferation: A Quantitative Test," *Journal of Conflict Resolution*, vol. 48, no. 6 (December 2004), 859–885.

10. See Chaim Braun and Christopher F. Chyba, "Proliferation Rings: New Challenges to the Nuclear Proliferation Regime," *International Security*, vol. 29, no. 2 (Fall 2004), 5–49; and Alexander H. Montgomery, "Ringing in Proliferation: How to Dismantle an Atomic Bomb Network," *International Security*, vol. 30, no. 2 (Fall 2005), 153–187.

11. For exceptions, see Kurt M. Campbell, Robert J. Einhorn, and Mitchell B. Reiss, eds., *The Nuclear Tipping Point: Why States Reconsider Their Nuclear Choices* (Washington, DC: Brookings Institution Press, 2004); Ariel Levite, "Never Say Never Again: Nuclear Reversal Revisited," *International Security*, vol. 27, no. 3 (Winter 2002–2003), 59–88; and Paul, *Power Versus Prudence.*

12. Also see George Perkovich, *India's Nuclear Bomb: The Impact of Global Proliferation* (Berkeley: University of California Press, 1999).

13. See Jacques Hymans, *The Psychology of Nuclear Proliferation: Identity, Emotions, and Foreign Policy* (Cambridge: Cambridge University Press, 2006).

14. See Šumit Ganguly, *Conflict Unending: India-Pakistan Tensions Since 1947* (New Delhi: Oxford University Press, 2002), 122–123; Jeffrey W. Knopf, "Recasting the Optimism-Pessimism Debate," *Security Studies*, vol. 12, no. 1 (Autumn 2002), 52; David J. Karl, "Lessons for Proliferation Scholarship in South Asia: The Buddha Smiles Again," *Asian Survey*, vol. 41, no. 6 (November–December 2001), 1020; Lowell Dittmer, "South Asia's Security Dilemma," *Asian Survey*, vol. 41, no. 6 (November–December 2001), 903; Feroz Hasan Khan, "Challenges to Nuclear Stability in South Asia," *Nonproliferation Review*, vol. 10, no. 1 (Spring 2003), 64; and P. R. Chari, "Nuclear Restraint, Nuclear Risk Reduction, and the Stability/Instability Paradox in South Asia," in Michael Krepon and Chris Gagné, eds., *The Stability/Instability Paradox: Nuclear Weapons and Brinksmanship in South Asia* (Washington, DC: Henry L. Stimson Center, 2001), 20–21.

15. Paul H. Nitze, "Deterring Our Deterrent," *Foreign Policy*, no. 25 (Winter 1976–1977), 195–210.

16. For evidence that senior military leaders did not share full information on the Kargil plan with Prime Minister Nawaz Sharif, see Owen Bennett Jones, *Pakistan: Eye of the Storm* (New Haven, CT: Yale University Press, 2002), 102–103.

17. Waltz, "More May Be Better," 4, 44.

18. Ibid., 45.

19. See Etel Soligen, *Nuclear Logics: Contrasting Paths in East Asia and the Middle East* (Princeton, NJ: Princeton University Press, 2007).

20. William C. Potter and Gaukhar Mukhatzhanova, "Divining Nuclear Intentions: A Review Essay," *International Security*, vol. 33, no. 1 (Summer 2008), 140.

21. Quoted in "Musharraf's Views Before the Coup: A Collation," South Asia Analysis Group, available at http://www.southasiaanalysis.org/%5Cpapers%5Cpaper92.html.

22. "The army appears convinced of the wisdom of keeping India bleeding in Kashmir. As long as India is busy in Kashmir, it cannot have the 3 to one ratio that is necessary for offensive options." Azhar Abbas, *Herald*, May 1999, as quoted in ibid.

23. David E. Sanger and William J. Broad, "US Secretly Aids Pakistan in Guarding Nuclear Arms," *New York Times*, November 18, 2007, A1.

24. For further discussion, see Thomas E. Ricks, "Calculating the Risks in Pakistan," *Washington Post*, December 2, 2007, A-20.

25. *Nightline with Ted Koppel*, transcript, June 24, 2003.

26. For different views on this issue, see T. V. Paul, ed., *The India-Pakistan Conflict: An Enduring Rivalry* (New York: Cambridge University Press, 2005); and Ganguly, *Conflict Unending*.

27. Robert Burns, "Abizaid: World Could Live with Nuclear Iran," *AP*, September 17, 2007, available at http://www.iranfocus.com/en/index.php?option=com_content&task=view&id=12455. Also see Barry R. Posen, "We Can Live with a Nuclear Iran," *New York Times*, February 27, 2006.

28. For more analysis of the dangers posed by a nuclear Iran, see Scott D. Sagan, "How to Keep the Bomb from Iran," *Foreign Affairs*, vol. 85, no. 5 (September–October 2006), 45–59; and Sharam Chubin, *Iran's Nuclear Ambitions* (Washington, DC: Carnegie Endowment for International Peace, 2006).

29. See Dong-Joon Jo and Erik Gartzke, "Determinants of Nuclear Weapons Proliferation," *Journal of Conflict Resolution*, vol. 51, no. 7 (February 2007), 167–194; and Singh and Way, "Correlates of Nuclear Proliferation," 873.

30. Kurt M. Campbell and Robert J. Einhorn, "Avoiding the Tipping Point," in Campbell, Einhorn, and Reis, *Nuclear Tipping Point*, 326–327.

31. See Perkovich, *India's Nuclear Arsenal*, 459–464, for an excellent discussion of this problem.

THE CAUSES OF NUCLEAR PROLIFERATION IN SOUTH ASIA

1 THE BJP AND THE BOMB

Kanti Bajpai

ON MAY 11 AND 13, 1998, India exploded a total of five nuclear devices in the Rajasthan desert. Since 1974, when India first tested a nuclear device, there had been an expectation that New Delhi would once again test and perhaps go nuclear outright. Yet the 1998 series of tests caught most Indians and the world by surprise. Why did India test after a gap of twenty-four years? Most accounts and explanations of the Indian nuclear tests—including the government's own public statements—have focused on the strategic rationale for India's nuclear program. Much less attention has been paid to the domestic roots of the decision to test. What role did domestic political considerations play in the Indian government's decision?

This chapter addresses two questions about domestic politics and the Indian nuclear bomb. First, what were the domestic political incentives for the Bharatiya Janata Party (BJP), which came to power in March 1998, to test barely six weeks later? Second, what were the domestic political effects of the BJP's decision to test nuclear weapons? Here, I focus on how the BJP remained politically unscathed despite a series of crises with Pakistan in the Indian part of Kashmir after the party took a series of positions and initiatives that were either palpable failures or that contradicted earlier stands. Why was the party not taken to task by the public and not hurt politically, including in the 1999 elections that occurred just after the Kargil War?

I have put the BJP at the center of my analysis. Although the BJP was only one of the twenty or so parties that made up the National Democratic Alliance (NDA) that came to power in March 1998, it was the single largest party in the alliance and indeed the largest party in India in terms of the number of seats in Parliament.[1] The prime ministership and the most important cabinet posts were with the BJP. There was an enormous struggle for domestic supremacy, primarily between the BJP and the Congress. Other parties may have been affected by the tests, but it was the BJP that made the decision to test and that stood to benefit or lose from it.

In bringing domestic politics into an understanding of India's nuclear tests and in asking how the consequences of post-test security policies can be explained, I do not intend to suggest that international politics played no role in the behavior of Indian leaders. It would be bizarre if Indian leaders' decision making on nuclear weapons was completely unrelated to their understanding of international politics and the challenges to national security. Conversely, in an increasingly globalized world, domestic politics are always influenced by the external world—by conflicts, pressures, and ideas stemming from foreign governments and societies. There can therefore be no purely external/ international and internal/domestic understanding of either international or domestic politics. Instead, what is needed is a careful weighing of the influence of different factors on important political decisions.

Put another way, political leaders are influenced both by international structural imperatives to assure the security of their societies in an anarchical world and by domestic constraints and opportunities. The decision to build a nuclear weapons program and to validate its effectiveness by testing may well arise out of the need to assure one's security in a self-help international system where there is no central authority either to adjudicate between member states or to enforce certain norms of behavior. Faced in particular by other states that possess nuclear weapons, especially those who are "rivals," governments will be pressed to seek a deterrent.

As Kenneth Waltz and other structural realists have argued, the incentive to follow such a course is strong. It is not, however, inevitable. States may choose to ignore structural pressures to balance themselves against rivals. They may eventually, as a result, be eliminated as sovereign entities in the international system or else, at the limit, be physically destroyed. Agents do have choices, however limited these may be. They must at some point make a decision to ensure their survival by investing in the requisite forms of military power (whether they do so by seeking another's protection or by their own efforts)—or face the possibility of capitulation or destruction.[2] The point at which they take this decision, indeed the nature of the decision itself (to seek protection or to rely on one's own strength, to seek security guarantees or to build a nuclear deterrent) depends on a variety of domestic resources, self-understandings, conjunctions, and circumstances.

Specifically, in respect to building a nuclear weapons program, a state must at the very least possess the science and technology and natural resources (e.g., uranium), the financial resources, the military sophistication, and the public's support to construct a deterrent. Public support for a nuclear deterrent may come from an understanding of national security imperatives, but it may also come from deeper wellsprings of identity—from nationalism, from the desire to display one's sovereignty, from conceptions of modernity.[3] Leaders may use national security arguments and/or powerful social-psychological emotions to affirm a national identity in their own narrower political interests—in the cut and thrust of domestic politics, to outmaneuver political rivals, ensure their own survival, enlarge their power, and stifle opposition. It is this last domestic perspective that we shall put forth in this chapter.[4] The argument is that India's decision to develop a nuclear weapons program may well reflect the long-term structural imperatives of security in a self-help world, but the timing of the 1998 tests, the tipping point, is better explained by domestic political considerations arising out of certain internal conjunctions and circumstances, including notions of political and national identity. The evidence presented in this chapter shows that the party interests of the BJP and, more specifically, of Prime Minister Atal Behari Vajpayee were critically important to the nuclear test decision of 1998 and that the domestic political situation after the tests influenced the public reception of the NDA government's handling of a series of national security decisions thereafter.

INTERNATIONAL POLITICS / STRATEGIC IMPERATIVES AND THE DECISION TO TEST

The policy community and the academic understandings of the Indian nuclear tests have focused on "first image" or "security model" analyses, that is, on the nature of international politics and the security imperatives facing New Delhi in 1998.[5] There are three basic first image explanations. The first relates to the increase in international pressure against nuclear proliferation in the aftermath of the Cold War and a closing window of opportunity for India in terms of testing and going nuclear. The second explanation focuses on the collapse of the Soviet Union—India's Cold War ally—and India's more vulnerable strategic position in the world in the 1990s. The third explanation is that the geopolitical changes in India's more immediate environment, in particular, military growth and increased cooperation between China and Pakistan, which directly impinged on Indian security, caused the tests.

How do we treat these explanations from the point of view of building a case for a domestic politics explanation of the tests? Are public officials who make these arguments simply lying? Are they ignorant of the "real" (i.e., domestic) reasons for the tests? Is all the first image scholarship on the tests wrong?

In this chapter, I sketch out each of these security model explanations and show that there are grounds for questioning each of them. Very little has been written from the domestic politics perspective on the 1998 tests and their aftermath.[6] There are many difficulties in developing a domestic politics view of India's nuclear tests. The empirical "base" is too thin. The principal actors involved in the tests will not speak openly enough. Their recollection of their own motives and interests may not be altogether credible. Documentation is therefore always difficult at best. By definition, nuclear politics is perhaps the highest of "high politics" and therefore the most shrouded in secrecy. There are few if any documents here, and even if documentation existed, India's secrecy laws are so stringent that virtually no one can get access to anything important. It is tempting therefore to "fall back" on first image security analyses and to throw up one's hands in terms of research possibilities. Research on the domestic politics of nuclear decision making cannot be suspended, however, for it is simply too consequential an area of public policy to be let alone. The researcher, like a detective deploying the tools of forensic science, must piece together the best evidence he or she can obtain in order to derive some conclusions. I will, like a good detective, therefore begin by raising questions about alternative explanations of the facts.

Closing Windows of Opportunity

The most common explanation of why India tested in May 1998 is that proliferation politics were closing "windows of opportunity" for India.[7] This is a view that Indian government officials and senior scientists expressed at the time of the tests. R. Chidambaram, the head of India's atomic energy establishment, reportedly told Prime Minister Atal Behari Vajpayee, for example, that with the Comprehensive Test Ban Treaty (CTBT) due for review in September 1999, "the more we delay, the more the danger grows of India losing its option altogether."[8] Those who make this argument suggest that the global nonproliferation effort had reached a tipping point. India's ability to conduct tests and to move forward in terms of a credible nuclear weapons program would have been severely constrained if it had not tested in 1998.[9] A series of developments, some of them explicitly aimed at India, were putting tremendous pressure on India. The Argentina-Brazil nuclear rapprochement; South Africa's opening up of its nuclear program; the dismantling/repatriation of Soviet nuclear remnants in Belarus, Kazakhstan, and Ukraine; the four-power deal on North Korea's nuclear program; the accession of China, France, and South Africa to the Nuclear Non-Proliferation Treaty (NPT); the indefinite extension of the NPT; the conclusion of the CTBT; the start of the Fissile Materials Control Treaty (FMCT) talks; a tightening of nuclear proliferation export controls (both nationally and multilaterally)—all these in combination presented New Delhi with a global nonproliferation regime in which it would have been diplomatically much more costly to test.

A rider to his argument is that Indian scientists would have gradually lost interest in nuclear weapons design as the nonproliferation regime tightened its hold. The longer India did not test, the more likely that the younger generation of Indian scientists would have turned away from a career in nuclear weapons laboratories. A day would have come when India would simply not have had enough bomb engineers.[10]

This argument assumed several things. First, it assumed that the various nonproliferation measures were primarily aimed at India. Second, it assumed that even if they were, India would be unable to resist pressures to cap or eliminate its weapons program and that India in particular would have been unable to test, which was crucial for the deterrent it was trying to build. Third, it assumed that without testing, India's nuclear weapons program would have lacked credibility as a deterrent. Fourth, it assumed that unless India's nuclear scientists carried out a series of test explosions, they would lose interest in a bomb program. All these assumptions are questionable.

Was the ramifying nuclear nonproliferation regime aimed *primarily* at India? There were countries far more worrisome in terms of proliferation in 1998: Iran, Iraq, Libya, and North Korea, to name those of greatest concern. The Western powers led by the United States would certainly have liked to end India's and Pakistan's nuclear programs—the Clinton administration spoke publicly about its aim to "cap, rollback, and eliminate" South Asia's nuclear capabilities—but this was not regarded as a serious, practical goal, and from an absolutist view of nonproliferation, there were more pressing concerns in the Middle East and Northeast Asia. The assertion that India was the major target of the NPT extension, the CTBT, and the putative FMCT was an exaggeration.

Would the Indian government have buckled and given up any hope of testing, and therefore of going nuclear, confronted as it would have been by these various treaties and measures? In the first place it is worth noting that since India had refused to sign the CTBT, India was not legally bound to refrain from testing. It is probably true that with only a few holdouts, the treaty would have made testing more difficult for India. However, although the leading powers and many others were keen that New Delhi should give up its right to test, the Indian government's refusal to sign the CTBT had demonstrated that India was not ready to give up testing and a weapons program. Calls for India to wind up or limit its nuclear program continued, but this was hardly new. During the time that the so-called window of opportunity was closing, successive Indian governments did indeed consider testing. The fact that they pulled back from such a drastic decision suggests that their assessment of the pressures of nonproliferation, if that was a consideration, was not so alarmist as to cause them to authorize testing.[11] One reason that earlier Indian governments perhaps resisted testing was that it is unclear how the international community could have forced India to end its bomb program.

Was testing vital for a credible nuclear deterrent? This is a difficult question to answer definitively, but we can note that New Delhi had not tested for twenty-four years after its first test in 1974, yet it was widely credited with having a nuclear weapons capability. An influential group of Indian analysts continued to argue in this period that India did not necessarily need to test, given what its scientists and engineers had learned in 1974 and given that a crude form of deterrence—the only kind, it was argued, that anyone needed—thereby already existed.[12] If so, India would have had the capacity to deter its enemies even if it had signed the CTBT. To the extent that testing was vital, there were credible nonexplosive forms of testing, such as subcritical tests or simulations. During the CTBT debates, Indian analysts had argued that these forms of testing, which the older nuclear powers had already perfected, were just as effective as the real tests and that the CTBT therefore would not achieve its nonproliferation goal. Indeed, leading Indian scientists were confident that they had the ability to use nonexplosive, subcritical tests such as hydronuclear and hydrodynamic testing.[13]

Finally, there was plenty of challenging work for nuclear weapons scientists and engineers to do, including the development and use of simulations and other forms of weapons design and testing. If India could not carry out nuclear test explosions, research in nonexplosive testing would become vital. Here was a huge field of investigation, inquiry, and experimentation, one that should be capable of enlivening the professional careers of Indian nuclear scientists.

Post–Cold War Strategic Vulnerabilities and Uncertainties

The second explanation of why New Delhi tested is related to the view that the world was a much more dangerous place after the Cold War and that India was far more vulnerable.[14] The tests were a sign to the international community at large, particularly the great powers, that India could defend itself and that it would take steps to redress a growing imbalance in power, real or perceived.

With the end of the Cold War, and specifically the collapse of communism in the Soviet Union, India no longer had diplomatic support of the kind it had enjoyed during the Cold War. Coincident with the disappearance of an ally was the rise of China, an old rival. Another rival, Pakistan, which had helped defeat the Soviets in Afghanistan, had come out of the Cold War with great confidence and had been part of the winning coalition along with the West and China. Most important, the United States had emerged as more powerful than ever before. India's relations with the United States were ambivalent at best in 1998. One of the most contentious areas between the two countries was nuclear nonproliferation. The Clinton administration saw nonproliferation as a major area of diplomatic effort with India and was determined to curtail New Delhi's nuclear program. Washington was also ranged against India on a number of other issues, most important, the Uruguay round of trade talks and human rights. On India's relations with Pakistan, Washington often tilted toward Islamabad's view of Kashmir. All in all, the broader geopolitical situation had deteriorated for India. The tests, in this view, were an attempt to recast the balance of power, arrest India's decline, and reduce its vulnerability in the larger geopolitical game.[15]

The crucial issue here is whether or not nuclear weapons constitute a strategic talisman. It is difficult to see how they could mitigate and redress the range of challenges that India supposedly faced. Nuclear weapons were perhaps relevant to the Kashmir issue, in the sense that tensions over Kashmir with Pakistan might escalate to military and perhaps even nuclear confrontation. Yet it was precisely the danger of confrontation that made the United States so fearful of any further proliferation in South Asia. Going nuclear could have been expected to alienate the United States even further on the Kashmir issue, with the accusation that India had ratcheted up tensions.

A variant of the vulnerability argument is that the nuclear tests were a way of dealing India back into the game of international politics at the highest level after the Cold War. In this view, it was not so much that India was weak and vulnerable but that it had become irrelevant in international politics after 1990. After the Cold War, there were only three ways to gain recognition in the new international order—to be a U.S. ally, to become a major economic player in a globalizing world and thus a market for the United States, or to oppose the United States and the norms it sought to propagate. By 1998, India was none of these things. To become a U.S. ally or to transform India into a major economic player was a long-term venture. To become an adversary was easier. Testing nuclear weapons had advantages here. It was in India's hands to do. It could be done immediately. And it would not go unnoticed. As an adversary, India could look forward to greater U.S. (and Western) attention and eventually to cutting deals (nuclear restraint in return for economic/technological or political deals) in key strategic areas.[16]

Was this India's reason for testing? This is a sophisticated explanation but also one that is fraught with problems. Was India irrelevant in the new international order? It was quite an important player in a series of multilateral negotiations—on environment, population, women, and more important, on trade and nuclear weapons. From the point of view of a rising China, India once again became relevant in Asia as a possible strategic counterweight. By 1998, becoming a quasi ally of the United States in relation to China was a distinct possibility.[17] When India tested in the summer of that year, its economic reforms were more than half a decade old, and it was already being touted as a newly emerging market.[18] Even before testing, therefore, India was a potential ally and attractive market. Would testing have been a better form of international recognition, if a negative one? Was it better to be a potential ally and U.S. market and to hope that "good," integrative behavior would get India what it wanted economically and technologically, or was it better to be an adversary and to expect that "bad," disruptive behavior would be rewarded?[19] Testing would certainly qualify as bad behavior, but as to whether it would primarily be rewarded or punished was uncertain. In the short term, punishment was certain. Beyond that, no one could say with certainty what the tests would bring.

Were the tests a way of propelling India into the forefront of international politics? Here the evidence seems more convincing. Statements by Indian leaders and commentators indicate that the tests were linked to a desire to be recognized in the power and prestige game of international politics. However, if this was so, why did India not test much earlier, say, in the late 1980s or early 1990s when, having been allied to the losing side in the Cold War and being wracked by internal political and economic instability, its standing in the international system was much lower? By 1998, whatever the internal politics of the country, the economy was exhibiting high rates of growth and the balance of payments crisis of the early 1990s had been surmounted. India as an economic player of some standing globally was much more a reality in 1998 than in 1989 or 1995, and to that extent New Delhi could look out far more confidently at the rest of the world. Relations with the major powers were also far steadier. In particular, India's relations with the United States, the preeminent power, were at an all-time high in 1998 despite the NPT and CTBT. In 1998, the Clinton administration was seriously considering a presidential visit to India, the first since Jimmy Carter had visited India in 1976. Those who argue the power-and-prestige case would say that real power and prestige come from military strength and ultimately from nuclear weapons, not from internal strengths, political and economic, or from good diplomatic relationships with leading powers. The question that must still be answered is why earlier governments had not comprehended such a simple, self-evident proposition and why they had failed to test as a way of signaling India's greatness.

Deteriorating Regional Security Environment
The third explanation of the tests is the most common one: in the 1990s, India's immediate geopolitical environment had become more dangerous; and by 1998, matters had reached a climax. In April 1998, Pakistan tested its Ghauri missile just after the BJP-led National Democratic Alliance (NDA) government had come to power. Pakistan's involvement in Indian Kashmir had continued to grow through the 1990s. China, too, was a growing security threat for several reasons. Over the years, Beijing had contributed clandestinely to the Pakistani nuclear program. China was increasingly involved in Central Asia and Myanmar as part of its "encirclement" of India, from Pakistan at one end to Southeast Asia at the other.[20] China's own nuclear arsenal was burgeoning. Audaciously, Beijing had carried out a series of tests after the permanent extension of the NPT and during the CTBT negotiations. In the treaty negotiations, it had insisted that the entry-into-force provisions of the CTBT must include a reference to India's accession.[21] In sum, Pakistan and China between them were working to hem India in strategically. The tests would demonstrate

that India had both the capacity and will to defend itself and that its patience was not unlimited.

How convincing is this as an explanation of the May 1998 tests? Did the security situation around India deteriorate as a result of Pakistan's and China's nuclear decisions in the years preceding India's tests? To the extent that both powers had increased their nuclear capabilities, India's security had to be more fraught. Yet Pakistan's and China's accrual of nuclear capacity was hardly new. Why then had earlier Indian governments not tested? Were they ignorant of Pakistan's and China's plans and policies? Were they unable to weigh the costs and benefits of testing rationally? Were they not committed to India's security? As soon as we ask such comparative questions, we move away from a strictly first image explanation of the tests and move instead toward a second image explanation, one that rests on a domestic politics view of decision making that differentiates among internal actors and their motives, goals, and capacities.

The regional security situation, arguably, was quite stable and no worse than in the previous ten years. During the Narasimha Rao period (1991–1996), India and Pakistan had identified eight areas for discussion. The so-called six-plus-two formula identified security and Kashmir as the two most important issues, thus balancing Indian and Pakistani concerns, respectively. These talks, with some interruption, had continued to be held since 1992. In 1993, the two countries had nearly reached agreement on three disputes: Sir Creek, Wullar, and Siachen.[22] The violence in Kashmir was unabated in this period, but it was only *after the tests*, in 1999, that the two sides went to war, in Kargil.[23] India-China relations also were more stable than they had been in many years. The two sides had embarked on a process that included confidence building, border talks, summitry, and trade. No military incidents of any significance had occurred for over a decade.[24] New Delhi succeeded in getting Beijing to repeat earlier statements that the India-Pakistan dispute over Kashmir should be settled peacefully and bilaterally.[25] The revelations relating to Pakistan-China nuclear and missile cooperation certainly caused India some alarm, but Islamabad and Beijing's strategic relationship was a complex one and certainly not directed at India alone.[26] In addition, there were tensions between Islamabad and Beijing over Pakistan's support of Islamic militancy in the region, including its own Xinjiang Province.[27] Most important, the Pakistan-China relationship, strategically and in the nuclear weapons field, was not new in 1998.[28] Finally, we should note that it was an even bet whether testing would drive Pakistan and China closer together, thereby *increasing* rather than reducing India's strategic problems. In sum, the security situation around India was, if anything, better than in many years. China and Pakistan had differences—for example, over Islam and Kashmir—that were well known. The China-Pakistan nuclear and missile relationship had been common knowledge for years. And it was quite possible to imagine that testing would add to India's woes. That India tested in response to a deteriorating regional security environment seems a rather strained if not inverted argument. As it turned out, the tests would worsen the security situation, culminating in the 1999 Kargil War with Pakistan and, later, the mobilization of troops by India and Pakistan in 2002.

DOMESTIC POLITICS AND THE DECISION TO TEST

Why then did India test when it did? I have suggested that international politics and security considerations cannot altogether account for what happened in May 1998. Rather, the decision and timing of the tests were related to domestic political developments. The foremost development was the BJP coming to power under the leadership of Atal Behari Vajpayee.

To reconstruct the BJP's decision to conduct the nuclear tests in May 1998, it is necessary to pay attention to two major factors: (1) the political and strategic culture of the BJP, which emphasizes the importance of "keeping promises" and which is obsessed with national power and prestige; and (2) the political survival of Prime Minister Vajpayee and his ability to consolidate power after a narrowly won election. We must take as given that India had been on the edge of testing for a long time. Previous governments had considered testing—in 1982, 1995, and 1996. Indeed, in 1996, Vajpayee himself had given the scientists permission to test. In the end, though, for a variety of reasons, each prime minister had drawn back, including Vajpayee. The political and strategic culture of the BJP impelled the party to face the issue of whether or not it should conduct a test once it was in power. This factor was certainly a structural driver of the tests, that is, a long-term imperative arising from a set of values and arguments that were so deeply internalized and normalized within the party that they were scarcely open to debate. These values and arguments had over time acquired a power that was beyond anyone's ability in the party to ignore. Even so, Vajpayee had backed away from testing in 1996, and it is therefore impossible to understand the 1998 tests without paying attention to the difficult political circumstances in which the new prime minister found himself, circumstances in which the tests became more attractive and that dictated they be carried out as soon as possible.

The Tests and the BJP's Political and Strategic Culture

To understand Vajpayee's decision to test in both 1996 and 1998, one has to comprehend the political and strategic culture of the BJP. At the level of political culture, the BJP is obsessed with the idea that it is an organization that delivers on its promises no matter what the cost to the party in terms of immediate political returns. Over the years, the BJP has convinced itself and has sought to convince others that, in comparison with other parties in India, it carries through policies that it believes to be right for the country. This assertion—that it is the only truly "principled" and "nationalist" party—is one that it works hard to sell to both its own members and the public. In effect, the party seeks to propagate an image of a political force that is above the petty, tactical cut and thrust of everyday politics.[29]

The tests very much fitted within this imagery. The BJP suggested in effect that in conducting the tests, it was only doing what the other parties knew was right for the country but did not have the courage to do because of the international repercussions of testing.[30] In a country that is hungry for politicians and leaders who stand for something, who do the right thing, who work for national welfare, and who inspire citizens, the tests were a badge of honor for the BJP. The BJP had carried through on its promise to make the controversy over the Babri Masjid/Ram Janambhoomi temple complex into a national issue. The nuclear tests would be another promise that had been redeemed, perhaps an even more important one.[31] After the tests, another Vajpayee aide explained that the vulnerability of the NDA government in the early days in power and the prime minister's desire to keep his promises were important considerations in the decision to test: "He [Vajpayee] wanted to come in with a bang at that time. It [testing] was also to say that he had kept his word on something he had been advocating India should do for the past thirty years."[32]

The tests particularly suited the BJP because the politics of promise keeping needs something that evokes themes of sacrifice and cost—to India and to the party. After the tests, Vajpayee noted to his aides: "I had faith in the country's inherent strength to withstand any difficulties that may arise out of the test. The fundamentals of the economy were strong and on such issues I believe our people are ready to make any sacrifice for the security of the country."[33] The fact that the tests would trigger international condemnation, calls to punish India and isolate it, and the imposition of sanctions actually played into the hands of the BJP. The public, whatever its feelings about nuclear weapons, would credit the party with having taken a daring step. The promise of sacrifice and costs for the nation would work to intertwine the fates of the BJP and the public. The party as well as the public would face a hostile world, at least for a period of time. Gradually, the world, seeing India's determination to live with punishment, would come round.[34] The party and the public would be challenged and would come out winners. The nation needed to go through a trial in order to strengthen its mettle. This powerful mythos of a people in search of its destiny, of trials and challenges, and finally of redemption and victory in the life of a nation and in the course of a nationalist renewal was at the heart of the politics of promise keeping.

Beyond the political culture of the BJP, there is its strategic culture. Related to the theme of sacrifice and cost in domestic politics, there was the BJP's obsession with a strategic culture of national power and status. In this strategic imagery, nuclear weapons are a vital component.[35] The tests themselves were named "Operation Shakti" (*shakti* means "strength" in Hindi). The BJP did not name the tests; the scientists and the military presumably did. The name is redolent, though, of the view that the BJP takes of nuclear weapons and the importance of military power. In his first interview after the tests, Vajpayee told *India Today*, "The greatest meaning of these tests is that they had given India *shakti*, they have given India strength and they have given India self-confidence."[36] In reply to Raja Ramanna, a leading nuclear scientist, who asked him why he wanted to test at that juncture, Vajpayee simply said, "I want to see India as a strong country and not a soft one."[37]

Within this strategic culture, there was nothing terribly problematic about the importance of nuclear weapons. It was obvious to its proponents and adherents that nuclear weapons must be an element, perhaps the greatest element, of national power and status. It is true that the Congress Party, among others, also holds nuclear weapons to be important. However, the grand old party of Indian politics has always had a rather ambivalent attitude toward a full-fledged nuclear weapons program. For Congress Party leaders from Jawaharlal Nehru to the present, nuclear weapons have at best been perceived as a regrettable necessity, a terrible weapon fit only for defense in extremis and constituting only one element of national security.[38] With the BJP, nuclear weapons are seen as vital for national power and status. As Brajesh

Mishra, Vajpayee's national security advisor, said in an interview, "I have always felt that you cannot in today's world be counted for something without going nuclear."[39]

Nuclear weapons are an instantaneous source of power and status in the BJP worldview. Everyone can agree that, in the long run, economic and technological power counts for a lot in terms of national capabilities and standing. However, these take time to assemble—years if not decades. Nuclear weapons are a spectacular announcement of power—latent power perhaps, but certainly a promise of power that is difficult to ignore. In the BJP's strategic thinking, it was not necessary for a state to wait for economic and technological power before developing military power. Rather, the reverse is true: national power comes primarily from military strength, with economic and technological power coming in the wake of military power. Thus, soon after the tests, a Vajpayee aide argued, "Narasimha Rao's policy of 'nothing but the economy' has been modified to read 'security first and the rest will follow.'"[40] In the prevailing order, where nuclear weapons were legitimate only in the hands of the Permanent Five (P-5), testing and deploying nuclear weapons were also subversive acts, a thumbing of the nose at those powers. Subversion of an established order is an assertion of power, pure and simple, even if one seeks to be assimilated into and accommodated by that order.

The BJP, as a conservative party, is quite at home with notions of power and status. Its theoreticians valorize strength and hierarchy in society, whether in domestic or international society.[41] The contrast with the Congress Party is quite stark. Congress pronouncements and the writings of its major figures show a discomfort with the politics and culture of power and status. Congress thinkers accept that India is a great nation with a proud past and a potentially proud future, but the valorization of power is a notion that resides uneasily in the strategic culture of the Congress.[42] In the BJP, there are no qualms about power—and military power in particular.

The political and strategic culture of the BJP predisposed the party to order the tests and was a powerful influence on Vajpayee. The importance of the cultural factor becomes clearer when we remember that Narasimha Rao of the Congress, Vajpayee's predecessor as prime minister, was also in a precarious position politically, both within his party and nationally in relation to other parties. Nonetheless, Rao chose not to test. That Rao did not test and that Vajpayee did so, it might be argued, occurred because of a different orientation toward risk taking, that is, Rao was a risk-averse leader, whereas Vajpayee was risk accepting. The decision to test or not to test, therefore, might have had little to do with the political and strategic culture of the two parties and more to do with the risk preferences of the two leaders. Although it is tempting to attribute the differences between the two to their risk "profiles," Rao's decision to refrain from testing is not necessarily evidence of risk aversion. To turn back from testing under U.S. pressure when it was public knowledge that he had wanted to test might have been the riskier course politically, the danger being a massive public loss of face at a time when he had a slender majority in Parliament. A risk-averse leader might just as well have chosen to test and reap the almost-certain political dividends of domestic approbation. Rao's decision to hold back the tests is thus more likely related to the nature of the Congress Party's strategic and political thinking than his risk-averse personality.

The Tests and Political Survival

If the political and strategic culture of the BJP made it almost certain that the party, at some point in power, would authorize nuclear testing and the building of an overt nuclear weapons program, this still does not explain why Vajpayee tested when he did. The prime minister and his advisors and supporters publicly argued that international politics—the politics of nuclear proliferation, nuclear politics in India's neighborhood (Pakistan, China), and national security—dictated the tests. The BJP's domestic political interests, however, though rarely mentioned in public, were crucial to the decision. In fact, Vajpayee's personal political survival and agenda played a major role.

After the February 1998 elections, the NDA government headed by Vajpayee came to power with a slim majority. Two years earlier, in a similar situation, the Vajpayee government had collapsed in thirteen days. To appreciate the impact of this collapse, it is vital to understand that the BJP leader had been in politics for over forty years when he became prime minister in 1996. He had finally become prime minister, only to lose power in less than two weeks. As he was sworn in for the second time, the events of 1996 could not have been far from Vajpayee's mind. His survival, once again, was by no means assured given the fractured nature of the electoral results. Political survival was an imperative. A collapse of the government, of the kind that had occurred in 1996, would in all probability have meant the end of his career and a debacle for the BJP, which had painstakingly cobbled together a winning, if noisy, coalition. The prime minister's survival and his consolidation of power were dependent on at least three factors: (1) managing the opposition and its allies after coming to power; (2) warding off the hard-liners within the Hindutva fold, including within his own party; and (3) changing the prime minister's image, which was that of a weak, rather ineffectual leader.

Before we proceed any further, it is important to note that the decision to test in 1998 was taken by Vajpayee and his closest advisor, Brajesh Mishra. Vajpayee personally was committed to making India a nuclear power, and he went ahead with the tests without a detailed policy review within the government. He made the decision on his own, having consulted senior scientists and a few senior BJP leaders.[43] Mishra, principal secretary to the prime minister and later national security advisor, also strongly advocated testing right after the NDA's assumption of power.[44] The decision to test did not come out of a review of nuclear policy that was discussed in the cabinet, with the Cabinet Committee on Security, or within the bureaucracy. During the election campaign, the NDA had promised to carry out a strategic review for India and had suggested that it would revisit the issue of going nuclear after a review. In the event, the new government did no such thing, and there is no evidence that they seriously planned to do so.[45]

Vajpayee, Mishra, and a few senior NDA, primarily BJP, leaders made the decision to test. According to one account, Vajpayee, his lieutenant in the party, Lal Kishan Advani, and Professor Rajendra Singh of the Rashtriya Swayamsevak Sangh (RSS) were involved in the decision to test, and Defense Minister George Fernandes was informed only after the decision was made.[46] The RSS is a right-wing Hindu organization that provides both workers and ideologues for the BJP and the various quasi-political Hindu organizations such as the Bajrang Dal and Vishwa Hindu Parishad.[47] *The Organizer*, the mouthpiece of the BJP, brought out a special issue, "Nuclear India," just hours before the May 11, 1998, tests were announced to the public.[48] Jaswant Singh, considered to be the most experienced and expert in matters related to defense, security, and foreign affairs, had talked over the nuclear problem with Vajpayee and knew that India would test. Home Minister L. K. Advani and Finance Minister Yashwant Sinha were informed the day before the first tests.[49] Vajpayee must surely have sought Advani's views, possibly also Sinha's at various times in the decision-making process. Neither they nor Jaswant Singh, however, knew the date of the tests.[50]

Testing was not a contested and controversial issue within the BJP, but it was more controversial within the NDA. Parties such as the Samata Party led by George Fernandes, the socialist leader who had publicly opposed the 1974 tests, and regional parties such as the Telegu Desam Party (TDP), could have opposed the tests.[51] It is not surprising that, from all available evidence, only the BJP stalwarts within the NDA were therefore consulted on the tests.

To the extent that the decision to test was not a controversial one inside the party, Vajpayee's actions in March and April 1998 do not require a lot of analysis. Testing was, in Cherian's terms, "an article of faith" for the BJP.[52] The BJP's precursor, the Jana Sangh, had called for India to develop nuclear weapons as early as 1964 after China's first nuclear test at Lop Nor. It was the first Indian political party to do so.[53] The party had congratulated Indira Gandhi of the Congress Party on conducting India's first test in 1974 and had frequently castigated both her and the Congress Party for not making India into a full-fledged nuclear weapons power.

Vajpayee and National Security Advisor Mishra were both nuclear advocates. There is no doubt that testing was a priority with them, going back at least to 1996. On his very first day in office in 1996, Vajpayee asked India's nuclear scientists to carry out a test.[54] In an interview with a leading Indian journalist, Mishra recalled that in a public discussion in the mid-1990s he had stated that if the BJP came to power, it would immediately test.[55] The test shafts in Pokhran had been prepared in 1995 during Prime Minister Narasimha Rao's term in office. Rao, concerned about the international condemnation and economic sanctions that testing would bring, had decided not to proceed. The scientists had subsequently left a device in one of the test shafts.[56] In 1996, therefore, they were in a position to conduct a test with some dispatch. Vajpayee promptly asked them to do so. He asked them to halt preparations soon afterward, however, when it became clear that he would not be able to win a parliamentary vote of confidence. Vajpayee reasoned that the international repercussions of the tests might be severe and a new government might have been left to cope with the aftermath.[57]

On March 20, 1998, the day after Vajpayee was sworn in as prime minister, he met India's nuclear scientists again and asked for a briefing on India's nuclear program. He did not immediately clear the tests but indicated his strong interest in testing.[58] Later that day, however, military engineers were asked to prepare the site for testing.[59] On April 9, three days after the test of Pakistan's Ghauri missile, he indicated that the scientists should go ahead and fix a date with Mishra. Once again, there is no evidence that Vajpayee consulted his senior colleagues. He appears to have relied entirely on Mishra. Mishra used the Ghauri missile test conducted by the Pakistanis on April 6 to clinch the issue. According to Raj Chengappa, Mishra's briefing to the prime minister on the test emphasized that "it [the Ghauri test] was having a demoralizing effect on the nation, especially the armed forces and India had to respond. One way was to use the Ghauri as a good enough excuse to go ahead with the nuclear tests."[60] This sequence of events suggests that the decision to test had little to do with Pakistani behavior in and around the tests. Vajpayee and Mishra had set in motion the test process from the day they had come to office. The Pakistani missile test was an "excuse," not the cause.

Why did Vajpayee have to move so quickly to test? The answer lies, I argue, in the politics of political survival as they faced Vajpayee in the aftermath of the fractured electoral verdict. To survive, Vajpayee had to manage his allies and the opposition, and he had to ward off extremists within his own party. To accomplish these two key tasks, he had to refurbish his political image.

Managing Allies and Opposition

Vajpayee's decision to test was related to his fear that his second stint as prime minister might not be very long, just as his first had been very brief. In 1996, the Vajpayee government had lasted less than two weeks. In 1998, many of the difficulties he had faced in 1996 continued to exist, and the longevity of his government was in considerable doubt. The question is whether he tested quickly because he feared that domestic politics would fail him and he would lose a second opportunity to consolidate India's nuclear program; or whether he decided to test to prolong the life of his shaky government. In all likelihood, both considerations played a role. Vajpayee could quite well have had more than one calculation in mind. Either way, domestic politics certainly played a role in the decision to test in May 1998.

Chengappa notes: "This time too [i.e., in 1998] there was a danger of the government falling not in thirteen days but possibly in six months. Vajpayee was aware that the clock was ticking and he moved fast [to test]."[61] Strong evidence exists to suggest that an interpretation focusing on Vajpayee's political survival is the most reasonable one. In 1998, the BJP was the largest single party in terms of the number of seats in Parliament, but it was nowhere near a majority. It needed the support of nearly twenty allied parties to secure a majority. Some of these allies were mercurial and volatile, and their votes could not be counted on for more than some weeks or months.[62] In the little time that he had before the conflicts between his allies and the BJP caused a collapse of the government, it was necessary to have an impact on the calculus of his alliance partners and the public mind.

Why nuclear tests? What were the domestic political advantages of nuclear weapons over other issues that might have been used to mobilize public opinion and rein in allies and opposition? Testing had several advantages. First, Vajpayee could count on the fact that testing was popular. Virtually all public opinion surveys on nuclear weapons suggested that testing and weaponization were popular.[63]

Second, Vajpayee could be assured that a series of nuclear tests would have an impact internationally and therefore nationally. Indeed, a negative international reaction could be counted on to help the BJP domestically.[64] International outrage over India's testing would only serve to rally Indians around the flag and the party in power. The BJP's allies within the NDA, as well as the opposition parties, would therefore find it difficult to criticize the tests *beyond some limit*. Clearly, at a time when the Indian public was rejoicing at India's going nuclear, it would be impossible for the BJP's allies to go so far as to destabilize the alliance. Gail Omvedt, a seasoned observer of Indian politics, noted just a month after the tests: "It [the decision to test] is a bid for popular support which seems to have fairly thoroughly won, at least for the moment. The tests also seem to have been rather useful in stilling at least temporarily the clamor of the BJP allies."[65] Since there was certain to be international condemnation in the short run at the very least, both allies and opposition had reason enough not to bring down the government. Their "playing politics" in the aftermath of the tests, when India was under siege from the United States and its Western friends, would be seen as a "stab in the back" by the public. After the tests, in the face of opposition questions on the tests, L. K. Advani, Vajpayee's unofficial deputy in the BJP, responding to criticism in the Indian Parliament, "brusquely questioned the opposition's patriotism and claimed it for his own party. BJP deputies followed his lead and advised Communist Deputy Somnath Chatterjee to emigrate to Pakistan."[66]

Third, the opposition parties had either tested or come close to testing themselves. They might question the timing of the testing but, not without embarrassment, its necessity. The Congress had conducted the tests of 1974. It had also come close to testing in 1982.[67] Although the 1982 episode was not well known, even within the party, it was common knowledge that in 1995 Prime Minister Narasimha Rao of the Congress had decided to test and then drawn back under U.S. pressure. That decision had been widely reported in the Indian press. The left-of-center government of Deve Gowda and Inder Gujral that succeeded Rao had also tacitly recognized the need for testing when it opposed India's signing the CTBT. At the time, India had insisted that it would not sign because of "security reasons," at least one of which, by implication, was the need to test.[68]

The tests, therefore, had a short-term and a longer-term meaning for Vajpayee. Their immediate impact would be to make it more difficult for his various allies to defect and for the opposition to mount a heavy political attack. In the longer term, even if the alliance began to fray and the opposition parties gained strength, the conduct of the tests under a BJP government would add to Vajpayee's political credibility. If the country were forced once again to go to elections, he could always claim that in the short time that he had been at the helm of affairs, he had taken a brave and momentous decision for the country.

Warding Off the Extremists Within

The second source of threat to Vajpayee's position as prime minister and his brand of relatively moderate politics was the extremists within his own party and the Sangh Parivar. These included members of the RSS, the Vishwa Hindu Parishad (VHP), Bajrang Dal, and the Swadeshi Jagran Manch (SJM).[69]

It is important to remember that in March 1998 Vajpayee was not as clearly the leading figure in the BJP as he was to become. His gentler brand of BJP politics was under pressure from those within the Sangh Parivar who felt that the more extremist BJP agenda that mobilized the party's cadres and energized supporters was the way of the future. Furthermore, in this view, it was extremist politics that served to polarize the electorate between the Hindu majority and various minority groups and to cause the secular parties to lose ground. Extremists argued that the secular parties would get the votes of the minority groups and would lose the Hindu vote to the BJP. Extremists were urging that issues such as the Ram Janambhoomi agitation be made into the centerpiece of BJP politics. They insisted that the BJP bring forward a bill proposing a uniform civil code. They wanted all special "deals" for the Muslim-majority state of Jammu and Kashmir to be revoked, most important, Article 370 of the Constitution, which guarantees the state a special status within the Union. Vajpayee was hard pressed on economic issues, and his appointees were being opposed by the hard-liners in the RSS and other Hindutva organizations such as the VHP and SJM.[70]

Vajpayee understood that if he gave in to the extremists on all these issues, his ability to garner broad public support for himself and the NDA government would be threatened and his term in office might once again be a very short one. The nuclear tests would discipline the extremists within his own camp as much as they would quiet the opposition and the unruly members of his coalition. On issues such as the Ayodhya crisis and a uniform civil code, which were dear to the extremists, Vajpayee had little room for flexibility. Any move to give in to the extremists here would have sparked a rebellion within the NDA from the more secular parties in the alliance. Nuclear testing was not a terribly divisive issue in the NDA, certainly not as controversial as Ayodhya and the civil code, and, crucially, it was attractive to the extremists.

The tests did serve to put Vajpayee's stamp on the NDA government. For at least the next year, Vajpayee and his supporters within the BJP were at the forefront. Brajesh Mishra and Jaswant Singh in particular were the point men for the nuclear program, defending it at home but, more important, abroad. Minister of Home Affairs Advani and Minister of Human Resources and Development (HRD) Murli Manohar Joshi, rival centers of power in the BJP and in the government, could play only a little role in nuclear affairs. The tests very quickly made external relations the focus of the government's energies, and this favored Vajpayee.

Reshaping Vajpayee's Image

How could Vajpayee manage the opposition, various factions within the governing NDA, and extremists within his own party? Vajpayee had to refurbish his image and to appear visionary, decisive, and determined. As a senior editor of one of India's leading magazines notes: "The perception [in 1998] was that Vajpayee, despite his eloquence, was going to be a weak and ineffective prime minister. Vajpayee was desperate to shed that image. He didn't want to go down as another Indian leader who flattered only to deceive."[71] Bharat Karnad, a conservative and well-informed critic of Indian security policy (and a longtime advocate of nuclearization), agrees: "There is little doubt that Prime Minister Atal Behari Vajpayee's decision to resume nuclear testing . . . at one level, sprang from his personal desire to disprove he was a weak leader."[72]

Vajpayee also had to more convincingly take on the mantle of a national figure. Prior to the tests, Vajpayee was not terribly well accepted as a *national* leader (things would be different after the tests). He was a senior leader of the BJP and primus inter pares in the Sangh Parivar, but there remained considerable doubt over how the vast majority of Indians saw him and his ability to govern: they had grown accustomed to his face, but could he run a government?

Vajpayee had little experience in administering and governing. In 1979, he had served as foreign minister in the Janata government under Morarji Desai, but only for two turbulent years before the Congress was returned to power. His tenure as foreign minister had not been particularly distinguished. In any case, by 1998, public memory of that period had faded. Certainly, neither the Indian media nor the public had memories of his earlier stint.

There was also doubt about Vajpayee's ability to stay at the top in the BJP. After the collapse of the V. P. Singh government in 1990, L. K. Advani, much more than Vajpayee, had rallied the party and changed its fortunes. In response to Singh's proposal to institute a reservations policy for the so-called Other Backward Classes (OBCs), Advani and the BJP had embarked on a campaign to build a Hindu temple at Ayodhya at the site of the Babri Masjid. Advani's famous "Rath Yatra" and his brand of agitational politics had popularized the BJP as never before.[73] Vajpayee's moderate politics were judged to have failed the BJP.[74]

The nuclear tests would be *Vajpayee's* tests and his contribution to both India's and the BJP's fortunes. They would project him as a strong, nationalist, and rational leader. To test at a time when the United States and its allies were trying to tighten the nonproliferation net would demonstrate Vajpayee's strength. The tests would be evidence also of his nationalism. Nuclear weapons would give India status and power and would be advertised as having bolstered its security. The tests would also show Vajpayee to be a rationalist—as against an agitational—politician. This last point deserves emphasis. The tests were a "secular" initiative; they were not "communal." In an unfriendly world, India needed reassurance. Nuclear weapons would supposedly give India that reassurance. This was a supremely "rationalist" response, unlike the Babri Masjid campaign, and would show Vajpayee as a responsible, moderate leader, one with whom Indians of all stripes could be comfortable.

DOMESTIC POLITICS AFTER 1998:
THE BJP'S "TEFLON" SURFACE

Before the tests both Vajpayee and the BJP were in a relatively precarious position. The tests served to change their vulnerability. After the 1974 tests, Indira Gandhi and the Congress Party, with a massive majority in Parliament, found themselves in political trouble. By 1975, things were so bad that Mrs. Gandhi had to impose an Emergency in India and jail thousands of her political opponents. After the 1998 tests, Vajpayee and the BJP, by contrast, improved their political position. Indeed, for the next six years, they developed immunity in both domestic and foreign policy that allowed them to weather a number of setbacks and crises. India's relations with Pakistan since 1998 and a series of tensions related to Kashmir illustrate this immunity well.

India's relations with Pakistan and New Delhi's Kashmir policy after the nuclear tests were turbulent, to say the least. Those who thought that the tests on both sides of the border would produce regional stability were mistaken. After 1998, India was on a roller coaster with Pakistan and on the issue of Kashmir, with cooperation and optimism being replaced rapidly by conflict and doubt, as can be seen in the following chronology of events:

February 1999: The Lahore summit

May–July 1999: The Kargil War

1999: The hijacking of an Indian Airlines flight from Kathmandu to Kandahar

July 2000–January 2001: The cease-fire with some Kashmiri militants

July 2001: The Agra summit

December 2001: The terrorist attack on the Indian Parliament

January 2002: The virtual break in diplomatic relations with Pakistan and the mobilization of Indian forces

2002: The terrorist attacks on the Indian army camp in Jammu and on the Akshardham temple in Gujarat

2003: The ending of India's military mobilization

2003: The return to the peace process

2004: The U.S. announcement that Pakistan is a major non-NATO ally

The BJP alternated between aggressiveness and moderation. Promises made to the Indian public—such as the Indian government's refusal to deal with Pakistan until terrorists had been turned over to India, the dismantling of Pakistan's terror network, and New Delhi's unwillingness to negotiate with terrorists—were broken as easily as they had been made.

Almost every initiative that Vajpayee took with Pakistan or related to Kashmir failed, yet his government remained unscathed. The prime minister argued that nuclear weapons in South Asia would bring about stability and cooperation with Pakistan; they palpably failed to do so. He went to Lahore and signed an agreement, only to be at war with Pakistan three months later. The conduct of the Kargil War was portrayed as a great success, but the Pakistani withdrawal came only after the United States intervened diplomatically.

Only months later, an Indian Airlines flight was hijacked to Kandahar by Kashmiri militants. The Indian foreign minister, Jaswant Singh, personally flew to Kandahar to negotiate an end to the hijacking. With him on the flight were several militants whom India had agreed to free in exchange for the passengers onboard the hijacked airplane. This most unusual mission also attracted little opprobrium. The cease-fire with Kashmiri militants in 2000 failed to produce a breakthrough. Few in India held the policy to be a failure, one that the government should account for in public. Vajpayee initiated and hosted the Agra summit, in which President Pervez Musharraf was widely credited with having stolen the limelight. Public opinion, nevertheless, did not hold Vajpayee or the NDA accountable. Nor was Vajpayee's image hurt by the terrorist attacks of 2001 and 2002 and the failure of the Indian military mobilization in 2002. The NDA also escaped criticism when, in 2004, the United States announced that Pakistan would henceforth figure as a major non-NATO ally, even though the Indian government had made India-U.S. relations the pivot of its foreign policy.

How did the BJP avoid punishment by the Indian public right through this period? One view is that foreign relations and security are seen as being above politics, as requiring consensus and nonpartisanship on the part of the public as well as politicians. The depoliticization of external relations, it may be argued, adds up to a forgiving situation for foreign policy and security managers. The BJP's predecessors in the 1990s, the Congress and the National Front, also weathered various foreign policy and security crises with a fair degree of ease. A second and related argument is that nuclear issues and, indeed, national security and external relations are of low salience in Indian politics and do not affect domestic politics, in particular electoral politics.[75] Two reasons for the low salience of external relations in India are worth noting. India is a big country and remains quite insular: although domestic politics are easily understood and regarded as consequential, foreign relations seem alien to many citizens and not immediately material. In addition, coverage of foreign affairs, while fairly high in the English-language press, tends to be far more intermittent in the regional-language press, which has the greatest number of readers.

The problem with these arguments is that external relations in India are by no means above criticism and contention, and at crucial moments they have been of very high rather than low salience. Thus, C. Raja Mohan in his survey of Indian foreign policy argues that "the assumption that there was a near national consensus on foreign policy since Independence also deserves some scrutiny. Many of India's initiatives . . . were all controversial when first mooted by the governments in New Delhi." Raja Mohan lists nonalignment, India's support of Soviet intervention in Afghanistan, Nehru's China and Soviet policy in the 1950s, and the Simla accord with Pakistan in 1972, among others.[76] In the aftermath of the nuclear tests, the BJP was involved in a number of dramatic episodes and decisions in external relations and in Kashmir that did attract criticism from opposition political parties, the media, and the intelligentsia; yet the BJP remained more or less untouched. These actors were unable to mobilize public opinion to the point that it became politically costly for the NDA government. The inability to mobilize political opinion, I argue, rests on two factors: (1) the weakness of the opposition parties led by the Congress, a party that was ill placed to lead; and (2) the strength of the BJP after and in part created by the May 1998 tests. The weakness of the opposition arose principally from anti-Congressism among the non-Congress parties as well as the disarray within all the major opposition parties. The strength of the BJP after the tests was a function of Vajpayee's growing popularity, the image of the BJP as the leading nationalist party, and the party's relationship to the media.

The Weakness of the Opposition

The BJP avoided public criticism and political penalties for its handling of foreign and security policy during this period due to the depth of anti-Congress feeling among sections of the electorate, especially the urban middle class, and among political parties. It was also helped by internal disarray among all the major opposition parties.

Many Indians during the 1990s took the view that it was time for a change, that the BJP was the only national alternative to the Congress, and that it should be "given a chance"—arguments that the BJP repeatedly made.[77] Indeed, the BJP election slogan, "*Sabko dekha baar-baar, hamko parkhen ek baar,*" translates as "You've looked at the others again and again; why not look at us once."[78] A fairly widespread view was that even if the BJP was making mistakes, the Congress had done so for many years. The National Front, which was the third option electorally, had collapsed in 1997. So the real choice was between the Congress and the BJP. Embarrassing the BJP, therefore, meant helping the Congress. For a number of regional parties and former opponents of the Congress at the national level (such as remnants of the old Janata Party that had defeated the Congress after the Emergency in 1977), the grand old party was the major threat.[79] The Congress was the primary electoral rival to them in various states and was still a force nationally. Several senior politicians of the opposition had suffered in the Emergency, including serving harsh jail terms. During their jail sentences, they had lived with members of the BJP. In 1977 and then again in 1989, some of these parties had governed with the help of the BJP. Criticizing the BJP would have played into the hands of the party that threatened their current electoral chances and that had threatened their very existence in the past. Opposition action against the BJP had to contend with another factor that helped the BJP considerably: both the electorate and political parties of various stripes were tired of elections. India had gone to the polls in 1989, 1991, 1996, 1998, and 1999, that is, five times in ten years. In this period, the country was led by seven prime ministers (V. P. Singh, Chandra Shekhar, Narasimha Rao, Atal Behari Vajpayee, Deve Gowda, I. K. Gujral, and Atal Behari Vajpayee). Bringing down the BJP meant more elections and more instability at the top.

In addition to the unpopularity of the Congress, the BJP benefited from the internal disarray among the opposition parties and their unwillingness or inability to mount sustained criticism of the BJP. Part of the problem was that the opposition parties more or less subscribed to the view that external relations and national security are "above politics." Having insisted on this when they were in power, they found it difficult to turn against the BJP. A larger part of the problem, though, was that these parties were in a mess internally. The Congress Party was still reeling from Rajiv Gandhi's assassination in 1991. Narasimha Rao had been prime minister from 1991 to 1996 at the head of a minority government that brought the Congress back into power after two years. However, internally, the party had not settled on its leadership. Sonia Gandhi was unsure of her role and position: she did not want to join active politics, but she feared that if she abnegated power, the party would break up.[80] A second rank of leadership was unable to assert itself against her or Rao or indeed able to decide who was next in line. Three second-rank leaders died unexpectedly—Madhav Rao Scindia, Rajesh Pilot, and Sitaram Kesri. In a tragic way, this did help clarify the leadership issue, but it left the party dangerously low on senior leaders and therefore on parliamentary and organizational talent. Worse was to follow. By 1996, Narasimha Rao had gone into eclipse, with corruption charges against him crippling his government.[81] After the Congress Party's election losses of 1996, he was effectively finished in the party and in politics. In 1998, another set of leaders left the party. There was a danger that this would lead to the party's complete collapse. First Mamata Banerjee, over the handling of Bengal politics, and then stalwarts Sharad Pawar, P. Sangma, and Tariq Anwar quit the party over Sonia Gandhi's foreign origins. Pawar, Sangma, and Anwar argued publicly that the BJP and its allies were correct in claiming that a person of foreign origin could not be prime minister of India.[82] Finally, whereas Sonia Gandhi increasingly took charge of the party and involved herself in the political hurly-burly (especially after winning a seat in Parliament in 1998), she was still very new to political activity. In 1999, when Jayaram Jayalalitha withdrew her support for the ruling NDA coalition, the Congress Party staked its claim to form a government. Sonia Gandhi showed her lack of experience when she announced that the party had enough support to take power. In the event, the Congress did not have sufficient support, and India went back to the polls.[83]

The rest of the opposition was also in disarray. The Samajwadi Party (SP) of Mulayam Singh in India's largest state, Uttar Pradesh, was pitted against not only the Congress but also Kumari Mayawati's Bahujan Samaj Party (BSP) and the BJP, both of whom were strong forces in the state. The Rashtriya Janata Dal (RJD) of Laloo Yadav in Bihar was also under pressure from the BJP and from Ram Vilas Paswan of the RJD. Laloo ran into legal trouble and was in jail during the BJP's rule. His wife, Rabri Devi, took over as chief minister of the state. In any event, Laloo was under political siege in his own state and was unable, like the other non-NDA parties, to mount a national opposition to the NDA government. All these caste-based formations were increasingly prone to factionalism, to caste-related tensions among themselves, and to cooptation by the Hindu right, including the BJP.[84] Finally, the Communist Party of India (CPI) and Communist Party Marxist (CPM) were beset by problems. The CPM, the larger of the two parties, had an aging leadership and increasingly faced difficulties in the two states where it had its base—West Bengal and Kerala. In both states, it was in competition with the Congress as well as new political forces: Mamata Banerjee's Trinamool Congress and a stronger state BJP in West Bengal; and the Congress, as well as BJP, in Kerala.[85]

The Growing Strength of the BJP: Vajpayee, Nationalism, and the Media

The weakness of the Congress in this period stood in contrast to the growing strength of the BJP. The BJP's strength came from Vajpayee's growing popularity and the party's effectiveness in portraying itself as a "nationalist" party. The nuclear tests played a considerable role in contributing through the media to project both images.

Vajpayee's Growing Popularity

After he became prime minister in 1998 and especially after the Pokhran II tests, Vajpayee's popularity rose to unprecedented heights. The tests and the media reaction to them played a considerable role in this change. Vajpayee had always been quite popular in Parliament among fellow politicians. Over the years, he had shown that he was a good public speaker, and, win or lose, he drew big crowds during election campaigns. But he was untested, and even though opinion polls from the late 1970s showed him to be the most admired politician after Indira Gandhi and Rajiv Gandhi, there was doubt about his ability to govern.[86] Janardan Thakur describes Vajpayee's attitude as one of "escapism and detachment": Vajpayee "perhaps lacked the grit and determination, the energy and the gusto which Indira Gandhi had in such great measure" and suffered from an "inbuilt phlegmatism and poetic pessimism."[87] Public perception was ambivalent because he had had very little experience in governing, and therefore his attractiveness as a politician was not based on anything he had done in office. Since he had never been active at the state political level, he had no experience of running even a provincial government. Nationally, he had been prime minister for thirteen days in 1996 and foreign minister in 1977–1979. In the first case he had had no time to make an impact on the public mind, and in the second case his tenure had not been particularly eventful. Until 1996, he had not led the BJP successfully in a national election: he was a "crowd catcher" but not a "vote catcher."[88]

Yet, after the tests, Vajpayee became something of a national hero. The media projected him as a Nehruvian figure, larger than life, with heroic and charming personal qualities.[89] A number of themes recurred in the public descriptions of the prime minister. Vajpayee was a great orator and parliamentarian. He was the consummate moderate, the only person capable of running India and the NDA coalition and of holding the Sangh Parivar extremists in check. He was politically crafty but essentially honest and gentlemanly in his dealings. The prime minister was a poet and artist (an image he often projected), above the hurly-burly of politics, a visionary who was comfortable with a pluralist, tolerant India.[90] A fairly typical view of Vajpayee was Thakur's statement that "[h]e [Vajpayee] is a simple, fun-loving man, without any pretensions, quite capable of seeing himself from the outside, with the eyes of a sensitive poet."[91] Vajpayee was painted as a folksy figure whose somewhat shambling, inarticulate manner on television was turned into a positive quality: he was not a shallow, media-driven politician out to be popular but rather a statesman who spoke from the heart, chose his words carefully, and above all, took "decisions not for petty political gain but in the national interest."[92] No one in his party, the ruling coalition, or the opposition was any match for him. India was safe in his hands. Even opposition politicians, the public was told, were comfortable with him and respected him: he was "moderate," "the right man in the wrong party," or "the wrong man in the Right."[93] If the NDA coalition was liable to criticism, it was the second rank of politicians who were the targets. L. K. Advani, the home minister and deputy prime minister; Jaswant Singh, the foreign and later finance minister; Yashwant Sinha, the finance and later foreign minister; George Fernandes, the defense minister; Murli Manohar Joshi, the minister for human resources and development, among the more senior figures; and Arun Jaitley, Pramod Mahajan, and Sushma Swaraj, among the younger ones, were blamed for all manner of things in domestic and external policy. The only thing that Vajpayee was blamed for was his indulgence of them and the Sangh Parivar.

Vajpayee's "Teflon" coating helped minimize criticism of the NDA. The prime minister's experience and interest in foreign policy meant that the relationship with Pakistan and the various ups and downs with it were hard to pillory. Vajpayee's famous "musings" were a masterstroke. These epigrammatic essays, which appeared in the press, were usually issued from a holiday retreat outside New Delhi.[94] They clothed the prime minister in the image of a philosopher-king, someone who stood above quotidian concerns and took the long view, a wise, generous elder who would not be easily deflected from his goal of peace and cooperation with adversaries, foreign or domestic.

Vajpayee's popularity rested also on a fairly generalized view that there was no one else who could lead. Here again, after the tests, there was a distinct shift in favor of Vajpayee as the only political leader within or outside the BJP who had the stature of prime minister. Poll after poll showed that none of the BJP leaders, such as Advani or Joshi, had much of a following. Nor did the Congress leaders, such as Sonia Gandhi, Scindia, Pilot, or Manmohan Singh. Outside the Congress, there was no one of any consequence—not George Fernandes, Laloo Yadav, Mulayam Singh, Sharad Pawar, Kanshi Ram, Mayawati, or Jayalalitha.[95]

The BJP as a Nationalist Party

By 1998–1999, the BJP had acquired another kind of political immunity. It had for years arrogated to itself the notion that it was India's most truly "nationalist" party. Increasingly, this image came to be fairly widely accepted. The nuclear tests and the changed attitude of the media played a crucial role here. Of some importance also were the very public tokens of legitimacy that came the party's way in the 1990s.

The BJP's nationalist credentials were built on a massive and sustained campaign against the other major parties, particularly the Congress and the left. The Congress was attacked on a number of fronts. Its much-vaunted secularism was portrayed as being false, as "pseudosecularism," a term coined by L. K. Advani, the BJP leader second only to Vajpayee.[96] In any case, secularism itself, the BJP argued, was an import, something that had come from the West. Real Indians did not practice Western secularism. Hindus in particular were innately "tolerant" and thus truly secular. Secularism was just an excuse to pander to the religious minorities and secure their votes. It was therefore dangerously divisive and antinational.[97]

The BJP represented the interests of Hinduism, and Hinduism was the "essential ingredient" of Indian culture; the party was therefore the most nationalist force in the country.[98] In 1999, the Congress was also attacked for falling into the hands of Sonia Gandhi, a "foreigner."[99] For millions of middle-class Indians, the "Sonia as foreigner" campaign resonated powerfully. Even those who were not particularly pro-BJP found themselves in agreement with the view that India could not be ruled by someone who had not been born in India. The Congress brand of politics also was attacked successfully. The BJP was able to construct a coalition of regional parties from all over India; the Congress was unable to do so.[100] The Congress's claim to national status was an anachronism. The old umbrella party had been trumped by the BJP, which had shown a capacity to work with others. It was the Congress that was domineering and intolerant, not the BJP. The Congress was dynastic and undemocratic, in contrast to the BJP. The BJP could accommodate other parties and leaders, and it was a cadre-based party in which the leadership had risen through the ranks by dint of hard work and political acumen.[101]

The left also was portrayed as less than nationalist. The Communists had loyalties elsewhere. They owed their ideas and inspiration to foreign thinkers and powers. Their internationalism was proof that they did not care about national interest and national welfare. They were obsessed with the interests and welfare of a particular class, which in any case was transnational. Moreover, the Indian left was not national enough in its political base. The party's electoral stronghold was in two states—West Bengal and Kerala. It was basically a regionalist party, made up of ethnic Bengalis and Keralites.[102]

The BJP's critique of the Congress and left had an impact in reinforcing the public's desire for change. The Indian public had grown tired of the Congress. The grand old party's fortunes had been in decline for years. Two assassinations had arrested the declining popularity of the party: Indira Gandhi's in 1984 and Rajiv Gandhi's in 1991. But by the middle 1990s the party was losing ground once again. The left, too, was in trouble. The end of communism globally, an aging leadership, policy pronouncements that seemed out of kilter with the times (socialism, secularism, anti-imperialism/antiglobalization, social justice), and an inability to confront some of the major issues facing India (the upsurge of caste-based voting and party formation, the rise of the religious right, insurgency and terrorism) had eroded support for the left.[103] The BJP's organization, backed by various elements of the Sangh Parivar, had élan and youth, and its stand on various issues challenged the shibboleths of Indian politics. Particularly among upper-caste, educated, urban, middle-class, young, and male voters, the BJP's arrival politically was a relief, even when there were doubts about the party's abilities and values.[104]

The BJP was helped by some very public tokens of legitimacy that came its way. In particular, a number of retired civil servants, former officers of the armed forces, actors and sportsmen, and politicians from other parties declared themselves for the BJP or actually joined the party. Brajesh Mishra, N. N. Jha, and Yashwant Sinha of the civil services, Shatrughan Sinha and Rajesh Khanna from the entertainment world, Kirti Azad from sports, and K. C. Pant (an erstwhile Congress stalwart) were some of the more prominent personalities to join the party. Among journalists, Chandan Mitra, Swapan Dasgupta, and Prabhu Chawla were clearly identified with the BJP and its worldview. The political conversion of these and other technocratic, popular, and formerly left-liberal figures to the BJP cause had considerable impact in normalizing the party in the perception of the urban, middle-class India that was in search of a well-organized political force that promised order and efficiency and that projected a coherent worldview in the fast-changing post–Cold War world.

The BJP and the Media

The BJP's relationship with the Indian media, particularly television, was a contributing factor to its political immunity. In India, as in other democracies, the media, tacitly or otherwise, gives new governments a honeymoon period when it withholds serious criticism of government policies. The media also, as in other countries, tends to give the government more room on external relations and in moments of national crisis, particularly war, when there is a rally-round-the-flag sentiment and dissent is unpopular with the public. The BJP benefited from this honeymoon mood in 1998 and the rally-round-the-flag effect both after the nuclear tests and then again during the Kargil War in the summer of 1999. It also benefited from the various terrorist attacks (particularly on Parliament and on the Akshardham temple) and the mobilization crisis in the summer of 2002.

The BJP's ability to manage the media went beyond the honeymoon period and periods of crisis. It was helped by the tendency of the media to accommodate itself to a new political force and political sensibility. As India became more conservative, the media learned to adapt to conservative politics. The BJP did not need, in this sense, to exert itself upon the media. As its popularity increased through the 1990s and as the media got used to the idea that the BJP was going to be a growing force, if not the government of the future, it began to change its commentary and focus. A more "balanced" coverage of the BJP's ideas, policies, and leaders emerged throughout the 1990s, and of course after 1998, without the party having to do much to expand its influence.

Once the BJP came to power, conservative media flourished. Conservative journalists came out into the open and were given column space even in centrist and left-of-center publications. Newspapers and magazines in the English-language press with a more conservative persuasion openly declared themselves—*India Today* and *The Pioneer*, for instance.[105] Well-established newspapers that regarded themselves as "establishment" publications, such as the *Times of India* and the *Hindustan Times*, adjusted to the growing conservative mood politically and the rise of the BJP.[106]

Behind the growing conservatism of the public and of the media's dilution of its criticism of conservative political forces, including the BJP, were a variety of developments. The explosion of television helped the conservative cause and the BJP. In particular, the television serials *Ramayana* and *Mahabharata*, depicting the eponymous classic Hindu epics, which aired in the mid-1980s, had both mirrored and helped construct the rising conservatism of middle-class and lower-middle-class India, which increasingly had access to television sets. The cable and video revolutions allowed a huge population to watch these serials with religious themes. A second development that brought the media closer to the BJP was the liberalization of the Indian economy and the promise that the media, too, would benefit from it in the form of foreign investment. The NDA government eventually passed a bill allowing foreigners to own up to a 26% share in an Indian media house.[107] A third factor that accounts for the media's differential treatment of the BJP was the growing fear of the BJP and the Sangh Parivar. The treatment meted out to the *Tehelka* newspaper, which, in a "sting operation" on a senior BJP member, had exposed the corruption in the party and in the NDA government, shook the media. During the Gujarat riots, the rather threatening public statements of BJP functionaries on the supposedly inflammatory role of television and the press also intimidated the media. The expectation that the BJP was going to be in power a long time, indeed that it might take over the mantle of the Congress Party as the "natural party of governance"—a phrase popularized by the BJP—was another disciplining factor on the media.

CONCLUSION

Domestic politics certainly played a major role in the decision to test, and afterward domestic politics continued to influence the BJP-led NDA government's handling of relations with Pakistan and the issue of Kashmir. The timing of the tests immediately after the coming to power of the BJP-led coalition is best explained by domestic political considerations. The political culture of the BJP, with its mythos of promise keeping, and the strategic culture of the BJP obsessed with power and prestige were the basic forces behind testing. Sooner or later, the BJP, if it were in power, would have tested. That it tested as soon as it did is explained by the rather weak political position it and its leader were in, at least in their own estimation.

The BJP played politics with the bomb. The tests of May 1998, in contrast to May 1974, benefited the party in power, at least long enough to consolidate the prime minister's hold on his party and his coalition and to strengthen his hand in relation to the opposition parties. Operation Shakti and its aftermath seemed to give Vajpayee and the BJP enough time to bring their strengths to bear. This explains why the BJP's failures and contradictory policies with respect to Pakistan and Kashmir went unpunished by the Indian public from May 1998 to 2004. The increasing perception of the BJP as the only truly nationalist party helped give it immunity from public criticism. More important, the increase in the prime minister's popularity after the tests and the weakness of the opposition were crucial in protecting the BJP politically in the course of a series of diplomatic failures and security crises.

What insight does this domestic political focus provide regarding the future of India's nuclear policies and its stance toward Pakistan and Kashmir? First, while the BJP conducted the tests, there is no prospect of rolling the weapons program back regardless of what party is in power in New Delhi. No Indian political force now opposes nuclearization. However, there are differences over the nature of the program (how many, what type, etc.). The BJP, with a political and strategic culture that emphasizes decisiveness and military power, will continue to argue for a bigger rather than smaller nuclear arsenal. India, by all estimations, is locked into a period of coalition government from New Delhi. These coalitions may or may not last the full five-year term, but it is probable in the future that a Congress-led government will be replaced by a BJP-led government with a fair degree of regularity. The electorate has shown, both at the state and national levels, a tendency toward voting the incumbents out. If the BJP returns to power, we can expect it to push ahead with plans for a more robust nuclear weapons program—not a large arsenal, compared to those of the U.S. and USSR Cold War arsenals, in terms of numbers, but a large, more diverse, and sophisticated arsenal, one that would be more active in character than would make the other political parties comfortable.

Second, instability within the coalition is likely to prompt whoever is in charge of the BJP to play politics with the bomb and security. Will a BJP government test again? It is quite plausible that a BJP-led government would once again test sometime in the future, especially if it is a government that is unstable. Even if the United States cut off nuclear cooperation with New Delhi in the event of a future Indian test, Russia and France would be likely to continue to supply nuclear fuel and technology. The fact that there is a fair degree of uncertainty over the success of the fusion device tested in 1998 could serve as a technical case for testing a more sophisticated device.[108] By contrast, it is unlikely that a non-BJP government will test. The Congress and other parties will cautiously take the nuclear program forward, but they have never been as effusive about the bomb as the BJP.

There is a good chance that a BJP-led government in the future will be unstable. The BJP's allies are fairly restive, especially Chandrababu Naidu's party, one of the biggest in the coalition. Relations with other members of the Hindu right wing, especially the RSS, are frequently turbulent. Vajpayee officially retired from political life in December 2005. In 2008, L. K. Advani, a relative hard-liner, took over the leadership of the party and is the party's prime ministerial candidate, but his age and his unpopularity within sections of the BJP remain vulnerabilities for him.[109]

A decade after the tests, it is clear that domestic politics plays a vital role in nuclear decisions. In 2006–2007, India under the Congress-led United Progressive Alliance (UPA) negotiated a deal with the United States that would separate its civilian and military nuclear reactors, bringing the former under IAEA safeguards and allowing the latter to produce fissile material for India's bomb program. The deal set the stage for the resumption of international involvement in India's civilian nuclear program. How the Indian government implements the deal, however, will depend crucially on domestic politics. The deal would seem to legitimate India's nuclear program and lay the foundation for a stronger civilian nuclear program that would help satisfy the burgeoning Indian demand for energy. Nonetheless, domestic politics will strongly influence the implementation of the deal. This underlines this chapter's claim that any understanding of nuclear decision making and strategic choices more broadly requires an appreciation of domestic political conjunctions and circumstances.

NOTES

1. The size of the NDA in terms of the number of parties varied over time, between eighteen and twenty-four. See Paranjoy Guha Thakurta and Shankar Raghunathan, *A Time of Coalitions: Divided We Stand* (New Delhi: Sage Publications, 2004), 39.

2. For this perspective, see Kenneth N. Waltz, *Theory of International Politics* (New York: Addison-Wesley, 1979). On the problem of agency in an anarchical international system, see Richard Little, "Rethinking System Continuity and Transformation," in Barry Buzan, Charles Jones, and Richard Little, *The Logic of Anarchy: Neorealism to Structural Realism* (New York: Columbia University Press, 1993), 82–168. The so-called agency-structure debate is a massive subfield of writing. See the early statements of Alexander Wendt, "The Agent-Structure Problem in International Relations Theory," *International Organization*, vol. 412, no. 3 (1987), 335–370; and David Dessler, "What's at Stake in the Agent-Structure Debate," *International Organization*, vol. 43, no. 3 (1989), 441–473.

3. On the role of identity issues in proliferation decisions, see Scott D. Sagan, "Rethinking the Causes of Nuclear Proliferation: Three Models in Search of a Bomb?" in V. A. Utgoff, ed., *The Coming Crisis: Nuclear Proliferation, U.S. Interests, and World Order* (Cambridge, MA: MIT Press, 2000), 17–50.

4. Peter B. Evans, Harold K. Jacobson, and Robert D. Putnam, eds., *Double-Edged Diplomacy: International Bargaining and Domestic Politics* (Berkeley: University of California Press, 1993), shows that government officials and leaders find themselves "negotiating" in two arenas—the international in relation to other states and the domestic in relation to other internal political actors. It is this kind of perspective that informs the analysis here, where Prime Minister Vajpayee and the BJP-led government made their calculations on the nuclear tests in relation to both the

international and domestic realms, where questions of national survival and political survival feature. Classically, the foremost examples of the statecraft perspective are Kautilya's *Arthashastra* and Machiavelli's *The Prince*. In modern American political science, a still-useful book on statecraft is W. Howard Wriggins, *The Ruler's Imperative: Strategies for Political Survival in Asia and Africa* (New York: Columbia University Press, 1969).

5. See Šumit Ganguly, "India's Pathway to Pokhran II: The Prospects and Sources of New Delhi's Nuclear Weapons Program," *International Security*, vol. 23, no. 4 (Spring 1999), 148–177. Ganguly deals with domestic political factors as an explanation of the long-term drift of Indian nuclear policy insofar as he includes the role of India's scientists in keeping the nuclear and missile programs moving forward. However, the burden of his analysis of the 1998 tests is that U.S. behavior in indefinitely extending the Nuclear Non-Proliferation Treaty (NPT) and passing the Brown Amendment in 1995, combined with the passage of the Comprehensive Test Ban Treaty (CTBT), plus Chinese and Pakistani military cooperation in the period 1995–1998, were responsible for the May 1998 tests. For an analysis of alternative "models" for nuclear weapons development in India and elsewhere, see Sagan, "Rethinking the Causes of Nuclear Proliferation."

6. George Perkovich, *India's Nuclear Bomb: The Impact on Global Proliferation* (New Delhi: Oxford University Press, 2000) deals with domestic political factors as a part of the story of Indian nuclear decision making since 1948 but remains incomplete since the book was finished shortly after the tests. Two articles deal explicitly with the domestic politics of the tests: Pramod K. Kanth, "The BJP and Indian Democracy: Elections, Bombs, and Beyond," in Ramashray Roy and Paul Wallace, eds., *Indian Politics and the 1998 Election: Regionalism, Hindutva and State Politics* (New Delhi: Sage Publications, 1999), 340–364; and Stuart Corbridge, "'The Militarization of All Hindudom'? The Bharatiya Janata Party, the Bomb, and the Political Spaces of Hindu Nationalism," *Economy and Society*, vol. 28, no. 2 (1999), 222–255. In addition, the writings of nuclear critics Achin Vanaik and Praful Bidwai situate the tests in domestic politics. See their *South Asia on a Short Fuse: Nuclear Politics and the Future of Global Disarmament* (New Delhi: Oxford University Press, 1999), 93–100.

7. For the concept of strategic "windows of opportunity," see Stephen Van Evera, *Causes of War* (Ithaca, NY: Cornell University Press, 1999), 73–104.

8. As quoted in Raj Chengappa, *Weapons of Peace: The Secret Story of India's Quest to Be a Nuclear Power* (New Delhi: HarperCollins Publishers India, 2000), 33.

9. For this view, see Jasjit Singh, "Why Nuclear Weapons?" in Jasjit Singh, ed., *Nuclear India* (New Delhi: Knowledge World in association with the Institute for Defence Studies and Analyses, 1998), 20–25; and K. Subrahmanyam, "Indian Nuclear Policy: 1964–98," in Singh, *Nuclear India*, 50–53. See also Ganguly, "India's Pathway to Pokhran II," 167–171.

10. This view is attributed to Chidambaram, quoted in Chengappa, *Weapons of Peace*, 34.

11. Both the Narasimha Rao and Gowda-Gujral governments had considered testing but refrained from doing so in 1995 and 1996–1997, respectively. On the other hand, the thirteen-day Vajpayee government of 1996 had given orders to test. The fall of the government, however, stopped the tests. On the Rao and Gowda-Gujral "near-testing" episodes, see Chengappa, *Weapons of Peace*, 390–407. On Vajpayee's first decision to test, see ibid., 31–32. Bharat Karnad claims that Rao had wanted to test in 1993 and then postponed the decision to 1994 and finally 1995. See Bharat Karnad, *Nuclear Weapons and Indian Security: The Realist Foundations of Strategy* (New Delhi: Macmillan India, 2002), 369–370.

12. Those who have articulated such a view include K. Subrahmanyam and Jasjit Singh. Other terms applied to this kind of thinking are "nonweaponized deterrence" and "recessed deterrence" (the latter is Jasjit Singh's term). See Perkovich, *India's Nuclear Bomb*, 339–340, 432.

13. See Karnad, *Nuclear Weapons and India's Security*, 382.

14. See C. Raja Mohan, *Crossing the Rubicon: The Shaping of India's New Foreign Policy* (New Delhi: Viking/Penguin India, 2003), xii–xxii.

15. See ibid., 14–28.

16. See ibid., 89–96.

17. See the evidence cited in Waheguru Pal Singh Sidhu, *Enhancing Indo-US Strategic Cooperation*, Adelphi Paper 313 (London: International Institute for Strategic Studies and Oxford University Press, 1997), 53.

18. Varun Sahni, "India in American Grand Strategy," in Kanti Bajpai and Amitabh Mattoo, eds., *Engaged Democracies: India-U.S. Relations in the 21st Century* (New Delhi: Har-Anand Publications, 2000), 43–46.

19. Mohan, *Crossing the Rubicon*, 90.

20. Brahma Chellaney, "The Dragon Dance," *Hindustan Times*, January 23, 2002, http://www.hindustantimes.com/nonfram/230102/detideo1.asp (no longer available).

21. Karnad, *Nuclear Weapons and India's Security*, 391.

22. J. N. Dixit, "Got a Grip, So Gently Now," *Hindustan Times*, January 14, 2004, available at http://meaindia.nic.in/opinion/2004/01/14op02.htm. Dixit notes that draft agreements on Sir Creek, Wullar, and Siachen were prepared during the period 1988–1996. In private conversations, the former foreign secretary revealed that in 1993, when he was at the helm of the Ministry of External Affairs, the two countries had completed agreements on the three disputes.

23. On the Kargil War, see Chapter 5 in this volume; Šumit Ganguly, *Conflict Unending: India-Pakistan Tensions Since 1947* (New Delhi: Oxford University Press, 2002), 114–133; and Kanti Bajpai, Afsir Karim, and Amitabh Mattoo, eds., *Kargil and After* (New Delhi: Har-Anand Publications, 2001).

24. The last India-China crisis of any significance was in 1986–1987. Indian and Chinese troops mobilized and were placed on high alert in the Sumdurong Chu area and along the northeastern border in the wake of the Indian military exercise "Chequerboard." See Kanti Bajpai, "Conflict, Cooperation, and CSBMs with Pakistan and China: A View from New Delhi," in Šumit Ganguly and Ted Greenwood, eds., *Mending Fences: Confidence- and Security-Building Measures in South Asia* (Boulder, CO: Westview Press, 1996), 29.

25. Rosemary Foot, "Sources of Conflict Between China and India As Seen from Beijing," in Ganguly and Greenwood, *Mending Fences*, 64, notes that as early as June 1980 Deng Xiaoping had stated that Kashmir was a bilateral problem that should be settled bilaterally and peacefully.

26. The Pakistan-China relationship was also aimed at the United States. For China, a close relationship with Pakistan was intended to ensure that Islamabad did not become a U.S. ally and a troublesome neighbor on China's southern periphery. For Pakistan, the relationship with China gave it leverage with the United States. See Kanti Bajpai, "Strategic Threats and Nuclear Weapons: India, China, and Pakistan," in M. V. Ramana and C. Rammanohar Reddy, eds., *Prisoners of the Nuclear Dream* (New Delhi: Orient Longman, 2003), 27–52.

27. Foot, "Sources of Conflict," 67, notes that Chinese concerns over Muslim separatism in Xinjiang Province were the cause of China's more balanced position on Kashmir.

28. See Anil Joseph Chandy, "Pakistan-China Relations," in Kanti Bajpai and Amitabh Mattoo, eds., *The Peacock and the Dragon: India-China Relations in the 21st Century* (New Delhi: Har-Anand Publications, 2000), 315–329.

29. Dina Nath Mishra, an ideologue of the BJP, commenting on the international and domestic reaction to the tests, noted just after the tests: "[A] considerable number of political commentators, including some belonging to political parties, can't see beyond the tip of their nose. They are prone to speculate politically even about the most vital decisions concerning security and [sic] future of India." See Dina Nath Mishra, "Towards Making India Invincible," *The Observer*, May 21, 1998, available at http://www.hvk.org/articles/0598/0095.html.

30. Ibid., 3.

31. Ibid., 3–4.

32. Quoted in Chengappa, *Weapons of Peace*, 31.

33. Ibid., 50.

34. Chengappa, ibid., 48–49, records that an Indian government analysis suggested that in the aftermath of the tests the United States would be the biggest concern in terms of sanctions but that the economy was "resilient enough to stand up for a year" and that "[i]f India plays its business and political cards well the worst should be over in six months."

35. I have taken the term "strategic imagery" from Stephen P. Cohen. See his early essay on Indian and Pakistani strategic culture, "The Strategic Imagery of Elites," in James M. Roherty, ed., *Defense Policy Formation: Towards Comparative Analysis* (Durham, NC: Carolina Academic Press, 1980), 153–173. See also his "Image and Perception in India-Pakistan Relations," in M. S. Rajan and Shivaji Ganguly, eds., *Great Power Relations, World Order and the Third World* (New Delhi: Vikas Publishing House, 1981), 281–290.

36. Chengappa, *Weapons of Peace*, 36.

37. As reported in ibid., 52.

38. On Nehru, see Kanti Bajpai, "Nehru and Disarmament," in *Nehru Revisited* (Mumbai: Nehru Centre, 2003), 353–393. See also Chengappa, *Weapons of Peace*, 70, 80–84, on Nehru's ambivalence to nuclear weapons. On Indira Gandhi's reluctance to sanction any further tests after 1974, see the narrative in ibid., 285–287. On Rajiv Gandhi's and Narasimha Rao's attitude to nuclear weapons, see ibid., 295 and 369–370, respectively.

39. Quoted in R. Swaminathan, "Pokhran II: Five Years Later," *South Asia Analysis Group*, Paper No. 690, 2, http://www.saag.org/papers7/papers690.html (no longer available).

40. Quoted in Perkovich, *India's Nuclear Bomb*, 442.

41. See M. S. Golwalker, *A Bunch of Thoughts*, 3rd ed. (Bangalore: Sahitya Sindhu Prakashan, 1996), and *We, or Our Nationhood Defined* (Nagpur: Bharat Publications, 1939); and V. D. Savarkar, *Hindutva: Who Is a Hindu?* (Mumbai: Swantantryaveer Savarkar Rashtriya Smarak, 1999). Also see Kanti Bajpai, "Hinduism and Weapons of Mass Destruction: Pacifist, Prudential, and Political," in Sohail H. Hashmi and Steven P. Lee, eds., *Ethics and Weapons of Mass Destruction: Religious and Secular Perspectives* (New York: Cambridge University Press, 2004), 308–320; and Kanti Bajpai, "Indian Strategic Culture," in Michael R. Chambers, ed., *South Asia 2020: Future Strategic Balances and Alliances* (Carlisle, PA: Strategic Studies Institute, U.S. Army War College, 2002), 245–303.

42. See in particular Jawaharlal Nehru, *The Discovery of India* (New Delhi: Nehru Memorial Fund and Oxford University Press, 1946), 536–548.

43. Vajpayee met two of the principal scientists associated with India's nuclear and space programs, A. P. J. Abdul Kalam and R. Chidambaram, on March 20, 1998, the day after his government was sworn in. See Chengappa, *Weapons of Peace*, 29–30.

44. Ibid., 47–48.

45. Ibid., 31, notes that on April 9, 1998, Prime Minister Vajpayee formed a high-level task force to work out the composition of a National Security Council that would author a nuclear doctrine for India. Neither the task force nor the National Security Council, however, conducted the review of nuclear policy that the BJP manifesto had promised.

46. Stuart Corbridge, "'The Militarization of All Hindudom'?" 241.

47. Bernard Imhasly, "A 'Hindu' Bomb for India? Political Exploitation of the Nuclear Tests," *Neue Zurcher Zeitung*, June 13–14, 1998, 1.

48. Kalpana Sharma, "The Hindu Bomb," *Bulletin of the Atomic Scientists*, vol. 54, no. 4 (July–August 1998), 1.

49. Chengappa, *Weapons of Peace*, 11–12.

50. Ibid., 11–12.

51. Cherian, "BJP and the Bomb," 8.

52. Ibid., 4.

53. Shyam Bhatia, *India's Nuclear Bomb* (Ghaziabad: Vikas Publishing House, 1979), 111.

54. Chengappa, *Weapons of Peace*, 31; Perkovich, *India's Nuclear Bomb*, 365–371, on the Rao government's decision to test and 371–376 on the BJP's first decision to test in 1996.

55. Swaminathan, "Pokhran II," 3.

56. Perkovich, *India's Nuclear Bomb*, 374.

57. For this series of events, see Chengappa, *Weapons of Peace*, 31–32; and Perkovich, *India's Nuclear Bomb*, 365–376.

58. Chengappa, *Weapons of Peace*, 29–34. Swaminathan, "Pokhran II," 4, reports that Mishra recalled discussions on testing "two weeks or so after the Prime Minister took oath, which would make it 4 April." It is unclear whether this refers to the briefing by the nuclear scientists or by others, including Mishra himself. The Pakistani missile test took place on April 6.

59. Chengappa, *Weapons of Peace*, 42.

60. Ibid., 44–45.

61. Ibid., 32.

62. On the precariousness of the NDA government and the link to the decision to test, see ibid., 32; Kanth, "The BJP and Indian Democracy," 350–353; and Corbridge, "'The Militarization of All Hindudom'?" 243.

63. Sharma, "The Hindu Bomb," 2, reports that 87% of those polled soon after the tests supported the government's decision. Public displays of celebration and the Indian media's reactions were indicative of a national mood of exhilaration and exuberance. Sandy Close, "Indians Take Bomb Tests in Stride As They Cross Bridge into the World of the 21st Century," *Jinn Magazine*, 2, available at http://www.pacificnews.org/jinn/stories/4.11/980602-india.html.

64. Kanth, "The BJP and Indian Democracy," 354, 356, makes a similar point.

65. Gail Omvedt, "The Hindutva Bomb," *The Hindu*, June 20, 1998, available at http://www.foil.org/politics/nonuke/gailomv.html.

66. This is reported by Imhasly, "A Hindu Bomb for India?" 3.

67. Perkovich, *India's Nuclear Bomb*, 242–244. See also Chengappa, *Weapons of Peace*, 246–261.

68. For a similar analysis of why the opposition could not challenge the tests, see Sharma, "The Hindu Bomb," 2.

69. Geeta Puri, *Hindutva Politics in India: Genesis, Political Strategies and Growth of Bharatiya Janata Party* (New Delhi: UBSPD, 2005), 364.

70. Vajpayee's nominee for the post of finance minister was his political ally within the BJP, Jaswant Singh. K. S. Sudershan, a senior RSS leader, "categorically told him [Vajpayee] to drop Singh. Vajpayee was forced to agree and told the president of India to remove Singh's name from the list [*sic*] to be sworn in as ministers the next day." See Chengappa, *Weapons of Peace*, 30.

71. Ibid., 30.

72. Karnad, *Nuclear Weapons and India's Security*, 399. Vajpayee was well aware of his image of weakness. Karnad quotes Vajpayee as saying that "people go around saying I am soft, I bend easily. When did I bend? On the nuclear test? We knew there will be sanctions but we withstood them."

73. A *rath yatra* is literally a "chariot journey or pilgrimage." Advani's 1990 Rath Yatra was in support of the construction of a Ram temple in Ayodhya. See Neena Vyas, "BJP to Observe Anniversary of Advani's Rath Yatra," *The Hindu*, April 8, 2005.

74. Janardan Thakur, *Prime Ministers: From Nehru to Vajpayee* (Mumbai: Eeashwar Publications, an imprint of Business Publications, 1999), 347–348, 358–362, on the Vajpayee-Advani relationship and Advani's role in propelling the BJP forward politically and electorally. See also Puri, *Hindutva Politics in India*, 373, on Advani's "ideological" politics as shaping the BJP from 1984 until the destruction of the Babri Masjid in 1992.

75. Public opinion surveys in India have shown that nuclear weapons are not considered a high priority. The Indian public rates nuclear weapons below a series of socioeconomic issues—economic growth, employment, inflation, communal peace, and social justice. See, for instance, David Cortright and Amitabh Mattoo, eds., *India and the Bomb: Public Opinion and Nuclear Options* (Notre Dame, IN: University of Notre Dame Press, 1996), 118.

76. Raja Mohan, *Crossing the Rubicon*, 267.

77. Kanth, "The BJP and Indian Democracy," 357, notes that over half of those who voted for the BJP in 1998 did so "to give the new party a chance."

78. V. B. Singh, "Rise of the BJP and Decline of the Congress," in Rajendra Vora and Suhas Palshikar, eds., *Indian Democracy: Meanings and Practices* (New Delhi: Sage Publications, 2004), 307.

79. Kanth, "The BJP and Indian Democracy," 359; and Singh, "Rise of the BJP," 305.

80. See Thakur, *Prime Ministers*, 327, on Sonia Gandhi's desire to project an image of reluctance to participate actively in politics. Thakur suggests that this was a "ploy."

81. See ibid., 332–341, on the corruption around the Congress Party before and during Rao's tenure as prime minister. See also Singh, "Rise of the BJP," 309.

82. See Thakurta and Raghuraman, *A Time of Coalitions*, 165–167, on the foreigner issue.

83. Singh, "Rise of the BJP," 313.

84. See Rajendra Vora, "Decline of Caste Majoritarianism in Indian Politics," in Vora and Palshikar, *Indian Democracy*, 279–296, on the limits of caste-based political parties and the difficulties they faced in the 1990s.

85. See Sandeep Pendse, "Predicament of the Left," in Vora and Palsikhar, *Indian Democracy*, 331–339, on the disarray of the leftist parties, primarily the CPM.

86. Thakur, *Prime Ministers*, 357, who mentions the polling results on Indian leaders and Vajpayee's standing.

87. Ibid., 357–358.

88. Ibid., 351.

89. Ibid., 351–352.

90. See ibid., 348, 350, on Vajpayee's appeal across party lines; and 351, on Vajpayee's political idealism and his distaste for "murky politics."

91. Ibid., 356.

92. See Vir Sanghvi, "In Defence of Vajpayee," *Mid-Day*, April 24, 2005, http://www.mid-day.com/columns/vir_sanghvi/2005/April/108053.htm (no longer available); and Vir Sanghvi, "India's Most Admired Politician," *BJP Today*, May 16–31, 2003, available at http://www.bjp.org/today/may_0203/may_2_p_6.htm.

93. Thakur, *Prime Minister*, 350, notes that even the Communists saw Vajpayee as moderate: "Even the Communists who detest the BJP, and more so the RSS, change their tone when they speak of Vajpayee. 'Ah, he is different. There is nothing of the Hindu fanatic about him. The RSS does not trust him.'"

94. Raja Mohan, *Crossing the Rubicon*, 176.

95. In 1998, Vajpayee was favored by 21.5% of those polled; Sonia Gandhi, by 13.6%; and serving prime minister I. K. Gujral, by 3.4%. This poll reported that 32% had never heard of Sonia Gandhi. As the election campaign got under way in 1999, more than a year after the nuclear tests, Vajpayee had the support of 51% of the voters, whereas Sonia Gandhi had 33%. Manmohan Singh, who became prime minister in a Congress-led government in 2004, had the support of only 2% of the electorate. Other candidates also had 2% or less. Another poll put Vajpayee at 57% and Sonia Gandhi at 27%. Yet another poll put the two leaders at 50% and 26%, respectively. The poll data are summarized in "The Thirteenth Election of India's Lok Sabha (House of the People)," 15–16, 21, on the Asia Society website, available at http://www.asiasociety.org/publications/indian_elections.13.a.html.

96. Advani on "pseudo-secularism" is quoted in Puri, *Hindutva Politics in India*, 292–293.

97. On "pseudo-secularism" as a way of pandering to the minorities and getting their votes, see Advani's presidential speech of 1995 as quoted in ibid., 292.

98. Ibid., 60.

99. Vir Sanghvi, "No Way to Treat a Lady!" *Rediff on the Net*, available at http://us.rediff.com/news/1999/oct/01vir.htm.

100. Prime Minister Atal Behari Vajpayee of the BJP at an election rally asserted: "[W]e have proved that only we [the BJP] can run a coalition." Quoted in Puri, *Hindutva Politics in India*, 436.

101. See ibid., 198–199. See also Thakurta and Raghuraman, *A Time of Coalitions*, 39–40, for the BJP's self-image as a democratic, cadre-based party, free of corruption—"a party with a difference."

102. For a typical BJP critique of the leftist parties, see Advani's speech as quoted in Puri, *Hindutva Politics in India*, 339–343.

103. Pendse, "Predicament of the Left," 339–345.

104. See Singh, "Rise of the BJP," 313–322, on the support bases of the BJP.

105. Prabhu Chawla, a senior editor with *India Today*, is a well-known sympathizer of the BJP. Swapan Dasgupta, a former leftist who became a conservative ideologue, was hired by *India Today* as the BJP rose to power and as the magazine inclined to the right in the 1990s. *The Pioneer* is a conservative newspaper sympathetic to and in part funded by the BJP and critical of the Congress Party.

106. Vir Sanghvi, editor of the *Hindustan Times*, became distinctly more sympathetic to the BJP after 1998, arguing that once in power the party would become more moderate. After the burning of a train compartment in Godhra, Gujarat, which was followed by the communal attacks on Muslims in the state, Sanghvi wrote that the secular parties and forces had not condemned Godhra sufficiently, an accusation that was highly questionable and that was not far from the BJP's own reaction to Godhra. See his "One Way Ticket," *Hindustan Times*, March 4, 2002, available at http://www.vskgujarat.com/godhraandaftermath/onewayticket.htm.

107. The bill was passed in February 2002. See Raju Bist, "Media Giants See Dollar Signs in India," *Asia Times Online*, http://www.atimes.com/atimes/printN.html (no longer available). On the policy, see Sukumar Muralidharan, "A Perilous Shift," *Frontline*, vol. 19, no. 14 (July 6–19, 2002), available at http://www.frontlineonnet.com/fl1914/19140190.htm.

108. Adam Berstein, Todd West, and Vipin Gupta, "An Assessment of Antineutrino Detection as a Tool for Monitoring Nuclear Explosions," *Science and Global Security*, vol. 9, no. 3 (2001), 235–255.

109. Somini Sengupta, "Former Premier Vajpayee Retires from Indian Politics at 81," *New York Times*, December 31, 2005, A8.

2 TESTING THEORIES OF PROLIFERATION IN SOUTH ASIA

Karthika Sasikumar and Christopher Way

WHY DO STATES ACQUIRE NUCLEAR WEAPONS? Answers to this question have proliferated over the years but have been grouped broadly under three approaches. Approaches emphasizing technological capabilities claim that once a country acquires the capacity to develop nuclear weapons, it is only a matter of time until it does so. Security-based explanations emphasize the need rather than the ability to build weapons: the probability of a state pursuing nuclear arms increases with the severity of external security threats. Finally, some explanations hold domestic political considerations responsible for nuclear proliferation.

Proponents of *all three approaches* have pointed to India's and Pakistan's acquisition of nuclear weapons as providing striking evidence supporting their claims. Can all of them be right? Do their explanations offer competing or complementary perspectives on South Asian proliferation? We address these questions by embedding the Indian and Pakistani cases in broader research investigating the correlates of nuclear weapons proliferation. In contrast to other chapters in this book, we look *outside* the region to understand what happened *inside* South Asia. We draw on our work of testing theories of nuclear proliferation with quantitative methods in order to situate the two South Asian cases in the broadest possible comparative context.[1] Drawing on a large-N survival model of proliferation covering 168 states from 1949 to 2001, we assess whether and to what extent India and Pakistan are surprising or unusual in the context of the broader "correlates of proliferation." To gauge the relative importance of specific variables to the two South Asian cases, we use a series of counterfactual simulations to generate hypothetical predictions for India and Pakistan under various scenarios.

Privileging one of the three approaches over another has important political and normative implications. Governments in India and Pakistan are united in their insistence that their programs were impelled by security needs; they see no reason why deterrence should not work in South Asia as elsewhere, and why their motives for acquiring weapons should be seen as different from those of existing nuclear weapons states.[2] For five decades, they point out, various proposals to restrict *vertical* proliferation have been rejected and marginalized by those who are now calling for elimination of nuclear weapons on the subcontinent. Both countries insist that their weapons programs are as legitimate as those of the Nuclear Weapon States (NWS) precisely because they are motivated by security concerns.

Scholarly work on the issue is divided. Some claim, in contrast to the positions of the two governments, that the threat environment cannot provide more than a retrospective justification for decisions that were motivated by a skewed understanding of national interest.[3] Other analysts, although sharing this skepticism of state elites who present security concerns as justifications, blame the nonproliferation regime for its selective enforcement practices and its blindness to the concerns of South Asian actors.[4] Yet others decry the "dismissal" of security imperatives and the privileging of explanations based on "status, prestige, and the exigencies of domestic politics."[5]

To enter into this debate, we first map the stakes in the debate over nuclear proliferation and then use a large-N hazard model to engage the contending positions, presenting a brief description of the model and our main results. The bulk of the chapter is then devoted to discussing and explaining the statistical results in the context of the cases of India and Pakistan and their implications for theory and policy.

THREE MODELS IN SEARCH OF A TEST:
THE DEBATE OVER NUCLEAR PROLIFERATION

The *technological determinants* literature claims that once a country acquires the latent capacity to develop nuclear weapons, it is only a matter of time before it does so. A country's level of economic and scientific development determines latent capacity to acquire nuclear weapons, and as it becomes easier to acquire nuclear weapons, it becomes more likely that a state will choose to do so. In some ways, this argument harmonizes with realist predictions that countries capable of developing a nuclear program will eventually do so. In other ways, it is congruent with accounts that stress the role of entrenched domestic actors.

The *external determinants* literature emphasizes intention rather than ability. Security threats are claimed to explain the desire to pursue nuclear weapons: the probability of a state pursuing nuclear arms increases with the severity of the external security threats that it faces. A third strand of scholarship shifts the focus from the external to *domestic determinants* of proliferation. Scholars have held a range of domestic factors—regime type, bureaucratic politics, economic policy preferences, political ideology, unsatisfied status aspirations—responsible for proliferation individually or jointly.

Among these three approaches, the "commonsense" understanding of proliferation as motivated primarily by security concerns predominates in policy and academic discourse. It is assumed that the states designated as NWS by the Nuclear Non-Proliferation Treaty (NPT) acquired nuclear weapons in order to meet security needs. These were legitimate security-seeking choices in an international system acknowledged to be anarchic. Even after Cold War threats faded, NWS retain nuclear weapons as insurance against threats emerging from "rogue states" or unanticapted future threats. Yet, in a striking contrast, the Indian and Pakistani programs are frequently depicted in the literature as motivated by domestic interests or by technological momentum. Those who would reverse their programs, therefore, aim to provide incentives to domestic factions to renounce nuclear weapons or to restrain the dissemination of the technology that underlies such programs.

THE CORRELATES OF NUCLEAR PROLIFERATION

Testing theories of proliferation, therefore, has crucial policy implications. Although we do not claim to resolve this debate, we enter it by drawing on our recent work aimed at providing a quantitative test of theories of proliferation. Seeking to complement the qualitative, comparative case-study methods that predominate in this area of research, we highlight some strengths of quantitative approaches. First, theories of nuclear weapons proliferation offer, either explicitly or implicitly, *probabilistic* hypotheses. Statistical models based on a probabilistic logic of inference fit this theoretical logic better than the deterministic logic associated with the Millian methods of agreement and difference of comparative case studies.[6] Moreover, it is likely that decisions to pursue nuclear arms have multiple, interacting determinants. Yet some studies implicitly rely on monocausal logics of inference, comparing competing explanations as if looking for the "magic bullet" that explains all cases, whereas others respond to the complexity by crafting idiosyncratic interpretations of individual cases in all their richness and complexity. The multivariable logic of inference embodied in statistical approaches walks a middle ground, recognizing the importance of multiple, potentially interacting determinants but also pursuing generalizability. Finally, because they sample on the dependent variable, most qualitative studies ignore or underemphasize the large number of countries that never pursued nuclear weapons. This runs the risk of underestimating the strength of causal effects (or, more rarely, erroneously accepting a relationship that does not hold up in a wider sample).[7] Equally important, sampling on the dependent variable discards much valuable information useful in drawing inferences about the "correlates" of proliferation. Quantitative analyses encourage us to include observations covering the full range of variance on both the dependent and independent variables.

To study proliferation quantitatively, we must use a method well suited to rare events and able to model the effects of time (such as "duration dependence"). We are interested in estimates of the likelihood that a country will begin to pursue nuclear weapons, given that it has not done so until that point. Moreover, since most countries never do pursue nuclear weapons, we need a method that accounts for this "right censoring" and avoids the selection bias resulting from excluding countries that never even seriously considered going nuclear.[8] Finally, a suitable model must accommodate explanatory variables that change in value over time.

Event history models (also called survival, hazard, or duration models) provide *estimates of the probability of an event occurring*—in our case, a state going nuclear at a particular time—given that it has not yet happened.[9] In the language of event history analysis, this likelihood is given by the hazard rate, the "risk" that a country will go nuclear in a specific time period. To facilitate the inclusion of both time-invariant and time-varying variables, we estimate parametric discrete-time hazard models using a Weibull distribution to characterize the baseline hazard function. The hazard rate is then given by

$$h(t|x_j) = pt^{p-1}\exp(\beta_0 + x_jB_x)$$

where $h(t)$ is the hazard rate for an event x, t is time, and $\beta_0 + x_jB_x$ are the estimated coefficients and variables; p is a shape parameter estimated from the data. When p equals one, the baseline hazard is constant over time; if p is less than one, it decreases over time; and if p is greater than one, hazard increases with time.

Dependent Variables

Although it may appear that the choice between acquiring nuclear weapons and exercising nuclear restraint is a binary decision, further reflection reveals greater nuance. There are many different stopping points on the pathway to proliferation: some states manufacture nuclear weapons, some states make serious efforts to build nuclear weapons but never actually build them, while others seriously consider building them yet stop short of actually taking firm, costly steps down that path. In order to be sensitive to these multiple stages and to allow for robustness checks across indicators, we devised three indicators of nuclear proliferation. Rather than think of nuclear weapons status as a dichotomous variable, we conceive of "degrees of nuclear-ness" arrayed along a continuum ranging from absolutely no effort or interest at one end, to possession of a nuclear weapons arsenal at the other. Operationally, we divide this continuum into three stages: no effort to acquire nuclear weapons, substantial efforts to develop weapons, and acquisition of weapons capability.[10]

First Explosion/Assembly of Weapons: Every country that has ever exploded a nuclear device, or assembled a nuclear weapon, is coded as a nuclear proliferator from the year of its first explosion or possession of a functional nuclear weapon, until the date that it abandons its program.[11]

Pursuit of Weapons: We count every country that has ever made an active effort to pursue nuclear weapons as a nuclear proliferator from the year of its first effort.[12] Thus, all countries with nuclear weapons programs are coded as nuclear proliferators until the date that their efforts cease.[13] To warrant inclusion in this category, states have to do more than simply explore the possibility of a weapons program. They have to take further steps aimed at acquiring nuclear weapons, such as a political decision by cabinet-level officials or movement toward weaponization.[14] Sweden, for example, is excluded from this category despite its exploration of the nuclear option in the 1950s because it failed either to take an explicit political decision demonstrating willingness to acquire weapons or to move beyond dual-use research.

Explanatory Variables

We include a battery of variables suggested by the three different approaches surveyed in the previous discussion. Here it is worth noting that our goal in using survival analysis is not to generate point predictions about particular cases but to map the general correlates of proliferation that have featured prominently in the literature. For that reason, we focus on variables that can reasonably be considered exogenous to the intention to pursue nuclear weapons. Although indicators such as the number of nuclear physicists and uranium production, for example, might help make better point predictions, they are also probably endogenous to incipient efforts to pursue nuclear weapons.

Table 2.1 summarizes the included variables, the indicators we use to study them, and theoretical expectations in the literature about their relation to proliferation. We group explanatory variables under three headings, corresponding to the three models just discussed.

Technological Determinants

This indicator measures a country's ability to construct nuclear weapons, using data on economic and industrial development.

GDP per capita: Although Gross Domestic Product provides an indicator of aggregate size of the economy, a per capita measure more accurately captures

Table 2.1. Theoretical expectations and measures

Explanatory variables	Anticipated direction of effect	Operationalization
Technological determinants		
Level of development	Positive	(1) GDP per capita and its square; (2) energy consumption per capita
Industrial capacity	Positive	Index based on steel production and electricity-generating capacity
Sparse resources / microstate	Negative	Dummy variable if population less than 1 million
External determinants		
Security threat	Positive	(1) Participation in enduring rivalry; (2) frequency of MID involvement
Security guarantee	Negative	Alliance with great power (NWS)
Integration into international system	Negative	Membership rate in international organizations
Internal determinants		
Democracy	Negative	Polity IV democracy scale
Democratization	Uncertain	Change in Polity IV democracy scale (over a 5-year period)
Exposure to global economy	Negative	(Exports plus imports) / GDP
Economic liberalization	Negative	Change in trade ratio (over a 5-year period)
Political instability	Positive	Index of antigovernment demonstrations, general strikes, and crises threatening government's survival

level of development. Purchasing-power-parity GDP data are taken from version 6.1 of the Penn World Tables.[15] We include a squared term to account for the possibility that the relationship between this variable and our outcome—pursuit of nuclear arms—is curvilinear (for example, if there is a threshold effect whereby prosperity encourages countries at low levels of development to go nuclear while additional increments of wealth do not increase the temptation for prosperous states).

Industrial capacity index: We use a dichotomous variable based on electricity generation and steel production. If the country produces steel domestically and has an installed electricity-generating capacity over 10,000 MW, this variable takes on a value of one, and zero otherwise.[16]

Energy and electricity consumption: To supplement the industrial capacity index, we used data on both aggregate and per capita energy consumption.[17]

External Determinants

Security threat: We use involvement in an enduring rivalry as an indicator of a significant security threat.[18] As T. V. Paul has emphasized, nuclear weapons are likely to be particularly attractive to states in a high-threat region characterized by enduring rivalries.[19] We draw on Bennett's coding to identify enduring rivalries,[20] recording whether or not a state was involved in an enduring rivalry in a given year.[21] Yet the challenge posed by all enduring rivals is far from equal; the magnitude of the threat depends on the size and capabilities of one's rival(s). To gauge the scale of the challenge, we use version 3.02 of the Correlates of War project's data on composite capabilities to create a measure of the balance of conventional capabilities between a state and its rival(s).[22] This consists of the ratio of capabilities controlled by the rival state(s) to the sum of those controlled by the home state and its rival(s): the resulting figure varies between nearly zero (if the home state enjoys overwhelming superiority) to nearly one (if the rival state[s] has overwhelming superiority). For example, in 1970 Bennett's data code India as having enduring rivalries with both Pakistan and China. Accordingly, the balance measure consists of the ratio of Pakistan and China's capabilities to those of India, Pakistan, and China combined. For every year in which a state is coded as involved in an enduring rivalry, we use this measure of the balance of capabilities within the rivalry; otherwise, the rivalry variable is coded zero.

Frequency of dispute involvement: To measure the intensity of security challenges, we calculate a five-year moving average of the number of militarized interstate disputes (MIDs) per year in which a state is involved, drawing on version 3.0 of the Militarized Interstate Dispute data set.[23]

Security guarantee: Does the state have a security guarantee in the form of a defense pact from a nuclear-armed great power? Such a guarantee may attenuate nuclear insecurity. Drawing on Singer and Small's standard list of great powers, we count the United States, USSR, United Kingdom (from 1952), France (from 1960), and China (from 1964) as possible allies of this type.[24] We count only defense pacts as providing guarantees (excluding ententes and neutrality treaties), based on the alliance coding from the Correlates of War data set (version 3.03).[25]

Integration into international system: Norms of nonproliferation embodied in the NPT have strengthened over time, shifting perceptions so that adherence to the NPT is arguably seen as a more compelling marker of modernity than is "going nuclear." Possession of nuclear weapons can play an important symbolic role in a state's self-image. According to this perspective, much of a state's behavior is determined by shared beliefs about conduct that is deemed appropriate and legitimate in international relations. If nonproliferation has indeed become a systemic norm and marker of modernity, then countries that have internalized systemic values should be less likely to pursue nuclear weapons. The key concept here is the extent of each country's acceptance of systemic values, and as a proxy we use the extent of participation in international organizations. This indicator was constructed using version 2.1 of the International Governmental Organizations Data Set, which contains information on membership of any organization with at least three states as members during 1816–2000.[26] We excluded all organizations that were restricted to countries of particular regions, such as the European Union. We also excluded geographically limited functional organizations, such as the association of tin-producing countries. Using the resulting set of truly systemic organizations, we calculated IO involvement for each country-year as the number of all organizations joined as a ratio of all organizations to which it could possibly belong. The resulting indicator varies from zero (no IO memberships at all) to one (membership in every possible IO).[27] Presumably, countries participating in a greater number of IOs are better socialized into systemic norms.

Domestic Determinants

Explanations for Indian nuclear policy have very often been located in the "domestic politics model," which holds that nuclear weapons serve the parochial interests of at least some actors within the state. Sagan, Perkovich, and Abraham argue that bureaucrats and scientists in the Department of Atomic Energy formed a secretive and influential "strategic enclave" that pushed the program forward; other versions of the argument emphasize dominant political ideologies.[28] Some analysts see the rise of the Bharatiya Janata Party (BJP), which headed the ruling coalition when India tested nuclear weapons in 1998, as either the cause or the symptom of a more aggressive and militaristic Indian nationalism. In the case of Pakistan, critics have claimed that the nuclear program was furthered by military officials and/or "militarized" civilian officials.[29]

Emphasizing the lack of transparency in civic life (rather than procedural democracy), these arguments point out the relative strengths of political and bureaucratic actors in South Asia, as well as general narratives about postcolonial development. It is difficult to operationalize these nuanced concepts for a large number of cases, and consequently our analysis is not able to take them into account. In effect, due to our desire to situate India and Pakistan within the broadest possible comparative context, we are not testing the most prominent domestic politics explanations for proliferation in South Asia. However, in recent years a vast literature in international relations has emphasized the importance of regime type for understanding foreign policy behavior, and we are able to test arguments emerging from this strand of work. If domestic politics influences proliferation through regime type, we should be able to gauge its effect.

Democracy and democratization: In recent years, democratization has sometimes been associated with a reassessment of nuclear weapons programs, for instance, in Latin America in the early 1990s and in South Africa. Consequently, the idea that democracies are less likely to want nuclear weapons programs has become established in some policy-making circles—as is evident in the current debate on Iran. We use the Polity IV data set to create two different variables related to arguments about regime type and proliferation. One variable measures democracy for each country-year with a derived measure of the level of democracy that combines Polity's two separate 11-point scales for democracy and autocracy. However, since periods of transition are known to be particularly volatile, making unconsolidated democracies more aggressive in foreign policy, we also measure movement *toward* democracy.[30]

Exposure to global economy and economic liberalization: Countries seeking or enjoying a high level of integration in the global economy may hesitate to pursue nuclear weapons.[31] Among possible measures of exposure to the global economy—international capital mobility, volume of foreign direct investment, tariff and nontariff trade barriers—the trade ratio both is the most straightforward and is available for the largest number of countries and years. Consequently, we use exports plus imports as a share of GDP as a measure of exposure to the international economy, drawing on data primarily from the Penn World Tables (version 6.1).[32] We also create a measure of trade liberalization analogous to our democratization variable by calculating the change in trade ratios over a number of years.[33]

Political instability: A long tradition in international relations scholarship identifies diversionary motives for foreign conflict. Governments facing trouble at home may seek to rally support by focusing attention on a foreign rival. In a similar vein, governments with an insecure hold on power may seek to rally support around assertive nationalism by going nuclear. The idea that assertive nuclear weapons policies may help shore up nationalist support is prominent in discussions of India's program, as well as in current discussions about Iran.[34] A reliable measure of political insecurity for 168 countries is difficult, if not impossible, to construct; nonetheless, we create a rough and ready proxy with an index of political instability consisting of a weighted sum of the number of general strikes, antigovernment demonstrations, and crises that threaten the downfall of the current government.[35]

Table 2.2 presents a snapshot of values on these variables for India and Pakistan at three different points in time: 1960, 1975, and 1990. Although snapshots of particular years necessarily obscure important cross-time variations, the figures in Table 2.2 indicate important similarities and differences between the two countries. They have very similar GDPs per capita, security environments, and rates of participation in international organizations; both lack a defense pact with a Nuclear Weapon State. Pakistan's Polity score, however, has varied widely over time, whereas India's has been very stable, despite the fact that both countries have featured a substantial amount of instability in terms of demonstrations and general strikes (especially prevalent in India after the increase in communal violence). India's greater size is evident in much greater energy consumption and population figures, whereas Pakistan has been much more exposed to the world economy with a trade ratio nearly three times that of India.[36]

Table 2.2. Selected values on variables for Pakistan and India

Variable	Pakistan			India		
	1960	*1975*	*1990*	*1960*	*1975*	*1990*
GDP per capita (in 1996 US$ at PPP exchange rates)	639	1,023	1,749	838	1,097	1,675
Energy consumption (thousands of metric coal-ton equivalents)	3,493	16,676	37,001	45,351	166,399	371,072
Population (thousands)	48,737	71,033	112,404	432,703	602,748	834,697
Urban population (thousands living in cities larger than 100,000)	6,496	11,987	20,169	35,036	61,453	117,059
Industrial capacity index (see text)	0	1	1	1	1	1
Balance of power with rivals (see text)	0.82	0.85	0.85	0.74	0.69	0.66
5-year moving average of MIDs (militarized interstate disputes)	2.4	0.8	1.2	3.2	1.0	1.6
Defense pact? (with Nuclear Weapon State)	0	0	0	0	0	0
Participation in international organizations (rate of participation in IOs)	0.525	0.67	0.71	0.65	0.72	0.66
Polity democracy scale (see text)	−7	8	8	9	7	8
Change in democracy scale (change in polity scale over past 5 years)	−12	8	12	0	−2	0
Volatility over 5 years (standard deviation in polity index score)	7.75	3.94	6.58	0	0.82	0
Political instability index (index of general strikes, demonstrations, and crises of government survival)	0.9	1.45	2.0	2.1	1.75	3.3
Trade ratio (exports plus imports as a share of GDP)	29.7	33.3	38.9	11.6	11.8	16.9
Change in trade ratio (change over past 5 years)	1.1	3.3	4.3	−1.5	3.9	3.3

GENERAL RESULTS

We performed survival analysis on a data set covering 168 states over the years 1949 to 2001. For present purposes, we focus on variables that prove statistically and substantively significant. To gauge the substantive meaning of the resulting findings, we discuss the *relative risk ratios* rather than the coefficients.[37] Relative risk ratios provide a useful way of understanding the results by indicating *how much* an increase in a given variable increases the odds of the occurrence of an event—in this case, the acquisition of nuclear weapons. For example, a coefficient of 3.2 on a dichotomous variable (such as our enduring rivalry participation variable) implies an increase of 220% in the likelihood of starting a nuclear weapons program.[38]

We first use relative risk ratios from our model to interpret the substantive role that different variables have played in the decision to *pursue* nuclear weapons (to cross the first of the two thresholds). The entries in the column labeled "Pursue" in Table 2.3 represent the percent change in the hazard rate for a given change in the explanatory variable. The entry in row one indicates that a country enjoying a defense pact with a great power is 58% less likely to acquire nuclear weapons than a similar country without an alliance. Even more striking, participation in an enduring rivalry with a powerful adversary increases the hazard rate nearly sixfold (495%).[39] The *intensity* of the rivalry also has a powerful effect: increasing the five-year moving average of militarized interstate disputes per year by two yields a 72% increase in the likelihood that a country will pursue the nuclear option. Taken together, these three results indicate that the external security environment strongly affects decisions to explore nuclear weapons acquisition, as realists have long emphasized.

Yet the results reported in the next three rows remind us of the importance of factors emphasized by the technological/economic capability approach. Breaching a minimal level of industrial development has a tremendous effect: a country over the threshold has a predicted hazard 702% higher than one below it. Level of general economic development, as proxied by GDP per capita, also plays a role. Interestingly, however, this effect is nonlinear. At very low levels of GDP, increasing GDP per capita by $500 produces a 62% increase in the probability a country will explore the nuclear option. However, once a country is already wealthy (above a threshold of about $9,000 per capita GDP), further increments of income *reduce* the chance it will go nuclear; a $500 increase in GDP per capita yields a 25% drop in the hazard rate.

Table 2.3. Substantive effects of the explanatory variables on likelihood of pursuing and acquiring nuclear weapons

Variable	Percent change from baseline hazard rate	
	Pursue (%)	Acquire (%)
Great power military alliance	−1	−58
Participation in ongoing enduring rivalry	+495	+490
Increase in frequency of MIDs (2 or more/year)	+72	+49
Industrial capacity threshold	+702	+1,650
Increase in per capita GDP ($500 at very low level)	+62	+22
Increase in per capita GDP ($500 at high level)	−25	−32
Higher level of democracy	+10	+30
Democratization	−9	−8
Increased participation in international institutions	−13	+15
Higher level of trade openness	−0	−20
Trade liberalization	+40	+10
Greater domestic political instability	+54	+40

NOTE: All results in italics are statistically significant; other results are not significant by conventional criteria (democracy and international institutions in both columns, and trade openness in the "Acquire" column).

The domestic politics variables produce weaker results. Regime type, a recent democratic transition, and greater participation in international institutions have no discernible effect; all fail to attain statistical significance. In contrast, greater political instability, in the form of an increase of 2 points on our political stability index, increases the hazard rate by 54%, and this effect is statistically significant. A higher level of trade openness—here, a trade ratio 20 points higher—is associated with a lower hazard rate, offering support to those who see an open and stable external economic environment as a disincentive to dabble with nuclear weapons.[40]

Turning to the *acquisition* of nuclear weapons (that is, crossing the second of the two thresholds), the broad pattern is similar, but there are interesting differences. Levels of statistical significance are generally lower, meaning that we have less confidence in estimates of substantive effects. Nonetheless, the security variables retain their substantive importance. Among the economic variables, crossing an industrial development threshold increases the hazard by a very large amount, and once again, the effect of GDP per capita is nonlinear. Trade openness proves less important for the acquisition threshold than for the pursuit threshold, falling short of statistical significance. The fragility of this result suggests we should interpret the restraining role of economic integration with caution. Regime type and participation in international organizations again fail to exhibit statistically distinguishable effects, whereas domestic political instability retains its importance.

These results are, of course, derived from the broadest possible universe of all countries for which data were available. Where do India and Pakistan fit in? Are they typical cases or outliers? Should we be surprised that these two countries pursued and eventually acquired nuclear weapons? Or were these developments highly likely, given what we know about proliferation globally?

As a first cut at answering these questions, we assess the predictions our statistical model would make for India and Pakistan. To do so, we simply compute the hazard rates predicted by our model for India and Pakistan for each year between 1949 and 2001. It is then a simple matter to compute the cumulative probability that India (or Pakistan) would acquire nuclear weapons by a given year. Calculating this figure for each year between 1949 and 2001 allows us to plot the cumulative probability over time of India (or Pakistan) acquiring nuclear weapons.

Using the model described in the column labeled "Acquire" in Table 2.3, Figure 2.1 plots for each year the cumulative probability of acquiring nuclear

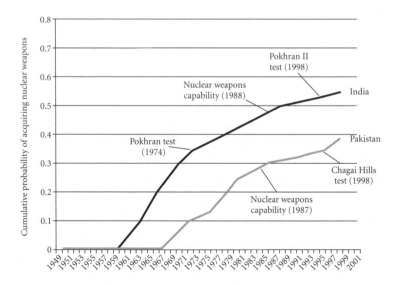

Figure 2.1. Predicted likelihood of acquiring nuclear weapons

weapons by that date.[41] The vertical axis records the cumulative probability of acquiring nuclear weapons, a number that ranges from zero (no possibility) to one (acquisition with certainty). The horizontal axis records each year from 1949 to 2001. For example, the chart indicates that the model predicts roughly a 30% chance that India would acquire nuclear weapons by 1970, and approximately a 55% chance it would have them by 2000. We can then conclude that it is not at all surprising that India had acquired nuclear weapons by 1990, although also far from a certainty that it would do so. Our model predicts about a 50% chance that it would do so.

Pakistan, on the other hand, presents a slightly different and more surprising picture. The model predicts notably lower likelihoods that Pakistan would acquire nuclear weapons, with only a 20% likelihood by 1980 and about a 40% chance it would have them by 2000. Although a sharp increase in the hazard rate does occur as Pakistan crosses the minimum industrial development threshold in the late 1960s (which is also about the time the government began seriously pursuing nuclear weapons), the model indicates a good chance of Pakistan not acquiring nuclear weapons: the predicted odds of it obtaining weapons before 2000 is less than fifty-fifty. We defer speculation about this somewhat surprising contrast between India and Pakistan to the next section.

INTERPRETING THE SOUTH ASIAN CASES

In this section we unpack the results for India and Pakistan by exploring a series of counterfactual scenarios in which we alter important attributes of the cases in order to gauge the relevance of several variables in turn.[42] For instance, to assess the importance of enduring rivalry, we hold all other variables constant and change the value on the rivalry variable. Comparing the results of this counterfactual scenario with those reported in Figure 2.1 allows us to estimate how much enduring rivalry "mattered" for the nuclearization of South Asia. Here we discuss only the final stage of proliferation: the decision to acquire nuclear weapons. The results for the model of the decision to pursue nuclear weapons are quite similar.

This section also highlights, in discrete terms, the strengths and weaknesses of our quantitative approach. As we stated previously, our goal is not to generate point predictions about particular cases but to map the general correlates of proliferation that have featured prominently in the literature. However, the model is only as good as its indicators. We use commonly employed proxies for the variables we wish to study, such as GDP per capita for level of development, trade ratio for degree of economic integration, and enduring rivalry for intensity of security challenges. In certain cases such indicators may not appear to convey much rich information compared to other data available for specific countries. Pakistan, for instance, exemplifies "atomic enclave development"—elites assigned substantial investments to specific institutions crucial to the development of nuclear technology, something not captured by crude measures of economic development. A large-N, large-T statistical model, however, is the only way to situate India and Pakistan within the broader "nuclear age" and to study systematically whether, and in what aspects, they were different from the rest of the world. This task requires us to use data available for the maximum number of countries and longest periods of time. Additionally, since we are primarily investigating arguments about the *causes* of interest in nuclear weapons technology, we eschew indicators that may be *endogenous* to that interest (such as the numbers of scientists in nuclear fields).[43]

External Threat Variables

One of the most important findings of our model is that external factors play a substantial role in predicting nuclear policy behavior in South Asia. Across the globe, countries involved in enduring rivalries have a drastically higher predicted likelihood of exploring nuclear weapons, and this effect is greater for countries facing a rival boasting superior conventional strength. To evaluate the importance of this variable for the South Asian cases, we explore the counterfactual of imagining that they did *not* participate in any enduring rivalries between independence in 1947 and 2000. This entails imagining that India and Pakistan were not engaged in an enduring rivalry either with each other or with China (for India) or Afghanistan (for Pakistan).[44] In doing so, we hold everything else about them constant; the only thing that varies is the value of the enduring rivalry variable.[45]

Figure 2.2 plots the results of this counterfactual simulation. As in Figure 2.1, the vertical axis records the cumulative probability of acquiring nuclear weapons, and the horizontal axis records each year from 1949 to 2001. The bold lines plot the predicted cumulative probabilities of going nuclear for Pakistan and India with nothing changed: these are the same curves as those in Figure 2.1. The dashed lines also plot cumulative probabilities for each country, but with one important difference: we now change the enduring rivalry variable to zero. The arrows indicate the shifts in the curves caused by this change. Clearly, the effect of participation in challenging enduring rivalries is substantial. Without any rivalries, the model predicts only about a 6% chance of India acquiring nuclear weapons by 1970 (compared to 30% in the baseline model) and a 13% chance of it doing so by 2000 (compared to 55%). The implications for Pakistan are even greater: under a no-rivalry scenario, Pakistan has over a 97% likelihood of remaining nonnuclear through 1980, and a slightly greater than 5% chance of acquiring nuclear weapons by 2000.[46] Without the security threat posed by enduring rivalries and a high-threat environment, a race toward nuclear weapons would have been unlikely in South Asia. Our model thus supports arguments for the primacy of external security threats in explaining the Indian and Pakistani nuclear programs.

In this counterfactual, we eliminated *all* rivalries from South Asia. Western commentators have emphasized the India-Pakistan rivalry as driving nuclear dynamics in the region. In contrast, Indian strategists have emphasized the threat posed by a conventionally powerful and nuclear-armed China as

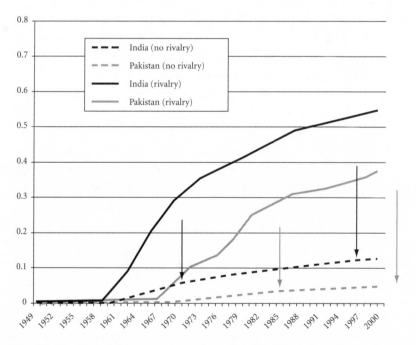

Figure 2.2. The effect of enduring rivalry on the predicted likelihood of acquiring nuclear weapons

the motive for nuclear acquisition. What does our model suggest is the relative weight of these two challenges facing India? To explore this question, we repeated the counterfactual, but this time we eliminated *only* India's rivalry with China, leaving its rivalry with Pakistan intact. This dramatically changes the conventional challenge facing India: whereas India is at a considerable disadvantage when facing the dual rivals of China and Pakistan, it enjoys a substantial superiority over Pakistan alone.[47] In this scenario, the dashed black line in Figure 2.2 shifts up a bit, but the lion's share of the change remains. Facing a rivalry with Pakistan only, there is a 19% chance of India acquiring nuclear weapons by 2000, compared with 13% under the no-rivalries scenario and 55% with the dual rivalries.

The intensity of such rivalries, as measured by a five-year moving average of military actions undertaken by either country (MIDs), is also significant. We assess the implications of cutting the rate of MID involvement by 50%. For both India and Pakistan, this reduction in the intensity of the security threat decreases the predicted likelihood of acquiring nuclear weapons by 2000 (from 56% to 47%, and for Pakistan the value falls from 39% to 33%). Thus, changes of intensity *within* a rivalry matter in addition to the simple presence or absence of a rivalry.

Some scholars and policy makers have argued that external threats can be mitigated if the country finds a powerful ally. A security guarantee from a nuclear-armed great power can partly substitute for nuclear deterrence. Indeed, our general findings revealed that a defense pact with a nuclear-armed great power cuts the likelihood of proliferation by a very large amount. To gauge this effect, we conducted a counterfactual analysis in which we gave each country a defense pact with a nuclear weapons state. Figure 2.3 presents the results, plotting the baseline cumulative probabilities of going nuclear alongside the results from the alliance scenario (with the arrows indicating the direction of change). The effect is dramatic: with an alliance, Pakistan has only a 5% predicted chance of acquiring nuclear weapons by 2000; without an alliance, that value increases dramatically to nearly 40%. With a solid security guarantee from a great power, India has less than a 10% predicted likelihood of acquiring nuclear weapons by 2000; without it, this figure shoots up to nearly 55%.[48]

The main findings from our investigation of security variables strongly support claims by both South Asian diplomats and scholars working in the realist tradition that nuclear programs are responses to national security

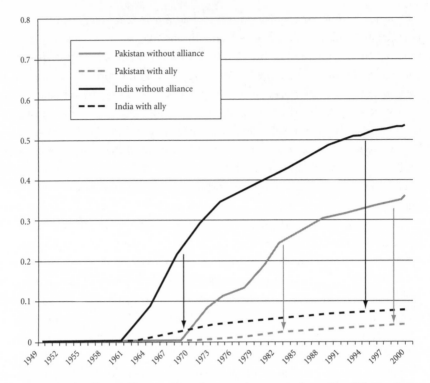

Figure 2.3. The effect of alliances with nuclear-armed powers on the predicted likelihood of acquiring nuclear weapons

threats. Moreover, the more intense the threat, the greater the predicted probability that the countries will pursue nuclear weapons. Our measure of external threat, however, cannot deal with a more comprehensive understanding of security challenges. For instance, the "tightening" of the nonproliferation regime in the 1990s is often cited as having accelerated South Asia's nuclear programs.[49] Although our model indicates that the security environment matters mightily, it cannot parse the specific, contextual features of the threat environment that motivate leaders.

Economic Variables

Etel Solingen's treatment of the Indian case states that early nationalist, inward-looking economic strategy encouraged a technological-military-industrial complex in India. A brief period of liberalization and nuclear rollback in the early 1990s ended with the advent of the "radical-confessional Hindu

BJP," representing import-competing groups and opposed to "Western regimes."[50] In this interpretation, India's failure to adopt an outward-looking, open economic strategy (and the related failure of a liberalizing coalition to prevail in domestic politics) played an important role in facilitating its nuclear weapons program. Our quantitative findings, combined with a qualitative interpretation of the Indian case, question this interpretation.[51] The key to our reservations lies in the curvilinear relationship between economic growth and weapons acquisition. Recall that at low levels of economic development, such as those found in India and Pakistan, additional increments of development make weapons acquisition much more likely, whereas at high levels of development, greater income makes proliferation less likely. The point of an open economic strategy is precisely to accelerate growth. The proliferation-enabling effects of higher growth must be weighed against the proliferation-inhibiting mechanisms of openness emphasized by Solingen.

To assess this balance, and the effects of economic development variables in general, we perform a series of counterfactual experiments with three types of economic variables, assessing different growth and integration scenarios. Our general results show the industrial threshold indicator has a very large effect: states that have yet to attain a minimal level of development are very unlikely to pursue nuclear weapons. To illustrate the magnitude of this effect, we ask, what if India's and Pakistan's development had been much slower? Specifically, what if they had not crossed the minimal development threshold embodied in our industrial capacity indicator until 1980?[52]

Figure 2.4 plots the results of this "delayed-development" scenario. Once again, solid lines represent the baseline curves from Figure 2.1, whereas dashed lines indicate the counterfactual scenario and arrows indicate the shift caused by changing the timing of crossing the threshold. The change is dramatic: both states would have been extremely unlikely to acquire nuclear weapons prior to 1980. In this counterfactual scenario, even by 2000 there is only a 25% chance of acquiring nuclear weapons for either nation. Later industrial development would have very likely delayed weapons development in South Asia. In turn, the opposite also holds: earlier development (especially for Pakistan, which lagged India on this count) would in all likelihood have spurred an earlier nuclear race. Figure 2.4 also points to an explanation for the difference between India and Pakistan noted in our earlier discussion of Figure 2.1. If both countries are set to cross the minimal industrial capacity threshold at the same time, the difference between them nearly vanishes. India's greater

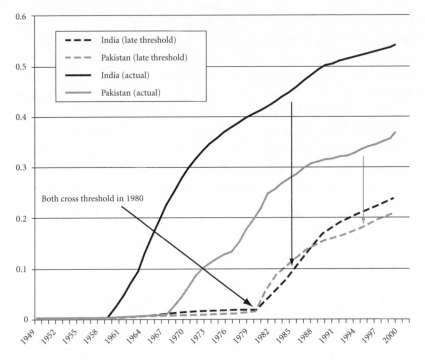

Figure 2.4. Predicted likelihood of acquiring nuclear weapons with delayed crossing of industrial threshold

predicted likelihood of acquiring nuclear weapons, as portrayed in Figure 2.1 and the solid lines in Figure 2.4, is almost completely a product of its earlier acquisition of the minimally necessary industrial/technological infrastructure. Once this difference is removed, the two countries have very similar predicted likelihoods of acquiring weapons.

For most of their postindependence history, both India and Pakistan have featured moderate economic growth at best. What if India and Pakistan had instead grown like the Asian "Tiger" economies? To assess this scenario, we imagine that both countries grew their economies at an average of 7% per year from 1949 to 2001 (instead of their actual growth rates, which were about half that figure). Since both countries are well below the tipping point beyond which growth reduces the likelihood of pursuing nuclear weapons, a nuclear program would be expected to become *more likely* with this higher rate of growth.[53] The tipping point occurs at per capita income of about $9,000; in comparison, India and Pakistan both had per capita income of barely over

$1,000 in 1975. At this level of development, faster growth significantly increases the chances of proliferation.

Figure 2.5 plots the results of this rapid-growth counterfactual. For both countries, the curve representing the cumulative likelihood of acquiring nuclear weapons by a given date shifts sharply upward, indicating that higher growth would have made the pursuit of nuclear weapons more likely than it was under actual historical growth rates. For example, under the high-growth scenario, the likelihood of India acquiring nuclear weapons by 1980 is 12 percentage points higher (54% instead of 42%); for 2000, the figure jumps by over 20 points (from 55% to 77%). The consequences of faster growth for Pakistan are equally dramatic: under the high-growth scenario, it has a 35% likelihood of acquiring weapons by 1980 (versus 20% under historic growth rates) and a 64% chance by 2000 (versus 40%). The implications are clear: faster economic growth would have in all likelihood spurred an earlier nuclearization of South Asia.

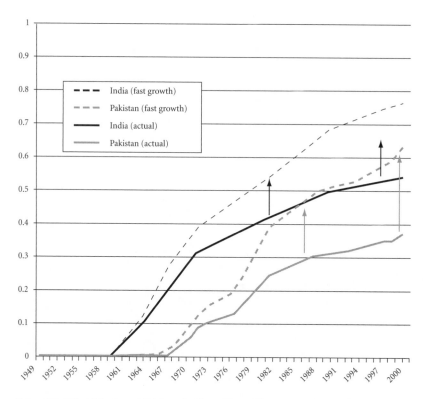

Figure 2.5. What if India and Pakistan had been Tigers? Fast-economic-growth scenarios

Turning from growth to economic openness, we imagine that India and Pakistan both pursued externally oriented strategies of economic integration and openness following independence. To construct this scenario, we increase their trade-to-GDP ratio by 20 points for each year from 1949 to 2001. This represents a substantial, but not completely fanciful, increase.[54] Figure 2.6 plots the results of the high-openness scenario. Both curves drop down, indicating a reduced likelihood of acquiring nuclear arms. A hypothetical externally oriented India has a 30% predicted likelihood of acquiring nuclear arms by 1980, a substantial decrease from the 40% implied by the baseline curve. For Pakistan, the change is somewhat less dramatic: the likelihood of acquiring nuclear weapons by 1980 drops from about 20% to about 12%. An important caveat is in order, however: unlike the other results discussed in this section, economic openness is not statistically significant by conventional criteria.[55] For that reason, the results of this counterfactual should be treated as highly speculative.

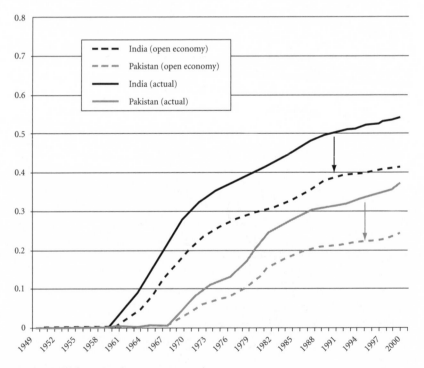

Figure 2.6. High-economic-openness scenarios

Although the economic-openness counterfactual seems to support arguments about the restraining influence of economic integration and liberalizing coalitions, viewing these results in tandem with those for economic growth complicates the picture. One of the primary motivations for opening the economy is the expectation of faster growth, an expectation supported by mainstream economic theory and substantial empirical evidence. By boosting growth, trade openness thereby loosens resource constraints. This indirect effect *runs counter to* its empowerment of liberal domestic constituencies.[56] Thus, whether or not increased openness reduces the likelihood of proliferation becomes a question of the net effect.

For the Indian case, at least, we believe there are reasons to be skeptical of making strong claims based on the trade-openness variable. First, economic nationalism does not necessarily imply mercantilism or protectionism. If global economic integration is seen as promoting autonomy and unity, nationalists can adopt it wholeheartedly.[57] Specifically, in the Indian case, it was *liberalizers* who advocated bringing the nuclear program "out of the closet."[58] Liberalizers presented economic integration as a "necessary element of India's pursuit of a larger global role for itself, *including a declared nuclear power status* and a larger voice in global economic and political forums, like the UN."[59] Second, both India and Pakistan were at the levels of development where additional increments of income have the *greatest* effect in making proliferation more likely. In the curvilinear relationship between economic development and nuclear weapons acquisition, the pro-proliferation effect of additional growth is greatest at very low levels of GDP per capita—especially between $500 and $2,500. As income rises, the marginal effect of an additional increment decreases. Eventually a tipping point is reached at about $9,000, after which additional development decreases the likelihood of weapons acquisition. India and Pakistan have been at income levels yielding the greatest pro-proliferation effect during the years when their rivalry was fiercest, suggesting that faster growth at those times (resulting from increased openness) would significantly fan the flames of proliferation.

Domestic Politics

Explanations for India's 1998 tests often focus on the ideology of the Bharatiya Janata Party. The widespread popular support for nuclear weapons acquisition in India and Pakistan suggests that democratic governments may be pandering to nationalist populations. But in fact the BJP government in India was only following a national consensus on nuclear policy,[60] and it is unclear whether dynamics unique to democratic politics play a role. The Indian program was developed enough to facilitate testing within a few days of the BJP taking over the reins of government in 1998, and India had possessed a nuclear weapons capability for many years before the tests brought the bombs "out of the basement." It is true that earlier governments did not test in the 1990s when they presumably could have—but this calls into question the importance of testing as opposed to the development of a nuclear program. We are trying to explain the latter. Various democratic governments in India kept the program alive and to different degrees promoted it.

Another approach potentially linking regime type to the likelihood of proliferation builds on the argument that the Indian program was sustained by a clique of technocrats, bureaucrats, and strategists who used secrecy and their command of scientific resources to strengthen capability and to influence the political leadership.[61] Similar arguments have been made for Pakistan.[62] In the vein of other bureaucratic politics arguments, this interpretation emphasizes the ability of particularistic interests to use security concerns and nationalistic rhetoric to promote a nuclear program.[63] Although we have no direct way of testing bureaucratic power, we can hypothesize that established democracies would see the power of parochial actors curbed by popular dictates. It is not implausible that elites will enjoy less autonomy, and that debate will be more transparent, in democracies than in nondemocracies. In the general analysis, however, a range of regime-type indicators—including the level of democracy and democratic transitions—fail to attain statistical significance. The level of democracy is not significant in explaining decisions on nuclear weapons. If domestic politics influences proliferation, it is probably not through regime type but through the influence of bureaucratic actors in the military and research laboratories. We find that India and Pakistan are no exception to the rule. India's score on the Polity IV index remains nearly constant. Pakistan oscillates wildly back and forth between highly authoritarian and mildly democratic scores. Even though the results are not statistically significant, in view of the importance attached to democracy in recent policy debates, we considered different counterfactual scenarios for each country, imagining that India had been consistently authoritarian and that Pakistan quickly developed into a politically stable, moderately democratic country.[64] In a crude sense, we are essentially switching their regime types, allowing Pakistan's Polity to look more like India's, and vice versa.

The results of this counterfactual are that democracy has a positive effect, increasing the likelihood of pursuing nuclear weapons, and consequently India's predicted likelihood of obtaining nuclear weapons by any given date drops in the counterfactual authoritarian scenario. In contrast, a consistently democratic Pakistan becomes *more* likely to pursue nuclear weapons. These effects are not trivial: an authoritarian India has a predicted 45% chance of acquiring nuclear weapons by 2000, contrasted with the 55% value for democratic India. A democratic Pakistan's chance of acquiring nuclear weapons by 2000, in contrast, rises to 47% from 40%. Although we caution about placing too much emphasis on these figures because of the lack of statistical significance underlying them, we can conclude that there is clearly no good evidence that increasing democracy *reduces* proliferation.

CONCLUSION: LESSONS FROM SOUTH ASIA

We now draw out some implications from our model and the history of efforts to stop proliferation in South Asia, and suggest lessons for the operation of the nonproliferation regime as it encounters other nuclear programs. We acknowledge that in many ways, India and Pakistan are exceptions: they are involved in an exceptionally fierce rivalry (often defeating attempts at security reassurance or conflict resolution), they were on opposing sides in the Cold War (discouraging the superpowers from pressuring them too hard), and their nuclear programs have become robust and self-sufficient. Yet our analysis suggests that India and Pakistan are in most ways not outliers from the broader universe of potential and actual proliferators. Just as the experience of other nations can illuminate events inside South Asia, so can the experience of Pakistan and India suggest lessons for other regions facing potential proliferation.

Theorists of proliferation have classified India under *each* of three main explanations for proliferation—security threats, technological imperatives, and domestic determinants—whereas Pakistan has most often been seen as reacting to nuclear provocation from India. Our analysis shows that variables emphasized by all three approaches are important, although given the limitations of our data, we can draw strong conclusions only about the security and economic development variables. Unless supported by a defense pact with a nuclear-armed great power, states facing a challenging security environment are *much* more likely to pursue nuclear weapons. Although states at low levels of development have acquired the bomb (China and North Korea providing the best examples), a minimal industrial infrastructure is nearly a necessary condition. More surprisingly, at low levels of development additional growth makes pursuit of nuclear weapons more likely, whereas at high levels of development further growth decreases the likelihood of proliferation. Turning to domestic politics, our strongest conclusions are negative ones: to the degree domestic politics influences proliferation, it is probably not through regime type or political instability. Variables capturing the degree of democracy, democratic transitions, and political instability are all inconsequential. Combining these negative results with the considerable qualitative evidence for the importance of powerful bureaucratic actors in the military and scientific establishments, we can speculate that to the extent domestic politics matters, it is not through regime type but rather via the influence of parochial actors who gain enough influence to promote their agenda. We discuss implications from each of these perspectives in turn.

Security Threats—Guarantees and Conflict Resolution

Our analysis suggests that an environment of heightened external threat plays a major, perhaps preeminent, role in stimulating nuclear ambitions. Counterfactual simulations based on our model of proliferation imply that if India and Pakistan had not faced challenging enduring rivalries, in all likelihood they would not have acquired nuclear weapons. Although it is too simple to conclude "no rivalry, no bomb,"[65] our analysis strongly supports efforts by the international community to foster reconciliation between India and Pakistan and to dampen rivalries elsewhere. Our indicator of dispute intensity—the number of MIDs—is positively associated both with nuclear exploration and acquisition. This implies that "ambiguous" deterrence may not always work and that stable conflict resolution may be the best policy to counter proliferation. The world—especially the United States as the leading great power—must not give up efforts at addressing disputes such as Kashmir. Reducing external threats reduces the primary cause of proliferation.

There is one danger in this approach. India and Pakistan may make strategic use of the imperative for intervention by the international community created by the nuclearization of the subcontinent. During the crises of 1999 (Kargil) and 2001–2002 (the border standoff), each country, correctly assuming that the United States shared a strong interest in avoiding an actual nuclear exchange, tried to stimulate American intervention in its favor. Paradoxically, the more credible the American resolve to stay involved, the lower the risks to India and Pakistan of pursuing a tough strategy.[66] A credible U.S. commitment to intervene to stop disputes from escalating to a nuclear exchange creates a "moral-hazard" problem. This moral-hazard problem also relates to the sponsorship of terrorism. Confident that the United States will step in to prevent a nuclear war, Pakistan need not rein in militant cross-border activists; instead, it can feel free to bolster their efforts under a nuclear umbrella that negates India's conventional superiority.

If we keep that caveat in mind, our model shows that security guarantees from great powers can also dampen the incentives to acquire nuclear weapons. Our counterfactual simulations suggest that nuclearization of South Asia would have been much less likely if both India and Pakistan had enjoyed defense pacts with nuclear-armed states. In the late 1960s India made some efforts to obtain a security guarantee from the superpowers: the U.S. offer was inadequate, the Soviet one even more so. The absence of a security guarantee associated with the NPT is often cited as one of the shortcomings of the nonproliferation regime.

Although Pakistan and India both had ententes or nonaggression pacts with the United States or Soviet Union for at least part of the past fifty years, the reassurance offered by these arrangements was too weak to help prevent proliferation. The U.S.-Pakistan relationship has been too volatile for the entente or American provision of conventional arms to provide a credible security guarantee. In the 1950s the United States, while keeping its doors open to India, incorporated Pakistan into its global containment strategy. However, Pakistan was disappointed with the lack of U.S. support in the 1965 war with India. The "special relationship" with Pakistan was strengthened in the aftermath of the Soviet intervention in Afghanistan, but with the end of the Cold War Pakistan's strategic value to the Americans diminished. Currently, Pakistan's links to terrorism and proliferation make American decision makers cautious. Similarly, though it has been claimed that India enjoyed a security guarantee by virtue of its 1971 friendship treaty with the USSR, if Pakistan's more robust treaty with the United States failed to provide sufficient reassurance, it is difficult to imagine India's much vaguer treaty with the Soviet Union doing so. Although great powers are understandably hesitant to offer defense pacts for fear of entrapment and moral hazard, our analysis does suggest that they can be effective in containing proliferation if used judiciously.

Technology Controls and Economic Sanctions

The dominant international response to nuclear proliferation has been to attempt controls on technology through supplier groups.[67] The 1974 Indian test in fact led to the formation of the first such group—the Zangger Committee—which evolved into the Nuclear Suppliers Group. Technology controls prevent potential proliferators from accessing specific dual-use technologies. However, they also function as de facto economic sanctions, thereby affecting the relative balance of power among different domestic actors in affected states, a point that we take up in the next section. What do our results tell us about the wisdom of this approach?

India and Pakistan are no exception to the effects of industrial capacity on nuclear propensity. If India and Pakistan had crossed the minimum industrial capacity threshold later than they actually did, resource constraints would have stymied nuclear ambitions. And at low levels of development, increases in GDP per capita dramatically increase the likelihood of pursuing nuclear weapons. At lower levels of economic development, potential proliferators face a higher technical/industrial hurdle and pay greater opportunity costs to vault it; economic growth brings the hurdle within reach and reduces the opportunity cost of jumping it.

Thus, our findings validate the basic logic behind technology controls—by targeting crucial sectors, imposing an economic cost, and tightening resource constraints, they reduce the likelihood of going nuclear.[68] However, potential proliferators may see such controls as implicit economic warfare—and thus a major security threat. Moreover, the damage to the domestic economy from controls and sanctions becomes a constant "opportunity cost," paradoxically reducing the costs of an open declaration of nuclear status. Unsurprisingly, reform-fueled economic growth in India in the 1990s actually bolstered the nuclear program.

Although historically very important, indigenous industrial and scientific capacity may prove less important for future proliferators as a result of the emergence of proliferation rings, such as the A. Q. Khan network, linking less developed states. In recent years, less developed states have increasingly begun to exchange nuclear weapons and missile-related technology, giving rise to "second-tier proliferation rings" in which states with varying technical capabilities trade among themselves.[69] This not only allows would-be proliferators to bypass supply-side approaches that attempt to limit the spread of technology by controlling exports from economically advanced states, but also reduces the importance of developing indigenous industrial, manufacturing, and scientific infrastructure as a prerequisite to acquiring nuclear weapons. Horizontal networks across developing states pose the threat of lowering the industrial/technological hurdle and reducing the costs of acquiring nuclear weapons. Although the effectiveness of these networks in advancing the efforts of would-be proliferators is open to question,[70] their existence raises the possibility that economic development and industrial capacity may play less of a role in the future than implied by our models.

Shaping Domestic Power Structures

Nonproliferation strategies have also attempted to manipulate the balance of power among domestic actors. A post–Cold War vision of world order in which free trade, prosperity, and peace reinforce each other has greatly influenced policy. In Iraq and Libya, for instance, the promise of improved economic ties with the rest of the world was presented as an incentive for abandoning nuclear weapons projects.[71]

Our findings show that increased economic openness may indeed make a difference, but that its potential for strengthening outward-oriented actors and tying down countries in a web of mutually beneficial interdependence may be outweighed by its stimulation of prosperity and more rapid development. In both India and Pakistan, increments in income freed up resources and actually *strengthened* support for the nuclear programs. Moreover, an earlier crossing of the industrial development threshold sharply increases the likelihood of proliferation, and faster economic growth resulting from openness should certainly accelerate this crossing. Openness cuts two ways, and the net effect on proliferation prospects is uncertain.

Although our model is not set up to capture institutional arrangements, or shifts in dominant political ideologies, it does show that democracy as measured in procedural terms does not promote nuclear restraint. In fact, in our counterfactual, democracy has a mild positive effect on nuclear propensity. Thus, the experience of the Latin American countries and South Africa may not be generalizable; certainly there is no basis for the equation in the current discourse between autocratic regimes and the pursuit of weapons of mass destruction (WMD). To the extent domestic politics matters for proliferation, regime type does not provide the primary mechanism of influence. In contrast to the great attention lavished on regime-type arguments in recent years, our analysis suggests that when it comes to nuclear proliferation, approaches that further unpack the state and examine the autonomy and influence of the military and scientific establishments are more promising.

APPENDIX: Sources Used in Coding Developments in India's and Pakistan's Nuclear Programs

Federation of American Scientists. 2005. *Nuclear Forces Guide.* Available at http://www.fas.org/nuke/guide/.

Jones, R. W., M. G. McDonough, T. F. Dalton, and G. D. Koblentz. 1998. *Tracking Nuclear Proliferation: A Guide in Maps and Charts, 1998.* Washington DC: Carnegie Endowment for International Peace.

Kapur, Ashok. 2001. *Pokhran and Beyond.* Oxford: Oxford University Press.

Marwah, O., and A. Schulz. 1975. *Nuclear Proliferation and the Near-Nuclear Countries.* Cambridge, MA: Ballinger Publishing.

Nuclear Age Peace Foundation. 2000. Countries with Nuclear Weapons Capabilities. http://www.napf.org/resources/nuclear_facts.html (no longer available).

Perkovich, George. 1999. *India's Nuclear Bomb: The Impact on Global Proliferation.* Berkeley: University of California Press.

Reiss, Mitchell. 1988. *Without the Bomb: The Politics of Nuclear Non-proliferation.* New York: Columbia University Press.

Russian Federation Foreign Intelligence Service. 1995. The Nuclear Potential of Individual Countries. Available at http://www.fas.org/irp/threat/svr_nuke.htm.

Smith, Chris. 1994. *India's Ad Hoc Arsenal.* New York: Oxford University Press.

Spector, Leonard. 1984. *Nuclear Proliferation Today.* New York: Vintage Books.

———. 1985. *New Nuclear Nations.* New York: Vintage Books.

———. 1987. *Going Nuclear.* Cambridge, MA: Ballinger Publishing.

———. 1988. *The Undeclared Bomb.* Cambridge, MA: Ballinger Publishing.

———. 1990. *Nuclear Ambitions.* Boulder, CO: Westview Press.

NOTES

1. See Karthika Sasikumar and Christopher R. Way, "Leaders and Laggards: When and Why Do Countries Sign the NPT?" Working Paper 16, Research Group in International Security, Montreal, 2004; Sonali Singh and Christopher R. Way, "The Correlates of Nuclear Proliferation: A Quantitative Test," *Journal of Conflict Resolution*, vol. 48, no. 6 (December 2004), 859–885.

2. Indian analyst Jasjit Singh writes that "logically, the reasons for possessing nuclear arsenals by one state" cannot be different from those of others. See Jasjit Singh, *Nuclear India* (New Delhi: Knowledge World, 1998), 5. B. R. Nayar echoes these sentiments. See Baldev Raj Nayar, "India and the Major Powers After Pokhran II," in Kanti

Bajpai and Amitabh Mattoo, eds., *The Foreign Policy, Peace, and Security Series* (New Delhi: Har-Anaud, 2001).

3. See George Perkovich, *India's Nuclear Bomb: The Impact on Global Proliferation* (Berkeley: University of California Press, 1999); Scott D. Sagan, "Rethinking the Causes of Nuclear Proliferation: Three Models in Search of a Bomb?" in V. A. Utgoff, ed., *The Coming Crisis: Nuclear Proliferation, U.S. Interests, and World Order* (Cambridge, MA: MIT Press, 2000).

4. Hugh Gusterson, "Nuclear Weapons and the 'Other' in the Western Imagination," *Cultural Anthropology*, vol. 14, no. 1 (February 1999), 111–143; David Mutimer, *The Weapons State: Proliferation and the Framing of Security* (Boulder, CO: Lynne Rienner Publishers, 2000).

5. Šumit Ganguly, *Conflict Unending: India-Pakistan Tensions Since 1947* (New York: Columbia University Press, 2001).

6. Stanley Lieberson, "Small N's and Big Conclusions: An Examination of the Reasoning in Comparative Studies Based on a Small Number of Cases," in C. C. Ragin and H. S. Becker, eds., *What Is a Case?* (New York: Cambridge University Press, 1992); Jasjeet Sekhon, "Quantity Meets Quality: Case Studies, Conditional Probability, and Counterfactuals," *Perspectives in Politics*, vol. 2, no. 2 (2004), 281–293.

7. Barbara Geddes, "How the Cases You Choose Affect the Answers You Get," *Political Analysis*, vol. 2, no. 1 (1990), 131–149; Gary King, Robert Keohane, and Sidney Verba, *Designing Social Inquiry* (Princeton, NJ: Princeton University Press, 1994); David Collier and James Mahoney, "Insights and Pitfalls: Selection Bias in Comparative Politics," *World Politics*, vol. 49, no. 1 (October 1996), 56–91; Douglas Dion, "Evidence and Inference in the Comparative Case Study," *Comparative Politics*, vol. 30, no. 2 (January 1998), 127–145.

8. Right censoring poses a problem because we know how many countries have gone nuclear up to our last observation in time, but we do not know how many *will* go nuclear in the future. Survival models deal with this problem more effectively than alternatives such as logit or probit.

9. Paul D. Allison, "Event History Analysis: Regression for Longitudinal Event Data," Sage University Paper Series on Quantitative Applications in the Social Sciences, 07-04 (Newbury Park, CA: Sage, 1984); Janet M. Box-Steffensmeier and Bradford S. Jones, "Time Is of the Essence: Event History Models in Political Science," *American Journal of Political Science*, vol. 41, no. 4 (October 1997), 1414–1461.

10. This is a truncated version of the four-stage coding developed and used in Singh and Way, "Correlates of Nuclear Proliferation." Sources for the coding are described in that article.

11. In practice the distinction between assembly and explosion is important in four cases. Pakistan is widely considered to have assembled ready-to-use nuclear devices long before finally testing in 1998, as is India. In this chapter, we use codings

emphasizing the *acquisition* of weapons instead of *tests*. We experimented with three alternative codings for India: first, coding it as crossing the threshold with the test in 1974; second, with the acquisition of ready-to-assemble weapons in 1988 or thereabouts; and third, as crossing it twice, in both 1974 and 1988. The results we report use the 1988 coding, since we are primarily interested in the decision to acquire nuclear weapons—results differ little if the alternative 1974 or dual codings are used instead. For Pakistan, we code 1987 as the year of acquisition of weapons capability. In addition to these two cases, South Africa assembled working nuclear devices but did not test them. Although the range of variation is narrow, there is some disagreement about when precisely Israel gained full-fledged weapons capability. In all cases, we assess sensitivity of our findings to the particular coding employed (see Singh and Way, "Correlates of Nuclear Proliferation"). Sources used for coding India and Pakistan are listed in the Appendix.

12. The Soviet successor states that inherited nuclear arms, and ultimately renounced them, are excluded from our analysis because they made no independent decisions to pursue nuclear weapons.

13. This indicator includes countries that have ongoing nuclear programs but that have not tested weapons or prepared nuclear devices for quick assembly.

14. In addition to decisions by cabinet-level officials, we also count the decisions of senior military leaders in the case of a military government.

15. Alan Heston, Robert Summers, and Bettina Aten, *Penn World Table Version 6.1*, Center for International Comparisons at the University of Pennsylvania (CICUP), October 2002.

16. We experimented with a range of possible thresholds; this one, which sets the threshold quite low, is, quite simply, the one that works best. To create the index, we used data on electricity-generating capacity from the *United Nations Energy Statistics Yearbook* and the *United Nations Statistical Yearbook*. We used data on steel production from the Correlates of War (COW) project's Composite Index of Capabilities, in J. David Singer, Stuart Bremer, and John Stuckey, "Capability Distribution, Uncertainty, and Major Power War, 1820–1965," in Bruce Russett, ed., *Peace, War, and Numbers* (Beverly Hills, CA: Sage, 1972); extracted using Scott D. Bennett and Allan Stam, *EUGene* version 3.1 [computer software], available at www.eugenesoftware.org; and updated through 2000 using the *United Nations Statistical Yearbook*. For a theoretical discussion of *EUGene*, see Bennett and Stam, "EUGene: A Conceptual Manual," *International Interactions*, vol. 26 (2000), 179–204.

17. Energy consumption data are from the Correlates of War project's Composite Index of Capabilities, in Singer, Bremer, and Stuckey, "Capability Distribution," extracted using Bennett and Stam, EUGene version 3.03. Population data covering 1945 to 2000 were gathered from Heston, Summers, and Aten, *Penn World Table Version 6.1*; the Correlates of War project; Angus Maddison, *The World Economy: A Millennial Perspective* (Paris: OECD, 2002); and the *United Nations Statistical Yearbook*.

18. Paul F. Diehl, *The Dynamics of Enduring Rivalries* (Urbana: University of Illinois Press, 1998).

19. T. V. Paul, *Power Versus Prudence* (Montreal: McGill-Queen's University Press, 2000).

20. Scott D. Bennett, "Integrating and Testing Models of Rivalry Duration," *American Journal of Political Science*, vol. 42, no. 4 (October 1998), 1200–1232.

21. Although precise definitions vary across authors, enduring rivalries are identified by frequent disputes between countries over a certain period. We employ the definition by Diehl and Goertz: at least three militarized interstate disputes in a fifteen-year span. Rivalries are coded as ending after a number of dispute-free years have passed.

22. J. David Singer, "Reconstructing the Correlates of War Dataset on Material Capabilities of States, 1816–1985," *International Interactions*, vol. 14 (1987), 115–132; Singer, Bremer, and Stuckey, "Capability Distribution"; Russett, *Peace, War, and Numbers*.

23. Faten Ghosn, Glenn Palmer, and Stuart Bremer, "The MID3 Data Set, 1993–2001: Procedures, Coding Rules, and Description," *Conflict Management and Peace Science*, vol. 21 (2003), 133–154.

24. J. David Singer and Melvin Small, *Resort to Arms* (Beverly Hills, CA: Sage, 1982).

25. Douglas M. Gibler and Meredith Sarkees, "Measuring Alliances: The Correlates of War Formal Interstate Alliance Data Set, 1816–2000," *Journal of Peace Research*, vol. 41, no. 2 (2004), 211–222.

26. Jon Pevehouse, Timothy Nordstrom, and Kevin Warnke, "Intergovernmental Organizations, 1815–2000: A New Correlates of War Data Set," version 2.1, 2003, http://cow2.la.psu.edu/ (no longer available); Jon Pevehouse, Timothy Nordstrom, and Kevin Warnke, "The Correlates of War 2 International Governmental Organizations Data Version 2.0," *Conflict Management and Peace Science*, vol. 21, no. 2 (2004), 101–119.

27. We recognize several possible objections to this indicator. First, does the indicator really measure the intensity of interest in participation? Many functional IOs count mainly the developed countries as members, and given the costs of IO membership, it is easy to see why. Second, joining an IO may not measure acceptance of the system as well as compliance would, but compliance is too hard to measure for such a broad range of countries and IOs. Third, formal organizations may not be necessary for states who wish to cooperate. Katzenstein, for example, argues that states of Southeast Asia cooperate without institutions thanks to network power.

28. Itty Abraham, *The Making of the Indian Nuclear Bomb* (Hyderabad, India: Orient Longman, 1998); Perkovich, *India's Nuclear Bomb*; Sagan, "Rethinking the Causes of Nuclear Proliferation."

29. Zia Mian and Ashis Nandy, *The Nuclear Debate: Ironies and Immoralities* (Colombo, Sri Lanka: Regional Centre for Strategic Studies, 1998); Perkovich, *India's Nuclear Bomb*; Sagan, "Rethinking the Causes of Nuclear Proliferation."

30. We experimented with movements over various time spans ranging from one year to ten years. In the results presented, we employ the variable measuring change in democracy score over the past five years.

31. Etel Solingen, *Nuclear Logics* (Princeton, NJ: Princeton University Press, 2007). Paul, *Power Versus Prudence*, also emphasizes the importance of economic interdependence for proliferation.

32. For countries not covered by Penn World Tables, we used data from the International Monetary Fund, drawing on Gleditsch's extension of the data using AMELIA interpolation software. Kristian Gleditsch, "Expanded Trade and GDP Data," *Journal of Conflict Resolution*, vol. 46, no. 5 (2002), 712–724.

33. As with democracy, we experimented with change over various lengths of time. In the results reported, change is over a five-year time span.

34. Vernon Hewitt, "Containing Shiva? India, Nonproliferation and the CTBT," *Contemporary South Asia*, vol. 9, no. 1 (2000), 25–39; Pramod Kumar Kantha, "The BJP and Indian Democracy: Elections, Bombs and Beyond," in R. Roy and P. Wallace, eds., *Indian Politics and the 1998 Election: Regionalism, Hindutva and State Politics* (New Delhi: Sage Publications, 1999); Dennis Kux, *India and the United States: Estranged Democracies, 1941–1991* (Washington, DC: National Defense University Press, 1992).

35. Data are from the Banks Cross-National Time-Series Data Archive. To be called general, a strike must aim at national government policies or authority; an antigovernment demonstration is for the primary purpose of voicing opposition to government policies; a government crisis is a rapidly developing situation that threatens the downfall of the present regime. The index weights government crises twice as heavily (0.50) as demonstrations and general strikes (each 0.25). Data are missing for a handful of countries; in those cases, we have assigned the average values from the general population for that particular year.

36. The rapid increase in India's involvement in the global economy mostly occurs after 1990 so is not represented in Table 2.2.

37. Technically, we are simply discussing the exponentiated coefficients rather than the coefficients themselves. This is only a difference in how the results are presented, not in the results themselves.

38. More precisely, countries in an enduring rivalry face a hazard 220% greater than those not in enduring rivalries.

39. This figure compares the hazard rate faced by a country with no enduring rivalry (a score of zero on our enduring rivalry variable) to that for a country facing a rival or rivals with slightly more than twice as many conventional capabilities (a score of 0.70 on our variable). This is roughly the situation faced by India in 1980. The increase in the hazard is lower if the rival is weaker, and greater if the rival is stronger.

40. Paul, *Power Versus Prudence*; Etel Solingen, "The Political Economy of Nuclear Restraint," *International Security*, vol. 19, no. 2 (1994), 126–169. Note, however, that the

process of trade liberalization—measured as the change in trade ratio over a five-year period—is not statistically significant.

41. Performing the same exercise for the "pursue" model yields very similar results.

42. With one exception, we discuss counterfactuals only for variables that were statistically significant. Thus, we do not provide counterfactuals for the effects of involvement in international organizations, democratic transitions, or economic liberalizations. The exception is regime type: due to the prominence of democracy in recent foreign policy debates, we include it in the set of counterfactuals. Among variables that are statistically significant, we do not discuss counterfactuals for microstate status or political instability, because of space constraints.

43. Another example: As part of our broader research, we collected time-series data on known uranium deposits. In the course of collecting this data, however, it became clear that known uranium deposits are partly endogenous to an incipient interest in nuclear weapons: states that are developing an interest in nuclear weapons often begin searching for uranium in their territory. In India, for example, uranium exploration began at almost exactly the same time the country began considering the pursuit of nuclear weapons.

44. Bennett codes both India and Pakistan as participating in two enduring rivalries: (1) with each other, (2) India with China and Pakistan with Afghanistan. According to our balance-of-capabilities measure derived from the COW project's composite capabilities data, the challenges faced by India and Pakistan were roughly comparable. Both were at a significant conventional disadvantage against the combined strength of their rivals: the rivalry variable takes on an average score of around 0.70 for India and around 0.83 for Pakistan. The counterfactual entails changing these scores to zero. Of course, India's disadvantage in regard to its rivals would be much reduced if one ignored the India-China rivalry and focused exclusively on Pakistan.

45. In terms of statistics, this amounts to stipulating that India and Pakistan did not participate in any enduring rivalries, although they are coded as participating in the same number of militarized interstate disputes. For this reason, this counterfactual understates the magnitude of the effect caused by removing the enduring-rivalry indicator.

46. Recall that because, according to the rivalry measure, Pakistan faced the more challenging situation, the corresponding reduction in external threat caused by changing the rivalry variable to zero is slightly greater for it than for India.

47. When facing both China and Pakistan, India receives an average score of around 0.68 on the enduring rivalry variable (0.50 indicates parity). Facing only Pakistan, this falls to about 0.18.

48. India's 1971 treaty with the USSR does not feature in our coding as a defense pact, nor do Pakistan's various arrangements (such as SEATO) with the United States. See Gibler and Reid Sarkees, "Measuring Alliances," 211–222.

49. Ashok Kapur, *Pokhran and Beyond: India's Nuclear Behaviour* (New York: Oxford University Press, 2001); C. Raja Mohan, *Crossing the Rubicon: India's New Foreign Policy* (New Delhi: Penguin Press, 2003).

50. Solingen, "Political Economy of Nuclear Restraint," 126–169.

51. Karthika Sasikumar, "The Political Economy of Nuclear Revisionism: Economic Integration and Nuclear Weapons in India," unpublished manuscript.

52. In the real world, India crossed this threshold in the mid-1950s, and Pakistan, in the late 1960s.

53. To isolate the effects of the GDP variable, we hold the industrial threshold variable at its actual value, thereby understating the effects of economic growth in this counterfactual. In reality, faster economic growth surely would have caused an earlier crossing of the minimum industrial capabilities threshold.

54. Quite a few countries similar in size had trade ratios 20 and more points greater than did India and Pakistan over this time period, making the counterfactual quite plausible. Although smaller countries generally have larger trade ratios, even an extremely large country such as China has reached a trade ratio of 70% as a result of following externally oriented policies. If India and Pakistan had followed more externally oriented development strategies, their trade ratios would have been substantially greater.

55. More precisely, the trade ratio variable is significant for models featuring the decision to pursue nuclear weapons as the dependent variable; it falls from significance when modeling acquisition of nuclear weapons.

56. Solingen, "Political Economy of Nuclear Restraint," 126–169.

57. See Rawi Abdelal, *National Purpose in the World Economy: Post-Soviet States in Comparative Perspective*, Cornell Studies in Political Economy (Ithaca, NY: Cornell University Press, 2001); Sanjaya Baru, *National Security in an Open Economy* (New Delhi: ICRIER, 1999); Stephen Shulman, "Nationalist Sources of International Economic Integration," *International Studies Quarterly*, vol. 44, no. 3 (2000), 365–390.

58. Sasikumar, "Political Economy of Nuclear Revisionism."

59. Sanjaya Baru, "National Security in an Open Economy," in *Strategic Consequences of India's Economic Performance* (New Delhi: Academic Foundation, 2006), emphasis added.

60. Kapur, *Pokhran and Beyond*; Paul, *Power Versus Prudence*.

61. Abraham, *Making of the Indian Nuclear Bomb*; Perkovich, *India's Nuclear Bomb*.

62. Mian and Nandy, *The Nuclear Debate*.

63. Scilla Elworthy, *How Nuclear Weapons Decisions Are Made* (New York: St. Martin's Press, 1986); Sagan, "Rethinking the Causes of Nuclear Proliferation."

64. We are cautious about counterfactuals using regime-type data from the Polity IV project, largely because this factor has attracted much attention in popular discus-

sions. Even though the coefficient is not distinguishable from zero by standard criteria of statistical significance, it is still our best guess about the effect of democracy.

65. Our model does predict a 13% chance of India acquiring nuclear weapons even without its rivalries with China and Pakistan.

66. See Chapters 5 and 6 in this volume.

67. Mutimer, *The Weapons State*.

68. Whether technology controls succeed in actually restricting the spread of sensitive technologies is outside the scope of our research. Recent revelations about technology transfer from China to Pakistan and Iran, and from Pakistan to Libya and North Korea lead us to doubt that they do. Still, even if controls are far from perfectly effective, there can be little doubt that they raise the costs of acquiring the relevant technologies.

69. Chaim Braun and Christopher F. Chyba, "Proliferation Rings: New Challenges to the Nuclear Nonproliferation Regime," *International Security*, vol. 29, no. 2 (Fall 2004), 5–49.

70. Alexander H. Montgomery, "Ringing in Proliferation: How to Dismantle an Atomic Bomb Network," *International Security*, vol. 30, no. 2 (Fall 2005), 153–187.

71. On Libya's economic integration as the main reason for its nuclear renunciation, see Joseph Cirincione, "Iran, Libya and North Korea," *Talk of the Nation*, National Public Radio, January 21, 2004. Also see recent advocacy of economic sanctions against Iran in George Perkovich and Silvia Manzanero, "Plan B: Using Sanctions to End Iran's Nuclear Program," *Arms Control Today*, vol. 34, no. 4 (May 2004).

3 CONTRA-PROLIFERATION

Interpreting the Meanings of India's Nuclear Tests
in 1974 and 1998

Itty Abraham

THE POLICY OF NUCLEAR NONPROLIFERATION seeks to prevent the spread of weapons-related nuclear technologies to countries not possessing them in 1967. For quite some time, it appeared that the policy was relatively successful. Although John F. Kennedy famously predicted in his third debate with Richard Nixon that, by 1964, "10, 15, or 20 nations [would] have a nuclear capacity," for nearly three decades from the entry into force of the Nuclear Non-Proliferation Treaty (NPT) in 1970, only one new country—India—made a public claim to being a nuclear power, when it set off a "peaceful nuclear explosion" in 1974. The hostile international reaction that followed that event, along with the imposition of a variety of sanctions, appeared to have worked. No new tests followed, and India's nascent nuclear weapons program, if there was one, seemed to be on hold. By the 1990s, much-touted successes like the removal of nuclear weapons from Belarus, Kazakhstan, and Ukraine following the demise of the Soviet Union; the renunciation of nuclear weapons programs by South Africa, Brazil, and Argentina; and the unexpected indefinite extension of the NPT led to the feeling that the policy had evolved into an international norm against the possession of nuclear weapons.[1] This optimism was reinforced by the recognition that these developments were taking place in spite of the fact that countries identified as nuclear weapon states (NWS) had done little to meet their disarmament obligations under Article VI of the treaty.

Then came May 1998. Eleven nuclear tests by India and Pakistan in the span of three weeks forced a major reconsideration of this optimism. A year later these new nuclear powers fought a war in Kargil that, although relatively limited in scope, included multiple threats of use of nuclear weapons by both sides.[2] More recently, ongoing multilateral negotiations seeking to prevent North Korea and Iran from developing nuclear weapons; reports that Brazil may be reconsidering its nonnuclear status; the uncovering of an elaborate underground network managed by Pakistan's Dr. A. Q. Khan supplying weapons-related nuclear technologies and blueprints around the world; the ongoing condition of Israel as an undeclared nuclear power; and indications that South Korea, Taiwan, and Egypt have tried, albeit at an experimental level, to master the technologies of fuel enrichment suggest that the optimism of the 1990s was entirely premature.[3] Basic flaws in the NPT architecture, especially the weakness of its primary trade-off—making civilian and peaceful nuclear technologies available to countries that renounce belligerent uses of nuclear power—have returned to our collective awareness.[4] Now, the unwillingness of NWS to substantially address their Article VI obligations, the desire of the George W. Bush administration to develop a new generation of tactical nuclear weapons, and the differential treatment of crises in North Korea and Iraq appear to have led to a reinforcement of the utility and value of nuclear weapons as political instruments of power and prestige. The norm against *possession* of nuclear weapons is now downscaled—at best and with no small amount of wishful thinking—into a possible norm against the *use* of nuclear weapons.

What went wrong? This chapter argues, first, that there are important conceptual shortcomings endemic to the concept of "nuclear proliferation" and, second, that the policy of nonproliferation has itself become a factor shaping decisions to possess nuclear weapons.[5] These closely related arguments are developed through an interrogation of the concept of nonproliferation, which is identified here as a "discourse of control" produced through the overlap of academic studies of "proliferation" and the objective of U.S. nonproliferation policy to contain the spread of nuclear weapons worldwide.[6] The effect of this framing of the "problem" of nuclear power has led to a conflation of the reasons why countries develop nuclear *weapons* and why they create nuclear *programs*. By contrast, this chapter offers an answer to the more general question of why countries develop nuclear programs rather than focusing on the much narrower policy issue of why countries develop nuclear weapons. Applying a global template to discrete conditions of nuclear development leads to the marginalization of important contextual considerations and distinct national histories; when context and history are considered, I propose, a very different understanding of the place of nuclear power in relation to state formation and legitimation emerges. Once we develop a critique of nonproliferation and its alternative, it becomes possible to offer a reading of India's nuclear tests of 1974 and 1998 as politically valent signs with very different meanings.

DISCOURSE OF CONTROL

Since 1945 and the acknowledged arrival of the United States as a global power, among the central concerns of U.S. foreign policy has been to prevent, and, when that proved impossible, to limit the number of countries that possess nuclear weapons. Recognizing the high likelihood that nuclear weapons would "proliferate" widely unless both the calculus of strategic choice and the symbolic weight of nuclear power were altered, the United States and other major powers created a legal regime that sought to address both conditions. The NPT was set up to reward countries that explicitly eschewed the search for weapons, while allowing them the benefits of nuclear power for nonbelligerent ends under strict conditions of international surveillance or safeguards. A sop given to nuclear renouncers was the promise, albeit without legally binding penalties or time frame, that nuclear weapons–possessing states would "work in good faith" toward nuclear disarmament (Article VI). From the point of view of the dominant interests promoting the NPT bargain, positive outcomes included the freezing of the existing strategic status quo, and thus the international distribution of power, as well as the management of racially inflected doubt about the reliability of diverse actors who might come into possession of these "doomsday" weapons.[7] It was also not lost on the creators of the treaty that an additional positive outcome of this international bargain would be a boost to the commercial interests of a growing civilian nuclear power industry seeking international markets. Balancing these two quite different ends at the same time made the construction of an effective NPT regime very difficult. Internationally imposed safeguards on nuclear material became the primary means of monitoring the bargain, even as the human capital base of nuclear-trained personnel grew across the world.

Nonproliferation as a discourse of control is a product, in the first instance, of an understanding of nuclear history that has internalized the policy prescription: to prevent the undesired outcome of nuclear weapons production from taking place. This discourse begins from the unexamined assumption that the same reasons used to explain nuclear weapons development in the United States and USSR—the first countries to develop nuclear weapons—hold true for succeeding generations. Following from the assumption of common origins, analysis proceeds by the elaboration of a narrative structure that takes the following conditions as given: (1) nuclear programs are *indigenous* and *national*; and (2) the primary intent of a nuclear program can be reduced to a simple dichotomy that it is either *for war* or *for peace*. Following from these conditions, and given the extent of official secrecy surrounding these programs, (3) unimpeachable proof of intent is best established through the technical means of a *nuclear test*. Each of these assumptions is examined in turn.

NATIONAL AND INDIGENOUS

One of the most enduring tropes of proliferation studies is the idea that atomic energy programs are always *national* programs. The close relation between nuclear power and national power has led to the assumption that, for reasons of security especially, nuclear programs must be uniquely identified with particular countries. Official histories and scientists encourage this belief, for obvious parochial reasons, but it is rarely true. No atomic program anywhere in the world has ever been purely indigenous, nor is it sensible to attribute singular national origins to the scientific efforts to create nuclear fission in laboratories. Given the continental scale of nuclear physics research in prewar years, where scientists from a dozen countries worked together in four or five different countries, it is difficult, and indeed intellectually pointless, to attribute either origins or original successes to one *country* over another. The scientific importance of nuclear-related discoveries all through the 1930s, at Cambridge, in Rome, in Soviet Russia, in Denmark, and in Germany, culminating in the discovery of nuclear fission by Otto Hahn and Fritz Strassman in December 1938 (published in 1939), guaranteed a wide interest in the latest news from nuclear physics among physicists from around the world.[8]

The first effort to create a "national" atomic energy program, the U.S. atomic energy bomb project, was inherently a multinational project, with important contributions from British, Canadian, Italian, and French scientists, as well as the extensive efforts of expatriate German refugees.[9] The Canadian and British atomic energy projects, the latter beginning with the loan of French uranium oxide, derived some of their legitimacy and expertise from experiences gained in the multinational U.S. program, and Canada and the UK were the only countries that the United States was permitted to collaborate with under the McMahon Act. John Lewis and Xue Litai remind us that Chinese scientists worked with Max Born in Edinburgh, in Joliot-Curie's lab, and at Pasadena's Jet Propulsion Lab during the war years and, after returning to China, helped build the Chinese nuclear program.[10] The Chinese program also began with Soviet help, and scores of Chinese engineers were trained in USSR schools and labs before relations between the two countries broke down. The French approached both the Norwegians and the Canadians for help in the early years of their program.[11] The Soviet program was built largely through the indigenous efforts of Russian scientists, supplemented by the clandestine work of British and American spies working in the U.S. program.[12] The Norwegians supplied the Israeli program with heavy water, worked closely with both France and Sweden in the early postwar years, and later worked with the Dutch, a relationship that would lead eventually to the formation of the European nuclear consortium, Urenco.[13] The Israeli program was closely tied to the French and Norwegian efforts as well.[14] It cannot be denied that to some extent international collaboration, especially for the French, was a self-help strategy driven by the legal exclusion of everyone except the UK and Canada from the American nuclear program, and even these two exceptions rarely felt themselves to be equal partners in the process.[15]

The Indian "national" program was no exception. In 1951 India and France signed an agreement to collaborate, but little else happened. A few years later, India's nuclear scientists, facing increasing political pressure at home for their lack of manifest achievements, turned, at Sir John Cockcroft's suggestion, to a British swimming-pool-reactor design that had been published in the trade magazine *Nucleonics*. In addition to design and engineering details, the enriched uranium fuel rods were also supplied by the UK.[16] Its second reactor (CIRUS) was based on a Canadian design, moderated by heavy water supplied by the U.S. Atomic Energy Commission. But in India, this multinational history would remain largely invisible. At the inauguration of the swimming-pool reactor Apsara in January 1957, Nehru said:

> We are told, and I am prepared to believe it on Dr. [Homi J.] Bhabha's word, that this is the first atomic reactor in Asia, except possibly the Soviet areas. In this sense, this represents a certain historic moment in India and in Asia. . . . We are not reluctant in the slightest degree to take advice and help from other countries. We are grateful to them for the help which they have given—and which we hope to get in future—because of their longer experience. *But it is to be remembered that this Swimming Pool reactor in front of you is the work, almost entirely, of our young Indian scientists and builders.*[17]

A local product, in other words, "almost entirely." The Indian Atomic Energy Commission (AEC) press release following reactor criticality had Cockcroft grumbling to his colleagues, "Did you see the press release from Delhi? . . . [T]his [characterization of India's achievement] seems rather ungracious in view of the advice and help we have given and are asked to give. Presumably, detailed plant designs and drawings do not constitute outside help!"[18] Recent revelations about the A. Q. Khan network and its illicit assistance to the North Korean and Libyan programs only reaffirm the fact that, far from being national and indigenous as commonly assumed, nuclear programs are almost always multinational efforts.

FOR PEACE OR FOR WAR?

Those responsible for the Indian nuclear program had long been aware of the possibility of atomic energy being used to build weapons. In yet another example of the intertwined histories of nuclearization across many sites, we find that both Indian and Soviet scientists became aware of the top-secret Manhattan Project before Hiroshima.

David Holloway, in his authoritative study of the Soviet nuclear program, writes:

> Early in 1942 Lieutenant [nuclear physicist Georgii] Flerov's unit was stationed in Voronezh, close to the front line. The university in Voronezh had been evacuated, but the library was still there. "The American physics journals, in spite of the war, were in the library and they above all interested me," Flerov wrote later. "In them I hoped to look through the latest papers on the fission of uranium, to find references to our work on spontaneous fission." When Flerov looked through the journals he found that not only had there been no response to the discovery that he and [Konstantin] Petrzhak had made, but that there were no articles on nuclear fission [at all]. Nor did it seem that the leading nuclear physicists [in the West] had switched to other lines of research, for they too were missing from the journals.[19]

Holloway reports that Flerov concluded that "the Americans were working to build a nuclear weapon."[20]

The story told by Flerov, of the "dog that didn't bark," finds an uncanny parallel in India. Govind Swarup, the radio astronomer, reported in an interview some years ago that Homi Jehangir Bhabha, a Cambridge-trained physicist who would become the founder of the Indian nuclear program, had

told him that by 1944 Bhabha, too, had become convinced that the Americans
had started a nuclear weapons program.[21] Bhabha's reasoning was similar to
Flerov's. He was in close touch with a number of physicists around the world,
largely by letter, during the war years when he was stuck in India, unable to
travel. Letters from colleagues in America, always slow because of distance,
a situation made worse by the war, had practically dried up by 1943. Bhabha
thought little of it at the time, assuming that the obvious reasons, distance
and war, had slowed his mail down. By 1944, still not having heard from his
colleagues in spite of his having written a number of letters, Bhabha sat down
and made a list of the people that would be likely candidates for a nuclear
program. He then made a list of his silent correspondents: the two lists were
almost exactly the same.

The near-simultaneous realization by Flerov and Bhabha (and undoubtedly others) that the United States was engaged in a highly secret process to
build an atomic weapon should come as no surprise. The potential military
implications of these discoveries was also no secret to anyone who had a basic
understanding of the fission process, though there was less than unanimity
on the exact outcome of a process of nuclear fission.[22] The nuclear physics
community in the interwar years was small, close-knit, and multinational.
New discoveries were emerging from a relatively small number of labs in Europe and the United States and were communicated immediately via letter
and travel to a transnational epistemic community that eagerly discussed the
implications of each new finding.[23]

In the unsettled first decade after Hiroshima, with Europe divided and
a hot war breaking out in Korea, many feared that nuclear weapons would
be used again. The horror of nuclear weapons led the UN General Assembly
to express its "earnest desire," in a resolution introduced by India in 1953, to
urge the "Powers principally involved" to sit down and thrash out a means
to "eliminate and prohibit" weapons of "war and mass destruction." Lester
Pearson, the influential foreign minister of Canada, spoke for many when he
noted: "A Third World War accompanied by the possible devastation by new
atomic and chemical weapons would destroy civilization."[24] The need to restrain the superpowers, seeing them as the primary source of world insecurity,
became for many, aligned and nonaligned alike, the driving consideration of
international affairs in the 1950s.

The use of nuclear weapons in Japan had a considerable impact on Indian
elites. Mohandas Gandhi of course denounced it in no uncertain terms. Re-

sponding in typical fashion to the suggestion that atomic weapons were so horrific that they would end war, he wrote:

> This is like a man glutting himself with dainties to the point of nausea and turning away from them only to return after the effect of nausea is well over. Precisely in the same manner will the world return to violence with renewed zeal after the effect of disgust is worn out. . . . The atom bomb . . . destroy[ed] the soul of Japan. What has happened to the soul of the destroying nation is yet too early to see. . . . A slaveholder cannot hold a slave without putting himself or his deputy in the cage holding the slave.[25]

The widespread public revulsion against nuclear weapons, especially once the effects of the hydrogen bomb became more widely known, and a desperate need to consider new roads to international peace and development altered the discourse around nuclear power. Only a short decade after average Americans polled in a 1946 survey glumly confirmed that "atomic energy means the atomic bomb,"[26] the combination of Atoms for Peace (1953), the first UN-sponsored conference on the peaceful uses of nuclear energy (1955), the Plowshares project, an effort to develop peaceful uses of nuclear explosions, and international competition in the sale of nuclear reactors broke the link between nuclear power and nuclear weapons, temporarily. In spite of the intense and repeated association of the nuclear revolution with the use of ever-greater forces of destruction, a divergent but parallel discourse of nuclear power for development and economic growth did emerge. Although few questioned the nostrum that the nature of war was now substantially altered as a result of the destructive potential of these weapons, weapons acquisition did not become the only or even primary consideration for countries now facing the real possibility of a global holocaust.

Even countries that began nuclear programs with an explicit intent to develop nuclear weapons, the United States and the Soviet Union in particular, sought to expand the scope of these programs after the war beyond narrowly defined military ends. In both cases, "civilian" technologies were borrowed directly from the military effort. The transfer of technology from the U.S. nuclear submarine project led to the building of civilian, private-sector, light-water reactors, whereas Soviet electric power reactors were based on designs taken from a military reactor designed to maximize the availability of plutonium. Not surprisingly, these new civilian programs struggled with their redefinition because of the weight of existing popular sentiments about the destructiveness of atomic power. In David Nye's discussion of the American "technological sublime," he develops a genealogy of American technological development that links the U.S. space program with the nuclear program. Nye notes dryly that "[c]onvincing the public that atomic energy was friendly proved difficult, but the space program was popular."[27]

In order for governments to make the difficult case that nuclear power could be used for peaceful ends, it was necessary to utilize the discursive mediation of other modern technological marvels. Spencer Weart reminds us of some of the remarkable possibilities offered by the peaceful use of atomic power, including "new lands flowing with milk and honey," transforming Africa into "another Europe" and deserts into irrigated land, which led "some Americans [to look] forward to a government operated civilian atomic energy program, an 'atomic TVA'. . . . After all, projects already underway, such as the monumental dams of the Tennessee Valley Authority were scarcely less astonishing."[28] These linkages were not merely rhetorical flourishes: *wunderkind* head of the TVA, David Lilienthal, would be appointed the first chairman of the U.S. Atomic Energy Commission in 1946. Who better to combine, as Weart puts it, the "White City of technology with the green hills of Arcadia"?[29] The Soviets, too, had begun to believe in the possibilities of nuclear power for nonmilitary ends. Given a history of promoting the virtues of communism through modern technology projects, including "the most ambitious programs in hydro-electric power and canal building in the 20th century, as well as the largest nuclear power plants ever built,"[30] the Soviets discussed using nuclear explosions to change the course of major rivers for irrigation and electricity-generating purposes. "Along with Marxism, a fierce national pride urged Russians to stand second to none in modern technological projects; huge reactors would join huge dams, rockets and steel mills as proofs of [international] pre-eminence."[31]

Even in Israel, a country where security imperatives would seem to override all others, atomic energy was more than just that. Avner Cohen quotes Shimon Peres saying, "Ben Gurion believed that Science could compensate us for what Nature has denied us," and goes on to say, "Ben Gurion's romantic, even mystical faith in science and technology sustained his utopian vision of a blossoming Negev desert and the use of nuclear power to desalinate sea water."[32]

By contrast, India claimed from the outset that it was developing a nuclear program with a difference. Unlike the programs being created in the West and the Soviet Union, where military ends preceded civilian uses, nuclear power for India was always represented primarily as a program for civilian use. For instance, in the Constituent Assembly legislative debates that created an atomic energy program as early as 1948, Jawaharlal Nehru began his remarks introducing the bill by affirming its peaceful ends. The assembly delegates agreed with this formulation, by and large, sometimes identifying this decision with the legacy of Mohandas Gandhi, at other times applauding the government for taking control of this resource and not leaving it in private hands. But even at this early stage, dissenting voices could be found, arguing that a peaceful orientation made no sense, given the prevailing orientation of nuclear power with belligerent ends everywhere else.[33] Nehru's formulation would prevail, however, and the peaceful Indian program soon began operation. With the passage of time, maintaining the peaceful ends of the Indian program became a struggle. Even as the official rhetoric of atomic energy sought to foreground India's distinctively peaceful energy program, secret decisions taken within the Department of Atomic Energy (DAE) ensured that the technical means for converting this program to other, less than peaceful purposes were not foreclosed.[34]

If the world's first few nuclear programs moved in the direction of adding peaceful ends from defense and weapons-related starting points, India's program was indeed distinctive in that it moved in the opposite direction. In all cases, however, what is important to note is that neither national defense nor peaceful ends were sufficient reasons to continue to develop nuclear programs. If programs began for defense, they acquired peaceful purposes as well; if they began for peaceful ends, defense objectives were never far from the thinking of some of those involved at the highest levels of decision making. Ambivalence about ends is the norm.

NUCLEAR TESTS, AMBIGUITY AND OPACITY

Since many of the technological means for the development of nuclear power systems are largely identical whether the ends of the program are peaceful or not, what becomes of crucial importance is establishing the "true" intent underlying a nuclear program: might seemingly peaceful behavior be a cover for other, more deadly, purposes? Given the inherent uncertainty of ends, policy analysts tend to work with a worst-case-scenario approach so that they may not be taken unaware. Hence, stray statements by political leaders are parsed carefully for deeper meaning, and intelligence services work overtime seeking hints and clues that some other purpose drives a nuclear program. As is now clear, however, camouflage and deception are also extremely well-developed state skills, even to the extent of making it appear, as in the case of Iraq after 1991, that programs exist where there are none!

Academic studies of nuclear proliferation turned to address this question, seeking to establish a deeper understanding of the reasons for and causes underlying the desire to possess nuclear weapons. The most useful statement on why states "go nuclear" was set out by Scott Sagan.[35] Sagan posits that there are three primary models explaining nuclear acquisition: a "security" or realist model, which argues that states build weapons for security and because others do; a "domestic politics" model, which sees nuclear weapons development as the outcome of actions by powerful coalitions within states that seek institutional power via this end; and a "norms" model, which argues that "weapons acquisition, or restraint in weapons development, provides an important normative symbol of the state's modernity and identity."[36] Sagan goes through these models, focusing especially on anomalous cases in relation to each explanation, and concludes that both "[n]uclear weapons proliferation and nuclear restraint have occurred in the past, and can occur in the future, for more than one reason: *different historical cases are best explained by different causal models.*"[37] In other words, the assumption that a single reason is adequate to explain why countries develop nuclear weapons cannot be sustained.

As a result of this ambiguity, analysts of foreign policy, national security strategy, and international relations turn toward what appears to be the most obvious sign that a military program is in the offing, that is, the explosion of a nuclear device. Whether called a "bomb," "test," "peaceful nuclear explosion," or "demonstration," this event is of primary significance in setting analytic calendars, as it is seen to mark the unambiguous moment when a country has crossed over a particular set of political and technological boundaries. The nuclear explosion is taken to mark a shift in the international distribution of power, leading to new scales of international threat and casting into question existing regimes of nuclear control.

Under conditions of uncertainty the very "legible" nuclear test might appear to be the most objective indication that a country's nuclear program is moving in a nonpeaceful direction.[38] After all, nuclear explosions would seem to have little to do with civilian ends, such as producing more electrical energy or improving the quality of nuclear medical devices. But even this event is not as unambiguous as it may appear. By identifying the nuclear test as the moment when a threshold has been crossed—the historic moment—the many histories of any nuclear program have been reduced to the path that led to this particular outcome. The many countries that have not conducted nuclear tests but that may have viable nuclear programs are dropped from the analytic universe.[39] The multiple meanings of nuclear power are shrunk into one register—the desire to produce weapons. From a practical standpoint, this approach highlights the prevailing intellectual bias that countries that seek to develop nuclear weapons are of special interest, thereby conflating scholarly interests with those of policy makers who necessarily have to be worried about new weapons. In turn, this reinforces the particular aura of nuclear weapons as objects to be coveted and desired, the very opposite effect sought by policy makers concerned with nuclear proliferation.

India conducted a "peaceful nuclear explosion" (PNE) test in 1974. The PNE was officially termed a "demonstration," a word that recurs in Indian technological history.[40] Once India had tested, based on the experience of every other country that had set off a nuclear explosion since 1945, it could be considered a nuclear power. But was it? India did "nothing" for the next twenty-four years, or, in other words, didn't test again or overtly weaponize until 1998. This "expected absence" came to be called a state of nuclear "ambiguity."[41]

Nuclear ambiguity is usually defined as uncertainty in the presence of suspicion about the existence of a nuclear weapons program. But as Frankel and Cohen point out, the term "nuclear ambiguity" "is [itself] ambiguous": it could either mean a lack of clarity on the part of others' knowledge of the extent and abilities of a country's nuclear program—do they have a weapons program or not?—or could mean a multiplicity of views on the part of a country's leadership about the utility, efficacy, and morality of nuclear weapons possession.[42] The conceptual weakness of this term is clear when we realize that when taken to the limit, all nuclear-capable countries could be said to be in a state of ambiguity until they explode a nuclear device. Ambiguity, however, is to be distinguished from "opacity." Avner Cohen defines opacity as a "situation in which the existence of a state's nuclear weapons has not been acknowledged by the state's leaders, but in which the evidence for the weapons' existence is strong enough to influence other nations' perceptions and actions."[43] The best example of this case is Israel, which has not officially declared its possession of nuclear weapons but has institutionalized opacity at the highest level of national strategy. Ambiguity, in other words, is about uncertainty and lack of knowledge for the outsider; by this definition, so is opacity, but here the uncertainty is "actionable" from a policy point of view.

Opacity can be understood as the outcome of (1) indecision at the highest levels of political decision making (e.g., India);[44] (2) a deliberate strategy of information denial (e.g., Israel);[45] or (3) an effort to finesse executive authority via calculated deception by a government agency or coalition of agencies (e.g., France during the Fourth Republic).[46] Nuclear opacity on both sides of a dyadic rivalry might even lead to an equilibrium state of tacit mutual strategic deterrence (e.g., India and Pakistan from the late 1980s through 1998). The only possible resolutions to this condition of uncertainty are a nuclear explosion or the public dismantling of the program, à la South Africa. In the case of nuclear ambiguity, a nuclear test is taken to mean that the technical means to do so have been converted into formal ability—whether expected by analysts or not; in the case of opacity, a test is taken to show that the decision has been made to "come out of the nuclear closet" and openly declare a nuclear power. Given these shades of meaning, there is little surprise that analysts turn to the material proof of a nuclear test to confirm their concerns about the direction of a country's nuclear program; but by the same token, once a test has taken place, ambiguity and opacity are no longer meaningful categories. "Ambiguity" and "opacity" effectively become threshold terms describing a liminal stage between intention and a yet-to-happen event, the long moment between the Fall and the Second Coming.

The narrowing of vision embodied in these terms, built around the expectation that an explosion is forthcoming, reinforces the idea of how limited the purposes and meaning of a nuclear program are assumed to be and how analytically devalued is the importance of understanding the political processes that ultimately result in these decisions. Yet, if it is important to establish when a country has decided to develop nuclear weapons, the moment of a nuclear explosion is convenient but may not necessarily be meaningful. If the counterexample of Israel—a country that is recognized to have a nuclear weapons program but has never openly tested a nuclear device—is not sufficient, an alternative approach might be based on a closer examination of the technical means to nuclear explosive potential. However, with this approach, the evidence offered by a single test is neither necessary nor sufficient to prove a nuclear weapons program.

A country's first nuclear test is, at best, a scientific experiment. Although the feasibility of the fission process has been known for more than half a century, setting off a first explosive device anywhere is still an act of scientific ability, combined with considerable engineering skills, involving trial and error, chance, luck, and not inconsiderable means. To successfully produce a single nuclear explosive device requires, at the minimum, the following expertise: mathematical and statistical modeling skills, sufficient fissile material, sophisticated materials-handling abilities, expertise in conventional explosives, electronics and instrumentation abilities, the organizational skills to bring all these different elements together effectively, and a place to do it.

However, for this first test to translate into a weapons program and a nuclear arsenal that can be used at will, at least two additional things must happen. First and foremost, a political decision has to be taken to go ahead, and second, ad hoc scientific procedures have to be replaced with an organized, ends-oriented technological process. The technologization of the nuclear explosive building process is a discrete step necessary to convert a latent scientific ability to make nuclear explosives into a tangible and reliable process. Every step of the process—fissile material extraction, weapon design and testing, and delivery—has to be converted into an industrial process, built around repetition, with uncertainty minimized, where scientific practices are converted into industrial routines and safety codes, and where internal security and safety practices are regularized and institutionalized. It may not always be possible for the same organization that produced the first explosive device as a one-off scientific event to industrialize the process. Certainly new forms of industrial and organizational management have to be employed and the process routinized sufficiently to reduce levels of error to a level where the explosive device meets the standards of military reliability. In other words, if the objective is to build a reliable nuclear weapons program, a number of tangible, material, organizational objectives have to be put into place.

Based on the technological criteria referred to previously, India probably became a nuclear weapons–capable state around 1986, when Rajiv Gandhi was prime minister.[47] From this point onward, India was certainly capable of using nuclear weapons in war and could be considered to have an effective, if crude, nuclear deterrent capability vis-à-vis Pakistan. Certainly India's nuclear scientific establishment had been keen to push ahead with more tests for some time, but the political leadership had not made up their minds about the value of doing so. It was not until the ascent to power of the right-wing Bharatiya Janata Party (BJP), a radically new political dispensation in government, that the political decision to reveal India's capabilities was taken, well after conditions on the ground existed. Although the decision to test again was the siren call of an über-nationalist government finally in power, for all practical purposes India was already a nuclear power. Previous governments, quite unlike the BJP nationalists ideologically, had ensured that India had converted a latent ability into a viable weapons option a decade before. The nuclear test, long assumed to be ultimate proof of a nuclear weapons program, turns out to be a sign with multiple meanings. Neither the 1974 test nor its 1998 successors were necessary to establish India as a nuclear weapons power from the point of view of strategic threat. Both events were, nonetheless, important declarative statements, or, as Roland Barthes would put it, signs.[48] The 1974 test is a sign best understood in relation to India's history of state building; the 1998 tests, in relation to the discourse of control.

NUCLEAR DEVELOPMENTALISM

The closest parallel to the Indian program with regard to the larger national-technological meaning of atomic power is that of France. Gabrielle Hecht reminds us that "[t]he fundamental premise of discussions about a future technological France was that, in the postwar world, technological achievements defined geopolitical power." She goes on to quote de Gaulle, saying, "A State does not count if it does not bring something to the world that contributes to the technological progress of the world."[49] Both to recapture the "radiance" of France and to offset American dominance in postwar Europe and the world, France needed technology, especially nuclear technology. In the discussion of the first French Five-Year Plan, atomic energy was justified by noting the country's lack of traditional energy sources (coal, oil, hydroelectric power). The planners noted: "[T]here is no doubt that in a few years the energy sources put at the disposition of people would so profoundly and radically transform their economic activity that the nations that do not have it will appear as helpless as the most backward nations of the world today appear in the face of modern nations."[50] Given the French image of itself, what choice did France have?

In a similar vein, establishing the base for an Indian atomic energy program was always much more than a scheme for building weapons. The fact that the first Indian atomic energy act was passed by the Constituent Assembly rather than waiting for the first elected parliament, the speed with which it was rushed through the assembly with a minimum of debate, and the considerable amounts of money dedicated by a resource-constrained peacetime economy to this unproven technology, suggest that something else—something more—was at stake. The atomic energy project for independent India was also a means for the newly independent state to establish its difference from its illegitimate predecessor, and for the former colonial possession to show that its scientists and engineers were on a par with the best in the world.[51]

It is difficult today to imagine the extent of anxieties related to the formation of a new state or the urgency felt by a new government to show that the coming of political independence would transform the lives of people emerging from over a century of colonial rule. The Indian government was deeply concerned, on the one hand, about meeting the demands for material needs such as goods, services, law and order—what might be called the daily plebiscite of good governance—as soon as possible; on the other hand, in equally swift manner, they also had to establish this new rule as legitimate and ideologically distinct from its past.[52] If so much of anticolonial rhetoric had been wrapped up in economic issues—from the early theory of economic drain and deindustrialization, battles over imperial preferences and terms of trade to debates over protection and the irresponsibility of a liberal laissez-faire state[53]—it comes as no surprise that among the first acts of independent India was to establish a state that controlled the "commanding heights" of the economy. Temporally simultaneous with the Atomic Energy Bill was the first Industrial Policy Resolution (1948), which set aside large sectors of the economy, especially heavy industry, infrastructure, and natural resources, as a state monopoly. Starting from the assumption of a weak and venal private sector, the new Indian government borrowed the model of five-year plans from the Soviet Union with the intention of setting in motion the massive capital investments needed for rapid industrialization and growth.[54] The set of policies expressed in the Second Five-Year Plan and the role imagined for the state in leading this transformation of the economy would come to exemplify what we now call the "developmental" state. This state was, by definition, the antithesis of the indifferent, illegitimate colonial political authority.[55] Modern technologies—steel mills, iron ore mines, massive dams, cities, buildings, and infrastructure—complemented by a newly trained technological cadre committed to national growth, and by extension, national pride, would transform the state and make it "developed." This was not just sensible policy; the very legitimacy of the state depended on it.

"So what should our role be in this dangerous and fast changing world?" Nehru would ask. "It is obvious that the first thing is to make ourselves strong and better off to face any danger."[56] If development meant the constant iteration of the themes of self-reliance, autonomy, and independence, atomic energy was the pinnacle of state achievement, visible proof that the future was as unlike the past as was possible. Not only was atomic energy the modern technology par excellence, posited as producing badly needed electrical energy at low cost using cheap and widely available inputs, but it was a technology that was both local and modern, to which few countries around the world had access. Atomic energy was national strength, uniqueness, and security all wrapped up in one package. To this day, India's left-wing parties, which are opposed to India's nuclear weapons policies, cannot bring themselves to oppose civilian nuclear power even in the face of its economically dismal and safety-plagued record of achievement.[57] The urgent political need for national development and state legitimation was intimately wrapped up in the idea of atomic energy, pointing to the techno-political meaning of atomic energy, which aligns it alongside other modern technological marvels such as dams, steel mills, modern factories, large-scale irrigation systems, and, later on, the space program.[58] India's atomic energy program represented the zenith of Indian developmentalism, technologically and symbolically. Under these conditions, that it was also associated with massive destruction could be finessed.

The intimate and proximate relation between the project of atomic energy and state legitimacy only magnifies its distance from the concerns of nuclear nonproliferation. If Indian independence was defined in relation to nuclear "developmentalism," then giving up the nuclear program becomes equivalent to giving up the project of a sovereign Indian state. For a former colonial state—even if it was not seeking the respect of and eventual parity with the great powers—political freedom had been won too recently and was felt too deeply to allow that to happen.

NONPROLIFERATION AS A REASON FOR GOING NUCLEAR

This chapter has argued that 1974 and 1998 are not the most important dates reflecting the condition of India's nuclear capabilities.[59] The delinking of the "obvious" meaning of the nuclear test and the moment at which a country becomes nuclear weapons capable is further established by what we now know about previous efforts to test nuclear weapons in India.[60] Best known is the desire of the Narasimha Rao government to conduct a round of tests in 1995. In the version recently made public by former U.S. deputy secretary of state Strobe Talbott, in early December 1995, and while U.S. Ambassador to India Frank Wisner was in Washington on a routine visit, U.S. satellite images spotted efforts under way at the Pokhran test site that seemed to indicate that India was preparing for another test. Wisner flew back to New Delhi with copies of these images and "warned [the prime minister's principal secretary] that a test would backfire against India, incurring a full dose of the sanctions under the terms of the Glenn amendment."[61] Rao backed down and canceled the tests. How different would be the spate of analyses that would have followed the test had it taken place in 1995? At the very least, it can be said that the now-dominant association of the tests with the rise of a Hindu nationalist ethos in India would not have been made, given that this was a (relatively) secular Congress government. If the meaning of an explosion can be so different depending on its timing, surely some skepticism regarding the unambiguous linkage usually inferred between an explosion and its meaning is justified?

A very different way of understanding the Indian decision to announce its arrival as a nuclear power comes by considering the effects of the discourse of control. As discussed previously, the discourse of control begins from the assumption that countries seek to develop nuclear weapons as a logical necessity of the self-help condition under conditions of anarchy. The NPT sought to mediate that strategic choice, offering countries the option of civilian nuclear technologies for those willing to eschew, legally, the possession of nuclear weapons. Under uncertain conditions of compliance and with a high degree of overlap in the technological means to produce either weapons or electricity, the primary analytic and policy impulse is to determine whether there is cheating going on. The only seemingly unambiguous sign that nuclear weapons status is being sought is the decision to test a nuclear device, an event that cannot be hidden from international scrutiny. The discussion has shown the limits of meaning that can be attributed to nonevents—opacity and ambiguity—and to explosions; Israel stands as a prime example of a country that is assumed to have nuclear weapons without openly testing. Clearly, even this seemingly unambiguous event is not.

Based on its history, size, and self-representation as a distinct and unique civilization, India has always expected and sought a special position for itself in the international community. Among its first steps following the end of British colonial rule was the articulation of a set of foreign policy positions that questioned and even sometimes rejected prevailing understandings of the nature of the international system, especially the role of force, and argued instead for the relevance and importance of justice and morality in international affairs.[62] This starting point made India's foreign policy quite distinct, especially in relation to the established great powers, during a time of global political hostility and fear. For a relatively weak military power with huge economic problems, what was less easy to establish was a consistent set of distinct practices corresponding to this sense of uniqueness, and, with the passage of time and events, the distinctiveness of Indian foreign policy waned.

From the outset, however, there has always been a vocal minority within India that, while fully accepting these claims to difference, found it difficult to conceive of national practices that did not correspond to international norms of power and prominence. As early as 1948, during the first major nuclear debate in India, there was considerable doubt among the majority who supported the creation of an Indian nuclear program that a policy of peaceful uses of nuclear power made any sense at all. Faced with this public doubt, Jawaharlal Nehru, independent India's first prime minister and sponsor of the Atomic Energy Bill, was forced to admit in debate that he could not distinguish between military and peaceful uses of nuclear power, even as he proposed the creation of a nuclear program dedicated to peaceful ends. Shibban Lal Saxena, a Constituent Assembly delegate from the United Provinces, spoke for many in expressing his grave doubts that such a policy would have its desired effect:

> Unless we are [a militarily powerful] nation and unless we can have a say in world affairs, I do not think we can make the world pacific. Our national genius being pacific I would then like to tell the world that we must ban the use of atomic energy for warfare and even outlaw war. But we cannot do it by preaching and good wishes alone. Unless we have the capacity to use atomic energy for destructive warfare, it will have no meaning for us to say that we shall not use atomic energy for destructive purposes.[63]

Saxena's doubts define international power in two ways, in terms of capability and relationally. As capability, in order to be meaningful, Saxena argued that the power-to-do had to precede the power-to-reject. Relationally, if the expressed idiom of power was not recognized as power but merely as "preaching and good wishes," was it power at all? Both senses of power come together to argue that the decision to adopt a peaceful nuclear program would not be understood by its intended recipients; hence, its larger purpose would fail. This slippage between meaning and intent is paralleled after 1974. The unintelligibility of a technological "demonstration," the first meaning attributed to India's 1974 test, soon mutated into the idea of a nuclear "option." The "option" meant that India had shown the capability to become a nuclear power and would choose, on its own terms, the time and place of doing so more explicitly. The international discourse of control, however, could not comprehend these meanings and translated them at once into the belief that India had made a claim to be a nuclear power. Rather than take these meanings as they were intended, namely, to demonstrate ability and at the same time express uncertainty about a desired course of future action, the combined forces of proliferation policy and academic studies treated India as a new nuclear power and, therefore, as a country that sought to undermine the regime of nuclear control established by the great powers.

As noted earlier, the accepted meanings of a nuclear test led to India being seen as a nuclear power, even if the meaning of that power was "ambiguous." India received none of the advantages it expected for showing this capability— including its cause of disarmament—and paid a steep price for violating the terms of an international agreement that it had not signed. As time went on, the gap between the domestic meanings of India's nuclear program and their reception abroad became greater. The more India claimed only to possess the option and have a peaceful program, the more these disavowals were read as cover for an illicit weapons program. The exposed fragility of the nuclear bargain embedded in the NPT led to the possibility of ever-increasing sanctions being applied to India, culminating in the provisions of the Comprehensive Test Ban Treaty (CTBT). Worse still, even if India did not sign the treaty, it would nonetheless be held accountable under the CTBT regime.[64]

By the 1990s, international meanings had come to dominate domestic understandings of the "peaceful" Indian nuclear program and its nuclear "option." This was the context within which Narasimha Rao first gave the order to go ahead with more tests and then revoked it. The BJP, always chafing at their perception of India as an unacknowledged great power, had no compunctions about meeting the norms expected of countries that conduct nuclear explosions. In May 1998, they tested five nuclear devices (including a boosted fission device that was erroneously described as a thermonuclear fusion weapon) and declared the country a nuclear power.[65] Framing the decision to go ahead with the May 1998 tests was the desire to reduce the multiple meanings of a "peaceful" nuclear program, to force nuclear ambivalence into a more familiar register. As defense minister and senior party strategist Jaswant Singh would write, almost as if responding directly to the concerns raised by Saxena half a century before:

> The problem . . . is entirely of India's making. In 1974, with the underground nuclear explosion, India demonstrated an ability, but disclaimed the intent.

In retrospect, the step is to be faulted on both counts—of having the capability and yet none of the advantages. India ought not to have held such an experiment at all—simply an explosion as a capability demonstrator— if it intended to deny the capability straight thereafter. By demonstrating the ability, India had effectively and explicitly entered the world of nuclear capability. Had we straight thereafter conducted a series of other such tests and established our ability, then it would have been easier to cope with all *the confusion of subsequent years*, these current international pressures, and all the other difficulties of today. Instead we went into a nuclear trance: pretence replaced policy. In consequence, India has suffered the ill effects of both: of being suspected of being a nuclear weapons possessing power, and not really being one.[66]

Jaswant Singh would later expand on this position:

[Given the changing security environment] India was left with little choice but to develop the capability that it had demonstrated in 1974, twenty-four years ago. . . . Restraint however has to arise from strength. It cannot be based upon indecision or doubt. The series of tests recently undertaken by India has led to the *removal of doubts*. . . . India is now a nuclear weapons state. This is a reality that cannot be denied.[67]

The immediate desire to discipline multiple meanings—to remove doubts and confusion—via nuclear explosions comes from the intersection of the discourse of control with the interests of the nuclear scientist seeking "sweet" solutions, more resources, and intellectual bravura in the name of national pride.[68] Each nuclear test reduces further the range of meanings of the Indian nuclear program, bringing it closer to conformity with received interpretations of what a "typical" nuclear program does. This excess of meaning, however, emerges in the first instance from the gulf between domestic interests of the nuclear project and the international discourse of control.

India's 1974 PNE was called, at the time, a technological "demonstration." This appellation was never taken seriously, and the prevailing assumption, both within and without the country, was that India had decided to become a nuclear power. Certainly Pakistan believed that: its nuclear history since that date has been a single-minded effort to achieve the same standard.[69] The long history of Indian nuclear restraint that followed the PNE gave rise to terms like "ambiguity" that sought to produce clarity out of confusion.

The confusion came from a general unwillingness to believe that India could in fact be having a real debate about the virtues and utility of continuing along the same path as the NWS. Undoubtedly there were those among the Indian nuclear scientists and strategic community who saw this debate as wholly unnecessary and a public exhibition of weakness. But they were by no means the only or even the dominant voices within Indian strategic debates. Within the ranks of the powerful civil service and among the intelligentsia there was a real reluctance to forgo the country's time-tested positions against nuclear weapons and in favor of general disarmament, not only because of the negative fallout on India's desired position of international leadership among developing countries but also because of sincere belief in the moral and ethical superiority of this stance. The influence of voices promoting nuclear restraint was clearly felt in the higher reaches of power and certainly within the Congress Party. But this domestic debate has to be set against the pressures from outside.

The presumption that India had embarked on a covert nuclear program from 1974 dominated international analyses. India found itself in a position where its expressed policy of restraint was met with deep skepticism from the major powers, who could see no other end for a nuclear program-cum-explosion than an effort to build nuclear weapons. Post-1974, India had hoped that its position on the need for general disarmament would be made even stronger by its self-imposed reluctance to go any further down the nuclear path. But this was not to be. It took awhile for New Delhi to understand the implications of what it had done from others' points of view. Over time, India found that not only was it being denied the presumed advantages of being a nuclear power, which were in any event hugely overrated in India, but also the country's very denials were taken to mean that it was in fact seeking this status. A quickly fashioned post-1974 policy was failing on two fronts in the international community. The last serious effort that India made to return to its old position on general disarmament, based on the presumption that its policy of restraint gave it a special status among nuclear-capable states, was Rajiv Gandhi's proposal to the United Nations in June 1988 calling for a new effort toward complete global disarmament. This effort, like others before it, went nowhere. India was, from the international point of view, a nuclear-capable state; neither its protestations to the contrary nor its self-imposed restraint made any significant dent in that belief. Complementing the many stories explaining the 1998 tests, this chapter argues they cannot be understood without reference to nonproliferation as a discourse of control. The nuclear explosions of May 1998 become a semantic tourniquet: they stem the proliferation of competing domestic meanings that circulated in the state of nuclear ambiguity and produce identity with a dominant international meaning attributed to the nuclear test.

NOTES

The "National and Indigenous" section of this chapter draws on my "The Ambivalence of Nuclear Histories," *Osiris: Science, Technology and International Affairs*, vol. 21 (2006), 1–37.

1. For a useful summary discussion of how norms emerge, see George Bunn, "The Status of Norms Against Nuclear Testing," *Nonproliferation Review*, vol. 6, no. 2 (Winter 1999), 21–23.

2. See Chapter 6 in this volume.

3. See Paul Kerr, "IAEA: Seoul's Nuclear Sins in Past," *Arms Control Today* (December 2004), available at http://www.armscontrol.org/act/2004_12/Seoul, and "IAEA Investigating Taiwan and Egypt," *Arms Control Today* (January–February 2005), available at http://www.armscontrol.org/act/2004_12/Seoul.

4. See Robert N. Schock, Eileen S. Vergino, Neil Joeck, and Ronald F. Lehman, "Atoms for Peace After 50 Years," *Issues in Science and Technology Online* (Spring 2004), available at http://www.issues.org/20.3/schock.html.

5. "Nuclear nonproliferation" indexes an international-legal discourse where five countries are given a special status as "nuclear weapon states"; the intent of the law is to prevent other states from acquiring the same (de facto and de jure) status. Quotes around the term are used to indicate this term is a form of "political language." See Murray Edelman, *Political Language: Words That Succeed and Policies That Fail* (New York: Academic Press, 1977). The distinction between "proliferation studies" and "nuclear histories" points to the political purpose of the former term.

6. Steve Smith, "The United States and the Discipline of International Relations: 'Hegemonic Country, Hegemonic Discipline,'" *International Studies Review*, vol. 4, no. 2 (Summer 2002), 67–85.

7. For instance, Michael Mandelbaum: "[T]he farther the bomb spreads from the industrial circumference, the greater are the chances that it could find its way into the hands of persons who would not show the prudence that the guardians of existing nuclear stockpiles have so far displayed." Cited in Devin T. Hagerty, "The Power of Suggestion: Opaque Proliferation, Existential Deterrence, and the South Asian Nuclear Arms Competition," in Zachary S. Davis and Benjamin Frankel, eds., *The Proliferation Puzzle: Why Nuclear Weapons Spread (and What Results)* (London: Frank Cass, 1993), 265.

8. See Atomic Scientists of Chicago, *The Atomic Bomb: Facts and Implications* (Chicago: Atomic Scientists of Chicago, 1946), 18, for a list of the key publications announcing the discovery of fission and the diverse nationalities of their authors.

9. Richard Rhodes, *The Making of the Atomic Bomb* (London: Simon and Schuster, 1995).

10. John Lewis and Xue Litai, *China Builds the Bomb* (Stanford, CA: Stanford University Press, 1988), 44–45.

11. Lawrence S. Scheinman, *Atomic Energy Policy in France Under the Fourth Republic* (Princeton, NJ: Princeton University Press, 1965).

12. David Holloway, *Stalin and the Bomb* (New Haven, CT: Yale University Press, 1996).

13. Astrid Forland, "Norway's Nuclear Odyssey: From Optimistic Proponent to Non-proliferator," *Nonproliferation Review*, vol. 4, no. 2 (Winter 1997), 1–16.

14. Cohen, *Israel and the Bomb*.

15. Margaret Gowing, *Independence and Deterrence*, vol. 1: *Policy Making* (New York: Macmillan, 1974).

16. Itty Abraham, *Making of the Indian Atomic Bomb: Science, Secrecy and the Postcolonial State* (London: Zed Books, 1998), 84–85.

17. Nehru, "Apsara," from *Jawaharlal Nehru's Speeches*, vol. 3, March 1953–August 1957 (New Delhi: Publications Division of the Government of India, 1958), 504–505, italics added. Homi J. Bhabha, "father" of the Indian nuclear program, was trained in England and worked at Cambridge University through much of the 1930s, when a series of important discoveries and experiments were taking place. He was a close friend and colleague with the Cavendish group, including John Cockcroft, Patrick Blackett, James Chadwick, Charles Wilson, and others. For more on the transnational networks of Anglo-Indian physicists during this period, see the forthcoming study by Robert Anderson, *Nucleus and Nation: Scientists, International Networks and Power in India* (forthcoming, University of Chicago Press).

18. Internal memo (undated), File AB6/1250, Public Records Office, UK.

19. Holloway, *Stalin and the Bomb*, 78.

20. Ibid., 48.

21. Govind Swarup, interview, October 15, 1995, Washington, DC. Swarup, one of the few Indian Fellows of the Royal Society, is India's most distinguished radio astronomer and initiated a number of major radio astronomy projects, including the Ooty radio telescope and the GMRT array near Pune.

22. Spencer R. Weart, *Nuclear Fear: A History of Images* (Cambridge, MA: Harvard University Press, 1988), 77–102.

23. Daniel J. Kevles, *The Physicists: The History of a Scientific Community in Modern America* (Cambridge, MA: Harvard University Press, 1971), 200–286.

24. Quoted in Nehru, "The Hydrogen Bomb," in *Speeches*, 248.

25. Mohandas Karamchand Gandhi, "The Atom Bomb, America and Japan," originally published in *Harijan*, July 7, 1946. Reprinted in Homer A. Jack, ed., *The Gandhi Reader: A Source Book of His Life and Writings* (New York: Grove Press, 1994), 349–350.

26. Weart, *Nuclear Fear*, 162.

27. David E. Nye, *American Technological Sublime* (Cambridge, MA: MIT Press, 1994), 225.

28. Weart, *Nuclear Fear*, 158–159.

29. Ibid., 160.

30. Loren R. Graham, *Science in Russia and the Soviet Union* (Cambridge: Cambridge University Press, 1993), 166.

31. Weart, *Nuclear Fear*, 165.

32. Cohen, *Israel and the Bomb*, 11, 353fn9.

33. Abraham, *Making of the Indian Atomic Bomb*, 48–54.

34. Ibid., 122.

35. Scott D. Sagan, "Why Do States Build Nuclear Weapons? Three Models in Search of a Bomb," *International Security*, vol. 21 (1996–1997), 73–85. See also Stephen M. Meyer, *The Dynamics of Nuclear Proliferation* (Chicago: University of Chicago Press, 1984); Bradley A. Thayer, "The Causes of Nuclear Proliferation and the Utility of the Nuclear Non-proliferation Regime," *Security Studies*, vol. 4 (1995), 463–519; Tanya Ogilvie-White, "Is There a Theory of Nuclear Proliferation?" *Nonproliferation Review*, vol. 4, no. 1 (1996), 43–60.

36. Sagan, "Why Do States Build Nuclear Weapons?" 55. It should be noted that Sagan uses the term "norms" in three distinct ways: as an ideational-symbolic form, as a form of international mimicry, and as a reflexive constraint on autonomous actions.

37. Ibid., 85, italics added.

38. The term "legible" is borrowed from James C. Scott, *Seeing Like a State: How Certain Schemes to Improve the Human Condition Have Failed* (New Haven, CT: Yale University Press, 1998).

39. Important exceptions include Ariel Levite, "Never Say Never Again: Nuclear Reversal Revisited," *International Security*, vol. 27, no. 3 (Winter 2002–2003); and T. V. Paul, *Power Versus Prudence: Why Nations Forgo Nuclear Weapons* (Montreal: McGill/Queen's University Press, 2000).

40. That a techno-political event is only a "demonstration" is an official hedge. It should be taken to mean a technical capability to do something that (1) stops short of defining national policy and (2) provides cover to the technologists in case of failure. Central to the meaning of the word are the various audiences—domestic and foreign—who are presumed to be seeking unambiguous meaning from this event.

41. See Devin T. Hagerty, *The Consequences of Nuclear Proliferation: Lessons from South Asia* (Cambridge, MA: MIT Press, 1999).

42. Avner Cohen and Benjamin Frankel, "Opaque Nuclear Proliferation," in Benjamin Frankel, ed., *Opaque Nuclear Proliferation: Methodological and Policy Implications* (London: Frank Cass, 1991), 14–44.

43. Avner Cohen, *Israel and the Bomb* (New York: Columbia University Press, 1998), ix.

44. George Perkovich, *India and the Bomb* (Berkeley: University of California Press, 1999).

45. Cohen, *Israel and the Bomb*.

46. Scheinman, *Atomic Energy Policy in France*.

47. Raj Chengappa, *Weapons of Peace: The Secret Story of India's Quest to Be a Nuclear Power* (New Delhi: HarperCollins, 2000), 291–305; Perkovich, *India's Nuclear Bomb*, 293–299.

48. Roland Barthes, *Mythologies*, trans. Annette Lavers (New York: Jonathan Cape, 1957).

49. Gabrielle Hecht, *The Radiance of France* (Cambridge, MA: MIT Press, 1998), 39.

50. Scheinman, *Atomic Energy Policy in France*, 75.

51. See Abraham, *Making of the Indian Atomic Bomb*, chaps. 2–3, for a longer discussion.

52. See Partha Chatterjee, "The National State," in *The Nation and Its Fragments* (Princeton, NJ: Princeton University Press, 1993).

53. Manu Goswami, *Producing India: From Colonial Economy to National Space* (Chicago: University of Chicago Press, 2004).

54. Vivek Chibber, *Locked in Place: State Building and Late Industrialization in India* (Princeton, NJ: Princeton University Press, 2003).

55. Chatterjee, *Nation and Its Fragments*.

56. Nehru, *Selected Works*, 30.

57. M. V. Ramana, Antonette D'Sa, and Amulya K. N. Reddy, "Economics of Nuclear Power from Heavy Water Reactors," *Economic and Political Weekly*, April 23, 2005.

58. See Abraham, "The Ambivalence of Nuclear Histories."

59. See Chapters 1 and 3 in this volume. Also see Praful Bidwai and Achin Vanaik, *South Asia on a Short Fuse* (New Delhi: Oxford University Press, 2000); M. V. Ramana and C. Rammanohar Reddy, eds., *Prisoners of the Nuclear Dream* (New Delhi: Orient Longman, 2003); Perkovich, *India's Nuclear Bomb*; Chengappa, *Weapons of Peace*.

60. Ashok Kapur, in *Pokhran and Beyond* (New Delhi: Oxford University Press, 2002), asserts that Indira Gandhi wanted to test in 1982, but as Perkovich notes, other than the formal request by the nuclear scientists, the rest of the story (Gandhi's agreement to go ahead, which was rescinded after twenty-four hours) has never been fully corroborated. *India's Nuclear Bomb*, 242–244. Chengappa, in *Weapons of Peace*, 390–395, also reports that in 1995 Prime Minister Narasimha Rao ordered a series of tests that were canceled following internal disagreements and U.S. pressure. Of his two

successors, Atal Behari Vajpayee ordered tests, but his first government fell in thirteen days; H. D. Deve Gowda felt that other matters were more pressing than nuclear tests, even though the test site was ready and explosives were in place. Perkovich, *India's Nuclear Bomb*, 375–376.

61. Strobe Talbott, *Engaging India* (Washington, DC: Brookings Institution Press, 2004), 37–38.

62. Itty Abraham, "From Bandung to NAM: Indian Foreign Policy, 1947–1965," *Commonwealth and Comparative Politics*, vol. 46, no. 2 (2008), 195–219.

63. Quoted in Abraham, *Making of the Indian Atomic Bomb*, 51.

64. In a very unusual condition for international treaties, India and forty-three other countries were named as needing to sign the treaty before it could "enter into [legal] force." India bitterly protested this step, as it correctly saw itself as one of the primary targets of the ruling. More cynical observers have suggested that the Permanent Five (P-5) countries encouraged this condition in order to scuttle the treaty but not appear responsible.

65. The yields of the May 1998 tests have been the source of considerable controversy, scientific disagreement, and official propaganda. For the official Indian position, see R. Chidarambaram, "The May 1998 Pokharan Tests: Scientific Aspects," South Asia Analysis Group paper no. 451, available at http://www.southasiaanalysis .org/%5Cpapers5%5Cpaper451.html. The Indian DAE was reluctant to release hard data on the tests until pressed by domestic critics such as M. V. Ramana and as doubts began to mount from foreign scientists, especially seismologists. For DAE results, see S. K. Sikka, Falguni Roy, and G. J. Nair, "Indian Explosions of 11 May 1998: An Analysis of the Global Seismic Body Wave Magnitude Estimates," *Current Science*, vol. 75, no. 5 (September 1998); and S. K. Sikka, Falguni Roy, G. J. Nair, V. G. Kolvankar, and Anil Kakodkar, "Update on the Yield of May 11–13, 1998, Nuclear Detonations at Pokhran," *BARC Newsletter*, no. 178 (November 1998). Queries about the methodology, lack of data, discordant interpretations of results, etc., may be found in A. Douglas, P. D. Marshall, D. Bowers, J. B. Young, D. Porter, and N. J. Wallis, "The Yields of the Indian Nuclear Tests of 1998 and Their Relevance to Test Ban Verification," *Current Science*, vol. 81, no. 1 (July 2001); Terry Wallace, "The May 1998 India and Pakistan Nuclear Tests," *Seismological Research Letters* (September 1998); William R. Walter, Arthur J. Rodgers, Kevin Mayeda, Stephen C. Myers, Michael Pasyanos, and Marvin Denny, "Preliminary Regional Seismic Analysis of Nuclear Explosions and Earthquakes in Southwest Asia," 1999, UCRL-JC-130745-Ext-Abs-Rev-1, Lawrence Livermore Laboratory, available at http://www.llnl.gov/tid/lof/documents/pdf/903991.pdf. See also other studies by Rodgers et al. on the Lawrence Livermore website. Based on this analysis, some even doubt that the fourth and fifth Indian tests took place.

66. It is important to note that the text from the first paragraph was written in May 1997, when Jaswant Singh was not in office. The latter excerpt was written as a

postscript, published in June 1998, when he was, after the BJP had come to office and had conducted five tests.

67. Jaswant Singh, "What Constitutes National Security in a Changing World Order? India's Strategic Thought," Occasional Paper No. 6, Center for the Advanced Study of India, University of Pennsylvania, June 1998, 23–24, 31–32, italics added.

68. Abraham, *Making of the Indian Atomic Bomb.*

69. Ashok Kapur, *Pakistan's Nuclear Development* (London: Croom Helm, 1987).

THE CONSEQUENCES OF NUCLEAR
PROLIFERATION IN SOUTH ASIA

4 PRIDE AND PREJUDICE AND PRITHVIS
Strategic Weapons Behavior in South Asia
Vipin Narang

SOUTH ASIAN SECURITY SCHOLARSHIP has overwhelmingly focused on the causes and consequences of India's and Pakistan's nuclearization. Insufficient attention has been paid to the other components of these states' strategic weapons decisions, a portrait of which may reveal a richer understanding of the motivations driving them. The May 1998 nuclear tests were certainly major strategic events, but there are multiple plausible explanations for these decisions. A more complete and accurate understanding of Indian and Pakistani strategic behavior can be gained by analyzing their ballistic missile flight-testing patterns, patterns related to nuclearization that can provide insights into the motives for both the nuclear tests and their broader strategic weapons decisions. Instead of weighing alternative explanations for one event—the 1998 nuclear tests—I examine the series of ballistic missile flight tests in the region that occurred repeatedly across a two-decade time frame under a variety of systemic and domestic conditions, providing new insights into the motivations for India's and Pakistan's strategic weapons decisions.

I begin with a survey of the South Asian nuclearization debate, demonstrating in particular that there are multiple plausible explanations for India's decision to cross the nuclear weapons threshold in May 1998. This debate focuses on several possible security, domestic political, and normative or prestige variables that might influence India's and Pakistan's strategic weapons behavior; but it is unable to resolve which variables are the most important, and when, due to limited observations. My examination of ballistic missile flight tests in the region relies on a greater number of data points, allowing me to confirm or disconfirm the hypotheses generated by the nuclearization

137

debate. The empirical analysis that follows employs events-data and content-analysis methods to test which variables produced these states' ballistic missile flight-testing decisions.

The evidence suggests that Pakistan is indeed motivated primarily by security concerns, forced to keep pace with India's strategic weapons advances since it is the much weaker of the two powers. I show that the variables that best account for India's strategic weapons decisions, however, are a combination of *domestic political ideology* and *position*. Specifically, the Congress and the Bharatiya Janata Party (BJP) conceive of Indian pride in different ways. For the dominant political party, the Congress Party, Indian pride takes the form of a "techno-nationalist" pride, seeking to demonstrate that India's technological capabilities are indigenously developed, sophisticated, and world class; its conception of pride is self-referential and derivative of the Nehruvian emphasis on Indian self-reliance. The BJP, on the other hand, conceives of Indian pride in highly oppositional and competitive terms, seeking to repudiate the perceived malignant agents—both Pakistan and a hypocritical international community writ large—that it believes aim to keep India weak. The position of these parties relative to each other determines which form of "prestige" India seeks at a given moment. This domestic political dynamic captures both India's ballistic missile flight-testing pattern and its 1998 decision to nuclearize and suggests that the Indian preference for prestige needs to be disaggregated to fully understand New Delhi's strategic weapons behavior.

The analysis in this chapter has significant implications for how India's strategic weapons decisions may unfold and how Pakistan might respond in the future. In particular, one should largely expect the BJP to be more provocative in its strategic weapons behavior than its Congress counterpart. Motivated by a techno-nationalist pride that privileges the indigenous development of what a superpower is believed to have—above all, technological and economic prowess—future Congress governments are unlikely to develop and test strategic weapons at times of potential international political offense, instead supporting the technical imperatives and testing sequence requirements of its prized strategic weapons programs. However, future BJP governments, motivated by an "oppositional nationalist" ideology, may be more likely to develop strategic weapons at a more rapid pace than Congress governments and test or deploy them in response to challenges from perceived malignant entities, notably Pakistan and the Western powers. The consequence is that the South Asian arms race is likely to be more intense when a strong BJP government is in power.

THE NUCLEARIZATION DEBATE

Much has been written about the nuclearization of South Asia, with particular focus on India's decision to test nuclear weapons when it did, since it was the region's first-mover on nuclear weapons in both 1974 and 1998.[1] In comparison to the literature on India, there is very little debate about Pakistan's decisions to initiate a nuclear weapons program and to finally test in 1998.[2] Once India openly demonstrated its nuclear capabilities, many scholars argue that Pakistan had no option but to develop and test nuclear weapons to demonstrate the reliability of the Pakistani deterrent to India and the rest of the world.[3] Although Pakistan had lived under a cloak of nuclear ambiguity for almost a decade, India's May 1998 tests forced Islamabad's hand. For two weeks in May 1998, Prime Minister Nawaz Sharif says he "carefully considered" what was in Pakistan's security interest, but "Indian belligerency . . . made the retaliatory action inevitable."[4] According to Samina Ahmed, the armed forces, "which were still in charge of the overall direction of Pakistan's nuclear policy," held the "predominant belief that Pakistan had no choice but to test. . . . [A] tit-for-tat response was almost inevitable."[5] Arguments that Pakistan tested for prestige purposes or to wield an "Islamic bomb" are difficult to square with the timing of the test—immediately after the Indian tests—and with the widespread belief that Pakistan's nuclear arsenal was the product of considerable Chinese assistance.[6]

There is substantial consensus that Pakistan's decision to nuclearize was an overwhelming product of Indian-generated security imperatives. The implication is that any other Pakistani leader faced with the same security pressures would have done the same. Although there was some initial internal debate about whether to respond, the discussion quickly turned to how many tests Pakistan would conduct and how best to weather the international sanctions that would follow.[7] As Pakistani foreign minister Shamshad Ahmad penned in *Foreign Affairs*, "[T]o restore strategic balance to South Asia, Pakistan was obliged to respond to India's May 1998 nuclear blasts."[8] When Pakistan finally responded, Sharif spoke of settling the score with India and of facing the "manifest Indian [nuclear] threat" with resolve and with nuclear-tipped Ghauri missiles.[9] The summary judgment on Pakistan's motivations to nuclearize is captured by Lowell Dittmer: "Pakistan's motive for the acquisition of nuclear weapons is . . . far less complex and more conventional: national security. As India's weaker rival, defeated in nearly all their military encounters and dismembered in the third, Pakistan has reason for concern."[10] Šumit Ganguly and Devin Hagerty concur, arguing that the "core aim of Pakistan's nuclear weapons program is to prevent a repetition of 1971 [when Bangladesh was born out of East Pakistan] . . . to deter an Indian attack that might reduce Pakistan's size even further, or perhaps even put the country out of existence entirely."[11] The critical puzzle is what therefore compelled India to openly test in May 1998, for the scholarship on Pakistan's nuclearization almost unequivocally concludes that no matter when India chose to test, Pakistan would have had little choice but to follow suit.

In contrast to the literature on Pakistan, the debate about India's motivations for nuclearizing in 1998 is quite wide ranging, with several plausible explanations for the BJP's decision. Realists, for example, emphasize the security pressures emanating from both international and regional actors that drove India to test. They argue that a confluence of security factors in the late 1990s created system incentives for India to exercise its nuclear option: the permanent extension of the NPT in 1995, the prospect of the Comprehensive Test Ban Treaty (CTBT) forever foreclosing India's capability to generate live test data, and the persistence of an increasingly powerful nuclear China (despite a short-term thaw in relations) assisting a thorny Pakistan on India's borders.[12] The organizations responsible for India's nuclear development—the Atomic Energy Commission (AEC) and Defense Research and Development Organization (DRDO)—pressed for tests because of the looming CTBT;[13] and Prime Minister A. B. Vajpayee, days after the tests, cited China as the *primary* motivation for nuclearization in writing to President Clinton: "[W]e have an overt nuclear-weapon state on our border, a state which committed armed aggression against India in 1962 . . . [and which] has materially helped another neighbor of ours to become a covert nuclear weapons state."[14] Indeed, an Indian test would force Pakistan's hand, with only net security gains for India: if Islamabad successfully tested in response, it would simply confirm what New Delhi already believed to be a de facto reality; if Islamabad failed to respond, the credibility of its nuclear deterrent would be severely undermined, to India's security advantage.

In response, those partial to the constructivist school of thought in political science have argued that India's quest to be considered a legitimate global power and concurrent desire for prestige on the international stage drove it to test in 1998 to break into what it perceived to be an exclusive club of great powers. To India, this exclusivity is legitimated by the fact that the five declared nuclear powers are also the five permanent members of the UN Security Council, and India wants a seat at the table.[15] This explanation has also been corroborated by multiple methods and observations. Brajesh Mishra, the BJP's national security advisor, exulted that India controlled its own destiny on nuclear weapons: "Who are the Americans to tell us how to take care of our security concerns?"[16] The implication was that all forms of colonialism were dead and that India had just as legitimate a right to enter the "club" of nuclear powers as did any great state.[17] The prestige motivation is also evident in the scientific enclaves responsible for India's nuclear weapons, who sought to demonstrate their scientific prowess to the world and become one of only a handful of states to have *indigenously* developed and tested nuclear weapons.[18] Thus, the quest for the two perceived sources of prestige—an indigenously developed nuclear arsenal, a mark of technological achievement, and acquiring that which the existing nuclear weapons states sought to deny New Delhi—is also largely consistent with the fact and the timing of India's tests.

Others have argued that domestic political considerations were largely responsible for the May tests, again pointing to a confluence of political and bureaucratic forces compelling India to nuclearize in 1998.[19] In particular, the rise of the nationalist BJP party on the right flank of the traditionally cautious Congress Party and the bureaucratic interests of India's scientific enclave generated coinciding interests to test.[20] The recently elected BJP had solidly defeated its rival for the first time and may have been looking to consolidate support around it with a dramatic act. Brajesh Mishra also highlighted this motivation when he declared, "We had to show a credible deterrent capability not only to the outside world, but to our own people."[21] The argument is that the BJP's need to generate a strong focal point around which to rally the Indian population led it to test nuclear weapons. The BJP had a brief two-week tenure two years earlier in March 1996 and reportedly aborted a nuclear test at the eleventh hour—Vajpayee lost a vote of no confidence before he could test, going so far as to purportedly place three nuclear devices in test shafts.[22] If true, this aborted test suggests another domestic political motivation that has been advanced: Vajpayee had incentives to test as soon as possible in his second tenure to stave off any thoughts of another vote of no confidence.[23] It also provides powerful evidence for the domestic politics hypothesis, because, if true, irrespective of when it succeeded in coming to power, the BJP seemed determined to test nuclear weapons. Because the counterfactuals (Congress victories in March 1996 and 1998) are impossible to test and because the nuclear tests were a unique event, this domestic political explanation cannot be conclusively excluded.

Some variants on these hypotheses have been formulated, most notably the "oppositional nationalism" conception of national identity, which emphasizes the combination of fear in one's enemy plus pride in oneself; the BJP, which defined itself by a Hindu nationalism seeking to reassert India's *shakti* (potency or power), was fundamentally more oppositional toward Islamic Pakistan than was the Congress Party and directed the nuclear tests toward Islamabad.[24] This combination of pride and fear embodied by the BJP, according to Jacques Hymans, created an "explosive" mix that made nuclearization both a symbol of national self-esteem and a means to provoke or challenge Pakistan, which was viewed as a "menacing Other."[25] This explanation relies on showing that nuclearization was a signal whose primary external target was Pakistan, not China, and that the BJP evinced an "imperious need for self-expression in interactions" with Pakistan.[26] Hymans marshals substantial evidence: for example, he notes that Vajpayee's final authorization for tests was solidified by a Pakistani flight test of its Ghauri missile on April 6.[27] But the argument hinges on two inconclusive and problematic propositions: first, that the BJP was driven to test solely because of its oppositional nationalist ideology toward Pakistan, and second, that the Congress was consistently reluctant to cross the nuclear Rubicon. On the first count, although Hymans is correct in arguing that the BJP's nuclear manifestos during the mid-1980s were exclusively centered on Pakistan, where the "failure to mention China is particularly telling," by 1998 the BJP was serving up a panoply of rationalizations for the nuclear tests.[28] In fact, Vajpayee *explicitly* cited China as the primary motivation for the tests in the open letter to Clinton, making it difficult to adduce an oppositional nationalist ideology as the driving force behind the tests. And on the second count, as Hymans concedes, the fact that it was Congress that held the reins of India's creeping nuclear weapons program prior to 1998 poses a serious challenge for the hypothesis.[29] In particular, Congress prime ministers had been at the helm in New Delhi during India's critical nuclear junctures: Indira Gandhi tested India's peaceful nuclear device in 1974, Rajiv Gandhi brought the program out of dormancy and accelerated India's strategic weapons developments in the late 1980s, and successive Congress prime ministers, notably Narasimha Rao, came within a hair's breadth of fully exercising India's nuclear option as late as 1995.[30] Without these efforts, the BJP would not have had anything to test in 1998. Therefore, the characterization of the BJP as radically and consistently different from the Congress with respect to India's nuclear weapons program becomes difficult to sustain empirically.

Certainly, the oppositional nationalism hypothesis captures a cornerstone of the BJP worldview, but it cannot conclusively demonstrate that this ideology caused India to become a declared nuclear power in May 1998.[31]

Whereas the literature on Pakistan's decision to nuclearize has focused almost exclusively on the security pressures forcing Islamabad to test, the literature on India's nuclearization provides a multiplicity of plausible explanations. This reflects the fact that India's more powerful position within the regional and international systems gives it some room to maneuver against structural security-seeking constraints. By almost any measure of power, India would be classified as a rising great power, and Pakistan can be classified as a relatively weaker power. For example, using the 2001 aggregate composite index of national capabilities measure from the Correlates of War Project as a crude but representative measure, the proportion of systemic power of India is about 0.07 that of Pakistan, about 0.014; of China, about 0.13; and of the United States, about 0.15.[32] India's human, economic, and conventional military capabilities dwarf its smaller neighbor's by almost an order of magnitude.[33] Although India stares up at China in terms of aggregate power metrics, India is sufficiently powerful within the regional subsystem to have some freedom to maneuver. Pakistan, on the other hand, is substantially less powerful and has been forced to divert a substantial percentage of its GDP to military expenditures and to pursue asymmetric "bleeding" strategies simply to balance its more powerful neighbor.[34] According to realists of all stripes, as a weak power facing a stronger polar neighbor, Pakistan—irrespective of domestic political configuration or personalities—should have no choice but to engage in security-seeking behavior by any means necessary, either by seeking external allies or by devoting significant domestic resources to developing its military deterrent.[35] India's relatively greater material power, though, affords it some elasticity in its security decisions whereby domestic-level variables may have a significant impact on its behavior.[36]

The nuclearization debate, however, successfully identifies several plausible unit-level intervening variables through which India's broader security policy decisions might be channeled. The narrow structural realist hypothesis is that India acts to maximize its material security in accordance with systemic pressures. This theory predicts that India's security decisions should be directly coupled to international instruments limiting ballistic missile or nuclear technology and to perturbations in India's material position relative to China. One possible intervening variable that might cause India to depart from strict security-seeking behavior is a preference for "prestige maximization" arising from India's quest to achieve great power status. According to this theory, the indigenous development of nuclear weapons and ballistic missiles is perceived to carry substantial international political currency and is thus a means to achieving international prestige. An alternative plausible intervening variable is the electoral position of India's domestic political parties. This would suggest that as the Congress Party weakened and faced a rising and substantial challenge from the BJP on its right flank, and as the BJP sought to solidify its base in the face of slim coalitions, India's parties made strategic weapons decisions for electoral purposes. The final possible intervening variable that might cause India to deviate from strict security-seeking behavior is captured by Hymans's hypothesis on oppositional nationalism and involves an oppositional domestic political ideology toward perceived hostile actors; this can be viewed as an interactive term combining the second and third intervening variables. Domestic political parties matter, but it is their respective worldviews and ideologies that drive India's foreign policy behavior. Figure 4.1 illustrates this preliminary framework for South Asia's strategic weapons decisions. According to this framework, Pakistan is forced by its power position to engage in strictly security-seeking behavior. India, however, has at least three major degrees of freedom beyond strict security-seeking behavior.

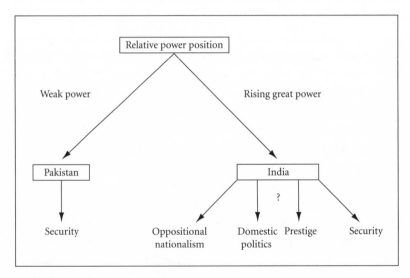

Figure 4.1. Framework for South Asian strategic weapons decisions based on the nuclearization debate

India's nuclearization therefore seems to be a case of true indeterminacy. In the absence of conclusive evidence one way or another, some scholars have started arguing that the confluence of simultaneous factors, or multiple causation, drove India to nuclearize.[37] This may indeed be true, but without examining the other components of India's strategic weapons decisions, such analysis may be premature. The following sections therefore turn to the ballistic missile flight-testing pattern in South Asia in order to help resolve this puzzle and to better understand strategic weapons behavior in the region. I first provide my rationale for why an analysis of India's and Pakistan's ballistic missile flight-testing patterns provides strong insights into their strategic weapons behavior. I then confirm that Pakistan has overwhelmingly engaged in security-seeking behavior in this realm. Finally, I examine which unit-level variables have been influential over time and across systemic and domestic conditions for India, showing that variable conceptions of "pride" between the BJP and the Congress—regulated by their domestic political positions—are critical to understanding India's strategic weapons behavior.

MOVING BEYOND NUCLEARIZATION

Ballistic missile flight tests in South Asia are both independent indicators for India's and Pakistan's strategic weapons decisions and tightly coupled to their nuclear weapons programs. Analyzing both the timing and the motivations for ballistic missile flight tests can thus help us proxy and understand the states' motivations for testing nuclear weapons.

Ballistic missiles are a key component of India's and Pakistan's strategic weapons arsenals.[38] Both states' postures on even their short-range ballistic missiles—as well as their longer-range forces, medium-range ballistic missiles (MRBM), and intermediate-range ballistic missiles (IRBM) (e.g., Agni, Ghauri, and Shaheen)—suggest primary linkages to strategic, rather than tactical, ends: deterrence, crisis signaling, high-value retaliation, and possibly preemption. The father of India's ballistic missile program, A. P. J. Kalam, explicitly notes that both the Prithvi and Agni families were designed as strategic weapons to be aimed at an adversary's high-value targets (cities, military and economic infrastructure, etc.) with either conventional or nonconventional warheads.[39] The development of nuclear-capable land- and sea-launched versions of the Prithvi is designed to equip all three Indian services with the ability to target both conventional and nuclear payloads at Pakistani strategic assets from a variety of short-range azimuths.[40] But the fact that the

Prithvi takes significant time to fuel, has a low terminal velocity, and has a rather high circular error probable (CEP) for its class has driven "a powerful section of the military [to argue] that the missile should be used only with nuclear warheads" and strictly as a strategic weapon.[41] When the Prithvi became operational in 1997, it was reportedly first deployed in Jalandhar, Punjab, which put some of Pakistan's major strategic targets, such as Islamabad and Lahore, within range.[42] Similarly, when the Pakistani government references targets within range of its ballistic missiles, it invariably includes India's strategic centers, such as New Delhi and Mumbai, not Indian military deployments in Kashmir. Although the short-range ballistic missiles in India's and Pakistan's inventories are suitable for both tactical and strategic uses, the fact that they can target key strategic infrastructure and can be configured to carry nonconventional warheads makes them an integral part of these states' strategic arsenals; the medium- and intermediate-range ballistic missiles in their inventories are strictly for strategic purposes.

Ballistic missile programs are also tightly coupled to a state's nuclear weapons program. Hence, I argue that the pattern of ballistic missile flight tests also helps explain a state's motivations to test nuclear weapons. Not only can they strike an adversary's high-value targets in their own right but ballistic missiles are the primary survivable delivery vehicle for nuclear warheads. Both ballistic missiles and nuclear weapons require technical sophistication, extensive design, and engineering testing, and they carry tremendous symbolism regarding a state's capabilities.[43] Without ballistic missiles, a state's nuclear weapons are limited by the range of its aircraft, which are then susceptible to air defenses, and as John Harvey has shown, for "nuclear missions, ballistic missiles are superior to strike aircraft in overall cost effectiveness."[44]

In South Asia in particular, both states' ballistic missile programs are critical to establishing a credible minimal deterrent, as set forth in their nuclear doctrines.[45] As Ben Sheppard observes, "[A] new and precarious form of nuclear deterrence has materialized between India and Pakistan, entailing the possession of nuclear-capable SSMs (surface-to-surface missiles) . . . away from the stable nuclear deterrence based on aircraft."[46] Many other scholars agree. W. P. S. Sidhu notes the inextricable "linkage in South Asia between missiles and nuclear weapons" at the symbolic, developmental, and operational levels.[47] Tara Kartha colorfully argues, "In our environment, nuclear deterrence requires a missile capability, without which a much vaunted [nuclear] test remains simply a loud bang in the ground."[48] In India, "the strategic enclave" places tremendous importance on missile testing, and the Agni is intended to be, according to Raj Chengappa, New Delhi's "workhorse nuclear delivery option."[49] Similarly, Ganguly and Hagerty note that Pakistan's "nuclear forces are . . . heavily geared towards delivery by ballistic missiles . . . [and] Pakistan's basic counter-city nuclear deterrent" rests primarily on its ballistic missile capabilities.[50]

If ballistic missile programs are indeed highly related to nuclear weapons programs in South Asia, an examination of tests for the former should yield insights into the motivations for tests of the latter. Thus, an analysis of *why* India and Pakistan flight-tested ballistic missiles *when* they did opens up an avenue of research that can potentially sharpen the nuclearization debate. From 1989 through June 2008, India flight-tested ballistic missiles 49 times, whereas Pakistan flight-tested ballistic missiles 37 times.[51] This time span covers a variety of domestic and systemic configurations, allowing me to isolate the particular conditions and motivations that drive Indian and Pakistani strategic weapons decisions. If ballistic missile flight tests are indeed a valid and reliable indicator for strategic weapons dynamics in South Asia, one can confirm or disconfirm whether Pakistan is in fact entirely constrained by its external security environment and whether the motivations for India's strategic weapons decisions are consistent with any of the security, domestic political, or prestige hypotheses advanced previously.

BALLISTIC MISSILES IN SOUTH ASIA

India and Pakistan have two of the world's most rapidly advancing ballistic missile programs. Indeed, this increasing missile sophistication coupled with the two states' geographic proximity has been the source of much concern regarding the strategic stability of the region.[52] India's ballistic missile families are, for the most part, indigenously developed by India's DRDO. India has two major families of ballistic missiles, both surface-to-surface systems, though it is in the early stages of developing more sophisticated sea-launched (SLBM) and cruise missile forces as well. The short-range Prithvi (Earth) family has 150-km, 250-km, and 350-km variants that are all single-stage, mostly liquid-fuel, missiles. Initially, these missiles employed strap-down radio guidance systems but they are now utilizing more advanced internal inertial navigation systems. Recently, the Indians developed GPS control for the Prithvi's guidance package as well, giving it an estimated CEP of about 100–300 m over its designated range.[53] Even though they are capable of being launched from mobile transporter erector launchers, the Prithvi I and II use liquid fuel, so they require some lead time to be placed on alert in the field. Researchers have experimented with a second-stage solid propellant and sea launches for the Prithvi III. If deployed on India's western border, the Prithvi is capable of striking most of Pakistan's urban centers.

The medium- and intermediate-range Agni (Fire) family has a recently developed 700-km variant (now designated Agni I) and a 2500-km two-stage member (Agni II), while a two-stage 3000+-km variant (Agni III) is currently undergoing testing. The Agni I, a single-stage, solid-fuel, mobile missile—which makes it a much readier delivery vehicle than the Prithvi—was developed after 1999 to fill range gaps in India's strategic missile capabilities. The Agnis II and III are designed to be rail- and road-mobile, two-stage, solid-propellant missiles; the Agni III is believed to be configurable for a third stage as well. The indigenously designed two-stage system was a significant advance for the Indian ballistic missile program, as the technical mastery of a successful stage separation is not a trivial matter. Like the Prithvi, the Agni family also employs GPS guidance for midcourse corrections and has a sophisticated terminal guidance system that gives it a claimed CEP of 25–50 m over its designated range, which would make it one of the world's most accurate IRBMs.[54] The Agni is capable of hitting any target in Pakistan, though its current operational range places Beijing out of reach with a standard 1000-kg warhead. The induction of the Agni III will be a major step toward catching up to China's capabilities and would give New Delhi substantial strategic reach against its larger neighbor. India is also working on a three-stage ICBM designated the Agni IV/V (aka Surya, or Sun), but it is currently only in development; some components that may appear in the Surya have been tested on India's satellite launch vehicles.

Pakistan's ballistic missile families are shrouded in much more secrecy than India's, perhaps to obscure their true capabilities or their foreign origins; it is widely believed that Pakistan has sought and received substantial assistance—including fully operational missiles—from both China and North Korea since 1990.[55] The various designations for Pakistan's missiles are less clear than India's, as Pakistan employs multiple and sometimes confusing designations that do not necessarily correspond to the range or technological origins of a given missile. The shortest-range missiles in Pakistan's inventory are the Hatf-I (Deadly Armor) and Hatf-II missiles (range of

100–300 km), which are believed to be derivative of French Eridan sounding rockets and assembled with substantial Chinese assistance circa 1989.[56] The Shaheen (Eagle) family is based on China's solid-fuel, M-class, export missiles (M-9, M-11, and M-18). The shortest-range member of the Shaheen family, the Ghaznavi (Hatf-III) (named after a Muslim ruler who invaded India), is largely believed to be either an operational M-11 missile or an upgraded version of the M-11 with an approximate range of 300 km.[57] Pakistan's unveiling of a sophisticated solid-fuel missile was an immediate indicator that it had received substantial international assistance for its missile program. It is believed that components for 30 to 90 M-11s were transferred to Pakistan between 1991 and 1996, and that Pakistan is capable of reverse-engineering and extending the original design parameters of the missile.[58] The Ghaznavi is Pakistan's closest variant to India's Prithvi, though the Ghaznavi's guidance system is less accurate. The Shaheen I (Hatf-IV) is estimated to have between a 600-km and 900-km range, suggesting that in addition to M-11s, Pakistan acquired the larger M-9 missiles.[59] The M-9 uses a strap-down inertial guidance system that gives it an estimated CEP of about 350 m over the designated range. A third variant of the Shaheen family, the Shaheen II (Hatf-VI), has been tested as well with a purported range of at least 2000 km, which puts it in the same class as the Agni; this missile is believed to be derivative of China's M-18 missile, which is a two-stage, solid-fuel missile based on the M-9 design.[60] The Shaheen family of missiles provides Pakistan with substantial range flexibility.

Pakistan's other major class of ballistic missiles is the Ghauri family (Hatf-V), which takes its name from the Muslim sultan who defeated the Rajput king Prithviraj Chauhan—like the Ghaznavi, the symbolism of the designation seems to have been intentional.[61] These missiles are so grouped because of their derivation from North Korea's No-Dong 1 missile. Unlike the solid-fuel M-class derivatives, the Ghauri is a single-stage liquid-fuel missile with a range of 1500 km. It is believed that up to 12 No-Dongs were transferred to Pakistan between 1993 and 1998, and more were possibly airlifted in 2001 and 2002, though the final destination of those shipments remains unclear.[62] The missile uses an inertial guidance system that gives it an estimated CEP of 2500 meters over a 1500-km range.[63] Extended versions of the Ghauri are being developed and flight-tested, with targeted ranges of up to 2000 km. This range would place the bulk of India's urban centers within striking distance of Pakistani ballistic missiles.

TESTING BALLISTIC MISSILES IN SOUTH ASIA

When and why have India and Pakistan tested ballistic missiles? Pakistan has flight-tested missiles under multiple domestic regimes: under the successive democratically elected governments of Benazir Bhutto and Nawaz Sharif as well as under Pervez Musharraf's military government. India's flight tests have occurred in a variety of domestic political configurations as well: under the dominant Congress Party, under the succession of weak Congress-allied governments in the mid-1990s facing a rising BJP challenger on their right flank, under a strong BJP government from 1998 through 2004, and finally under the resurgent Congress government from mid-2004 to the time of writing. The international systemic pressures have also varied over that same time period for both countries, with perturbations occurring in their relationship with each other (including the 1999 Kargil War); with other powers, including China; and with the international community at large. These various domestic and international configurations allow me to set up critical tests to confirm and disconfirm some of the plausible hypotheses accounting for each state's strategic weapons decisions.

I use two methods to systematically explore the pattern of ballistic missile flight tests in South Asia and to test these hypotheses for both Pakistan and India. The first is a straightforward events-data analysis that focuses on the *timing* of their flight tests. I have constructed a chronologically organized data set comprising all of India's ($N = 49$) and Pakistan's ($N = 37$) flight tests, in addition to all publicly available reports of Chinese flight tests ($N = 18$) for reference (total $N = 104$).[64] This data set, noting critical events surrounding flight tests, is shown in the Appendix to this chapter. India had a virtual monopoly on ballistic missile flight testing in the region until 1997, as Pakistan was forced abroad for ballistic missile technology. Since 1997, Pakistan has essentially matched India's tests one for one.

My analysis for this method centers on classifying the timing correlate for each flight test—the event most closely correlated with a given flight test. The critical assumption is that analyzing the timing pattern of flight tests sheds some light on motivations. Although ballistic missile flight tests certainly generate critical data for design validation and reliability, they have also been used on the subcontinent as a form of political signaling and so-called missile diplomacy.[65] Both Indian and Pakistani leaders have delayed tests whose political costs far outstripped whatever technical benefits might accrue; and conversely, they have sometimes pushed for a test if they wanted to send a sig-

nal at a specific time.[66] This assumption rejects the pure technological determinism of ballistic missile flight tests, which holds, for example, that the test
series is driven *solely* by DRDO's need to acquire technical data on the missile's
flight parameters. Given the provocative nature of ballistic missile flight tests
in South Asia, political considerations have remained largely paramount in
India's and Pakistan's flight-testing decisions.[67] Although some tests might be
outliers, the political nature of test decisions allows me to derive motivational
insights based on the overall timing pattern of flight tests in the region.

The second method I use is a form of content analysis that involves systematically coding public texts subsequent to flight tests to establish *why* India and
Pakistan tested missiles when they did. I have gathered post-test press releases
(printed or quoted in various sources) and expert or governmental analysis after
each flight test and coded which motivational hypothesis each test supports. I
used exactly three articles per test: one newswire report with the government's
announcement for the test, one article from a major daily newspaper from the
country in question,[68] and analysis by leading domestic strategic analysts in
dailies or weeklies as a third source where possible; where this last source was
lacking, I used a randomly selected third article from the newswires or another
local daily. Gathering three articles per test allowed me to triangulate terms
and motivations before coding a flight test under a given hypothesis, preventing one source from driving the analysis for any particular flight test.

PAKISTAN: KEEPING UP WITH THE KUMARS

The hypotheses I derived earlier suggest that Pakistan's strategic weapons
decisions should be driven almost exclusively by security concerns vis-à-
vis India. Therefore, its ballistic missile flight-testing pattern should largely
represent responses to India's advances and military capabilities. Given that
Pakistan was forced to seek international assistance for its missile program
and in fact acquired already-operational missiles from both China and North
Korea, Pakistan did not necessarily need to test for technical validation purposes (until entering the reverse-engineering and modification phases). In
addition, given that a flight test of an imported missile that is not in domestic
production depletes Pakistan's inventory, testing can indeed be a very costly
signal for Islamabad.

The realist prediction for this behavior is that Pakistan has no choice but
to match India's testing pattern when possible to maintain the credibility of
its deterrent against New Delhi. This pattern should be invariant in relation to

domestic political considerations or personality. The security-seeking hypothesis suggests that under both democratic regimes and military governments, Pakistan should be forced to keep pace with India's ballistic missile programs and to deter Indian military moves. In the absence of flight tests, the realist explanation must be that Pakistan is searching for balancing missile capabilities, either domestically or abroad. The timing of the tests and the motivations revealed in subsequent texts and press releases should thus overwhelmingly identify Indian-generated security concerns as the engine driving Islamabad's decisions. The variable domestic configurations under which Pakistan flight-tested its missiles should provide a good test for this hypothesis, since behavior that varies under regime type would deal a severe blow to the realist prediction. As a weak state—precisely the relative power tier over which realism's predictions should hold greatest leverage—the international systemic constraints on Pakistan should be so binding that it has no option but to acquire and demonstrate, through any means necessary, that its strategic weapons can match its more powerful neighbor's. If the motivations for Pakistan's flight-testing pattern are shown to be security driven, as was the case for its nuclearization decision, this would lend weight to my approach of using missile flight-testing patterns as an indicator for a state's broader strategic weapons decisions.

For the events-data analysis, I have distilled the chronology from the Appendix into Table 4.1 to give a contextual account for each of Pakistan's flight tests. Events surrounding Pakistani tests fall into four broad categories, three of which relate to realist motivations for testing: tests during a crisis to deter Indian military action; tests immediately following a critical shift in the material balance in favor of India (e.g., a tit-for-tat response to an Indian flight test or the Indo-Israeli missile defense deal); and tests where Pakistan is playing material "catch-up" with India's capabilities but did not—or could

Table 4.1. Events-data analysis for Pakistan's ballistic missile flight tests

Number of tests correlated with period	Crisis signaling (security)	Tit-for-tat test (security)	Catch-up test (security)	Total security	Domestic politics	Total
Period 1 (Bhutto)	0 (0%)	0 (0%)	2 (100%)	2 (100%)	0 (0%)	2
Period 2 (Sharif)	1 (25%)	2 (50%)	1 (25%)	4 (100%)	0 (0%)	4
Period 3 (Musharraf)	9 (29%)	9 (29%)	9 (29%)	27 (87%)	4 (13%)	31
Total	10 (27%)	11 (30%)	12 (32%)	33 (89%)	4 (11%)	37

NOTE: $N = 37$

not—test a system immediately after India did so. I broke up Pakistan's tests into three major periods to disaggregate potential variability in the timing of Pakistani flight tests: the initial Bhutto tests, the Sharif government from February 1997 through October 1999, and the Musharraf government since then. Unsurprisingly, a full 33 of 37 Pakistani tests (89 percent) fall into one of the three security categories, revealing that Pakistani ballistic flight tests are overwhelmingly timed in response to Indian-induced security concerns.

Indeed, a detailed analysis of the events data suggests that Pakistan's flight tests were largely responses to Indian-generated security pressures. The initial flight test of the Hatf-I in 1989 came a year after India's first Prithvi flight test, since Pakistan needed to adapt the French Eridan designs to a ballistic missile configuration.[69] After an international search for ballistic missile capabilities, Pakistan finally acquired operational M-class and No-Dong missiles by 1997, and the tit-for-tat flight-testing pattern became more salient, as Pakistani tests often followed on the heels of Indian tests. The second gap, between 2000 and 2002, corresponds to the period when Pakistan was believed to be acquiring additional shipments of No-Dongs from North Korea—all the available evidence suggests that Pakistan may not have been capable of matching India's Agni tests in this period until it received additional No-Dongs (the first flight test after this gap was indeed a Ghauri).[70] In addition, Pakistan often tested missiles during downward perturbations in its relationship with India as a form of deterrence signaling. For example, the April 6, 1998, Ghauri test was an explicit demonstration of resolve by the Sharif government against the newly elected BJP in India, whose fiery rhetoric against Pakistan created security incentives for Pakistan to test.[71] In May 2002, during India's Operation Parakram, tension in Kashmir again escalated over terrorist attacks, and the international community believed that India may have been mobilizing for war, as it poised its three offensive strike corps in the Rajasthan desert.[72] In response, President Musharraf ordered a succession of three ballistic missile flight tests over a four-day period as a deterrent to Indian military action. The second battery of three successive flight tests in October 2003 correlates with India's announcement that it had struck a deal with Israel to purchase its Phalcon early-warning system and potentially the Arrow missile defense system.[73] Furthermore, since Pakistan emphasized matching India's nuclear tests exactly one for one, a one-upmanship in the ballistic missile flight-testing pattern might be expected as well. Indeed, an examination of the number of flight tests between India and Pakistan under the BJP's tenure—when Pakistan's security position vis-à-vis India was most threatened—Pakistan flight-tested 14 missiles to the BJP's 13.[74] In large part, the timing of Pakistan's flight tests mostly suggests that they were driven by Indian-generated security pressures, as they only rarely correlate with domestic political events or larger international systemic changes.

Content analysis further confirms that Pakistan's behavior is indeed security seeking with respect to India. For Pakistan, I analyzed a total of 111 articles, exactly 3 per test, and used these to code which hypothesis each flight test supports (37 total codings)—security seeking, oppositional nationalist, domestic political, or other. The terms used to code a test under the realist security-seeking hypothesis include focus on Pakistan's national security needs in reference to India. In order to qualify as a realist explanation, these texts must reference the material or military balance in the region or Pakistan's need to maintain a deterrent against India. To test alternative theories, I include categories for other possible explanations. Because Hymans's oppositional nationalism theory could apply equally to Pakistan, I look for any evidence that Pakistani missile tests were characterized by an emotive "othering" toward India; unlike the realist explanation, these texts would reference India in a more emotive and vitriolic "othering" language and in a nonmaterial fashion. Terms used to code a test under the domestic politics explanation involve reference to elections or demonstrations of resolve to a Pakistani audience. Any other motivations that emerged were classified in the "Other" category. The results of this coding analysis appear in Table 4.2, and each test is individually coded in the Appendix.

It is starkly evident that Pakistan's ballistic missile flight tests are motivated by Indian-generated security concerns. Just as in the events-data analysis, I find that 89 percent of Pakistan's post-test explanations center on the military threat posed by its more powerful neighbor. This motivation is in-

Table 4.2. Results of coding analysis for Pakistan's ballistic missile flight tests

Tests content-coded by period	Security	Oppositional nationalism	Domestic politics	Other	Total
Period 1 (Bhutto)	2 (100%)	0 (0%)	0 (0%)	0 (0%)	2
Period 2 (Sharif)	4 (100%)	0 (0%)	0 (0%)	0 (0%)	4
Period 3 (Musharraf)	27 (87%)	0 (0%)	4 (13%)	0 (0%)	31
Total	33 (89%)	0 (0%)	4 (11%)	0 (0%)	37

NOTE: $N = 37$

STRATEGIC WEAPONS BEHAVIOR IN SOUTH ASIA   155

variant across multiple Pakistani regimes—both strong and weak, democratic and military. The following motivations repeatedly appear in the post-flight analysis: "If India wants a missile race . . . Pakistan can't give up the [ballistic missile] option";[75] and "We will take all necessary measures to counter [the Indian] threat."[76] As Pakistan tested longer-range missiles, its claims increasingly focused on the restoration of the strategic balance. Upon the unveiling of the Ghauri, the Pakistani government claimed that it has the "capability of carrying nuclear warheads and targeting every major Indian city";[77] Dr. A. Q. Khan noted that mutual vulnerability had been reestablished since "Pakistan could [now] target any city in India,"[78] while Prime Minister Sharif defended the Ghauri's development on the basis of "its legitimate security needs. . . . Pakistan cannot compromise on defence given the past 50 years of tension in the region."[79] After a tit-for-tat exchange in April 1999, Prime Minister Sharif said, "We do not believe in a match with India but we will certainly do what we deem necessary," and Foreign Minister Sartaj Aziz argued that "Pakistan has to maintain a reasonable deterrence in all areas, be it strategic or other weapons, and an indigenous missile program is part of that effort."[80] Another official said the tests are "an essential element of our policy of maintaining deterrence in the interest of our security."[81] This line of reasoning is offered after almost every Pakistani flight test, with the majority of the explanations including the claim that Pakistan could now "target every major Indian city" in light of "the security situation created in the region by aggressive Indian designs" in Kashmir—where Pakistan faces substantial conventional military inferiority.[82] Pakistan's overriding commitment was, according to its foreign minister, to "exploiting all resources to maintain this balance."[83]

President Musharraf was not immune to sometimes using flight tests to his domestic political advantage, however, as two flight tests in October 2002 coincided with the third anniversary of Musharraf's coup as well as with upcoming Pakistani elections. According to a *Dawn* editorial, the "missile test is the military's way of showing that the country needs a strong general at the helm."[84] And again in 2008, upon the election of a new government, Prime Minister Gilani witnessed two back-to-back tests of the Shaheen II, noting that the "strategic program . . . enjoys complete national consensus" and "the defense needs of the country will remain a high priority with the elected government."[85]

But these are the only tests for which Indian-generated security imperatives do not appear as the primary motivation during Musharraf's tenure. The reports of the battery of flight tests in October 2003 explicitly cited the Israeli-

Indian arms deal as a motivation. Even when the Congress returned to power in 2004, Pakistan invariably cited the military balance as the motivation for tests; the December 8, 2004, Shaheen test came a week after India tested its Akash surface-to-air missile, with the Shaheen designed to demonstrate "the government resolve to consolidate and strengthen Pakistan's nuclear deterrence capabilities" against India.[86] The November 2006 Ghauri test came two days after talks on Kashmir stagnated, with the Pakistani prime minister noting that "peace . . . comes from a position of strength and operational readiness,"[87] and analyst Khaled Mahmood suggesting that the test was "a signal to India that [Pakistan] would 'not compromise on its defense.'"[88] And one day after India tested an Agni III in May 2008, Pakistan responded with a test of its short-range nuclear-capable Ra'ad cruise missile (Hatf-VIII).[89] Almost invariably, a shift in the India-Pakistan security balance prompts a response from Islamabad—often with a missile flight test if the hardware is available. I find no evidence of the kind of emotive language that would support the oppositional nationalism explanation for Pakistan's strategic weapons decisions.

Pakistan's ballistic missile flight-testing pattern is a relatively easy case to analyze, as predicted by the realist school writ large. Faced with a significant conventional force imbalance and trailing India's strategic capabilities, Pakistan has no choice but to keep pace with India's strategic weapons advances to deter its more powerful neighbor. The events data and content analysis both confirm that Pakistan's flight tests are tightly coupled to perturbations in the Pakistani-Indian military balance and crises and are largely unrelated to domestic political configuration or personality. This result, though perhaps unsurprising, is an important confirmation for the realist school, which holds that, at the very least, the behavior of weaker powers in the system should be security driven. But if Pakistan was responding to India's moves, what drives India's ballistic missile flight-testing pattern?

INDIA: TECHNO-PRIDE AND OPPOSITIONAL PREJUDICE

Unlike the prediction for Pakistan, which is strongly security seeking, the predictions generated by the various hypotheses from Figure 4.1 suggest very different patterns of behavior for India's ballistic missile flight-testing decisions. If India is indeed a realist security-seeking state, one might expect India to flight-test missiles when faced with international efforts to roll back its ballistic missile or nuclear weapons program—as a substitute for testing nuclear weapons during review conferences for the NPT or CTBT negotiations, India could time a ballistic missile flight test. In addition, with respect to regional dynamics, structural constraints are stronger on those countries that are relatively weaker in relation to other actors; that is, India's program should be aimed at mitigating China's capabilities—not Pakistan's, over whom India has both a conventional and strategic military advantage. The range of its tests should therefore be aimed at demonstrating a capability to strike Chinese strategic centers.[90] With respect to Pakistan, because India does have a substantial conventional and strategic deterrent advantage, the realist hypothesis must be that India flight-tests missiles when the material balance shifts *away* from India toward Pakistan. Tests coinciding with perturbations in the India-Pakistan relationship that are independent of the material balance are not security motivated in this view.[91]

If the prestige hypothesis is correct, I would expect India to, in general, conduct its ballistic missile flight tests *independent* of changes in structural incentives to test. In terms of generating timing patterns for flight tests, one might expect this theory to be closest to *technological determinism*, where Indian scientists test missiles strictly for data-collection purposes and according to the technological requirements of a missile-testing sequence so that their indigenously designed missile families—hypothesized to be a major source of Indian pride—can be showcased to the international community. Technical needs could be delayed during times when flight testing might be an overly provocative signal; I would therefore expect tests conforming to the prestige motivation to occur during periods of stability and under noncrisis conditions. In addition, I would expect there to be a high premium on emphasizing technological sophistication (multistage separation technology, advanced guidance packages, etc.)—a source of prestige—in the flight-test announcements. The structural explanation would have little to say about this—it is mostly concerned with showing that one can throw a payload at a more powerful adversary, irrespective of the particular guidance package one uses to do so. The prestige hypothesis would therefore predict that India's flight tests should be largely uncorrelated with perturbations in its relationships with Pakistan *and* China but would seek to emphasize the *indigenous* and *sophisticated* technological achievements represented by its ballistic missile advances and the fact that those capabilities place India in an elite club of global powers.

The domestic politics hypothesis would primarily predict that the Indian government uses ballistic missile flight tests as a *domestic* signal to prove national-security credentials in the context of internal political events. For example, through the mid-1990s, successive waves of the United Front and Janata Dal governments, weak Congress-supported governments, were out-flanked on their right by the strengthening and hawkish BJP. This hypothesis would therefore suggest that flight tests should strongly correlate with the rise of the BJP in the mid-1990s and weak coalition leaders attempting to guard their right flank. The BJP, once it comes into office, might use flight tests as a mechanism to solidify its base. And once the Congress is voted back, this lens would predict that they might try to remove national security issues—of which the Prithvi and Agni are major symbols—as a campaign issue. The pat-tern generated if this unit-level intervening variable is operating is that flight tests would not correlate with Pakistan or China but with electoral events and configurations.

The variant on this, the oppositional nationalism hypothesis, would pre-dict that the period of the BJP's tenure was unique in the timing of ballis-tic missile flight tests, since they harnessed what Hymans calls the explosive combination of "fear of one's enemy plus pride in oneself" into a nationalism opposed directly to Pakistan.[92] This theory rests on the BJP's and Prime Min-ister A. B. Vajpayee's particular form of oppositional nationalism and sug-gests that India's decision to test nuclear weapons, and thus also to flight-test ballistic missiles, was a product of the specific BJP tenure from 1998 through 2004. In this period, if this hypothesis is correct, we should expect to see a BJP-provoked tit-for-tat flight-test pattern between India and Pakistan, or Indian testing as a signal of military intimidation during military standoffs against Pakistan in Kashmir—flight tests should correlate to perturbations in India's relationship with Pakistan, not with China. Critically, the BJP's provocations should not be in response to advances in Pakistani *material* capabilities but rather to challenges to the BJP's sense of superiority over Pakistan. Further-more, *outside* this period, we should not see a tit-for-tat pattern or demonstra-tions of resolve against Pakistan, since Hymans argues that the Congress and the Janata Dal were both secular "sportsmanlike nationalists" and were more wary of testing nuclear weapons and provocatively flight-testing missiles. Outside the BJP's tenure, then, if Hymans is correct, we should see a different motivation for flight testing emerge than the Pakistani threat.

I use the same two methods as before to analyze India's ballistic missile flight-testing pattern. The first is the events-data analysis that contextualizes India's tests within regional security dynamics (Appendix). I have broken up the flight tests into four time periods: 1988–1996, when the Congress was relatively firmly in power; 1996–1998, when weak Congress alliances faced a rising BJP on their right flank; 1998–2004, when the BJP was firmly in power; and mid-2004–2008, when the Congress firmly reestablished itself. This disaggregation should reveal which unit-level intervening variables are operating and when. Table 4.3 summarizes the context surrounding India's flight tests as deduced from the events-data analysis, separated according to the party in office.

The events-data analysis suggests characteristic differences between when the Congress and the BJP test ballistic missiles: Congress governments seem to test missiles at times that are largely uncorrelated with structural events and with India's relationship with Pakistan, suggesting that the timing of their tests might best be considered technological demonstrations or advancements; the BJP's timing pattern correlates much more closely to nonmaterial perturbations in the India-Pakistan relationship, lending support to the oppositional nationalism hypothesis. Largely absent is evidence for security-seeking behavior as defined by Indian responses to shifts in the material balance with either China or Pakistan.

Indeed, in the first period, the data seem to accord most closely to the prestige motivation during strong Congress tenures.[93] Each successive test appears to be a proof-of-concept for increasingly sophisticated technology, honing key flight parameters and demonstrating them to the international community. The tests, through 1994, seem to be largely uncorrelated with international systemic incentives (especially China's flight tests), perturbations in India's relationship with Pakistan, and domestic political events. Under the weak Janata Dal coalition governments between 1996 and 1998 one sees a marked drop in the frequency of flight tests. However, the two tests conducted

Table 4.3. Results from events-data analysis for Indian ballistic missile flight tests

Number of tests correlated with period	China or international pressure (security)	Pakistan (security)	Pakistan (nonsecurity)	Domestic politics	None of these (prestige/ techno-pride)	Total
Period 1 (Congress)	2 (12%)	0 (0%)	2 (12%)	1 (6%)	12 (70%)	17
Period 2 (Janata Dal– Congress)	0 (0%)	0 (0%)	0 (0%)	2 (100%)	0 (0%)	2
Period 3 (BJP)	1 (8%)	0 (0%)	7 (54%)	0 (0%)	5 (38%)	13
Period 4 (Congress)	2 (12%)	0 (0%)	0 (0%)	0 (0%)	15 (88%)	17
Total	5 (10%)	0 (0%)	9 (19%)	3 (6%)	32 (65%)	49

$N = 49$, $X^2 = 47.98$, DF $= 9$, $p < .001$

in this period correlate strongly with upcoming elections and domestic political events, reflecting the increasing strength of the BJP opposition. Pakistan was just developing ballistic missile capabilities during this period, but Indian tests are not correlated to dips in the India-Pakistan relationship.

During the BJP's reign, there is substantial evidence for the oppositional nationalism hypothesis: provocative tests correspond to periods of heightened tensions with Pakistan, even though India's missile capabilities remained a full generation ahead of Pakistan's. The BJP responded to Pakistan's maiden flight test of the Ghauri with the nuclear tests. The subsequent year, the BJP restarted the Agni flight tests after a five-year hiatus, which forced Pakistan abroad again for upgraded missile capabilities and triggered the tit-for-tat response that marks the bulk of the BJP's tenure. The critical test for this hypothesis is after the BJP falls in 2004. The Congress does indeed appear to set its own timetable of flight testing and returned to testing as a proof of concept, including demonstrations of a solid propellant in the Prithvi III and the first sea launches for the Prithvi, in addition to extended-range Agni II tests and the maiden Agni III flight test. Importantly, it was a Congress government that concluded a Memorandum of Understanding with Pakistan in October 2005 pledging structured mutual pre-flight-test notification to reduce tensions in the relationship and in the realm of ballistic missile flight testing specifically.[94] This analysis of India's ballistic missile flight-test timing pattern thus reveals systematically different correlations based on the domestic political configuration in New Delhi, with the BJP's tests being significantly more Pakistan-centric than the Congress's.

To directly assess India's motivations for each flight test, I now present the results from the content-analysis method. I analyzed a total of 147 tests, again exactly 3 for each of the 49 flight tests, trying to capture the broadest mix of wire reports, newspaper articles, and strategic analysis where available to triangulate codings to see which hypothesis a given test supports. I have coded each test to see whether it supports the realist, prestige, domestic politics, or oppositional nationalist hypothesis. Terms used to code a test as realist security-seeking behavior include references to China as the primary external threat, references to any material imbalance in Pakistan's favor, and references to international efforts to limit India's ability to develop ballistic missiles. Terms used to code a test under the prestige hypothesis include references to technological sophistication, the fact that its ballistic missiles place India in an exclusive club of great powers, and Indian self-sufficiency. Terms used to code a test under the domestic political hypothesis include mention of domestic opposition pressure and references to upcoming national elections. Finally, terms used to code a test as oppositional nationalist focus on the Pakistani threat independent of material pressures and references to a "hypocritical" international system intent on excluding India from great-powerdom.[95] Tests were coded by the primary hypothesis they supported; in cases where terms for multiple explanations were present, I used contextual analysis to determine the primary thrust of the explanation. The results of this coding analysis appear in Table 4.4.

These results largely confirm the conclusions derived from the events-data analysis, though in some cases the content analysis reveals a motivation for a test that was not readily apparent from the events data. In particular, the oppositional nationalism hypothesis gains even more support during the BJP tenure when using this method. These results suggest that the Congress is primarily motivated by a preference for benign prestige, whereas the BJP systematically tests as a provocative signal against Pakistan and a perceived hypocritical international community.

When the Congress had a relatively firm grip on power prior to 1996, the Indian government press releases after ballistic missile flight tests overwhelmingly emphasize indigenous development—a perceived source of Nehruvian self-sufficiency and prestige—and that "there was no foreign know-how or collaboration . . . [which] is an important technological achievement."[96] Other notable press releases stated, "The big power monopoly over advanced weapons

Table 4.4. Results of coding analysis for India's ballistic missile flight tests

Tests content-coded by period	Security	Oppositional nationalism	Domestic politics	Prestige	Total
Period 1 (Congress)	3 (17%)	2 (12%)	1 (6%)	11 (65%)	17
Period 2 (Janata Dal–Congress)	0 (0%)	0 (0%)	2 (100%)	0 (0%)	2
Period 3 (BJP)	1 (8%)	9 (69%)	0 (0%)	3 (23%)	13
Period 4 (Congress)	2 (12%)*	0 (0%)	0 (0%)	15 (88%)	17
Total	6 (12%)	11 (23%)	3 (6%)	29 (59%)	49

$N = 49, X^2 = 55.86, DF = 9, p < .001$

* These two tests correspond to the two successful Agni III tests, in which various motivations were present. Although the capability gives India strategic reach against China, the prestige motivations were very strong in these tests. Note that these X^2 and p values are slightly unstable due to the low frequency counts in some of the cells; nevertheless, the systematic nature of the hypotheses during different time periods emerges, and we can draw valid inferences from them.

technology has been gradually eroding, and new centers of military and economic power are emerging in the world. India is one of them";[97] "India joins a private circle" after "spectacular" Agni flight test;[98] and "unique technical achievement" for advancements in Prithvi and Agni guidance systems.[99] Some of the nonprestige codings in this period followed from flight tests that reacted to domestic events as well as those in China and Pakistan. For example, the May 29, 1992, Agni flight test followed a May 21 Chinese nuclear test that occurred while India's president was visiting Beijing, spurring a test for a missile that "can strike the Chinese heartland."[100] In August of that same year, India flight-tested a Prithvi on the eve of talks with Pakistan to address tensions along the Kashmiri Line of Control. And in 1994, Narasimha Rao faced criticism from the BJP for delaying Prithvi tests, leading to a test on June 4; U.S. criticism immediately after this test seems to have spurred Rao to test a second Prithvi on June 6 in defiance of American efforts to freeze India's ballistic missile program.[101] However, these few flight tests are largely outliers for the Congress in this period, as other such perturbations in the respective relationships did not result in a flight test. The overwhelming pattern of flight tests during the Congress's tenure during this period emphasized the technological achievements of India's scientists, the indigenous nature of the program, and the fact that India's sophisticated missile designs placed it in an elite club of global powers. This suggests that the Congress's strategic weapons behavior is largely motivated by prestige, with a conception of prestige particularly derived from India's own technical achievements—a "techno-nationalism"—and not directed against a malignant international system or Pakistan.

As the Congress—and later, weaker Janata Dal–Congress coalitions—started facing pressure on their right flank with the rise of an increasingly popular BJP in late 1995, their flight testing became less frequent but increasingly correlated to domestic political events (e.g., elections) as they attempted to wrest national security away from the BJP as an election issue. Unsurprisingly, they guarded their right flank by mimicking the BJP's rhetoric, and one can see the increasing salience of Pakistan in post-test statements—even though Pakistan had not yet flight-tested its longer-range Shaheen or Ghauri missiles. In February 1996, facing elections in less than six weeks, Narasimha Rao succumbed to pressure to "deploy a home-made surface-to-surface missile ... and keep an 'open option' on testing [the] Agni," since a key component of the BJP platform was to reopen testing on the Agni, which had been placed on a flight-testing moratorium for two years.[102] This occurred shortly after

Rao found himself on the verge of exercising India's nuclear option before aborting the tests at the eleventh hour. The BJP openly criticized the Congress for its lack of national security muscle, and especially for "freez[ing] current missile development programs";[103] the tests and deployment decisions during this period seem to correspond to the increasing domestic political pressure. Still weak in 1997 and facing a stronger BJP, the Janata Dal–Congress alliance reportedly deployed the Prithvi for the first time at an air force base in Punjab near the Pakistani border under pressure from "inflamed Indian nationalist passions" ignited by perceived U.S. bullying on India's strategic weapons.[104] India's ballistic missile moves in this period can thus be seen as being driven by domestic political pressure, as the Congress and its allies sought to neutralize the BJP on national security issues.

When the BJP unseated the Congress alliance in March 1998, its ballistic missile flight-testing pattern became tightly coupled to relations with Pakistan, even though India enjoyed both conventional and strategic military superiority. Whereas China was in fact mentioned as an intended audience of the nuclear tests, Pakistan was usually mentioned as the target of the BJP's ballistic missile tests, with rhetorical salvos often simultaneously launched at an international community characterized by hypocrisy. The Indian defense minister George Fernandes declared that the Prithvi's range "covers every inch of Pakistan."[105] Vajpayee referred to the Agni as a "symbol of that resurgent India . . . capable of striking targets deep inside Pakistan."[106] One should also note that almost all of the BJP tests through 2000 coincided with increased tensions with Pakistan along the Line of Control (e.g., the Kargil War in the spring and summer of 1999) or as provoking, then responding to, a tit-for-tat exchange with Pakistan. Some tests were designed to demonstrate technological sophistication or mobile launch capacity, but through the end of their tenure, the BJP's flight-testing pattern was largely motivated by the desire to challenge or provoke Pakistan.

The BJP also spearheaded the development of a short-range Agni (Agni I) to "fill-the-gaps between Prithvi" and the longer-range version of the Agni. The target envisioned for a 700-km range Agni is clear: Pakistan.[107] Indeed, the BJP provocatively tested this missile for the first time as India was mobilizing its conventional forces in response to the December 2001 Parliament attacks. Brahma Chellaney, a leading Indian security scholar, noted at the time that "[t]his is a special Agni designed for use against Pakistan. So obviously, even though India may not like to say it, there is a strong message here for Pakistan."[108] Press reports about that test also suggested that it constituted "a powerful warning to Islamabad" following the terrorist attacks in New Delhi.[109] Similarly, in March 2003, the BJP "defiantly conduct[ed] missile tests" after the massacre of 24 Hindus in Kashmir.[110] This sustained pattern of activity largely supports Hymans's argument about the unique nature of the BJP and its oppositional nationalist conception of pride that evinces itself despite Indian military superiority over Pakistan. The BJP, one official stated, also often chafed at "Western powers led by the US preach[ing] restraint, an attribute they themselves singularly lack."[111] According to Vajpayee, unlike "all previous governments," the BJP refused to "bow down to any foreign pressure" on India's strategic weapons programs.[112] Conflicting statements about the nuclear test create some ambiguity as to whom the intended external target was meant to be. However, the pattern of ballistic missile flight tests leaves little doubt that the BJP's strategic weapons decisions were primarily driven by its view of Pakistan, but also by its view of a perceived group of hypocritical Western powers. This adversarial approach to ballistic missile testing largely confirms that the BJP's conception of pride is much more oppositional and intensely driven by an emotive cocktail of fear and arrogance toward particular entities.

The critical test for the hypothesis that there are characteristic differences in how the Congress and the BJP conceive of Indian pride is the period when the Congress returned to power in April 2004. Post-launch releases again begin emphasizing "indigenous" development and "high-accuracy" designs—a nod to the key source of prestige, technological sophistication, which characterizes the Congress's conception of Indian pride.[113] The Prithvi III (Dhanush) tests were India's first live tests of a sea-launched ballistic missile and underwater launch technology (for submarine launches), which is considered a rather large step in its effort to develop a world-class missile triad.[114] Others were refinement launches demonstrating a "sophisticated onboard computer and an advanced inertial navigation system which can use both solid and liquid propellant" or user-trial tests in accordance with the testing sequence's technical imperatives.[115] Indeed, while the BJP referred to its Agni I test as Pakistan-specific, Prime Minister Manmohan Singh's announcement following a refinement test of the same missile soon after India and Pakistan had successfully concluded confidence-building measures read: "The test should not be viewed as a threat to any country. Absolutely not . . . it marks yet another step forward in India's efforts to achieve self-reliance in high technology defense capabilities."[116] He similarly lauded the 2004 Agni II launches as "a step in India's quest to become self-reliant," capturing the Nehruvian ideology that underlies the Congress's conception of Indian pride.[117] On the heels of the partially successful maiden Agni III flight test, Minister of Defense Pranab Mukherjee described the motivation for developing and testing the missile: "Superpower means gaining superior technology. That is why Pandit Nehru wanted to kindle the scientific temperament in the country."[118] Even though the missile would certainly give India strategic reach against China and therefore has clear security imperatives, the Congress government continually deemphasizes any Chinese motivation, instead lauding the fact that the indigenously developed missile placed India in a "select group of countries";[119] meanwhile, strategic analysts, such as Uday Bhaskar, note that it would be "misleading to see the Agni test in a unifocal manner as anti-China."[120] And when India successfully intercepted its own Prithvi in a live anti-ballistic missile defense test in November 2006, Raj Chengappa exclaimed that "India has become the youngest member of a select band of nations—the US, Russia and Israel—who have the capability" to develop such a sophisticated system.[121]

Pakistan is rarely mentioned as a motivation for any of these tests—even after terrorist attacks in Kashmir and Mumbai. These flight tests thus accord with a deeper version of theories emphasizing the importance of prestige and pride. The Congress is characteristically different from the BJP in its view of Indian pride and how strategic weapons fit into Indian identity. Specifically, it conceives of the *source* of Indian pride differently than does the BJP. For the Congress, Indian pride mostly takes the form of a benign yet confident techno-nationalist pride, aimed at demonstrating the sophistication of Indian technological prowess that places India in an elite club of global powers.

The events-data and content-coding analysis I have performed here broadly suggests that the varying sources of pride between the Congress and the BJP, combined with their respective domestic political positions, offer the best explanation for India's strategic weapons behavior. With respect to ballistic missiles, the Congress's conception of Indian pride centers on demonstrating India's indigenous sophistication and leads it to test largely according to technical imperatives and for international prestige purposes without a malignant "othering"; the timing of tests also suggests that the Congress is more cautious about sending provocative signals to external actors. The BJP, however, has a more virulent form of nationalism that leads it to test ballistic missiles as a provocative signal, primarily to Pakistan—relations with whom it views through what Manoj Joshi calls "communalized spectacles"[122]—but also to the traditional global (mostly Western) powers, which the BJP believes seek to deny India rights and capabilities that they themselves enjoy. The dramatic demonstration of *shakti* and superiority to these actors through strategic weapons tests is one of the cornerstones of the BJP's conception of Indian pride.

This analysis thus suggests that the oft-cited characterization that India is "prestige seeking" needs to be disaggregated because the Congress and the BJP conceive of Indian prestige in *different* ways, leading to variation in their strategic weapons testing behavior. Further, the domestic political configuration in New Delhi *regulates* these conceptions of Indian pride. When either party was relatively firmly in power, India's flight-testing pattern largely accorded with these hypotheses; when a weak Congress was challenged by the BJP, however, Congress was forced to become more aggressive to guard its right flank, even coming close to testing nuclear weapons during this period. Most scholars have unfortunately given short shrift to the relative domestic political positions of the Congress and the BJP as a driver for India's behavior.

This evidence can help resolve the puzzle over India's decision to nuclearize. Hymans's hypothesis about prestige and pride is largely confirmed but with a richer understanding of how the two parties conceive of Indian pride and how domestic politics intervenes to determine which conception is influential. The BJP does have a more virulent form of nationalism vis-à-vis Pakistan, but it also conceives of the role of India's strategic weapons differently—not in terms of technological sophistication qua sophistication, but because they allow India to break the perceived shackles of Western nuclear "apartheid" and boldly brandish that which the international community seeks to deny it. Hence, the Congress may have been satisfied with the prestige generated by the 1974 peaceful nuclear explosion and with nuclear ambiguity thereafter because it did not seek Western approval for its nuclear program and was confident in Indian technical prowess without needing to cross an explicit threshold. When Congress prime ministers stood on the precipice of testing nuclear weapons in the mid-1990s, they may have been driven to the cliff by the domestic political threat of the BJP. But for the BJP itself, openly testing nuclear devices achieved dual goals: tapping into a nationalist sentiment by challenging Pakistan and defiantly proving to the world that Indian nuclear policy was made in New Delhi, not Washington. Thus, by exploring the pattern of ballistic missile flight tests—discrete indicators for India's strategic weapons decisions and a proxy for India's nuclearization—over a 15-year time span that, to date, has not been well studied, one can gain a clearer understanding of what drives India in these issue areas (this understanding is displayed in Figure 4.2).

My analysis therefore suggests that India's strategic weapons behavior is largely constituted by the party in office and its position relative to the opposition. This result generates testable predictions for India's future strategic weapons behavior. On the one hand, strong Congress governments will likely seek to demonstrate India's technological advances and sophistication without provocation toward Pakistan or the international community. Their secular and Nehruvian ideology largely comports with a techno-nationalist pride aimed at launching India onto the plane of great powers; this includes guiding Indian economic growth and, in the strategic weapons arena, showcasing that India's capabilities are indigenous and world class.[123] On the other hand, the evidence reveals that strong BJP governments have been particularly provocative toward Pakistan and the Western powers; its communalist nationalist ideology is more antagonistic toward these actors, and its strategic weapons decisions are, therefore, intensely driven by a desire to provoke and defy them.[124]

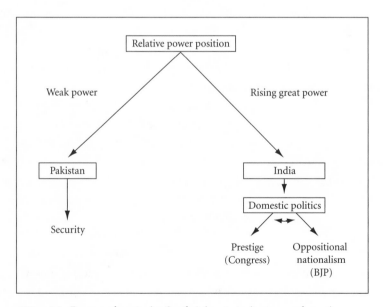

Figure 4.2. Framework capturing South Asian strategic weapons dynamics

CONCLUSION

India, because of its superior relative power, should be the first-mover in South Asia's strategic environment because its power advantage allows New Delhi to set the pace of South Asia's security dynamics. Pakistan, because of its conventional military inferiority, has no choice but to match India's advances. This was confirmed by my analysis of Pakistan's nuclear and ballistic missile behavior. So what drives India's strategic weapons decisions? Because India has the requisite power to sometimes maneuver around or thwart structural constraints, its strategic weapons behavior may be driven by other unit-level variables. The nuclearization debate generated three plausible intervening variables that might cause India to deviate from strict security-seeking behavior; these were then systematically tested against India's ballistic missile flight-testing pattern to derive an explanation for its decisions.

I found that domestic politics and party ideology are the primary variables driving India's strategic weapons testing decisions. In particular, India's conception of pride and prestige needs to be disaggregated, with different conceptions reigning depending on the domestic political configuration in New Delhi. The Congress's conception of pride takes the form of a more benign techno-nationalist pride, centering on demonstrating Indian self-sufficiency and technological prowess as a vehicle to being considered a legitimate global power. The BJP's conception of pride, on the other hand, can be characterized as oppositional nationalist and is intensely driven by a defiance against two perceived malignant entities: an aggressive Pakistan and a hypocritical club of global powers seeking to exclude India from great-powerdom. Less stable coalition governments on either side may tend to move to the center, as a weak Congress alliance attempting to wrest away the more muscular BJP conception of pride for electoral purposes suggests. This dynamic domestic political explanation captures both India's ballistic missile testing pattern and the 1990s nuclear testing story.

The evidence suggests that the pace and tone of India's future strategic weapons behavior—and Pakistan's consequent responses—are critically dependent on whether, and how firmly, the Congress or the BJP is in power. My analysis suggests that it is unlikely that future Congress governments will, for example, unilaterally reopen testing of nuclear weapons and risk India's growing international economic position and access to nuclear energy. Short of a renewed nuclear testing effort by other powers (e.g., the United States or China), a strong Congress government will likely adhere to the self-imposed moratorium on nuclear testing, choosing instead to rely on whatever limited database was generated in 1998 for simulations. In addition, the Congress will probably continue down the highly defensive doctrinal path of nuclear-component separation and is unlikely to deploy nuclear assets in the field under most realistic contingencies. Instead, the party will likely seek to steward India's gradual indigenous development of the capabilities that the superpowers have: more accurate long-range missiles (though ICBM tests are likely much farther down the road), satellite and space capabilities, the gradual evolution of a triad, missile defense proof of concepts, and above all, economic power. Because the latter is dependent on strong international confidence in South Asian stability, the Congress may be reluctant to make strategic weapons decisions that might provoke Pakistan, China, or the United States.

This chapter suggests, however, that the role of strategic weapons in the BJP's ideology—motivated especially by its view of Pakistan and the Western powers—may possibly cause future BJP governments to be more aggressive than the Congress in developing, testing, and deploying strategic weapons to assert India's *shakti*. They may be more willing to unilaterally reopen India's nuclear testing program, especially of thermonuclear devices, since the claimed May 1998 thermonuclear test was of dubious success. Tests of thermonuclear devices might achieve the BJP's dual goals of proving to the West that India has the capacity and the will to develop megaton-yield devices and signaling to Pakistan that India is a militarily superior power. The BJP may be more proactive about this especially if it is faced with either strong international pressure over its nuclear program or significant tension with Pakistan. Thus, in addition to using ballistic missile testing as a provocative signal against these actors, the BJP may be more assertive in both expanding and guarding the sovereignty of India's nuclear arsenal. Perhaps more alarming is the possibility that the BJP may be more willing than its Congress counterpart to deploy nuclear assets in the field or make nuclear and ballistic missile threats, particularly in the event of conflict with Pakistan. Though it remains unclear whether any nuclear assets were moved during the Kargil War, my findings suggest that any future India-Pakistan conflict is more likely to be characterized by greater ballistic missile and, perhaps, nuclear activity if the BJP rather than the Congress is in power.

Because Pakistan has little choice but to follow India's lead on strategic weapons, this chapter thus suggests that due to fundamental ideological differences between the Congress and the BJP, the South Asian arms race and the general risk of regional escalation are critically tied to the domestic political configuration in New Delhi. Because of its more provocative view of the sources and nature of Indian pride, those risks will likely be more intense if a strong BJP government is in power.

APPENDIX: Chronology of South Asia's ballistic missile flight tests

Date of Test	Country	Missile type	Comments	Events-data correlate	Content-analysis coding
2/25/1988	India	Prithvi I	Rajiv Gandhi (Congress) is PM	None	Prestige
9/27/1988	China	JL-1		—	—
2/6/1989	Pakistan	Hatf-I	Benazir Bhutto government	Catch-up	Structure
2/6/1989	Pakistan	Hatf-II		Catch-up	Structure
5/22/1989	India	Agni Tech Demonstrator		None	Prestige
9/27/1989	India	Prithvi I		None	Prestige
2/11/1991	India	Prithvi I		None	Prestige
7/4/1991	India	Prithvi I	Narasimha Rao government begins	None	Structure
8/7/1991	India	Prithvi I		None	Prestige
2/13/1992	India	Prithvi I (failed)		None	Prestige
4/29/1992	China	DF-31 (failed) / DF-21?		—	—
5/5/1992	India	Prithvi I		None	Prestige
5/29/1992	India	Agni Tech Demonstrator	Chinese nuclear test	China	Structure
8/18/1992	India	Prithvi I	Kashmir talks	Pakistan (NM)	Opp Nat'l
8/29/1992	India	Prithvi I		None	Prestige
2/7/1993	India	Prithvi I		None	Prestige
6/12/1993	India	Prithvi I	Prithvis deployed on Pakistani border	Pakistan (NM)	Opp Nat'l
11/30/1993	India	Prithvi I		None	Prestige
2/19/1994	India	Agni Trial		None	Prestige
6/4/1994	India	Prithvi I		Dom Pol	Dom Pol
6/6/1994	India	Prithvi I	U.S. pressure to freeze Indian BM programs	International Pressure	Structure
6/1/1995– 7/1/1995	China	DF-31 + DF-21 (4 tests reported)		—	—
11/10/1995	China	DF-21		—	—
1/10/1996	China	DF-31 (reentry vehicles)		—	—

Date of Test	Country	Missile type	Comments	Events-data correlate	Content-analysis coding
1/27/1996	India	Prithvi II	Rao term ends; BJP rise	Dom Pol	Dom Pol
3/8/1996	China	M-9	Taiwan Straits war games	—	—
12/28/1996	China	DF-31 / DF-21?		—	—
2/23/1997	India	Prithvi II	BJP pressure on Janata Dal	Dom Pol	Dom Pol
7/3/1997	Pakistan	Ghaznavi (Hatf-III)	Nawaz Sharif government	Catch-up	Structure
4/6/1998	Pakistan	Ghauri (Hatf-V)	BJP wins	Crisis Sig	Structure
4/11/1999	India	Agni II	BJP restarts Agni	Pakistan (NM)	Opp Nat'l
4/14/1999	Pakistan	Ghauri II (Hatf-VA)		TFT	Structure
4/15/1999	Pakistan	Shaheen I (Hatf-IV)	Kargil War begins in May 1999	TFT	Structure
8/1/1999	China	DF-31		—	—
10/15/1999	China	DF-41 simulation tests		—	—
2/7/2000	Pakistan	Hatf I	Pervez Musharraf government	Catch-up	Structure
4/11/2000	India	Prithvi III (failed)		None	Prestige
6/16/2000	India	Prithvi II		None	Opp Nat'l
11/4/2000	China	DF-31		—	—
12/16/2000	China	DF-31		—	—
1/17/2001	India	Agni II	Premier Li Peng visits India	China	Structure
3/31/2001	India	Prithvi II		None	Prestige
9/21/2001	India	Prithvi III		None	Prestige
12/12/2001	India	Prithvi II	Attack on Indian Parliament 12/13/01	None	Opp Nat'l
1/1/2002	China	DF-31 (failed)		—	—
1/25/2002	India	Agni I	Parakram I	Pakistan (NM)	Opp Nat'l
5/25/2002	Pakistan	Ghauri (Hatf-V)	Kashmir crisis / Operation Parakram	Crisis Sig	Structure
5/26/2002	Pakistan	Ghaznavi (Hatf-III)		Crisis Sig	Structure
5/28/2002	Pakistan	Hatf-II		Crisis Sig	Structure
8/21/2002	China	DF-4 (rumored)		—	—
10/4/2002	Pakistan	Shaheen I (Hatf-IV)	Parakram stalemate; withdrawal 10/16	Dom Pol	Dom Pol
10/8/2002	Pakistan	Shaheen I (Hatf-IV)		Dom Pol	Dom Pol

Date of Test	Country	Missile type	Comments	Events-data correlate	Content-analysis coding
1/9/2003	India	Agni I		None	Opp Nat'l
2/9/2003	China	DF-21 MIRV	In response to U.S. NMD Tests	—	—
3/26/2003	India	Prithvi I	Kashmir massacre	Pakistan (NM)	Opp Nat'l
3/26/2003	Pakistan	Hatf-II		Crisis Sig	Structure
4/29/2003	India	Prithvi I		Pakistan (NM)	Opp Nat'l
6/2003	China	DF-31, DF-21, JL-2	Series of tests reported	—	—
10/3/2003	Pakistan	Ghaznavi (Hatf-III)	Indian-Israeli arms deal	TFT	Structure
10/8/2003	Pakistan	Shaheen I (Hatf-IV)		TFT	Structure
10/14/2003	Pakistan	Shaheen I (Hatf-IV)		TFT	Structure
1/23/2004	India	Prithvi I	Peace talks with Pakistan approaching	Pakistan (NM)	Opp Nat'l
3/9/2004	Pakistan	Shaheen II (Hatf-VI)		TFT	Structure
3/19/2004	India	Prithvi II		Pakistan (NM)	Opp Nat'l
5/29/2004	Pakistan	Ghauri (Hatf-V)		TFT	Structure
6/4/2004	Pakistan	Ghauri (Hatf-V)		TFT	Structure
7/3/2004	India	Agni I	Manmohan Singh government (Congress) in power; CBMs concluded with Pakistan	None	Prestige
8/29/2004	India	Agni II		None	Prestige
10/12/2004	Pakistan	Ghauri (Hatf-V)		Catch-up	Structure
10/27/2004	India	Prithvi III (first sea launch)		None	Prestige
11/7/2004	India	Prithvi III (sea launch)		None	Prestige
11/29/2004	Pakistan	Ghaznavi (Hatf-III)	India conducts tests of Akash surface-to-air missile	TFT	Structure
12/8/2004	Pakistan	Shaheen I (Hatf-IV)		TFT	Structure
3/19/2005	Pakistan	Shaheen II (Hatf-VI)		Catch-up	Structure
3/31/2005	Pakistan	Hatf-II		Catch-up	Structure
5/12/2005	India	Prithvi II		None	Prestige
6/17/2005	China	JL-2		—	—

Date of Test	Country	Missile type	Comments	Events-data correlate	Content-analysis coding
12/28/2005	India	Prithvi III (Dhanush SLBM)		None	Prestige
2/19/2006	Pakistan	Hatf-IIA (M-11?)	Musharraf visiting China	Catch-up	Structure
4/30/2006	Pakistan	Shaheen II (Hatf-VI)	CBM negotiations break down	Crisis Sig	Structure
7/9/2006	India	Agni III	Maiden test, partial failure	None	Prestige
9/6/2006	China	DF-31		—	—
11/16/2006	Pakistan	Ghauri (Hatf-V)	Flight-tested by army during Kashmir peace talks	Crisis Sig	Structure
11/19/2006	India	Prithvi II	Planned air defense exercises (Pakistan prenotified)	None	Prestige
11/29/2006	Pakistan	Shaheen I (Hatf-IV)	Tested two days after successful Indian BMD test	TFT	Structure
12/9/2006	Pakistan	Ghaznavi (Hatf-III)		Catch-up	Structure
1/11/2007	China	ASAT Missile Test		—	—
2/23/2007	Pakistan	Shaheen II (Hatf-VI)		Catch-up	Structure
3/3/2007	Pakistan	Hatf-II		Catch-up	Structure
3/30/2007	India	Prithvi III (Dhanush SLBM)		None	Prestige
3/31/2007	Pakistan	Hatf-II		Catch-up	Structure
4/12/2007	India	Agni III	Catch-up with China but prestige motivation also highlighted	None	Structure
5/9/2007	India	Prithvi I	User trial	None	Prestige
10/5/2007	India	Agni I	User trial	None	Prestige
10/24/2007	India	Agni I	User trial	None	Prestige
12/6/2007	India/ Pakistan*	India tests series of missile interceptors 12/6/2007	Pakistan tests nuclear-capable Babur cruise missile 12/11/2007	N/A	N/A
1/25/2008	Pakistan	Shaheen I (Hatf-IV)	Western pressure	Crisis Sig	Structure
2/1/2008	Pakistan	Ghauri (Hatf-V)	Western pressure	Crisis Sig	Structure
2/13/2008	Pakistan	Ghaznavi (Hatf-III)		Catch-up	Structure

Date of Test	Country	Missile type	Comments	Events-data correlate	Content-analysis coding
2/26/2008	India	Prithvi III (Dhanush SLBM)		None	Prestige
3/23/2008	India	Agni I	User trial	None	Prestige
4/19/2008	Pakistan	Shaheen II (Hatf-VI)	New government	Dom Pol	Dom Pol
4/21/2008	Pakistan	Shaheen II (Hatf-VI)	New government	Dom Pol	Dom Pol
5/7/2008	India	Agni III	Catch-up with China but prestige motivation also highlighted; Pakistan responds on 5/8/2008 with a test of the nuclear-capable Ra'ad cruise missile	None	Structure
5/23/2008	India	Prithvi I	User trial	None	Prestige

India ($N = 49$); Pakistan ($N = 37$); China ($N = 18$); Total $N = 104$
*Not included as ballistic missile tests
TFT = Tit-for-Tat test; Pakistan (NM) = Pakistan Nonmaterial; Crisis Sig = Crisis Signaling;
Dom Pol = Domestic Politics; Opp Nat'l = Oppositional Nationalism

NOTES

1. See George Perkovich, *India's Nuclear Bomb* (Berkeley: University of California Press, 1999); Šumit Ganguly, "The Pathway to Pokhran II: The Prospects and Sources of New Delhi's Nuclear Weapons Program," *International Security*, vol. 23, no. 4 (Spring 1999), 148–177; Jasjit Singh, ed., *Nuclear India* (New Delhi: Institute for Defence Studies & Analysis, 1998); K. Subrahmanyam, "India and the International Nuclear Order," in D. R. SarDesai and Raju Thomas, eds., *Nuclear India in the Twenty-first Century* (New York: Palgrave, 2002), 63–84; T. V. Paul, "India, the International System and Nuclear Weapons," in SarDesai and Thomas, *Nuclear India*, 85–104; Jaswant Singh, "Against Nuclear Apartheid," *Foreign Affairs*, vol. 77, no. 5 (September–October 1998), 41–52; Stephen Cohen, "Nuclear Weapons and Conflict in South Asia," paper presented at Harvard/MIT Transnational Security Project, November 23, 1998, available at http://www.brook.edu/views/cohens19981123.html; Raj Chengappa, *Weapons of Peace* (New Delhi: HarperCollins, 2000); Jacques Hymans, "Why Do States Acquire Nuclear Weapons?" in SarDesai and Thomas, *Nuclear India*, 139–160; Scott D. Sagan, "Why Do States Build Nuclear Weapons? Three Models in Search of the Bomb," *International Security*, vol. 21, no. 3 (Winter 1996–1997), 54–86.

2. Pakistan's search for nuclear weapons was triggered after the 1971 war in which Bangladesh was severed from Pakistan; the program then accelerated after India's 1974 peaceful nuclear explosive (PNE) test and matured in the late 1980s.

3. Samina Ahmed, "Pakistan's Nuclear Weapons Program: Turning Points and Nuclear Choices," *International Security*, vol. 23, no. 4 (Spring 1999), 178–204; Samina Ahmed and David Cortright, eds., *Pakistan and the Bomb* (South Bend, IN: University of Notre Dame Press, 1999); Zia Mian, *Pakistan's Atomic Bomb and the Search for Security* (Lahore: Gautam Publishers, 1995); Ayesha Siddiqa-Agha, *Pakistan's Arms Procurement and Military Buildup: In Search of a Policy* (Houndsmill, UK: Palgrave, 2001), chap. 9; Hasan-Askari Rizvi, "Pakistan's Nuclear Testing," *Asian Survey*, vol. 41, no. 6 (November–December 2001), 943–955; Lowell Dittmer, "South Asia's Security Dilemma," *Asian Survey*, vol. 41, no. 6 (November–December 2001), 897–906; Shamshad Ahmad, "The Nuclear Subcontinent: Bringing Stability Back to South Asia," *Foreign Affairs*, vol. 78, no. 4 (July–August 1999), 123–125; Sumita Kumar, "Pakistan's Nuclear Weapon Programme," in Singh, *Nuclear India*, 157–187.

4. Nawaz Sharif quoted on Pakistan Television (PTV) following May 28, 1998, nuclear tests in "Pakistan Stages Five Nuclear Tests, Imposes State of Emergency," *Deutsche Presse-Agentur*, May 28, 1998.

5. Ahmed, "Pakistan's Nuclear Weapons Program," 194.

6. Ibid., 186–187. Also see T. V. Paul, "The Causes and Consequences of China-Pakistani Nuclear/Missile Cooperation," in Lowell Dittmer, ed., *South Asia's Nuclear Security Dilemma: India, Pakistan, and China* (Armonk, NY: M. E. Sharpe, 2005), 175–188; and Kumar, "Pakistan's Nuclear Weapon Programme," 163–168.

7. Rizvi, "Pakistan's Nuclear Testing," 948–955.

8. Ahmad, "Nuclear Subcontinent," 123.

9. Sharif quoted in Ashley Tellis, *India's Emerging Nuclear Posture* (Santa Monica, CA: RAND, 2001), 3.

10. Dittmer, "South Asia's Security Dilemma," 900.

11. Šumit Ganguly and Devin Hagerty, *Fearful Symmetry: India-Pakistan Crises in the Shadow of Nuclear Weapons* (Seattle: University of Washington Press, 2005), 123.

12. See Tellis, *India's Emerging Nuclear Posture*; Singh, *Nuclear India*; K. Subrahmanyam, "India and the International Nuclear Order," in SarDesai and Thomas, *Nuclear India*, 63–84; T. V. Paul, "India, the International System and Nuclear Weapons," in SarDesai and Thomas, *Nuclear India*, 85–104; Ganguly, "Pathway to Pokhran II."

13. AEC Chairman R. Chidambaram quoted in "India Poised to Become Nuclear Power," *Japan Economic Newswire*, March 4, 1998.

14. Prime Minister A. B. Vajpayee, "Indian's Letter to Clinton on the Nuclear Testing," *New York Times*, May 13, 1998, A14.

15. See, for example, Singh, "Against Nuclear Apartheid"; Cohen, "Nuclear Weapons and Conflict in South Asia"; Chengappa, *Weapons of Peace*.

16. Quoted in Perkovich, *India's Nuclear Bomb*, 417.

17. See Singh, "Against Nuclear Apartheid," 49.

18. See A. P. J. Abdul Kalam, *Wings of Fire* (Hyderabad, India: Orient Longman, 2000).

19. Scott D. Sagan has argued that both India's 1974 PNE and the 1998 tests fall largely into his domestic politics model for why states build nuclear weapons. See Scott D. Sagan, "Why Do States Build Nuclear Weapons?" in Victor Utgoff, ed., *The Coming Crisis: Nuclear Proliferation, U.S. Interests, and World Order* (Cambridge, MA: MIT Press, 1999), 17–50. Also see Chapter 1 in this volume.

20. See Perkovich, *India's Nuclear Bomb*.

21. Quoted in Raj Chengappa and Manoj Joshi, "Hawkish India," *India Today*, June 1, 1998.

22. See Chengappa, *Weapons of Peace*, 31.

23. See Mohammed Ayoob, "India's Nuclear Decision: Implications for Indian-US Relations," in Thomas and Gupta, *India's Nuclear Security*, 134–135.

24. See Jacques Hymans, "Why Do States Acquire Nuclear Weapons?" in SarDesai and Thomas, *Nuclear India*, 139–160; Jacques Hymans, "Pride, Prejudice, and Plutonium," PhD diss., Harvard University, 2001; and Jacques Hymans, *The Psychology of Nuclear Proliferation: Identity, Emotions, and Foreign Policy* (Cambridge: Cambridge University Press, 2006), chap. 7.

25. Hymans, "Pride, Prejudice, and Plutonium," 37, 451.

26. Ibid.

27. "Threats of War from Pak Led to Pokhran: Mishra," *Economic Times*, November 11, 2000; and Hymans, *Psychology of Nuclear Proliferation*, 196.

28. Hymans, "Why Do States Acquire Nuclear Weapons?" 151; Hymans, *Psychology of Nuclear Proliferation*, 199.

29. Hymans, *Psychology of Nuclear Proliferation*, 195.

30. Ibid., 193. This was recently confirmed by K. Santhanam, who was in charge of the aborted test, in an interview: "India Aborted N-Test Last Minute in 1994," *Timesnow*, April 1, 2008, available at http://timesnow.tv/NewsDtls.aspx?NewsID=6911; also see K. Subrahmanyam, "Narasimha Rao and the Bomb," *Strategic Analysis*, vol. 28, no. 4 (2004), 593–595; K. Subrahmanyam, "From Indira to Gowda It Was Bomb All the Way," *Times of India*, April 17, 2000; Saba Naqvi Bhaumik, "Blast from a Far Past," *Outlook India*, May 19, 2008. Hymans disputes that Rao was on the precipice of testing, but most other scholars and analysts contend that weaponization was in fact completed under Rao's tenure and only last-second U.S. pressure prevented Rao from pulling the trigger on tests in 1995.

31. Furthermore, as a theory of nuclearization, Hymans's characterization of oppositional nationalism seems to apply *equally to Pakistan*, whose fear of India and pride in itself as the Islamic bulwark against Hindu expansion should have driven its nuclearization behavior. According to the indicators in Hymans, "Pride, Prejudice, and Plutonium," 61, one could easily classify Pakistan led by Sharif as "oppositional

nationalist" toward India. Yet it would be extremely difficult to deny that India forced Pakistan's hand, in accordance with the realist hypothesis.

32. The National Material Capabilities Data Set, v. 3.02, Correlates of War Project, available at http://www.correlatesofwar.org/.

33. This is not to deny that India's aggregate power advantage can be "truncated" in certain theaters, e.g., Kashmir, where terrain and tactics can help Pakistan blunt India's advantage locally. See T. V. Paul, "Why Has the India-Pakistan Rivalry Been So Enduring? Power Asymmetry and an Intractable Conflict," *Security Studies*, vol. 15, no. 4 (October 2006), 600–630.

34. Pakistan has historically diverted almost double the percentage of its GDP and government budget to military expenditures as has India. See, e.g., *SIPRI Yearbooks: Armaments, Disarmament and International Security* (New York: Oxford University Press, various years).

35. Randall Schweller, *Deadly Imbalances: Tripolarity and Hitler's Strategy of World Conquest* (New York: Columbia University Press, 1998), 17–18, characterizes the constraints on weaker powers, which I have adapted here to describe Pakistan.

36. This observation has been best treated by the neoclassical realist school, which argues that the more powerful states in the system are precisely those over which the international structure holds the least amount of leverage. Determining their security behavior therefore often requires an analysis of unit-level, or domestic, independent variables through which their foreign policies might be filtered. Because these more powerful states possess greater material capabilities, they are better able to absorb the "cost" of non-security-seeking behaviors. Understanding the domestic-level determinants of these states' foreign policies is critical to understanding the behavior of the great powers. See, for example, Gideon Rose, "Neoclassical Realism and Theories of Foreign Policy," *World Politics*, vol. 51, no. 1 (1998), 144–172; Schweller, *Deadly Imbalances*; William Wohlforth, *The Elusive Balance: Power and Perceptions During the Cold War* (Ithaca, NY: Cornell University Press, 1993).

37. See, for example, Ganguly, "Pathway to Pokhran II"; Bhumitra Chakma, "Toward Pokhran II: Explaining India's Nuclearisation Process," *Modern Asian Studies*, vol. 39, no. 1 (Spring 2005), 189–236.

38. See Feroz Hassan Khan, "Nuclear Signaling, Missiles, and Escalation Control in South Asia," in Michael Krepon, Rodney Jones, and Ziad Haider, eds., *Escalation Control and the Nuclear Option in South Asia* (Washington, DC: Henry Stimson Center, 2004), 75–100.

39. Kalam, *Wings of Fire*, chaps. 13–14. Though the Prithvi I is certainly suitable for both strategic and tactical uses, its primary mission—and that of the Prithvis II and III—appears to be for strategic use; in particular, the large CEP and the fact that the operational missiles are all configured to carry nuclear payloads suggest that its

primary purpose is for strategic use. See T. S. Gopi Rethinaraj, "Nuclear Diplomacy Returns to South Asian Security Agenda," *Jane's Intelligence Review*, May 1, 2002.

40. See, for example, "IAF Increasing Prithvi Arsenal," *Statesman* (India), September 9, 2004. The Indian army has custody of the Prithvi I surface-to-surface missile (SSM); the air force operates the Prithvi II SSM.

41. See V. K. Sood and Pravin Sawhney, *Operation Parakram: The War Unfinished* (New Delhi: Sage Publications, 2003), 132.

42. It is believed that the bulk of India's Prithvis were later withdrawn from Jalandhar and placed in storage near Hyderabad. See Doug Richardson, "India's Prithvi Store May Be Found," *Jane's Missiles and Rockets*, August 1, 2000.

43. Aaron Karp, *Ballistic Missile Proliferation: The Politics and Technics* (Oxford: SIPRI, 1996); also see John Harvey, "Regional Ballistic Missiles and Advanced Strike Aircraft," *International Security*, vol. 17, no. 2 (Autumn 1992), 41–83.

44. Harvey, "Regional Ballistic Missiles," 74.

45. See Office of the Secretary of Defense, *Proliferation: Threat and Response*, United States Department of Defense (January 2001), 25–30, available at http://www.fas.org/irp/threat/prolifoo.pdf; "Draft Report of National Security Advisory Board on Indian Nuclear Doctrine," August 17, 1999, available at http://www.indianembassy.org/policy/CTBT/nuclear_doctrine_aug_17_1999.html. Also see Ben Sheppard, "Ballistic Missiles: Complicating the Nuclear Quagmire," in SarDesai and Thomas, *Nuclear India*, 189–210; Sidhu, "Missiles and Nuclear Risk-Reduction Measures"; and P. R. Chari, "India's Nuclear Doctrine: Confused Ambitions," *Nonproliferation Review* (Fall–Winter 2000), 123–135.

46. Ben Sheppard, "South Asia's Ballistic Missile Ambitions," in Raju G. C. Thomas and Amit Gupta, eds., *India's Nuclear Security* (Boulder, CO: Lynne Reinner, 2000), 181. Also see Ben Sheppard, "Regional Rivalries Are Replayed As India and Pakistan Renew Ballistic Missile Tests," *Jane's International Defence Review*, May 1, 1999; and Kent Biringer, "Missile Threat Reduction and Monitoring," in Michael Krepon, ed., *Nuclear Risk Reduction in South Asia* (New York: Palgrave Macmillan, 2004), 101.

47. W. P. S. Sidhu, "Missiles and Nuclear Risk-Reduction Measures," in Krepon, *Nuclear Risk Reduction*, 71. For both nations, ballistic missiles and nuclear weapons are key sources of national pride; in addition, the same organizations are responsible for the development of both ballistic missiles and nuclear weapons—the AEC and DRDO in India and Khan Research Laboratories (KRL) in Pakistan—and the decision-making authority rests with the same bodies as that for nuclear weapons.

48. Tara Kartha, "Ballistic Missiles and International Security," in Singh, *Nuclear India*, 115.

49. Interview with author, July 25, 2006. Also see Perkovich, *India's Nuclear Bomb*, 293.

50. Ganguly and Hagerty, *Fearful Symmetry*, 195–197.

51. These tests are strictly surface-to-surface ballistic missile tests and do not include India's tests of air-defense or cruise missiles, e.g., Trishul, Brahmos, Nag, and Akash, or Pakistan's nonballistic missile tests, e.g., Babur and Ra'ad, on the grounds that ballistic missiles are more tightly coupled to these states' nuclear weapons programs; and I seek to avoid introducing excess noise by including, e.g., air-to-surface missile tests.

52. See, for example, Scott D. Sagan, "The Perils of Proliferation in South Asia," *Asian Survey*, vol. 41, no. 6 (November–December 2001), 1064–1081; S. Paul Kapur, *Dangerous Deterrent: Nuclear Weapons Proliferation and Conflict in South Asia* (Stanford, CA: Stanford University Press, 2007); and Biringer, "Missile Threat Reduction," 105–106.

53. See Anupam Srivastava, "India's Growing Missile Ambitions: Assessing the Technical and Strategic Dimensions," *Asian Survey*, vol. 40, no. 2 (March–April 2000), 321–322.

54. Ibid., 322. Also see "Agni," *Jane's Strategic Weapon Systems*, June 8, 2005. It should be noted that the international community harbors doubts about the accuracy of this claimed CEP.

55. Siddiqa-Agha, *Pakistan's Arms Procurement*, chap. 5.

56. See John Pike, "Hatf-2," Globalsecurity.org, available at http://www.global security.org/wmd/world/pakistan/hatf-2.htm; also see Biringer, "Missile Threat Reduction," 103–104.

57. Siddiqa-Agha, *Pakistan's Arms Procurement*, 151; also see "Shaheen," *Jane's Strategic Weapon Systems*, July 19, 2005; and John Pike, "Shaheen," available at http://www.globalsecurity.org/wmd/world/pakistan/hatf-3.htm.

58. See Sheppard, "South Asia's Ballistic Missile Ambitions," 174–175; R. Jeffrey Smith, "China Linked to Pakistani Missile Plant," *Washington Post*, August 25, 1996, 1. It is believed that M-11 guidance systems and launch vehicles were transferred in the early 1990s, that full systems were transferred between 1993 and 1996, and that Pakistan has been capable of reverse-engineering the M-class missiles since 1998.

59. "Shaheen," *Jane's Strategic Weapon Systems*, July 19, 2005; Pike, "Shaheen-I," available at http://www.globalsecurity.org/wmd/world/pakistan/hatf-4.htm.

60. Biringer, "Missile Threat Reduction," 104; also see Robin Hughes, "Pakistan Test-Fires Hatf 6 Ballistic Missile," *Jane's Defence Weekly*, May 10, 2006.

61. See "Ghauri," available at http://www.pakdef.info/pakmilitary/army/missile/ghauri.html. One confounding issue is that, similar to the parallel tracks taken by Pakistan in the development of nuclear weapons, the Ghauri project is overseen by KRL, whereas the Shaheen projects are overseen by the Pakistan Atomic Energy Commission's National Development Complex, and the two may actually be in direct competition with each other for funding and development.

62. "Ghauri," *Jane's Strategic Weapon Systems*, July 19, 2005; also see Gordon Corera, *Shopping for Bombs: Nuclear Proliferation, Global Insecurity, and the Rise and Fall of the AQ Khan Network* (Oxford: Oxford University Press, 2006), 89–90.

63. "Ghauri," *Jane's Strategic Weapon Systems*, July 19, 2005; with GPS guidance, this CEP can fall to as low as 50 m.

64. For reported Chinese tests, see Hans M. Kristensen, Robert S. Norris, and Matthew G. McKinzie, *Chinese Nuclear Forces and U.S. Nuclear War Planning*, Federation of American Scientists & National Resources Defense Council, November 2006, 107, available at http://www.nukestrat.com/china/chinareport.htm. I supplemented the table with news reports of other tests.

65. See Khan, "Nuclear Signaling," 83–90.

66. Both states' political leaders have in fact delayed or timed tests in response to certain events. For example, when Musharraf was army chief of staff, he was quoted as saying in 1999, "We are ready [to flight-test] and we can do it. I leave it to the government. It is purely a government decision," in "Pakistan PM Vows 'Necessary' Response over Indian Missile Test," *Agence France Presse*, April 13, 1999. Similarly, Narasimha Rao ordered a second flight test of a Prithvi in June 1994 to send a signal to the United States.

67. See especially Khan, "Nuclear Signaling," 88–89, which describes the series of missile flight tests during Operation Parakram in 2002.

68. For Pakistani tests, this included *Dawn*, the *Nation*, and the *Pakistan Newswire*; for Indian tests, this included the *Hindustan Times*, the *Hindu*, *Economic Times*, *Indian Express*, and the *Times of India*.

69. See "Hatf-1," *Jane's Strategic Weapons Systems*, July 19, 2005.

70. Pakistani scientist Samar Mubarakmand claims that Shaheen tests were suspended by President Musharraf, but the reason was not specified. The first flight test after this period was a Ghauri. See "Pakistani Scientist Reveals Moratorium on Missile Tests," *Japan Economic Newswire*, March 23, 2001.

71. Andrew Koch and W. P. S. Sidhu, "South Asia Goes Ballistic Then Nuclear," *Jane's Intelligence Review*, June 1, 1998.

72. Celia Dugger, "Still Raw from Recent Attack, India Is Girding Itself for War," *New York Times*, May 18, 2002.

73. "Pakistan Testfires Nuclear-Capable Missile," *Agence France Presse*, October 14, 2003.

74. See Andrew Koch, "South Asian Rivals Keep Test Score Even," *Jane's Intelligence Review*, August 1, 1999.

75. Pakistani president Farooq Leghari quoted in "Pakistan to Retain Missile Option," *United Press International*, June 24, 1995.

76. Pakistani foreign secretary Najmuddin Sheikh, "Pakistan to Meet Indian Missile Threat," *Associated Press*, January 28, 1996.

77. "Pakistan Develops Nuclear-Capable Missile," *BBC Summary of World Broadcasts*, January 5, 1998.

78. A. Q. Khan paraphrased in "Radio Commentary Says Pakistan's Ghauri Missile Not Indigenous," *BBC Summary of World Broadcasts*, April 8, 1998.

79. Prime Minister Sharif paraphrased in "Pakistan Defends Its Missile Test," *Advertiser*, April 9, 1998.

80. "Pakistan PM Vows 'Necessary' Response over Indian Missile Tests," *Agence France Presse*, April 13, 1999.

81. "Pakistan Successfully Test-Fires Ghauri-II Missile," *Xinhua News Agency*, April 14, 1999.

82. "Pakistan to Test Fire Shaheen III Missile," *BBC Worldwide Monitoring*, May 21, 2002.

83. Foreign Minister Khurshid Mahmud Kasuri quoted in "Pakistan Military Statement Cited on Test-Fire of Nuclear-Capable Missile," *Financial Times*, October 14, 2003.

84. "Pakistan Tests Second Missile," *Dawn*, October 8, 2002.

85. Prime Minister Syed Gilani in "Pakistan Test Fires Ballistic Missile Hatf VI (Shaheen II)," *Pakistan Newswire*, April 19, 2008.

86. "Pakistan Tests Surface-to-Surface Nuclear-Capable Missile," *Deutsche Presse-Agentur*, December 8, 2004; also see "Pakistan Stages New Missile Test," *BBC News*, April 29, 2006.

87. Pakistani prime minister Shaukat Aziz quoted in "Pakistan Tests Intermediate Range Missile," *Reuters*, November 16, 2006.

88. Khaled Mahmood quoted in "Pakistan Test-Fires Medium-Range Missile," *Associated Press*, November 16, 2006.

89. "Pakistan Test-Fires Nuclear Capable Cruise Missile," *Associated Press*, May 8, 2008.

90. For a description of range characteristics, see Tellis, *India's Emerging Nuclear Posture*, 60–61.

91. Some may argue that Indian tests of weapons systems should be classified as realist security seeking toward Pakistan because India aims to maintain escalation dominance over Pakistan. The problem with this hypothesis is that it is effectively unfalsifiable—no matter what India tests and when it chooses to do so, the tests could be classified as Indian attempts at keeping ahead of Pakistani capabilities and achieving escalation dominance. Hence, I take a narrow view of structural realism that requires Indian security-seeking behavior to be a response to shifts in the material balance *away* from India; the virtue of this formulation is that it is testable and falsifiable.

92. Hymans, "Why Do States Acquire Nuclear Weapons?" 145.

93. The weak Congress-supported Janata Dal governments tested only one missile during their 18-month term from December 1989 through June 1991.

94. "Pakistan, India Sign Security Measures," *Los Angeles Times*, October 4, 2005. Though both India and Pakistan informally observed the terms of the Memorandum of Understanding for several years, charges of improper notification procedures on both sides led to the formal conclusion of this Memorandum in 2005.

95. The terms used to code Indian tests under this category often mirror the language under which I categorized Pakistani tests as security seeking. The reason why similar terminology leads to different categorizations for India and Pakistan, however, results from India's large material superiority over Pakistan; Pakistan referring to the Indian threat is classified as security seeking, but India referring to its ability to destroy Pakistani cities is, in my view, not motivated by security but by a nonsecurity variable. An appropriate analogy might be the relationship between the United States and Canada. Canada developing weapons because of a need to maintain a deterrent against the United States could be classified as security seeking; but because of the substantial U.S. material advantage over Canada, the United States citing the Canadian threat as motivation for developing strategic weapons could not be classified as being motivated by security but by some other consideration.

96. Prime Minister Rajiv Gandhi quoted in "India Successfully Launches Surface Missile," *United Press International*, February 25, 1988.

97. Brahma Chellaney, "India Shoots for Military Self-Sufficiency," *Christian Science Monitor*, March 21, 1988.

98. K. K. Chadha, "India Joins a Private Circle," *Aerospace America*, November 1989.

99. "India Developing Four 'Sophisticated Missile Systems,'" *BBC Summary of World Broadcasts*, May 13, 1992.

100. Quoted in "Missile Diplomacy," *Economist*, June 6, 1992.

101. See "US Criticizes Indian Missile Test," *United Press International*, June 8, 1994.

102. Senior Indian defense officials quoted in "India to Deploy Controversial Missile Despite US Opposition," *Agence France Presse*, February 2, 1996.

103. A. B. Vajpayee paraphrased in "Hindu Party Vows to Build Nuclear Arsenal If in Power," *Agence France Presse*, April 20, 1996.

104. Brahma Chellaney, "Read All About It: India Is Deploying Its Missiles," *International Herald Tribune*, June 13, 1997; also see Retd. Chief of Army Staff K. Sundarji, "Prithvi in the Haystack," *India Today*, June 30, 1997.

105. Quoted in "Indian Missile Covers 'Every Inch' of Pakistan: Defence Minister," *Agence France Presse*, April 10, 1998.

106. Quoted in "India Launches Missile Despite Call for Restraint," *Associated Press*, April 12, 1999.

107. "Agni," *Press Trust of India*, December 31, 2002.

108. Brahma Chellaney quoted in Giles Hewitt, "Indian Missile Test Poses New Strategic Threat to Pakistan," *Agence France Presse*, January 25, 2002; also see Celia Dugger, "India Test-Fires Intermediate Range Missile," *New York Times*, January 25, 2002, A5.

109. Hewitt, "Indian Missile Test Poses New Strategic Threat to Pakistan," *Agence France Presse*, January 25, 2002.

110. Pratap Chakravarty, "Nuclear Enemies Conduct Rival Missile Tests," *Agence France Presse*, March 26, 2003.

111. Senior government officials paraphrased in "Going Ballistic," *Statesman* (India), May 8, 1999.

112. Prime Minister Vajpayee quoted in Pratap Chakravarty, "India Will Conduct Fresh Nuclear, Missile Tests If Needed: PM," *Agence France Presse*, May 11, 1999.

113. "India Tests Nuclear-Capable Missile," *Agence France Presse*, August 29, 2004.

114. "Dhanush to Be Put on Trial Soon," *Statesman* (India), October 10, 2004; "India's Prithvi Missile Goes to Sea," *United Press International*, January 3, 2006.

115. "India Test-Fired Nuclear Capable Surface Missile," *Deutsche Presse-Agentur*, May 12, 2005.

116. Manmohan Singh quoted in Pratap Mohanty, "India Tests Nuclear Capable Missile," *Agence France Presse*, July 4, 2004.

117. Manmohan Singh paraphrased in ibid.

118. Pranab Mukherjee quoted in "Agni-III Was Partially Successful: Pranab," *Hindu*, July 11, 2006.

119. T. S. Subramanian and Y. Mallikarjun, "Agni III Test-Fired Successfully," *Hindu*, May 8, 2008.

120. Uday Bhaskar quoted in Pratap Mohanty, "India Successfully Tests Missile Able to Hit China," *Agence France Presse*, April 12, 2007.

121. Raj Chengappa, "The New Guardian," *India Today*, December 11, 2006, 33.

122. Manoj Joshi, interview with author, July 21, 2006.

123. Congress's prioritization of economic growth and technology was continually emphasized in author interviews in New Delhi with Pratap Mehta, July 19, 2006; Manoj Joshi, July 21, 2006; and Raj Chengappa, July 25, 2006.

124. See, for example, BJP Election Manifestos, 1991, 1996, and 1998; Bharatiya Janata Party, *Foreign Policy Resolutions and Statements 1980–1999*; Thomas Blom Hansen, *The Saffron Wave: Democracy and Hindu Nationalism in Modern India* (Princeton, NJ: Princeton University Press, 1999); Dr. C. P. Thakur and Davendra Sharma, *India Under Atal Behari Vajpayee: The BJP Era* (New Delhi: UBS Publishers, 1999).

5 REVISIONIST AMBITIONS, CONVENTIONAL CAPABILITIES, AND NUCLEAR INSTABILITY

Why Nuclear South Asia Is Not Like Cold War Europe

S. Paul Kapur

THE PRESENCE OF NUCLEAR WEAPONS in South Asia threatens to make regional conflict catastrophically costly. Nonetheless, the subcontinent has remained volatile, with violence ranging from a Pakistan-supported guerrilla war in Indian Kashmir, to protracted combat between Indian and Pakistani armed forces. Given the risks inherent in such confrontation between nuclear-armed adversaries, policy makers have sought to stabilize the Indo-Pakistani security relationship both at the strategic and at the tactical levels, minimizing the danger of nuclear war while simultaneously reducing the likelihood of lower-level violence. For example, the 1999 Lahore Declaration, signed by Indian prime minister Atal Behari Vajpayee and Pakistani prime minister Nawaz Sharif, stated that India and Pakistan would adopt policies "aimed at the prevention of conflict" in both "the nuclear and conventional fields."[1] And as Indian and Pakistani officials prepared for high-level peace talks in early 2004, they considered the negotiation of "a joint agreement to lower the threat of a nuclear or conventional war" between the two countries.[2]

Although the goals of promoting strategic and tactical stability are desirable in themselves, an important tension may exist between them. Policies seeking to maximize strategic stability in South Asia could make the Indo-Pakistani nuclear relationship safer, but they could also significantly increase the likelihood of lower-level conflict on the subcontinent. Most scholars attribute ongoing violence in the region to a phenomenon known as the "stability/instability paradox." According to the paradox, strategic stability, meaning a low likelihood that conventional war will escalate to the nuclear level, reduces the danger of launching a conventional war.[3] But in lowering the potential costs of conventional conflict, strategic stability also makes the outbreak of such violence more likely.[4]

This chapter asks whether continuing violence in a nuclear South Asia has in fact resulted from the stability/instability paradox. The answer to this question will have important implications for the regional security environment. If the stability/instability paradox is responsible for ongoing conflict, attempts to stabilize Indo-Pakistani relations at both the nuclear and the subnuclear levels could be futile, or even dangerous, as increased strategic stability allows more low-level conflict. If, by contrast, ongoing violence in South Asia has not resulted from the stability/instability paradox, then recent conflict would not demonstrate any necessary incompatibility between tactical and strategic stability in the region or suggest that danger inheres in current attempts to minimize the likelihood of nuclear war.

Determining the stability/instability paradox's impact on South Asia will also have implications well beyond the region. If we find that this paradox explains ongoing South Asian violence, it would suggest that the relationship between strategic and conventional stability that held for the United States and Soviet Union during the Cold War also applies to emerging nuclear conflict dyads.[5] But if we conclude that continuing Indo-Pakistani conflict runs counter to the expectations of the stability/instability paradox, then the relationship between strategic and tactical stability, and its resulting dangers, may be quite different for future proliferants than it was for the United States and Soviet Union.

This chapter argues that the stability/instability paradox does not explain continuing conflict in a nuclearized South Asia. Regional violence has been characterized by aggressive Pakistani attempts to revise territorial boundaries in the region, and relatively restrained Indian efforts to preserve the status quo; Pakistani forces or their proxies have repeatedly crossed de facto international borders to launch limited conventional attacks on Indian territory, while India has refused to retaliate with cross-border strikes of its own. The chapter explains that, contrary to the expectations of the stability/instability paradox, a very small probability of lower-level conflict escalating to the nuclear threshold would not encourage such behavior. A low likelihood of nuclear escalation would reduce Pakistani nuclear weapons' ability to deter a conventional attack. This reduction in deterrence would leave weaker Pakistan less protected from India's conventional advantage in the event of conflict and thus would discourage Pakistani aggression. Simultaneously, it would encourage vigorous Indian action to defend the status quo and defeat any Pakistani adventurism.

Pakistani boldness and Indian restraint have in fact resulted from a different strategic environment, in which instability in the strategic realm encourages instability at lower levels of conflict. In this environment, limited conventional conflict is unlikely to provoke an immediate nuclear confrontation.[6] However, in the event that a limited conventional confrontation subsequently spirals into a full-scale conventional conflict, escalation to the nuclear level becomes a serious possibility. This danger of nuclear escalation allows nuclear powers to engage in limited violence against each other. In the South Asian context, weaker Pakistan can undertake limited conventional aggression against India, in hopes of altering regional boundaries while deterring a full-scale Indian conventional response. In addition, nuclear danger draws international attention, potentially securing for weaker Pakistan third-party mediation of its territorial dispute with India and a diplomatic settlement superior to any that Pakistan alone could achieve. Thus, contrary to Cold War stability/instability logic, the outbreak of lower-level violence in South Asia has required the existence of a substantial degree of strategic *instability*.[7] Ironically, the characteristic of the regional strategic environment that Cold War logic predicts should impede subnuclear conflict has actually facilitated ongoing violence.[8]

In this chapter, I assess the South Asian security literature's discussion of the stability/instability paradox. I show that although scholars overwhelmingly agree that this paradox is responsible for ongoing conflict in South Asia, they are unclear as to how the phenomenon has actually caused such violence. In order to clarify the workings of the stability/instability paradox, the chapter's next section examines the phenomenon in detail, paying particular attention to its emergence in the context of the Cold War. The chapter then explains the nature of recent instability in South Asia, compares this instability to the logic of the stability/instability paradox, and demonstrates that stability/instability logic has not in fact facilitated ongoing Indo-Pakistani violence. I show instead that a significant danger of nuclear escalation has promoted low-level violence on the subcontinent. Finally, the chapter's conclusion explores the implications of my findings.

THE STABILITY/INSTABILITY PARADOX IN THE SOUTH ASIAN SECURITY LITERATURE

Scholars are virtually unanimous in their belief that the stability/instability paradox explains continuing conflict in a nuclear South Asia. Šumit Ganguly, for example, argues that the 1999 Indo-Pakistani border war at Kargil "conformed closely to the expectations of the 'stability/instability paradox,'" according to which nuclear weapons "create incentives for conventional conflicts in peripheral areas as long as either side does not breach certain shared thresholds."[9] Kenneth Waltz accounts for ongoing South Asian conventional violence by explaining that, under the stability/instability paradox, nuclear weapons "tempt countries to fight small wars."[10] And Jeffrey Knopf claims that "flareups in South Asia since the Indian and Pakistani nuclear tests of 1998 indicate the continued relevance of Glenn Snyder's 'stability/instability paradox.'"[11]

Despite scholars' agreement as to the stability/instability paradox's destabilizing effects, the literature is unclear as to how the paradox actually causes instability in South Asia. Some scholars suggest that the possibility of lower-level conflict spiraling to the nuclear threshold facilitates regional violence. For example, Ganguly broadly attributes the stability/instability paradox's effects to a "fear of nuclear escalation."[12] Similarly, Lowell Dittmer states that "fear of escalation to the nuclear level . . . facilitates the resort to violence" under the stability/instability paradox.[13] Other scholars, by contrast, claim that the paradox allows lower-level violence in South Asia through a *lack* of escalatory potential. Waltz, for example, maintains that under the stability/instability paradox "[t]he impossibility of fighting at high levels" creates "the possibility of fighting at low levels."[14] And Scott Sagan argues that conventionally aggressive behavior turns on the belief that "a stable nuclear balance . . . [permits] more offensive actions to take place with impunity."[15]

The literature's lack of clarity is problematic, because in order to determine whether the stability/instability paradox explains South Asian violence, we need first to understand how the paradox actually works. I therefore briefly revisit the stability/instability paradox's emergence during the Cold War.[16] I show that the paradox's destabilizing impact arises from a very small probability of subnuclear conflict escalating to the nuclear level, which erodes nuclear weapons' conventionally deterrent effects and thus makes lower-level violence more likely.

STABILITY/INSTABILITY LOGIC DURING THE COLD WAR

The issue of the stability/instability paradox first emerged during the mid-1950s, as America sought to extend nuclear deterrence to its European allies. The United States realized that growing U.S. and Soviet arsenals would make a nuclear conflict between the two states catastrophically destructive. This posed a problem for the conventionally weaker United States, which sought to deter Soviet conventional aggression against Western Europe with the threat of nuclear retaliation.[17] The difficulty was that the Soviet Union's increasing strategic power made this threat less credible. Although the United States might resort to nuclear war in defense of its homeland, it was unlikely that it would launch a full-fledged nuclear conflict, and invite catastrophic destruction on its home territory, to protect France or Germany from a Soviet invasion.[18]

Despite American threats, a conventional war in Europe was unlikely to escalate to the nuclear level. Therefore, it was possible that the Soviet Union, as the conventionally stronger power,[19] would initiate a conventional conflict in Europe, emboldened by the belief that it could prevail over NATO and seize Western European territory without triggering a nuclear war.[20] Strategic stability thus threatened to create conventional instability during the Cold War by eroding American extended nuclear deterrence and undermining the ability of the United States to defend the European status quo.

The United States dealt with this stability/instability problem by adopting policies at both the tactical and the strategic levels designed to *increase* the probability that a Soviet conventional attack on Western Europe would result in nuclear war. In the tactical realm, the United States threatened to initiate a process of escalation that would automatically create the risk of a strategic nuclear response from NATO, even without a deliberate American decision to launch a nuclear war.[21] To this end the United States introduced conventional ground forces, as well as tactical and eventually intermediate-range nuclear weapons to the Continent. The purpose of stationing these assets in Europe was not simply to defend against the Soviet military but also to ensure that the Soviet Union understood that the United States would be automatically engaged in the event of any aggression against Western Europe. The mission of American conventional ground forces in this regard was to act primarily as a trip wire to trigger nuclear escalation.[22] Similarly, the deployment of American tactical nuclear weapons was intended automatically to involve U.S. nuclear forces in any European conflict; in case of war with the Warsaw Pact, American nuclear weapons in Europe would either be attacked by invading forces or be used.[23]

At the strategic level, the United States built into its force structure and doctrine measures to make the deliberate American use of nuclear weapons more likely. For example, the United States adopted limited nuclear options (LNOs), under which it would attack restricted Soviet target sets, leaving other targets that the Soviets valued unscathed, and hostage to future American strikes.[24] The United States also sought to make its nuclear threats more credible through counterforce, which would destroy enemy nuclear assets rather than civilian targets. Counterforce could be used to enhance U.S. LNOs;[25] or it could be used to create incentives for a U.S. preemptive nuclear attack during a crisis.[26] Despite their differences, both LNOs and counterforce served the same strategic purpose, making the deliberate American use of nuclear weapons during a European conflict more likely.

Two key points emerge from this brief discussion of the Cold War case. First, the Cold War makes clear that a very small probability of subnuclear conflict spiraling to the nuclear threshold facilitates low-level violence under the stability/instability paradox. The unlikelihood of nuclear escalation reduces nuclear weapons' ability to deter conventional conflict, thereby making low-level aggression more likely.[27] Second, a low likelihood of nuclear escalation encouraged Soviet aggression because the Soviets, the potentially revisionist power in Cold War Europe, were conventionally stronger than NATO.[28] Since American nuclear escalation was very unlikely, the conventionally strong Soviet Union could have defeated NATO and seized Western European territory without fear of triggering a nuclear conflict. If the Soviet Union had been conventionally weak relative to NATO, it would have been unlikely to prevail over the alliance in a strictly conventional conflict, and a low likelihood of nuclear escalation would not have encouraged aggressive Soviet behavior.[29]

Do these conditions, through which the stability/instability paradox could have facilitated conventional violence during the Cold War, apply to contemporary South Asia? The answer is no. Indeed, the strategic conditions that gave rise to Cold War stability/instability dangers are precisely reversed in South Asia. Pakistan, the revisionist state in the Indo-Pakistani conflict dyad, is conventionally weak relative to India. A highly stable strategic environment, in which nuclear escalation was extremely unlikely, would undermine Pakistani nuclear weapons' conventionally deterrent effects. This would leave Pakistan more vulnerable to Indian conventional strength and make aggression exceedingly dangerous for Pakistan; India could crush any Pakistani adventurism with a full-scale conventional response, confident that the ensuing conflict was unlikely to escalate to the nuclear level.

Unlike in Cold War Europe, then, in contemporary South Asia a high degree of strategic stability does not encourage conventional violence. Rather, a significant degree of strategic instability on the subcontinent actually permits instability at the lower levels of conflict. A brief examination of the nature of the South Asian security environment and the behavioral incentives that varying levels of strategic stability create for India and Pakistan helps to explain why this is the case.

INSTABILITY IN SOUTH ASIA

Ongoing conflict between India and Pakistan is rooted in their dispute over the territory of Kashmir.[30] In the Indian view, the territory has been an integral part of the Indian Union since the maharaja of Kashmir signed an instrument of accession and joined India in 1947.[31] The Indian government believes that Pakistani support for the Kashmir insurgency, and Pakistan's cross-border incursions at Kargil, are simply the latest in a long list of Pakistani attempts to take this vital territory by force.[32] The Pakistani government, for its part, believes that Kashmir's accession to India was illegal and undemocratic. Further, the Pakistanis argue that India's continued refusal to hold a plebiscite on the question of accession denies the Kashmiri people their right to self-determination.[33] Support for the insurgency, and the ultimate achievement of Indian Kashmir's "liberation," is a central national project,[34] and the Kashmir dispute, in the Pakistani government's view, constitutes the "core issue" in Indo-Pakistani relations.[35]

Why is Kashmir so important to India and Pakistan? The region's significance lies in both strategic and domestic political factors. At the strategic level, Pakistani control of Kashmir's mountains would open the plains of Indian Punjab, Haryana, and potentially New Delhi to attack. Indian control of Kashmir, by contrast, could leave Islamabad vulnerable to assault, given the Pakistani capital's close proximity to the region. Pakistani leaders also believe that the incorporation of Kashmir's territory would give their country badly needed strategic depth, reducing the danger of catastrophic defeat at the hands of superior Indian conventional forces. Additionally, Kashmir contains the headwaters of several rivers important to both sides, including the Indus, and the five rivers of the Punjab. Finally, Kashmir borders directly on China and Afghanistan, states in which India and Pakistan have considerable strategic interest.[36]

At the domestic political level, the Kashmir dispute directly engages the core principles of India's and Pakistan's state-building projects. Pakistan was created out of South Asian Muslims' perceived need for a religiously based home. India, by contrast, was conceived as a homeland for the full spectrum of

South Asia's religious and ethnic groups. The disposition of Muslim-majority Kashmir thus has profound implications for both India and Pakistan.[37] Pakistan's abandoning its claims to Indian Kashmir would suggest that South Asian Muslims do not need a religiously based homeland and could in fact live in a polyglot Indian state. This, in turn, could call into question Pakistan's very reason for existence. On the other hand, India's ceding its portion of Kashmir to Pakistan would suggest that Muslims cannot live within a heterogeneous Indian Union and that statehood in South Asia should in fact be a function of religion or ethnicity. For a state as diverse as India, this would be a dangerous suggestion.[38] Thus, at both the strategic and the domestic political levels, Indian and Pakistani leaders view possession of Kashmir as crucial, and neither side is willing to relinquish its claims to the territory.

Regardless of the relative merits of competing Indo-Pakistani claims to Kashmir, Pakistan has been responsible for most of the recent cross-border aggression on the subcontinent.[39] Unlike the Indians, who would be willing to accept a permanent division of territory along the Line of Control (LOC) currently separating Indian from Pakistani Kashmir,[40] Pakistani leaders are deeply dissatisfied with the status quo in the region and seek to wrest further Kashmiri territory from Indian control.[41] To this end, Pakistan supports the ongoing Kashmir insurgency. Although the Pakistani government maintains that it offers only moral and political backing to the insurgents, it in fact has provided them with extensive material assistance, including training, arming, and infiltration and exfiltration of fighters across the Line of Control. Indeed, Pakistan's backing for the Kashmiri jihad has become a major factor in its foreign policy and has fundamentally shaped the nature of the Kashmir conflict. Through this support for the insurgency, the Pakistanis seek to "bleed" India and coerce the Indians into negotiating a diplomatic settlement on Kashmir.[42] Persistent Pakistani denials notwithstanding, Pakistan Army forces also clearly crossed the Line of Control at Kargil in 1999,[43] taking a swath of Indian territory 8 to 12 kilometers deep along a 150-kilometer front and triggering the first Indo-Pakistani war in 28 years.[44] Despite the operation's failure, President Musharraf later refused to rule out the possibility that "another Kargil" could occur in the future.[45]

Could a high degree of strategic stability have facilitated such aggressive Pakistani behavior, as the stability/instability paradox would predict? In order to answer this question, let us briefly consider Pakistan's military position relative to India's. Despite overall Indian conventional superiority, rough military parity prevails in the vicinity of the Indo-Pakistani border, with dispersed peacetime deployment patterns limiting India's ability to bring its forces to bear on Pakistan. In fact, in the short term, Pakistan may be able to field a somewhat larger force in the border region than the Indians.[46] Additionally, Pakistan's doctrine of "offensive defense" would respond to an Indian attack with a combination of holding actions and Pakistani counteroffensives, blunting the Indian advance and carrying the fight back into Indian territory. "However many of us they kill," argued Pakistani president and chief of army staff Pervez Musharraf, this policy of "strategic defense through tactical offense" will enable Pakistan to "kill enough [Indians] to make their losses unacceptable."[47] Pakistani attacks on Indian territory would likely be directed at the area between Poonch and Pathankot in an attempt to sever India's road links with Kashmir. In addition, Pakistan could launch diversionary offensives to the south, in Rajasthan and the Punjab.[48]

Pakistan thus could enjoy an advantage for the first few weeks of a conventional conflict with India, particularly if the Pakistanis were able to achieve strategic surprise. However, in a protracted Indo-Pakistani conflict, India's vastly superior resources would become decisive. Drawing on an active-duty force nearly double that of the Pakistan military,[49] and enjoying a roughly 2:1 advantage in combat aircraft and a 1.7:1 advantage in main battle tanks,[50] India over time could deploy sufficiently robust assets to the region to "achieve escalation dominance" and defeat the full spectrum of Pakistani defenses.[51] Within three weeks India could reach a force ratio of roughly 25 divisions against Pakistan's 21, and by approximately six weeks into a crisis, India's force advantage would be roughly 28 to 21 divisions.[52] Although these ratios are not overwhelming, they would be sufficient for India to begin driving armor and mechanized infantry into southern Pakistani Punjab, while simultaneously fighting holding actions to fix Pakistani forces in northern Punjab and Kashmir. The Indians could also launch deep-penetration attacks from Rajasthan toward Rahimyar Khan and the Indus River; Suleimanki or Bahawalpur; and Sukkur or Hyderabad.[53] Over a period of months such offensives would enable India to destroy key Pakistani military assets, sever vital lines of communication, and capture critical territory in Kashmir, West Punjab, and Sindh, thereby achieving decisive victory.[54] Thus, despite its extensive military capabilities, Pakistan suffers from a significant degree of conventional insecurity in relation to India—a fact that Pakistani policy makers are keenly aware of and that, in their view, makes nuclear deterrence essential to Pakistan's defense policy.[55]

Given these facts, would a high level of strategic stability facilitate Pakistani aggression, as expected by the stability/instability paradox? If a high degree of strategic stability prevailed, Pakistan would face strong incentives to avoid aggressive behavior. This is the case because a very small possibility of subnuclear Indo-Pakistani conflict spiraling to the nuclear level would reduce the ability of Pakistani nuclear weapons to deter an Indian conventional attack. If both sides understood that the probability of nuclear use was actually very low, it would be difficult for Pakistani leaders credibly to threaten to employ nuclear weapons in a crisis. Such a reduction in deterrence would encourage Pakistani caution, since it would leave Pakistan less protected from the full weight of India's conventional advantage and more vulnerable to catastrophic defeat in the event of a full-scale Indo-Pakistani conflict. Additionally, reducing the danger of conflict escalating to the nuclear level would lower the likelihood of outside diplomatic intervention, undercutting an important incentive for Pakistani aggression. India, by contrast, would be emboldened by such a highly stable strategic environment. If it were the case that a large-scale conventional conflict was very unlikely to escalate to the nuclear level, Indian leaders would be less likely to be deterred from launching a major conventional response to end Pakistani aggression and preserve the status quo.[56]

Pakistani adventurism would be encouraged only if nuclear escalation became a serious possibility in the event that a limited Indo-Pakistani confrontation spiraled to the level of full-scale conventional conflict. Now Pakistani leaders could engage in limited conventional aggression, believing that India would probably be deterred from launching a full-scale conventional response. Additionally, third parties, which might otherwise be uninterested in an Indo-Pakistani conflict, would likely become concerned and possibly seek to mediate the Kashmir dispute in an effort to prevent a nuclear confrontation. Thus, Pakistani aggression would be likely in a South Asian security environment where instability at the strategic level enabled limited conventional instability.

This is not to argue that continuing violence in a nuclear South Asia has resulted solely from the structure of the regional security environment. Other nonstructural variables, particularly organizational pathologies, have led to poor strategic decision making, which in turn has played an important role in promoting ongoing regional conflict. For example, during the Kargil War, the organizational biases of the Pakistan Army resulted in aggressive Pakistani policies that sought tactical advantage at the expense of broad strategic success, that overestimated nuclear weapons' coercive value, and that failed to incorporate appropriate cautionary lessons from past conflicts.[57] Such problems emerged, however, in an environment already structurally predisposed to low-level violence. Thus, despite their importance, organizational and other nonstructural variables have not been essential to continuing violence in South Asia; a significant amount of limited conflict in the region was likely even without them. Nonetheless, these nonstructural factors have helped to make the South Asian security environment even more dangerous than it would otherwise have been.

Figure 5.1 summarizes my argument regarding the difference between the effect of strategic stability on subnuclear violence during the Cold War and in contemporary South Asia. During the Cold War, high strategic stability encouraged lower-level violence, as the stability/instability paradox would predict; a small probability of nuclear escalation made aggression safe for the conventionally strong Soviet Union. In South Asia, however, a high degree of strategic stability does not encourage lower-level violence, since a small probability of nuclear escalation increases the odds that a conventionally weak Pakistan will face Indian retaliation. Rather, a significant degree of strategic *instability* has allowed ongoing Indo-Pakistani conflict. The danger of nuclear escalation enables Pakistan to engage in low-level violence while insulated from Indian retaliation; it also attracts outside attention.

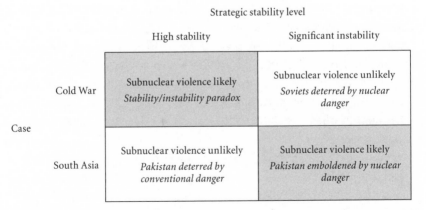

Strategic stability level

	High stability	Significant instability
Cold War	Subnuclear violence likely *Stability/instability paradox*	Subnuclear violence unlikely *Soviets deterred by nuclear danger*
South Asia	Subnuclear violence unlikely *Pakistan deterred by conventional danger*	Subnuclear violence likely *Pakistan emboldened by nuclear danger*

Case (row label)

Figure 5.1. Strategic stability and subnuclear violence: Cold War Europe versus nuclear South Asia

RECENT INDO-PAKISTANI BEHAVIOR

An analysis of recent Indo-Pakistani conflict illustrates my argument. With Pakistan's achievement of a de facto nuclear capability during the late 1980s,[58] Pakistani policy makers decided that any full-scale conventional conflict with India was likely to escalate to the nuclear level. Former Pakistani prime minister Benazir Bhutto explained that she and other Pakistani leaders concluded that "having nuclear capability would ensure that India could not launch a conventional war, knowing that it if did, it would turn nuclear, and that hundreds of millions would die. . . . It would have meant suicide not just for one, but for both nations."[59]

Pakistani leaders soon came to believe that this danger of nuclear escalation, by insulating Pakistan from Indian conventional attack, would allow Pakistan not simply to ensure its own security but also to pursue a strategy of limited conflict against Indian rule in Jammu and Kashmir. Bhutto recalled that in 1989, during her first term as prime minister, Pakistan's emerging nuclear capacity's "ability to ward off [an Indian] conventional act may have led to the conclusion that a low-scale insurgency in the disputed area of Jammu and Kashmir could focus international attention on the oldest item on the United Nations agenda which had remained unresolved. . . . Perhaps a low-scale uprising could convince India and the rest of the world community, including the United Nations, to address this very important dispute."[60] Pakistani decision makers believed that Pakistan's emerging nuclear capacity had in fact begun deterring India years earlier. According to former foreign ministers Aga Shahi and Abdul Sattar, and former air chief marshal Zulfikar Ali Kahn, "The [deterrent] value of nuclear capability was illustrated" twice during the 1980s: first, during the mid-1980s, when the Indian government contemplated an attack on Pakistani nuclear facilities at Kahuta, but ultimately decided not to strike; and second, when India abandoned plans to attack Pakistan during its "Brasstacks" war games in 1986–1987.[61] By 1989, Pakistani leaders had sufficient confidence in their nuclear capacity to begin an extensive project of providing political, material, and military support for the anti-Indian insurgency in Kashmir.[62] According to Bhutto, top Pakistan Army officers were convinced that India "could not resort to conventional war" in retaliation for these Pakistani provocations "because we had nuclear deterrence." In the Pakistan Army's view, the Indians "knew that if they resorted to conventional war and we suffered a setback, we could use the nuclear response."[63]

Throughout most of the 1990s, Pakistan restricted its involvement in the Kashmir insurgency to supporting Kashmiri and foreign militants struggling against Indian rule. After the 1998 Indian and Pakistani nuclear tests and the acquisition of an overt nuclear capacity, however, Pakistan exceeded those previous limits. In early 1999, Pakistan Army forces crossed the LOC at Kargil, seizing territory that enabled them to threaten vital Indian lines of communication in Kashmir and provoking a limited Indo-Pakistani war.[64] Pakistani leaders undertook the Kargil operation based in part upon their belief that Pakistan enjoyed a local tactical advantage over India and that Pakistan would receive international support for its position in the confrontation.[65] Apart from these tactical and diplomatic factors, however, Pakistani leaders' willingness to launch the Kargil conflict turned upon their nuclear capability; the Pakistanis believed that their new, overt nuclear status would enable them to deter the Indians even more effectively than their de facto nuclear capacity had previously done, while attracting the attention of third parties anxious to defuse a potential nuclear confrontation in South Asia. As Jalil Jilani, director general for South Asia in Pakistan's Ministry of Foreign Affairs, explained, "Since Pakistan's acquisition of [an overt] nuclear capacity, Pakistan has felt much less threatened" by Indian conventional capabilities, and thus "more confident" vis-à-vis India. This increased confidence has enabled the Pakistanis to adopt policies that "put a check on Indian ambition" in South Asia. At Kargil, Pakistan was able "to block the supply of [Indian] troops in Kashmir. And there [were] limits as to what India could do in response." Simultaneously, Kargil said to the outside world that "India's adverse possessions" in Kashmir "should be looked at."[66]

The Kargil operation, like Pakistan's earlier Kashmir policy, assumed the existence of sufficient stability in the Indo-Pakistani strategic relationship to allow Pakistan or its proxies to launch limited conventional attacks against India without immediately triggering a nuclear war. Beyond this background assumption of initial strategic stability, however, Pakistan's policy exploited the possibility of subsequent nuclear escalation in a full-scale Indo-Pakistani conventional confrontation. As Jilani put it, central to Pakistani strategy has been the recognition that "it is always possible for [conventional conflict] to get out of hand." This recognition has "deterred India" and made clear to the international community that it "has a stake in achieving peace in this region."[67]

Pakistani leaders' efforts to "put a check on Indian ambition" in South Asia have been neither risk- nor cost-free. Their support for the Kashmir insurgency has drained Pakistan economically and damaged its international reputation. Pakistan also paid a heavy price for its Kargil incursions; it lost hundreds of soldiers, was diplomatically isolated, experienced increased civil-military tension, which contributed to the October 1999 coup, and in the end withdrew from the area.[68] Finally, Pakistani adventurism has risked setting off a conflict with India that could end in nuclear war. Nonetheless, the Pakistanis have been willing to pay the costs and run the risk inherent in such a policy. Indeed, nuclear risk is precisely what has made limited Pakistani aggression feasible, forcing Indian leaders to choose between exercising restraint and launching a conventional war that could result in a nuclear confrontation. Thus, by exploiting instability in the Indo-Pakistani strategic balance, and giving India the "last clear chance" to avert potential disaster,[69] Pakistan has pursued its objectives in Kashmir insulated from the full extent of India's conventional military advantage and has attracted attention from third parties anxious to avoid a nuclear confrontation on the subcontinent.

While this escalatory danger has emboldened Pakistan, the risk of conventional conflict spiraling to the nuclear level has encouraged Indian caution. As a recent analysis explains, Indian leaders believe that Pakistan might use nuclear weapons during a conflict in any number of ways, including "in a pre-emptive mode, early in a war, when the going gets tough, or when ultimately pushed to the wall by India's conventional forces. This has instilled uncertainty amongst Indian planners," who believe "Pakistan's rash military leadership cannot be trusted with nuclear weapons."[70]

This sense of uncertainty has helped to dissuade India from launching full-scale conventional efforts to end Pakistani or Pakistan-backed aggression. For example, despite its conventional advantage, India has refrained from attacking insurgent bases and infrastructure in Pakistani Kashmir. And during the Kargil conflict, the Indian government ruled out full-scale war even in response to incursions into Indian territory by Pakistan Army forces, thereby abandoning India's long-standing policy of retaliating against Pakistani attacks on Kashmir with all-out horizontal escalation.[71] In both cases, Indian caution resulted at least in part from concern over the possibility of a Pakistani nuclear response.[72]

In the wake of the Kargil conflict, however, the Indian government began to take a more optimistic view of strategic stability on the subcontinent. Indian civilian and military leaders became increasingly convinced that Pakistan's aggressive behavior was based on "bluff and bluster," "exaggerating the likelihood of nuclear escalation" in order to "blackmail" India and the international community.[73] In truth, according to a senior Indian Army officer and strategic analyst, many Indian policy makers came to believe that "Pakistan will not use nuclear weapons until it is half gone."[74] Pakistan would be very unlikely to launch a nuclear strike on India, former Indian defense minister George Fernandes argues, because if it did so, India would retaliate in kind. Given the size disparity between the two countries, the effects of such an exchange would be grossly unequal; a nuclear confrontation would be extremely costly to India but would probably mortally damage Pakistan. As Fernandes puts it, after an initial Pakistani nuclear strike on India, "We may have lost a part of our population." But after India's retaliatory strike on Pakistan, "Pakistan may have been completely wiped out."[75]

This strategic asymmetry, combined with Pakistan's diplomatic, economic, and conventional military weakness, led Indian policy makers to conclude that India could probably fight a limited conventional conflict against Pakistan without escalation to the nuclear level.[76] Ironically, Pakistan's own actions in Kashmir may have provided India with the most compelling evidence of the feasibility of limited war in a nuclear South Asia. As former Indian Army chief of staff V. P. Malik explained, "Kargil showed the way. If Pakistan could do Kargil [without escalation to the strategic level], India could do something similar" in response to continued Pakistani provocations in Kashmir without fear of a nuclear confrontation. Thus, post-Kargil, there was "increasing realization in India that stability exists in the strategic balance. How low or high stability is will always be a question mark. But it's there."[77]

As their confidence in the subcontinent's strategic stability grew, Indian leaders threatened to become more aggressive in their efforts to defend the Kashmiri status quo and end Pakistani provocations in the region. India adopted a policy of compellence, vowing to launch limited conventional war against Pakistan if Pakistan did not curb cross-border violence in Kashmir. Possible Indian action ranged from attacking terrorist camps and Pakistani military assets within Pakistani Kashmir, to destroying military targets and seizing territory within Pakistan proper.[78]

The results of India's compellent strategy were mixed. In the policy's most dramatic application, following a December 2001 terrorist assault on the Indian Parliament, India massed roughly 500,000 troops along the Line of Control and the international border,[79] and it demanded that Pakistan turn over to New Delhi twenty criminals suspected to be residing in Pakistan, unequivocally renounce terrorism, shut down terrorist training camps in Pakistani territory, and check militant infiltration into Jammu and Kashmir.[80] Most important, the buildup was meant as a warning against any follow-on terrorist attacks, which the Indians feared were imminent. As Fernandes explains, "There were intelligence reports that there could be more such attacks on different targets in the country. So the message that went by mobilizing our forces and keeping them there for a length of time was that if anything should happen from any quarter . . . we would have taken [Pakistan] on in a conventional war."[81]

Indian threats initially met with a degree of Pakistani compliance. In January 2002, President Pervez Musharraf banned the militant organizations Lashkar-e-Toiba and Jaish-e-Mohammed and publicly promised not to allow Pakistani territory to be used as a launching ground for terrorism in Kashmir.[82] In the spring of 2002, American officials reported that Musharraf had assured them that terrorist training camps in Pakistani Kashmir would be shut down permanently and cross-border infiltration brought to an end. These developments coincided with a notable decrease in terrorist infiltration into Indian Kashmir.[83]

Ultimately, however, Pakistan failed to accede to Indian demands. Despite a temporary lull in cross-border infiltration, by mid-2002 the flow of militants into Jammu and Kashmir had begun to increase once again.[84] On May 14, 2002, terrorists launched another major attack, killing 32 people at an Indian Army camp at Kaluchak in Jammu.[85] And the Pakistani government flatly refused to turn over to New Delhi the Indians' list of 20 wanted fugitives. Despite this noncompliance, India eventually demobilized its forces without attacking Pakistan. Having lost the element of surprise, anxious to avoid angering the United States by attacking America's key ally in the Afghan War, and concerned with the conventional costs and nuclear risks of a large-scale Indo-Pakistani conflict, the Indians began withdrawing from the international border and the LOC in October 2002.[86] Significantly, however, the withdrawal did not mark an abandonment of India's compellent policy. Rather, Indian leaders hoped that the "strategic relocation" of their forces would enable them to husband their resources and, if necessary, fight later under more favorable circumstances.[87]

India's adherence to this approach has coincided with the emergence of more restrained Pakistani behavior, with Pakistan gradually taking steps to reduce, though not eliminate, cross-border violence.[88] The ensuing thaw in Indo-Pakistani relations has seen the initiation of a cease-fire along the Line of Control; a resumption of transportation and trade links between India and Pakistan; a written commitment by Pakistan not to allow its territory to be used for terrorist activity; meetings between the Indian government and leaders of the Kashmiri separatist All Parties Hurriyat Conference; and peace talks between Indian and Pakistani foreign secretaries. Meanwhile, violence in Kashmir has declined significantly. According to the Indian government, terrorist-related incidents fell by 22 percent from 2004 to 2005, and by an additional 16 percent in 2006.[89]

Thus, contrary to the stability/instability paradox, a growing perception of strategic stability did not lead to increased regional conflict in South Asia. Rather, it emboldened Indian leaders to threaten more assertive efforts to end Pakistani challenges to the territorial status quo. Although this threat did not lead to the achievement of specific Indian security goals, it broadly coincided with the emergence of more moderate Pakistani behavior and a decline in Indo-Pakistani tensions.

CONCLUSION

Contrary to the predictions of the stability/instability paradox, ongoing violence in South Asia has not been facilitated by a very low likelihood of subnuclear Indo-Pakistani conflict escalating to the nuclear level. Rather, South Asian violence has resulted from a strategic environment in which nuclear escalation is a serious possibility in the event that a limited Indo-Pakistani confrontation spirals into a full-scale conventional conflict. This environment has enabled Pakistan to launch limited conventional attacks against India while insulating itself against the possibility of full-scale Indian conventional retaliation and attracting international attention to the Kashmir dispute. Thus, a significant degree of *instability* at the strategic level, which Cold War logic predicts should discourage lower-level violence, has actually promoted tactical instability on the subcontinent. The fact that the stability/instability paradox has not facilitated recent conflict in the region suggests that Indo-Pakistani tactical stability and strategic stability are not mutually incompatible and that policies seeking to achieve such dual stability in the region will not necessarily be futile or dangerous.

More generally, our findings suggest that the relationship between strategic and tactical stability for new nuclear powers may be different than it was for the United States and the Soviet Union during the Cold War. In assessing the dangers of nuclear proliferation for states such as North Korea or Iran, we must consider the possibility that *instability* in the strategic realm could have destabilizing effects at the lower levels of conflict. If the leaders of newly nuclear states are dissatisfied with the territorial status quo, they may engage in limited aggression, believing that the danger of nuclear escalation will reduce the risk of full-scale conventional retaliation by stronger adversaries and will attract international attention. Such behavior would result not from organizational pathologies or irrationality on the part of nuclear proliferants but from calculations based upon their strategic environments, conventional military capabilities, and territorial preferences. In these cases, the strategic approach most likely to minimize conventional violence would be the reverse of the strategically destabilizing policies that the United States and NATO pursued during the Cold War; arms control and confidence-building measures designed to increase strategic stability and lower the likelihood of nuclear escalation would undercut a new proliferant's ability to engage in aggressive conventional behavior from behind a shield of nuclear deterrence.

Just as important as these strategic and technical measures, however, will be energetic diplomatic attempts to ameliorate ongoing territorial disputes. Such efforts can help to reduce a key incentive for aggression by newly nuclear states, thereby lowering the potential costs of future nuclear proliferation. This approach appears to be paying dividends in South Asia. As noted previously, the Indo-Pakistani peace process has made progress in improving relations between the two countries and in reducing violence in Kashmir. This could lower the likelihood of future nuclear crises in the region. What accounts for these recent diplomatic gains after decades of Indo-Pakistani deadlock? One possible explanation is that nuclear learning has occurred; India and Pakistan have discovered that conventional violence in a nuclear environment is unproductive and dangerous. Thus, after an initial period of instability, nuclear deterrence may finally be having a stabilizing effect on South Asia.

Close examination, however, reveals that this is not the case. Improvements in the Indo-Pakistani relationship have resulted primarily from nonnuclear factors. The Pakistanis initially reduced their support for the Kashmir insurgency because of pressure from the United States to join American antiterror efforts after September 11, 2001. The Pakistani government subsequently cracked down further on militants who had turned against it in retaliation for cooperating with the United States.[90] The Indians, for their part, have pursued improved Indo-Pakistani relations primarily for economic reasons. India's main national priority has become continued economic growth, which the government believes is necessary to combat poverty and join the first rank of nations.[91] Indian

leaders therefore seek to keep the peace rather than squander precious resources on further Indo-Pakistani conflict.[92] Also, recent anti-Indian terrorism
has been less provocative than previous attacks such as the Parliament assault.[93]
The Indians therefore have opted for restraint despite ongoing violence.

This is not to argue that nuclear learning has not occurred in South Asia.
Nuclear learning has taken place, and it has had an important impact on India
and Pakistan's strategic calculations. However, it is not responsible for recent
improvements in the regional security environment. In fact, as Russel Leng
points out, the learning that has occurred has been "largely dysfunctional"
and "dangerously hawkish." Thus, it could actually undermine ongoing progress in Indo-Pakistani relations.[94] For example, key Pakistani leaders and
strategists have concluded that Pakistani brinksmanship is a useful policy and
that provocations like Kargil achieved important successes. Pervez Musharraf argues that "whatever movement has taken place so far in the direction
of finding a solution to Kashmir is due considerably to the Kargil conflict."[95]
Jalil Jilani believes that Kargil effectively "made the point that India's adverse
possessions [in Kashmir] should be looked at." Therefore, he maintains, the
operation was "justified."[96] And Sharin Mazari characterizes Kargil as "a tremendous military success . . . totally undermined by the Sharif government's
confused and panicked approach from beginning to end."[97]

The Indians, by contrast, believe that the lesson of South Asian nuclear crises is that India must be prepared to fight limited conventional conflicts under
a nuclear umbrella. As V. P. Malik argues, the Pakistanis launched the Kargil
operation because they "believed India would not resort to war for fear of escalation." Thus, in order to prevent future Kargils, India "must seriously cater for
conventional and subconventional conflicts." Such wars "have to be conducted
within the framework of carefully calibrated political goals and military moves
that permit adequate control over escalation and disengagement."[98]

This logic of limited war has not merely led to Indian coercive diplomacy
against Pakistan; it is now driving major changes in India's conventional
military doctrine. As noted previously, India's conventional superiority over
Pakistan was traditionally mitigated by the location of Indian peacetime deployments. Indian offensive forces, stationed deep in the interior of the country, were slow to mobilize against the Pakistanis, requiring several weeks to
launch a large-scale offensive.[99] This allowed Pakistan time to prepare its defenses and gave the international community an opportunity to discourage
India from launching military action.

In response to these problems, the Indians are formulating a new Cold Start doctrine. Cold Start will augment India's offensive capabilities close to the international border and enable it to move quickly against Pakistan. Within 72–96 hours of a mobilization order, the Indians plan to drive six to eight brigade- and division-sized armor and infantry units 15–20 kilometers into Pakistan, seizing a long, shallow swath of territory. The Indians will seek to inflict significant attrition on enemy forces; to retain Pakistani territory for use as a postconflict bargaining chip; and, by limiting the depth of Indian incursions, to avoid triggering a Pakistani strategic nuclear response. Indian strategists hope that such a robust limited war capability, unfettered by long mobilization times, will deter future Pakistani adventurism. But even if deterrence fails, India will now be able to punish Pakistan far more effectively than it previously could have.[100]

Unfortunately, Cold Start will not only increase Indian military effectiveness. By threatening Pakistan, it is also likely to exacerbate regional security dilemma dynamics. Pakistan will now face increased incentives to maintain a higher state of readiness and to resort to more arms racing and asymmetric warfare. Such behavior could trigger aggressive Indian responses, which would further heighten Pakistani insecurity and increase the probability of crises between the two countries.

Thus, learning has occurred in the Indo-Pakistani nuclear relationship, but it is likely to reduce, rather than enhance, regional stability. Important segments of Pakistan's strategic elite are convinced that nuclear brinksmanship works. And Indian strategists have decided that rapid conflict escalation is the antidote to Pakistani adventurism. Nuclear learning and logic, then, are pushing South Asia toward a nuclear future that could be as unstable as its past. Ironically, nonnuclear factors such as economics, domestic political calculations, and international pressure have played the most important role in stabilizing India and Pakistan's nuclear relationship. And they probably have the best chance of playing such a role in the years to come.

NOTES

An earlier and somewhat different version of this article appeared as S. Paul Kapur, "India and Pakistan's Unstable Peace: Why Nuclear South Asia Is Not Like Cold War Europe," *International Security*, vol. 30, no. 2 (2005), pp. 127–152.

1. Text of the Lahore Declaration, United States Institute of Peace, Peace Agreements Digital Collection, available at http://www.usip.org/library/pa/ip/ip_lahore 19990221.html.

2. "AFP Asia-Pacific News Summary," *Agence France Presse*, February 17, 2004.

3. Although one could imagine other plausible definitions of strategic stability, I adhere to this definition throughout the chapter; for my purposes, strategic stability refers to the probability that conventional conflict will escalate to the nuclear level. This is the meaning of strategic stability originally embedded in the stability/instability paradox, and it is the one that we must employ if we are actually to analyze the paradox, rather than some other phenomenon. Note that the probability of conventional conflict escalating to the nuclear level is not an objective fact but a function of decision makers' perceptions, which may change over time.

4. Charles L. Glaser, *Analyzing Strategic Nuclear Policy* (Princeton, NJ: Princeton University Press, 1990), 46. See also Robert Jervis, *The Meaning of the Nuclear Revolution: Statecraft and the Prospect of Armageddon* (Ithaca, NY: Cornell University Press, 1989), 20. For the original discussion of the stability/instability paradox, see Glenn H. Snyder, "The Balance of Power and the Balance of Terror," in Paul Seabury, ed., *The Balance of Power* (San Francisco: Chandler, 1965), 198–199.

5. Clearly the Cold War case differs from the current South Asian security environment in a number of significant respects. For example, neither India nor Pakistan seeks to extend nuclear deterrence to a third party; Indo-Pakistani strategic behavior is subject to far more international pressure than U.S. and Soviet nuclear policy was during the Cold War, and this pressure may act as a check on conflict escalation in South Asia. In addition, India and Pakistan maintain small nuclear arsenals, lacking the large array of tactical and strategic forces that the superpowers deployed during the Cold War. Nonetheless, many scholars and policy makers believe that the same basic logic that governed superpower nuclear behavior during the Cold War should hold for new nuclear states such as India and Pakistan. See, for example, Kenneth N. Waltz, "For Better: Nuclear Weapons Preserve an Imperfect Peace," in Scott D. Sagan and Kenneth N. Waltz, *The Spread of Nuclear Weapons: A Debate Renewed* (New York: W. W. Norton, 2003), 117; John J. Mearsheimer, "Back to the Future: Instability in Europe After the Cold War," *International Security*, vol. 15, no. 1 (Summer 1990), 37–40; Scott D. Sagan, "For the Worse: Till Death Do Us Part," in Sagan and Waltz, *Spread of Nuclear Weapons*, 91; and Jaswant Singh, "Against Nuclear Apartheid," *Foreign Affairs*, vol. 77, no. 5 (September–October 1998), 43.

6. By "limited" conventional conflict I mean either conflict involving guerrilla or proxy forces or conflict involving states' regular militaries that does not cross official international borders on a scale sufficient to inflict catastrophic defeat on the loser. By "full-scale" conventional conflict I mean conflict that involves states' regular militaries, that crosses official international boundaries, and that is of sufficient magnitude to threaten the loser with catastrophic defeat.

7. This is not to claim that the stability/instability paradox rules out the possibility of subnuclear aggression where a substantial likelihood of nuclear escalation exists.

A state highly motivated to alter the status quo could engage in aggressive behavior despite a substantial likelihood of triggering nuclear conflict. Under the stability/instability paradox, however, such a high likelihood of nuclear escalation is an impediment to lower-level violence; increasing the probability of nuclear escalation makes lower-level violence less likely. In South Asia, by contrast, increasing the likelihood of nuclear escalation—up to a point—facilitates lower-level aggression. In fact, in this environment, the outbreak of lower-level violence actually requires a significant degree of strategic instability.

8. Of course, an *extremely* high level of strategic instability would discourage subnuclear violence in South Asia. If the Indo-Pakistani strategic balance were so unstable that even limited conventional aggression was likely immediately to result in nuclear escalation, limited aggression would be excessively risky, and thus unlikely. As noted previously, however, this is not an accurate description of the South Asian strategic environment. Limited conventional aggression on the subcontinent is unlikely immediately to escalate to the nuclear level.

9. Šumit Ganguly, *Conflict Unending: India-Pakistan Tensions Since 1947* (New Delhi: Oxford University Press, 2002), 122–123. India and Pakistan fought for approximately eight weeks in the Kargil sector of the Line of Control. For additional discussion of the stability/instability paradox's effects on the subcontinent, see Šumit Ganguly, "Conflict and Crisis in South and Southwest Asia," in Michael E. Brown, ed., *The International Dimensions of Internal Conflict* (Cambridge, MA.: MIT Press, 1996), 170; Šumit Ganguly, "Indo-Pakistani Nuclear Issues and the Stability/Instability Paradox," *Studies in Conflict and Terrorism*, vol. 18, no. 4 (October–December 1995), 325–334; and Šumit Ganguly and R. Harrison Wagner, "India and Pakistan: Bargaining in the Shadow of Nuclear War," *Journal of Strategic Studies*, vol. 27, no. 3 (September 2004), 479–507.

10. Waltz, "For Better," 122.

11. Jeffrey W. Knopf, "Recasting the Optimism-Pessimism Debate," *Security Studies*, vol. 12, no. 1 (Autumn 2002), 52. See also David J. Karl, "Lessons for Proliferation Scholarship in South Asia: The Buddha Smiles Again," *Asian Survey*, vol. 41, no. 6 (November–December 2001), 1020; Lowell Dittmer, "South Asia's Security Dilemma," *Asian Survey*, vol. 41, no. 6 (November–December 2001), 903; Feroz Hasan Khan, "Challenges to Nuclear Stability in South Asia," *Nonproliferation Review*, vol. 10, no. 1 (Spring 2003), 64; P. R. Chari, "Nuclear Restraint, Nuclear Risk Reduction, and the Stability/Instability Paradox in South Asia," in Michael Krepon and Chris Gagné, eds., *The Stability/Instability Paradox: Nuclear Weapons and Brinksmanship in South Asia* (Washington, DC: Henry L. Stimson Center, 2001), 20–21; and Sagan, "For the Worse," 97.

12. Ganguly, *Conflict Unending*, 122–123.

13. Dittmer, "South Asia's Security Dilemma," 903.

14. Waltz, "For Better," 122.

15. Sagan, "For the Worse," 97. Other scholars who mention lack of escalatory potential in their discussions of the paradox include Khan, "Challenges to Nuclear Stability in South Asia," 64. I do not claim that these authors offer fully developed arguments, or embrace two entirely coherent schools of thought, on the workings of the stability/instability paradox in South Asia. My point is that the literature contains two broad categories of discussion on this issue, one of which emphasizes the danger of nuclear escalation and the other of which emphasizes the lack of such danger.

16. I offer this brief overview for illustrative purposes only and do not purport to provide a comprehensive discussion of American strategic nuclear policy during the Cold War.

17. George H. Quester, *Nuclear Diplomacy: The First Twenty-five Years* (New York: Dunellen, 1970), 96; and Richard Smoke, *National Security and the Nuclear Dilemma: An Introduction to the American Experience in the Cold War* (New York: McGraw-Hill, 1993), 51.

18. Smoke, *National Security and the Nuclear Dilemma*, 84; Bernard Brodie, *Escalation and the Nuclear Option* (Princeton, NJ: Princeton University Press, 1966), 28; and John Lewis Gaddis, *Strategies of Containment: A Critical Appraisal of Postwar American National Security Policy* (New York: Oxford University Press, 1982), 165–166.

19. In 1955 NATO had fewer than 25 effective fighting divisions, against approximately 28–30 Soviet divisions in Eastern Europe and 60–70 additional Soviet divisions in the western USSR. See Stephen J. Flanagan, *NATO's Conventional Defenses* (Cambridge, MA: Ballinger, 1988), 14. Analysts therefore broadly agreed that the Soviets enjoyed a substantial conventional advantage over NATO during this period. See, for example, ibid., 9–14; Smoke, *National Security and the Nuclear Dilemma*, 66, 85; Gaddis, *Strategies of Containment*, 168; Brodie, *Escalation and the Nuclear Option*, 124; and Ronald E. Powaski, *The Cold War: The United States and the Soviet Union, 1917–1991* (Oxford: Oxford University Press, 1998), 102–103. The U.S. government, for its part, estimated that in the event of conflict during this period, the Soviets would have been able quickly to capture most of Western Europe. See text of NSC-68, available at http://www.fas.org/irp/offdocs/nsc-hst/nsc-68.htm. Note that this view of Soviet conventional superiority was subsequently called into serious question. See, for example, Barry R. Posen, "Measuring the European Conventional Balance: Coping with Complexity in Threat Assessment," *International Security*, vol. 9, no. 3 (Winter 1984–1985), 47–88; Barry R. Posen, "Is NATO Decisively Outnumbered?" *International Security*, vol. 12, no. 4 (Spring 1988), 186–202; John J. Mearsheimer, "Why the Soviets Can't Win Quickly in Central Europe," *International Security*, vol. 7, no. 1 (Summer 1982), 3–39; and Matthew A. Evangelista, "Stalin's Postwar Army Reappraised," *International Security*, vol. 7, no. 3 (Winter 1982–1983), 110–138.

20. Nikita Khrushchev explicitly used this argument to threaten the United States with Soviet action against Berlin between 1958 and 1962. See Alexander L. George and Richard Smoke, *Deterrence in American Foreign Policy: Theory and Practice* (New York: Columbia University Press, 1974), 395–396. See also Robert Jervis, *The Illogic of American Nuclear Strategy* (Ithaca, NY: Cornell University Press, 1984), 66, 67; John Lewis Gaddis, *We Now Know: Rethinking Cold War History* (Oxford: Oxford University Press, 1997), 137; and Quester, *Nuclear Diplomacy*, 94.

21. See Brodie, *Escalation and the Nuclear Option*, 101, 130; Thomas C. Schelling, *Arms and Influence* (New Haven, CT: Yale University Press, 1966), 43–44. This chapter does not address the question of how inadvertent nuclear escalation could have occurred in Cold War Europe or in contemporary South Asia. For valuable analyses, see Barry R. Posen, *Inadvertent Escalation* (Ithaca, NY: Cornell University Press, 1991); and V. R. Raghavan, "Limited War and Nuclear Escalation in South Asia," *Nonproliferation Review*, vol. 8, no. 3 (Fall–Winter 2001).

22. Powaski, *The Cold War*, 103. See also Walter LaFeber, *America, Russia, and the Cold War 1945–1992* (New York: McGraw-Hill, 1993), 125–126; Quester, *Nuclear Diplomacy*, 95; Marc Trachtenberg, *History and Strategy* (Princeton, NJ: Princeton University Press, 1991), 217; Gaddis, *Strategies of Containment*, 168; and Schelling, *Arms and Influence*, 47.

23. Jervis, *Illogic of American Nuclear Strategy*, 92. See also Gaddis, *We Now Know*, 137; and George H. Quester, "The Continuing Debate on Minimal Deterrence," in T. V. Paul, Richard J. Harknett, and James J. Wirtz, eds., *The Absolute Weapon Revisited: Nuclear Arms and the Emerging International Order* (Ann Arbor: University of Michigan Press, 1998), 169.

24. The threat to employ LNOs was deemed more credible than threats to launch all-out nuclear attacks against the Soviet Union because LNOs, by sparing a range of enemy targets, created Soviet incentives not to respond to a U.S. attack with a full-scale retaliatory strike. See Glaser, *Analyzing Strategic Nuclear Policy*, 216–217. See also Schelling, *Arms and Influence*, 190–192, 202–203.

25. Since counterforce would strike Soviet nuclear weapons while sparing civilian targets, it could provide the United States with a means of attacking a restricted target set and thereby avoiding all-out Soviet retaliation. As Glaser points out, however, counterforce was probably not necessary to enhance limited nuclear options. See Glaser, *Analyzing Strategic Nuclear Policy*, 216–222. Also, it is not clear that the Soviets would have been able to distinguish discrete counterforce strikes or LNOs from a full-scale American nuclear attack. For a discussion of the limitations of Soviet early-warning systems, see Bruce G. Blair, *The Logic of Accidental Nuclear War* (Washington, DC: Brookings Institution, 1993), 201–202, 204–208, 211–213. On Soviet false-warning dangers, see Scott D. Sagan, *The Limits of Safety: Organizations, Accidents, and Nuclear Weapons* (Princeton, NJ: Princeton University Press, 2003), 135–146.

26. By striking first with counterforce, and destroying a significant number of Soviet nuclear weapons, the United States could in theory limit damage to itself by reducing the Soviets' retaliatory capability. Jervis, *Illogic of American Nuclear Policy*, 70; Glaser, *Analyzing Strategic Nuclear Policy*, 224; Schelling, *Arms and Influence*, 193–194. Note that many analysts doubted this logic. See, e.g., Glaser, *Analyzing Strategic Nuclear Policy*, 32–35; and Jervis, *Illogic of American Nuclear Policy*, 54–55.

27. For this reason the United States adopted tactical and strategic measures designed to increase the likelihood of nuclear escalation during the Cold War. A high probability of conventional conflict reaching the nuclear level would make conventional conflict more dangerous, thereby reducing the likelihood of Soviet aggression. The Soviet Union's failure to attack Western Europe thus does not mean that the stability/instability paradox did not apply to the Cold War or that the Soviets did not actually believe the logic of the paradox. Rather, it suggests that U.S. and NATO efforts to increase the likelihood that a conventional conflict would escalate to the nuclear level, and thereby mitigate the stability/instability paradox's conventional dangers, were effective.

28. By "revisionist" I mean a state whose leaders are dissatisfied with existing territorial boundaries and wish to alter them. The leaders of a "status quo" state, by contrast, are satisfied with existing territorial boundaries and wish to maintain them. See Arnold Wolfers, "The Balance of Power in Theory and Practice," in Wolfers, *Discord and Collaboration: Essays on International Politics* (Baltimore, MD: Johns Hopkins University Press, 1962), 125–126; and Randall L. Schweller, "Bandwagoning for Profit: Bringing the Revisionist State Back In," *International Security*, vol. 19, no. 1 (Summer 1994), 72–107. My purpose here is not to make definitive claims about actual Soviet intentions regarding Western Europe. My point is that the principal Cold War danger as perceived by the United States and NATO was that the Warsaw Pact would attempt to seize territory in Western Europe. As the literature previously cited makes clear, the Western alliance's primary goal during the Cold War was to confine the Pact to Eastern Europe and prevent the Pact from seizing territory in Western Europe.

29. Note that relative Soviet weakness would have been unlikely to encourage NATO aggression, since the alliance's goal was to contain Soviet power and defend Western Europe rather than to seize territory in Eastern Europe. Thus, NATO would probably have used conventional superiority to maintain the status quo rather than to alter it.

30. The Kashmir dispute is the subject of innumerable scholarly and polemical works, and I do not discuss it at any length here. For detailed analysis, see, e.g., Robert G. Wirsing, *India, Pakistan, and the Kashmir Dispute: On Regional Conflict and Its Resolution* (New York: St. Martin's, 1998); Joseph Korbel, *Danger in Kashmir* (Oxford: Oxford University Press, 1954); Alastair Lamb, *Kashmir: A Disputed Legacy, 1846–1990* (Karachi: Oxford University Press, 1991); Prem Shankar Jha, *Kashmir, 1947: Rival Versions of History* (New Delhi: Oxford University Press, 1996); and Lars Blinkenburg,

India-Pakistan: The History of Unsolved Conflicts, vol. 1 (Odense, Denmark: Odense University Press, 1997).

31. Since a 1947–1948 Indo-Pakistani war over Kashmir, India has controlled roughly two-thirds of the territory (Jammu and Kashmir), while Pakistan has controlled approximately one-third of the region (Azad Kashmir and the northern areas).

32. See Ashley J. Tellis, C. Christine Fair, and Jamison Jo Medby, *Limited Conflicts Under the Nuclear Umbrella: Indian and Pakistani Lessons from the Kargil Crisis* (Santa Monica, CA: RAND, 2001), 16, 50. Pakistan also launched wars to take Kashmir in 1947 and 1965. For concise discussions of these wars, see Ganguly, *Conflict Unending*, 15–50.

33. Indian prime minister Jawaharlal Nehru promised in 1947 to hold a plebiscite in Kashmir to ratify the territory's accession to India, but the vote was deferred until normal conditions could be reestablished in the territory. India has yet to hold the plebiscite. See Ganguly, *Crisis in Kashmir*, 10.

34. "Excerpts from Pakistani President Pervez Musharraf's Address to the Nation," May 27, 2002, BBC Monitoring, available at http://news.bbc.co.uk/1/hi/world/monitoring/media_reports/2011509.stm.

35. K. J. M. Varma, "Pak Not Ready to Sideline Kashmir: Musharraf," *Press Trust of India*, June 17, 2003.

36. Cohen, *India*, 212–213; Talbot, *Pakistan*, 114; Lamb, *Kashmir*, 148; and Singh, "The Kashmir Issue," in Singh, ed., *Kargil 1999*, 2–3.

37. The Indian state of Jammu and Kashmir is approximately 64 percent Muslim and 32 percent Hindu. Kashmir Valley, the heart of Jammu and Kashmir state, is approximately 95 percent Muslim. See Wirsing, *India, Pakistan, and the Kashmir Dispute*, 125.

38. On these points, see Ganguly, *Crisis in Kashmir*; Cohen, *India*, 215; Lamb, *Kashmir*, 149–150; and Talbot, *Pakistan*, 114.

39. This is in no way to argue in favor of India's position on Kashmir or to maintain that India has not behaved aggressively in the region. Indeed, the Kashmir insurgency emerged during the late 1980s in reaction to decades of Indian misrule in the region, which included the arrest of popularly elected officials, the rigging of elections, and a steady erosion of Kashmir's autonomous status within the Indian Union. India has been widely condemned for systematic human rights abuses against the Kashmiri population in its efforts to quell the rebellion. See, e.g., Ganguly, *Crisis in Kashmir*; Sumantra Bose, *Kashmir: Roots of Conflict, Paths to Peace* (Cambridge, MA: Harvard University Press, 2003); Victoria Schofield, *Kashmir in Conflict: India, Pakistan, and the Unending War* (London: I. B. Tauris, 2003). India has also proven willing to seize contested territory in Kashmir, such as Siachen Glacier, long after the Simla Agreement and establishment of the Line of Control—though the capture of Siachen probably did not technically violate the LOC. See V. R. Raghavan, *Siachen: Conflict*

Without End (New Delhi: Viking, 2002); and Wirsing, *India, Pakistan, and the Kashmir Dispute*, 75–83. My point here is simply that Indian transgressions in the region have generally not taken the form of cross-border aggression. Pakistan and its proxies, by contrast, have repeatedly engaged in such activity, and scholars arguing that the stability/instability paradox explains ongoing conventional violence in South Asia are in fact attempting to account for this aggressive behavior.

40. Cohen, *India*, 219; Wirsing, *India, Pakistan, and the Kashmir Dispute*, 219–220; Tellis, Fair, and Medby, *Limited Conflicts*, 69.

41. Cohen, *India*, 219; Tellis, Fair, and Medby, *Limited Conflicts*, 46. See also Thomas Perry Thornton, "Pakistan: Fifty Years of Insecurity," in Selig S. Harrison, Paul H. Kreisberg, and Dennis Kux, eds., *India and Pakistan: The First Fifty Years* (New York: Cambridge University Press and the Woodrow Wilson Center, 1999), 184; Ganguly, *Conflict Unending*, 128; Hagerty, *Consequences of Nuclear Proliferation*, 135. As Pakistani president Pervez Musharraf put it, "LOC is the problem and can not be a solution." Press Trust of India, "LOC Is the Problem, Not Solution: Musharraf," *Times of India*, June 17, 2003.

42. Wirsing, *India, Pakistan, and the Kashmir Dispute*, 118–124, 134; John Lancaster and Kamran Khan, "Extremist Groups Renew Activity in Pakistan; Support of Kashmir Militants Is at Odds with War on Terrorism," *Washington Post*, February 8, 2003.

43. Although Pakistan repeatedly claimed that only irregular mujahideen had crossed the LOC at Kargil, the intruders in fact were members of the Pakistan Army's Northern Light Infantry, supported by civilian insurgents. See Brian Cloughley, *A History of the Pakistan Army: Wars and Insurrections* (Oxford: Oxford University Press, 2000), 376–377. The Pakistani government has finally admitted that its forces entered Indian territory at Kargil but maintains that they did so only after the fighting was already under way. See "Troops Were in Kargil, General Doesn't Rule Out Repeat," *Indian Express* (Mumbai), June 14, 2003.

44. The Kargil conflict resulted in over 1000 battle deaths and thus meets the standard social science definition of a war. See J. David Singer and Melvin Small, *The Wages of War, 1816–1965, A Statistical Handbook* (New York: John Wiley and Sons, 1972); and Faten Ghosn and Glenn Palmer, "Association Document for the Militarized International Dispute Data, Version 3.0," Correlates of War 2 Project, 3. For battle-death estimates, see Kargil Review Committee, *From Surprise to Reckoning: The Kargil Review Committee Report* (New Delhi: Sage Publications, 1999), 23, 98; Amarinder Singh, *A Ridge Too Far: War in the Kargil Heights 1999* (New Delhi: Motibagh Palace Patiala, 2001), 101–103; Sumantra Bose, "Kashmir: Sources of Conflict, Dimensions of Peace," *Survival*, vol. 41, no. 3 (Autumn 1999), 150; K. Alan Kronstadt, "Nuclear Weapons and Ballistic Missile Proliferation in India and Pakistan: Issues for Congress," Congressional Research Service, Report RL30623, July 31, 2000, 5. For detailed discussions of the Kargil conflict, see Kargil Review Committee, *From Surprise to*

Reckoning; Singh, *A Ridge Too Far*; Y. M. Bammi, *Kargil 1999: The Impregnable Conquered* (Noida, India: Gorkha Publishers, 2002); Ashok Krishna, "The Kargil War," in Ashok Krishna and P. R. Chari, eds., *Kargil: The Tables Turned* (New Delhi: Manohar Publishers, 2001), 77–138.

45. "Troops Were in Kargil."

46. Ashley J. Tellis, *Stability in South Asia* (Santa Monica, CA: RAND, 1997), 20–21. See also V. K. Sood and Pravin Sawhney, *Operation Parakram: The War Unfinished* (New Delhi: Sage Publications, 2003), 145–152; Kanwar Sandhu, "Can India's War Machine Deliver the Killer Punch?" *Hindustan Times*, January 10, 2002, 11.

47. Author interview of President Pervez Musharraf, Rawalpindi, Pakistan, April 2004. See also Mirza Aslam Beg, "Deterrence, Defence, and Development," *Defence Journal*, vol. 3, no. 6 (July 1999), 5; Ayaz Ahmed Khan, "Armed Forces Wargaming," *Defence Journal*, vol. 6, no. 1 (August 2002); Tellis, *Stability in South Asia*, 17–18; and Stephen P. Cohen, *The Pakistan Army* (Karachi: Oxford University Press, 1998), 145. Kanwar Sandhu, "Pak Strategy Will Be to Sever Link with J&K," *Hindustan Times*, January 11, 2002, 11.

48. Sandhu, "Pak Strategy."

49. The Indian armed forces consist of approximately 1,173,000 active-duty service members and 840,000 reservists; and Pakistan's, of 550,000 active and 513,000 reservists. R. K. Jasbir Singh, ed., *Indian Defence Yearbook 2002* (Dehra Dun: Natraj Publishers, 2002), 311, 317.

50. International Institute for Strategic Studies, *The Military Balance 2003–2004* (London: International Institute for Strategic Studies, 2003), 136–138, 140–142. India possesses 32 squadrons of ground-attack aircraft and 6 fighter squadrons for a total of 744 combat aircraft, versus Pakistan's 6 ground-attack and 12 fighter squadrons for a total of 374 combat aircraft. And India fields approximately 3900 main battle tanks and 1660 armored infantry fighting vehicles and armored personnel carriers, versus Pakistan's 2300 main battle tanks and 1200 armored personnel carriers. Also, India's larger defense industrial base, and supply of advanced weaponry from Russia, give its forces a qualitative advantage over those of Pakistan. Anthony H. Cordesman, *The India-Pakistan Military Balance* (Washington, DC: Center for Strategic and International Studies, 2002), 4. Economic, demographic, and geographic factors favor India as well. India's $505 billion gross domestic product is approximately eight times Pakistan's $68 billion GDP; its $15.6 billion defense budget is roughly five times that of Pakistan's $2.8 billion budget; its population of over 1 billion dwarfs Pakistan's approximately 147 million people; and its vast size gives it strategic depth that Pakistan sorely lacks. See International Institute for Strategic Studies, *Military Balance 2003–2004*, 288, 289; Cordesman, *India-Pakistan Military Balance*, 3.

51. Author interview of General V. P. Malik, Indian chief of army staff (retired), New Delhi, April 2004.

52. Tellis, *Stability in South Asia*, 23. The Kargil War illustrates this point, though on a much smaller scale. During the conflict, India shifted ground forces to the region from elsewhere in the country, giving India sufficient numbers to launch successful offensive operations in a highly defense-dominant tactical environment. Indian force levels in the Kargil sector went from approximately 9 infantry battalions in May 1999 to approximately 52 infantry battalions by late July. Because they had deployed there from outside the area of operations, many of these troops had to undergo high-altitude acclimatization upon arrival in Kargil. See Kargil Review Committee, *From Surprise to Reckoning*, 85–86; Singh, *A Ridge Too Far*, 68; Krishna, "The Kargil War," 110. India also moved elements of its Eastern Fleet to join its Western Fleet in the North Arabian Sea, enabling it to contain the Pakistan Navy in Karachi and to threaten a blockade of that crucial port. Kargil Review Committee, *From Surprise to Reckoning*, 22, 101; Singh, *A Ridge Too Far*, 70–71; and Krishna, "The Kargil War," 135–137.

53. This was essentially the strategy of India's Operation Parakram during the crisis following the December 2001 attacks on the Indian Parliament. See Sood and Sawhney, *Operation Parakram*, 80–83.

54. Tellis, *Stability in South Asia*, 7, 23; Kanwar Sandhu, "India's Strategy: Attack Across a Wide Front," *Hindustan Times* (New Delhi), January 12, 2002, 11. Tellis argues that even in the event of a Pakistani first strike employing tactical nuclear weapons, Indian conventional superiority is such that it should enable India to draw out the war, steadily mass its forces, and eviscerate Pakistani military capabilities. See Ashley J. Tellis, *India's Emerging Nuclear Posture* (Santa Monica, CA: RAND, 2001), 133.

55. Author interview of director general for South Asia in Pakistan's Ministry of Foreign Affairs, Jalil Jilani, Islamabad, Pakistan, April 2004. See also, for example, Waltz, "For Better," 111; Ganguly, *Conflict Unending*, 101–102; Pervez Hoodbhoy, "Pakistan's Nuclear Future," in Samina Ahmed and David Cortright, eds., *Pakistan and the Bomb: Public Opinion and Nuclear Options* (South Bend, IN: University of Notre Dame Press, 1998), 70; and Neil Joeck, "Maintaining Nuclear Stability in South Asia," Adelphi Paper 312 (London: International Institute for Strategic Studies, 1997), 37–38.

56. Note that since India is satisfied with the territorial status quo in Kashmir, high strategic stability would not be likely to encourage Indian aggression beyond that necessary to defeat Pakistani adventurism and restore existing regional boundaries.

57. See Sagan, "For the Worse," 96–98.

58. By "de facto" I mean that even though Pakistan did not actually possess nuclear weapons, it probably could have assembled them on short order. India achieved a de facto nuclear capability at roughly the same time as Pakistan. See Hagerty, *Consequences of Nuclear Proliferation*, 126; and Leonard Spector, *The Undeclared Bomb: The Spread of Nuclear Weapons, 1987–1988* (Cambridge, MA: Ballinger, 1988), 69–70.

59. Author interview of former Pakistani prime minister Benazir Bhutto, August 2004.

60. Ibid. While the Pakistan government has consistently sought to attract international mediation of the Kashmir conflict, Indian leaders have rejected any third-party involvement, maintaining that the two countries must resolve their disagreements on a purely bilateral basis. See Cohen, *India*, 219; Stephen P. Cohen, *The Pakistan Army*, 145; and Owen Bennett Jones, *Pakistan: Eye of the Storm* (New Haven, CT: Yale University Press, 2002), 80, 107. On the issue of internationalizing Kargil, see also Kargil Review Committee, *From Surprise to Reckoning*, 89; D. Suba Chandran, "Why Kargil? Pakistan's Objective and Motivation," in Krishna and Chari, *Kargil*, 23–38; Tellis, Fair, and Medby, *Limited Conflicts*, 38; Mirza Aslam Beg, "Kargil Withdrawal and 'Rogue' Army Image," *Defence Journal*, vol. 3, no. 8 (September 1999), 8–11; A. Rashid, "Responsibility for Kargil," *Dawn*, July 22, 2000; Zahid Hussain, "On the Brink," *Newsline*, June 1999, 30.

61. Aga Shahi, Zulfikar Ali Khan, and Abdul Sattar, "Securing Nuclear Peace," *News International*, October 5, 1999, in *Strategic Digest*, vol. 30, no. 1 (2000), 16.

62. This is not to argue that Pakistan invented the Kashmir insurgency; as noted previously, the insurgency has deep indigenous roots. Pakistani backing came only after there was already an existing current of discontent in Kashmir to exploit. See Wirsing, *India, Pakistan, and the Kashmir Dispute*, 114–118; Ganguly, *Crisis in Kashmir*, 14–42.

63. Author interview of Benazir Bhutto, August 2004. For a similar assessment of Pakistani strategy, see Shireen Mazari, "Kashmir: Looking for Viable Options," *Defence Journal*, vol. 3, no. 2 (February–March 1999), available at http://defencejournal.com/feb-mar99/kashmir-viable.htm. See also Samina Ahmed, "Pakistan's Nuclear Weapons Program," *International Security*, vol. 23, no. 4 (Spring 1999), 189–190; Hoodbhoy, "Pakistan's Nuclear Future," 71; Ganguly, *Crisis Unending*, 92; and Raghavan, "Limited War," 4.

64. Fighting at Kargil continued from March through July 1999, when, under a U.S.-brokered arrangement, Pakistani forces withdrew from the Line of Control. As part of the agreement, President Bill Clinton promised to take a "personal interest" in encouraging bilateral Indo-Pakistani efforts to resolve the Kashmir dispute. See Bruce Reidel, "American Diplomacy and the 1999 Kargil Summit at Blair House," Center for the Advanced Study of India, University of Pennsylvania (2002), available at http://www.freerepublic.com/focus/news/685898/posts.

65. On these points, see S. Paul Kapur, "Nuclear Proliferation, the Kargil Conflict, and South Asian Security," *Security Studies*, vol. 13, no. 1 (Autumn 2003), 87–88. Although Pakistani forces were ultimately forced to abandon the area, the Pakistanis' views on the tactical environment at Kargil were not wholly unfounded. Dug high into the sector's mountain peaks and overlooking the exposed approaches to their positions, Pakistani forces proved extremely difficult for the Indians to dislodge. However, Pakistani expectations of international support for the Kargil adventure

were disastrously wrong and seem to have been based upon little more than wishful thinking. Ganguly notes that in launching Kargil, "the Pakistani leadership simply assumed that the United States and other major states would step in to prevent an escalation of the crisis. . . . There is little or no evidence that the leadership had any tangible basis for their belief in international support." Ganguly, *Conflict Unending*, 122. As Tellis, Fair, and Medby put it, "Pakistan made unrealistic assumptions about the range of possible outcomes. Fundamentally, Pakistan did not anticipate the intolerance that the international community . . . would demonstrate for its attempts to alter the status quo." Tellis, Fair, and Medby, *Limited Conflicts*, 38–39. And Ejaz Haider similarly maintains that "no causal logic" underlay the Pakistani leadership's expectation of international support at Kargil. Their expectations were based simply on faith that the international community would see the justice of the Pakistani position on Kashmir. Author interview of Ejaz Haider, news editor, *Friday Times*, Lahore, Pakistan, April 2004.

66. Author interview of Jalil Jilani, April 2004. Kapur, "Nuclear Proliferation," 88–89; Ganguly, *Conflict Unending*, 92; Raghavan, "Limited War," 4; Karl, "Lessons for Proliferation Scholarship in South Asia," 1020; Tellis, Fair, and Medby, *Limited Conflicts*, 49; Kargil Review Committee, *From Surprise to Reckoning*, 89; Jasjit Singh, "The Fourth War," in Jasjit Singh, ed., *Kargil 1999: Pakistan's Fourth War for Kashmir* (New Delhi: Institute for Defence Analysis, 1999), 123, 132–133; interviews of retired Indian generals, New Delhi, India, May 2001; and Shireen Mazari, "Re-examining Kargil," *Defence Journal*, vol. 3, no. 11 (June 2000), 44–46. Other Pakistani goals at Kargil probably included undermining the legitimacy of the Line of Control and bolstering the anti-Indian insurgency in Kashmir, which in recent years had been flagging. See Kargil Review Committee, *From Surprise to Reckoning*, 89–90; J. N. Dixit, "A Defining Moment," in Rahul Bedi, Bharat Bhushan, Pamela Constable, Moti Dar, Saurabh Das, Sunanda K. Datta-Ray, J. N. Dixit, Muzamil Jaleel, Suketu Mehta, and Sankarshan Thakur, *Guns and Yellow Roses: Essays on the Kargil War* (New Delhi: HarperCollins, 1999), 188–191; F. S. Lodi, "Kargil: Its Aftermath," *Defence Journal*, vol. 3, no. 6 (July 1999), 7–8; Nasim Zehra, "Anatomy of Islamabad's Kargil Policy," *Defence Journal*, vol. 3, no. 7 (August 1999), 2–4; Ganguly, *Conflict Unending*, 121–122; Dixit, "A Defining Moment," 189; Tellis, Fair, and Medby, *Limited Conflicts*, 38; Husain, "Kargil"; Ayaz Amir, "What Is the Political Leadership Up To?" *Dawn*, July 2, 1999; Hussain, "On the Brink," 24; and Shaukat Qadir, "An Analysis of the Kargil Conflict 1999," *Royal United Service Institution Journal*, vol. 147, no. 2 (April 2002), 3.

67. Author interview of Jalil Jilani, April 2004.

68. See Tellis, Fair, and Medby, *Limited Conflicts*, x, 41, 55; Husain, "Kargil"; Hussain, "On the Brink"; Jones, *Pakistan*, 104; Irfan Husain, "The Cost of Kargil," *Dawn*, August 14, 1999; Shireen M. Mazari, "Kargil: Misguided Perceptions," Pakistan Institute for Air Defence Studies, http://www.piads.com.pk/users/piads/mazari1.html (no

longer available); Samina Ahmed, "Pakistan's Nuclear Weapons Program: Moving Forward or Tactical Retreat?" Joan B. Kroc Institute for International Peace Studies, Occasional Paper #18:OP:2 (February 2000), 17, http://www.nd.edu/~krocinst/oc papers/op_18_2.pdf (no longer available); and "Statement of Nawaz Sharif in ATC-1," *Dawn*, March 9, 2000.

69. As Schelling explains, "Skillful diplomacy . . . consists in arranging things so that it is one's opponent who is embarrassed by having the 'last clear chance' to avert disaster by turning aside or abstaining from what he wanted to do. . . . The risk of disaster becomes a manipulative element in the situation." Schelling, *Arms and Influence*, 101, 102.

70. Sood and Sawhney, *Operation Parakram*, 147–148.

71. For example, India escalated horizontally in response to Pakistan's attack on Kashmir in 1965. See Ganguly, *Crisis Unending*, 33, 38, 44, 48. Also note that combat at Kargil occurred in glacial conditions at altitudes generally higher than 15,000 feet. Attempts to eject Pakistani intruders from the sector's mountain heights forced Indian troops to advance uphill under withering artillery and machine-gun fire. See Kargil Review Committee, *From Surprise to Reckoning*, 83; and Gurmeet Kanwal, "Pakistan's Military Defeat," in Singh, *Kargil 1999*, 153. Expanding the conflict horizontally could have enabled the Indians to attack the Pakistanis elsewhere under more favorable conditions.

72. Author interview of V. P. Malik, April 2004; P. R. Chari, Pervaiz Iqbal Cheema, and Stephen Philip Cohen, *Perception, Politics, and Security in South Asia: The Compound Crisis of 1990* (London: Routledge Curzon, 2003), 143.

73. Author interview of senior Indian scholar and nuclear policy advisor closely involved with the formulation of Indian nuclear doctrine, New Delhi, April 2004.

74. Author interview of senior Indian Army officer, New Delhi, April 2004.

75. Author interview of former Indian defense minister George Fernandes, New Delhi, August 2004.

76. See Gaurav Kampani, "India's Compellance Strategy: Calling Pakistan's Nuclear Bluff over Kashmir," Monterey Institute of International Studies, available at http://www.cns.miis.edu/pubs/week/020610.htm, 3.

77. Author interview of V. P. Malik, April 2004. See also address by V. P. Malik at National Seminar on the Challenge of Limited War: Parameters and Options, Institute for Defence Studies and Analysis, New Delhi, January 6, 2000. Discussions with senior serving Army and Ministry of External Affairs personnel evinced a similar viewpoint.

78. Kampani, "India's Compellance Strategy," 11; and Karl, "Lessons for Proliferation Scholarship," 1021. See also Khan, "Challenges to Nuclear Stability," 64–65. On the conceptual roots of the "Limited War" policy, see C. Raja Mohan, "Fernandes Unveils 'Limited War' Doctrine," *Hindu*, January 24, 2000. Note that any

Indian attacks on Pakistan proper would have been highly circumscribed in nature to avoid threatening Pakistan with catastrophic defeat. Author interview of V. K. Sood, August 2004.

79. This was the largest mobilization in Indian history.

80. See Praveen Swami, "Beating the Retreat," *Frontline*, October 26–November 8, 2002.

81. Author interview of George Fernandes, August 2004.

82. See President Pervez Musharraf's Address to the Nation, January 12, 2002, http://www.jang-group.com/thenews/spedition/speech_of_musharraf/index.html (no longer available). The Indian government blamed Lashkar-e-Toiba and Jaish-e-Mohammed for the December 2001 Parliament attack. See Rana Lakshmi, "Indians Blame Attacks on Pakistan-Based Group; Fears of Renewed Tension Increase," *Washington Post*, December 15, 2001, A23; Ewan MacAskill, "India Says It Has Evidence Linking Pakistan with Raid," *Guardian*, December 17, 2001, 13; Sayantan Chakravarty, "The Plot Unravels," *India Today*, December 31, 2001, 6–8. For detailed discussions of these and other militant groups in Kashmir, see K. Santhanam, Sreedhar, Sudhir Saxena, and Manish, *Jihadis in Jammu and Kashmir: A Portrait Gallery* (New Delhi: Sage Publications, 2003).

83. Fahran Bokhari and Edward Luce, "Western Pressure Brings Easing of Kashmir Tension," *Financial Times*, June 8, 2002, 7; C. Raja Mohan, "Musharraf Vows to Stop Infiltration: Armitage," *Hindu*, June 7, 2002; Sood and Sawhney, *Operation Parakram*, 95, 98–99; and Shishir Gupta, "Advantage India," *India Today*, June 24, 2002, 40–42. Indian defense minister George Fernandes claimed in November 2002 that cross-border infiltration during the first 10 months of that year was down to 53 percent of what it had been during the same period in 2001. See "India: Fernandes Says Forward Mobilization of Troops Achieved Objectives," *World News Connection*, November 21, 2002; and "Government Carrying Out Strategic Relocation of Army," *Press Trust of India*, November 20, 2002.

84. V. Sudarshan and Ajith Pillai, "Game of Patience," *Outlook*, May 27, 2002; Shishir Gupta, "Keeping the Heat On," *India Today*, May 20, 2002, 40–41; "The General's Broken Promise," *Washington Post*, May 15, 2002, A26; and author interviews of retired Indian generals, New Delhi, August 2004. According to the Indian Ministry of Home Affairs, 4038 terrorist incidents occurred in Jammu and Kashmir during 2002, an overall decline of approximately 11 percent from 4522 total incidents in 2001. See Government of India Ministry of Home Affairs, *2003–2004 Annual Report*, 12. According to the Indian Army, 1063 non-Kashmiri terrorists were killed in 2002 by security forces in Jammu and Kashmir, and 1198 were killed in 2001, an overall decline of roughly the same percentage. For Indian Army statistics, see http://www.armyinkashmir.org/v2/statistical_facts/ft_actual_data.shtml (no longer available).

85. Most of the victims were family members of Army personnel stationed at

Kaluchak. See Raj Chengappa and Shishir Gupta, "The Mood to Hit Back," *India To-day*, May 27, 2002, 27–30.

86. Sood and Sawhney, *Operation Parakram*, 80, 82, 87; Sudarshan and Pillai, "Game of Patience"; Shishir Gupta, "When India Came Close to War," *India Today*, December 19, 2002; and interviews of retired Indian generals, New Delhi, April 2004.

87. Sood and Sawhney, *Operation Parakram*, 11.

88. See Sujit Chatterjee, "Pak Has Taken Steps to Put Down Cross-Border Terror: Fernandes," *Press Trust of India*, February 11, 2004; Vasantha Arora, "India Might Reconsider Stand on Troops for Iraq: Natwar," *Indo-Asian News Service*, June 11, 2004; Chidanand Rajghatta, "India, US Pledge Stronger Ties," *Times of India*, June 12, 2004; "Natwar, Powell Discuss Bilateral, Regional Issues," *Press Trust of India*, June 11, 2004; and Simon Denyer, "India Says Kashmir Infiltration Lower but Not Over," *Reuters*, June 18, 2004.

89. Government of India, Ministry of Home Affairs, *Annual Report 2006–2007*, 6, 143. See also *Reuters*, "Kashmir Violence Falls to All-Time Low—Official," April 1, 2007.

90. See S. Paul Kapur, "The Decade After: Ten Years of Instability in a Nuclear South Asia," *International Security*, vol. 33, no. 2 (Fall 2008), 71–94.

91. Indian GDP growth jumped from 5.6 to 8.4 percent between 1990 and 2005 and is expected to continue above 8 percent in 2008. See S. Paul Kapur and Šumit Ganguly, "The Transformation of US-India Relations: An Explanation for the Rapprochement and Prospects for the Future," *Asian Survey*, vol. 47, no. 4 (July–August 2007), 648–649.

92. See Shivshankar Menon, "India-Pakistan: Understanding the Conflict Dynamics," speech at Jamia Millia Islamia, April 11, 2007.

93. For example, the 2005 Diwali bombings killed approximately 60 people on the eve of a major Hindu religious festival. And in 2006, bombings killed approximately 180 people in railway stations and aboard commuter trains in Mumbai. Indian authorities implicated the Pakistan-backed Lashkar-e-Toiba and Jaish-e-Mohammed, as well as the Students Islamic Movement of India, in these attacks. See Amelia Gentleman, "Delhi Police Say Suspect Was Attack Mastermind," *International Herald Tribune*, November 13, 2005; "LeT, JeM, SIMI Helped Execute Terror Plan," *Times of India*, October 1, 2006. Although the New Delhi and Mumbai bombings were more deadly, the Parliament and Kaluchak attacks were widely viewed as a greater national affront, as they targeted the foremost symbol of the Indian state and the family members of Indian military personnel.

94. Russel J. Leng, "Realpolitik and Learning in the India-Pakistan Rivalry," in T. V. Paul, ed., *The India-Pakistan Conflict: An Enduring Rivalry* (Cambridge: Cambridge University Press, 2005), 103, 120.

95. Pervez Musharraf, *In the Line of Fire* (New York: Free Press, 2006), 98.

96. Author interview of Jalil Jilani, April 2004.

97. Mazari, "Re-examining Kargil," 46.

98. V. P. Malik, *Kargil: From Surprise to Victory* (New Delhi: HarperCollins, 2006), 355, 363, 365.

99. Tellis, *Stability in South Asia*, 20–21; interview with Center for Land Warfare Studies Director Gurmeet Kanwal, New Delhi, India, December 2007.

100. See Kapur, "The Decade After"; Walter C. Ladwig, "A Cold Start for Hot Wars? An Assessment of the Indian Army's New Limited War Doctrine," *International Security*, vol. 32, no. 3 (Winter 2007–2008), 158–190; Subhash Kapila, "India's New 'Cold Start' War Doctrine Strategically Reviewed," Parts I and II, South Asia Analysis Group Papers No. 991, May 4, 2004, and No. 1013, June 1, 2004; Tariq M. Ashraf, "Doctrinal Reawakening of the Indian Armed Forces," *Military Review* (November–December 2004), 53–62.

6 THE EVOLUTION OF PAKISTANI AND INDIAN NUCLEAR DOCTRINE

Scott D. Sagan

NEITHER THE GOVERNMENT IN NEW DELHI nor its counterpart in Islamabad had a fully developed nuclear doctrine when it ordered nuclear weapons tests in May 1998. Although both governments had maintained a latent nuclear weapons capability for many years, it was only after their momentous decisions to become declared nuclear weapons states that leaders in India and Pakistan began planning the unthinkable in earnest: how should nuclear arsenals be used in peacetime for deterrence and, if necessary, in war? New and more detailed military planning was further encouraged after two serious conflicts—the 1999 Kargil War and the 2001–2002 crisis—erupted between the new nuclear powers in South Asia.

This chapter analyzes the evolution of Pakistani and Indian nuclear doctrines. Although officials in both Islamabad and New Delhi similarly state that the central purpose of their arsenals is to provide "credible minimum deterrence," the term is highly, and deliberately, ambiguous. The word *minimum* is used to signal both domestic and international audiences that the Indian and Pakistani governments do not intend to enter into an arms race leading to massive nuclear arsenals, as occurred during the Cold War between the United States and the USSR. The word *credible* is added, however, to provide extreme flexibility regarding responses both to each other's nuclear arsenal developments and, in the case of India, to China's nuclear deployments as well.

Most security studies scholars and policy analysts focus primary attention on the strategic threats that governments face. Such a "realist" approach leads analysts to note that, under the same label of "credible minimum deterrence," the governments in Islamabad and Delhi have developed very different operational doctrines for potential use of nuclear weapons. Pakistan, as the weaker power in terms of conventional military capabilities, maintains an explicit nuclear first-use doctrine, which might include limited nuclear strike options, to provide a credible threat of nuclear escalation to deter an Indian conventional attack. The Indian government, as the conventionally stronger power in the South Asian rivalry, has maintained an explicit "no-first-use" nuclear doctrine against Pakistan, which could place the onus of nuclear escalation during a conventional war on the government in Islamabad.

That simple description, however, obscures a more complex and more disturbing picture of emerging nuclear doctrines in South Asia. For when one looks behind the rhetoric of official nuclear declaratory policy, lifting the veil of "minimum credible deterrence," both governments can be seen to be developing more complex and flexible nuclear-use doctrines that could lead to nuclear weapons use in response to less than imminent threats to national existence. This chapter will demonstrate that the nuclear doctrines of India and Pakistan have led to dangerous behavior and interactions in past crises and could also encourage the two governments to expand the size and character of their nuclear arsenals in the future.

In order for us to understand the evolution of nuclear doctrines in South Asia, it is necessary to focus on the organizational interests and biases common among professional military officers in both countries and on the influence of international norms on military planners and political decision makers. Any government in Islamabad would be likely to have a first-use doctrine, but the specific details of Pakistani nuclear doctrine reflect common organizational biases stemming from the central role of the professional military in making policy and the weak institutional checks and balances on its authority over nuclear matters. Organizational biases of the Pakistani military can be seen in the variety of conditions in which war planners and leaders are willing to threaten nuclear weapons use, including conditions that are less than life-threatening for the nation. The military's parochial interests and a common organizational tendency to conflate means with goals are also reflected in Pakistani statements about nuclear weapons. The result of such biases is that although authorities in Islamabad have stated that Pakistani weapons will only be used as "a last resort," the definition of last resort has become elastic, subject to different interpretations and potentially deadly misunderstandings. This chapter will also demonstrate that the Pakistani military's nuclear doctrine has led it to initiate dangerous military operations and nuclear alert measures in past crises and could encourage dangerous actions in the future.

Indian nuclear weapons doctrine, in contrast, is almost entirely determined by senior civilian authorities. As the state with conventional military superiority in the Indian-Pakistani rivalry, any government in New Delhi would have an interest in declaring a no-first-use doctrine against Pakistan, a doctrine that places the onus of nuclear escalation on Islamabad in any future war. Yet this chapter will present evidence on how India's nuclear doctrine in 2003 moved, subtly but clearly, away from the pure form of no first use that was previously espoused toward a more flexible and potentially "offensive" nuclear doctrine. These doctrinal changes in India were produced in part by Indian civilian leaders' reactions to the 1999 Kargil War and the 2001–2002 military crisis with Pakistan. But I will also demonstrate how, in making these changes, the Indian military leadership and nuclear strategists have been strongly influenced by cultural norms, especially through copying perceived innovations in U.S. nuclear weapons doctrine.

This chapter therefore both describes the key elements of the Indian and Pakistani nuclear doctrines and seeks to explain their causes and consequences. The chapter has five sections. The first section outlines different theories that have been developed elsewhere to explain the origins of military doctrine. The second section presents and analyzes the evolution of Pakistani nuclear doctrine since 1998 and discusses the impact of Pakistani nuclear weapons doctrine and operations on the 1999 Kargil conflict. The third section focuses on the nuclear threats and counterthreats between the governments in Islamabad and New Delhi during the 2002 crisis caused by the terrorist attack in New Delhi in December 2001. This section both illuminates the domestic disagreements in both countries about the use of such nuclear threats and highlights the dangers produced by such saber rattling. The fourth section focuses on the evolution of Indian nuclear doctrine, examining in detail the changes in doctrine announced in January 2003 in response to the 2001–2002 crisis. Finally, the chapter concludes with an assessment of how the emerging nuclear doctrines in Pakistan and India will place pressures on both governments to expand their nuclear arsenals and could lead to further dangerous misunderstandings in future crises or conflicts.

THE SOURCES OF MILITARY DOCTRINE

Military doctrine refers to the underlying principles and specific guidance provided to military officers who produce the operational plans for the use of military forces. Nuclear weapons doctrines can differ on several critical dimensions. Does the government plan to initiate the use of nuclear weapons in a crisis or conventional war, or does it have a strict no-first-use policy? Are preventive wars and preemptive strikes contemplated, or are only options for retaliation planned? Do military plans focus only on decisive uses of nuclear weapons, or are more limited nuclear options contemplated and exercised? What kinds of targets are emphasized in nuclear war plans: conventional military targets, an adversary's nuclear forces, enemy leadership targets, or cities filled with industrial targets and noncombatant citizens?

Four Theories in Search of a Doctrine

Four theories exist that explain why governments choose different kinds of military doctrines.[1] First, realist theory in political science conceives of military doctrine as the rational product of civilians and military officers determining together how best to protect the national security interests of the state against foreign threats. A nation's geographical position, the military resources at its disposal, the capabilities of its potential enemies, the strategic objectives of the government in power, and its alliance relations are the primary determinants of whether the government will adopt an offensive or defensive posture and whether it will stress limited or decisive uses of military force. Realists predict that states will adopt first-nuclear-use plans if they face adversaries with stronger conventional capabilities and that only a conventionally superior power could afford to adopt a no-first-use posture. Limited nuclear options will also be in the interest of weaker states because they provide a more credible threat of escalation if a stronger power attacks and is winning a conventional war. Realists also stress that the most important decisions a state leader can make are whether and how to go to war, and civilian authorities should therefore be deeply reluctant to give authority to initiate the use of nuclear weapons to military officers lower down in the chain of command. In short, for realists, military doctrine is designed to safeguard the national security interests of a country based on its position in the international system and with a focus on the military balance with its primary rivals. Realists accept that organizational learning can take place in a competition between rivals; indeed, states have strong incentives to monitor each other's doctrines, adjust their own to counter rivals' actions, and learn from others about which doctrines are most effective and which are not.[2]

Realist theory would therefore predict that India would have a no-first-use policy against Pakistan (but not necessarily against China). It would predict that Pakistan would maintain a first-use doctrine, given its conventional inferiority. Pakistan would, however, adopt a last-resort doctrine, preparing to use nuclear weapons only if use was absolutely necessary to prevent defeat in a major war and the destruction of Pakistan. Islamabad would also have strong incentives to develop limited nuclear options, both to add to the credibility of first-use threats and to increase the probability that such threats, if implemented, would lead to war termination and not to uncontrolled nuclear escalation.

Second, organization theory suggests that nuclear doctrine reflects the biases and parochial interests of military organizations, not just the national interests, and is strongly influenced by officers' desire to protect their own organizational strength, autonomy, and prestige. Cold War research about U.S. and Soviet military organizations, for example, demonstrated that officers often have biases in favor of offensive doctrines because they permit taking the initiative, often require larger budgets and longer-range forces, and can produce more decisive and glorious results. Military leaders prefer simple and decisive uses of military force, which maintain autonomy and control over operations, rather than more complicated and more "political" limited war options that cede authority to civilians and depend upon constraints being followed by both sides in a conflict. Military leaders tend to support counterforce doctrines that target enemy strategic forces rather than an adversary's cities. They also tend to hold strong preferences in favor of building more nuclear weapons to pad their organizational budget and enhance their offensive capabilities but are not inclined to spend limited resources on developing secure second-strike forces of their own volition. Military officers value operational autonomy and therefore prefer delegative command and control systems that give senior officers the authority and ability to use nuclear weapons promptly if necessary. Finally, leaders of military organizations, like other organizational leaders, often suffer from what W. Richard Scott has called "the common curse" of "goal displacement": they conflate means with ends, becoming fixated on the operational requirements that have been set for success and ignoring whether these means are really necessary for achievement of the goal.[3]

Organization theory would lead analysts to focus on the biases of the Pakistani military since they have virtually complete autonomy over military operations and war planning in Pakistan. Doctrine in India would presumably be less strongly influenced by such biases, given India's historical tradition of strict civilian control over the professional military. An organizational lens would encourage the analyst, however, to look at doctrinal developments in New Delhi in 2003 after the government created an independent Strategic Forces Command and approved "alternate chains of command for retaliatory nuclear strikes in all eventualities" to see if this produced more opportunities for direct military influence on strategic doctrine in India.[4]

The third theory about the origins of military doctrine focuses on the effects of national strategic culture. This theory focuses on how a state's unique history, religious traditions, and widely held perceptions of itself and its military rivals can influence the military doctrines adopted by its decision makers. Decision makers may think that they are responding with pure logic and objectivity to their strategic environment, but what appears as the appropriate or logical response to specific threats is filtered through a cultural lens. As Alistair Iain Johnson has noted, strategic culture produces "pervasive and long-lasting strategic preferences by formulating concepts of the role and efficiency of military forces in interstate political affairs, and by clothing these conceptions with such an aura of factuality that the strategic preferences seem uniquely realistic and efficacious."[5] During the Cold War, for example, leaders in both Washington and Moscow were influenced by their nation's recent history of suffering "surprise attacks" by the Japanese at Pearl Harbor and by the Germans on the Eastern Front in 1941 and developed nuclear doctrines emphasizing the need for instant response to warnings of attacks. Even more dramatically, specific leaders may reject specific types of weapons altogether as immoral or inconsistent with their unique religious traditions. For example, after the Iranian Revolution, the Ayatollah Khomeini shut down the Shah's nascent nuclear program on the grounds that the use of nuclear weapons was against Islamic principles; and Morarji Desai similarly objected, on Gandhian principles, to any plan for his government to build nuclear weapons when he was Indian prime minister in the mid-1970s.[6] Similar beliefs could also, obviously, have an influence on whether government officials accept or object to specific countercity nuclear-targeting doctrines with their emphasis on holding innocent civilians at risk for the sake of deterrence.

Pakistani nuclear doctrine, through this cultural lens, would be expected to be influenced by the teachings of the Koran and by common beliefs that will power and Islamic faith can serve as a force multiplier to enable materially weaker Islamic militaries to defeat stronger non-Muslim forces. Indian doctrine, in contrast, would be expected to reflect strict civilian control, because of distrust of professional military officers due to their history of collaboration with colonial powers; and India's no-first-use doctrine would reflect the moral tradition of Gandhi's nonviolent resistance due to its success in the struggle against British imperialism.[7]

The fourth theoretical approach focuses on global strategic culture, arguing that international models of organization and norms of behavior strongly influence military doctrines. These cultural theorists envision military officers and civilian strategists seeking the kinds of weaponry and mimicking the doctrines of other leading military organizations that they believe to be prestigious, modern, and effective, regardless of whether the specific weaponry or doctrines in question are necessary or effective in their nation's strategic environment.[8] In contrast to realism, this perspective would predict that organizational learning is uncoupled from measures of effectiveness and is produced instead by efforts to copy the actions of other professional militaries that officers admire and with whom they identify.[9] This theoretical lens, for example, would lead an analyst to predict that Pakistani officers could be influenced by their training in the United States during the 1970s, and that Indian doctrine might become more like American nuclear doctrine in the post–Cold War period as civilian nuclear strategists and retired military officers in New Delhi— the "engines of isomorphism"—read recent U.S. nuclear doctrine statements and encourage their government to adopt similar ideas and military plans.

Table 6.1 summarizes the logic behind these different theoretical lenses and the resulting predictions about both the sources and types of nuclear doctrines that will be adopted by Pakistan and India.

Caveats and Concerns

How do the Pakistani and Indian governments plan to use nuclear weapons? Why have these doctrines been chosen? This chapter seeks to answer these questions, but the analysis is necessarily tentative for five basic reasons. First, in some cases these theories predict similar outcomes, so we can't use the basic outlines of Indian and Pakistani nuclear doctrine as a conclusive test of each theory's power. It is therefore particularly important to pay attention to the causal process by which the doctrine is produced, since these theories focus

Table 6.1. Four theories in search of a doctrine

Theory	Key influence/logic	Prediction	Pakistan	India
Realism	Strategic environment	Conventional superiority = no first use (NFU) Conventional inferiority = first use (FU)	FU Limited nuclear options (LNOs) Counterforce targeting (CF)	NFU Invulnerable second-strike forces Countervalue targeting (CV)
Organization theory	Parochial interests and bias of military	Offensive, CF and FU, preventive war, decisive options, budget promotion and goal displacement	Military autonomy increases biases	Strict civilian control limits biases
National strategic culture	Historical experience / cultural traditions	Unique to each country	Islam as force multiplier; martial race bias	Postcolonial distrust of military; Gandhian nonviolence
Global strategic culture	Mimicry of most modern and prestigious actors	Isomorphism	Mimic U.S. doctrine?	Mimic U.S. doctrine?

attention on very different causes of doctrinal change and adoption.[10] When possible, therefore, I trace the origins of nuclear doctrines in both countries and analyze the intellectual ideas and political forces that led to resistance and change. Given the classified nature of nuclear policy deliberations in both countries, such process tracing is extremely difficult even when guided by the useful lens of these theories.

Second, although political and military leaders in both New Delhi and Islamabad have made important pronouncements outlining nuclear doctrine, neither government has ever released extremely detailed strategy guidance documents or declassified military operational plans that are the products of official doctrine. Outside analysts of nuclear policy in South Asia simply lack access to details of decision making inside the government comparable to the level of knowledge that exists in the United States from unclassified and declassified government reports and military plans, leaked contemporary documents, and official testimony to Congress.[11] This chapter must therefore offer interpretations of official statements made by senior political and military leaders and also unofficial statements about doctrine by lower-ranking officers, speaking to the press when in uniform or writing themselves during retirement.

Third, Indian and Pakistani government officials' statements about when, where, and how military forces will be used could be deliberately misleading since such pronouncements may be designed primarily to influence public opinion, allies' perceptions, or adversaries' calculations, and not necessarily reflect real military plans and proclivities. In other words, "declaratory policy" may differ significantly from nuclear doctrine since it can serve as a signaling device for friends and foes alike. Although this difference is noteworthy, it is nevertheless helpful to focus on public statements since such rhetoric can directly impact diplomacy and crisis interactions, even if it does not directly reflect actual plans.

Fourth, there are strong internal and external reasons why senior government leaders might not want to spell out in advance, in public or even in classified documents, the details of when or how they intend to use military force, especially nuclear weapons, in a crisis or conflict. Leaders may be concerned that such pronouncements or planning documents could limit their flexibility in internal decision making in crises or conflict situations and might become a source of military advantage to an enemy.

Finally, I note that nuclear doctrine in new nuclear states, such as India and Pakistan, is a moving target, as political and military leaders are seeking to develop plans and procedures in new and unfamiliar strategic conditions. Indeed, the degree of change that has occurred in nuclear doctrines in South Asia is an explicit focus of this chapter. In such a fluid situation, it is perhaps understandable that there are apparent tensions or contradictions in some doctrinal statements emerging from the governments in New Delhi and Islamabad. Although some degree of contradiction and confusion in public statements about nuclear weapons may well reflect deliberate obfuscation or strategic ambiguity for signaling purposes, we should not rule out the possibility that sometimes confusion and contradiction in doctrinal statements are genuine signs of confusion within governments and contrary positions taken by members of different government bureaucracies.

PAKISTAN'S NUCLEAR DOCTRINE AND THE KARGIL CONFLICT

In his May 1998 announcement of the Pakistani nuclear tests, Prime Minister Nawaz Sharif blamed India for altering the strategic landscape of South Asia and argued that Pakistan's arsenal be used solely for deterrent purposes:

> [The nuclear tests] have demonstrated Pakistan's ability to deter aggression. Pakistan has been obliged to exercise the nuclear option due to weaponization of India's nuclear programme. This had led to the collapse of the "existential

deterrence" and had radically altered the strategic balance in our region. Immediately after its nuclear tests, India had brazenly raised the demand that "Islamabad should realize the change in the geo-strategic situation in the region" and threatened that "India will deal firmly and strongly with Pakistan."[12]

Sharif concluded that "these weapons are to deter aggression, whether nuclear or conventional," implying that Islamabad would develop a first-use nuclear doctrine.[13]

Since the May 1998 tests, Pakistani leaders have been forced to think the unthinkable—how best to deter aggression and what to do if deterrence fails—more often and in more depth than when Sharif laid out the fundamental goals of deterring conventional and nuclear attacks.[14] Neither the military nor civilian leadership in Islamabad, however, has ever issued an authoritative and detailed statement on Pakistan's nuclear doctrine and war-planning assumptions about precisely when and against what targets Pakistani nuclear forces might be used.[15] The reasons for this continued ambiguity are understandable: Pakistan has a first-use nuclear doctrine designed to deter Indian conventional attacks; yet if Islamabad spelled out the precise conditions that would produce a nuclear first strike, such a "red line" declaration might tempt Indian armed forces to move just up to the red line, could encourage an Indian preemptive strike just before that red line was crossed in extreme circumstances, and would also limit Pakistani options if the red line were crossed deliberately or inadvertently. Thus, while Islamabad's nuclear doctrine's opacity may be partly attributable to the secretive mind-set of the Pakistan military, a deeper structural reason is clear and acknowledged by Pakistani leaders themselves.[16]

This ambiguity, however, leaves a number of crucial questions unanswered. First, how far does the nuclear writ run in the opinion of Islamabad leaders? For example, do nuclear weapons provide Pakistan with a shield behind which its armed forces can engage in more limited forms of aggression against India? Second, when and under what specific conditions do Pakistani authorities contemplate or threaten to use nuclear weapons if deterrence fails? Third, what kinds of nuclear war options are contemplated by Pakistani senior authorities and built in to war plans by Pakistani military officers? Are Pakistani military plans and operational deployments designed to create large-scale preemptive options against Indian command and control or military forces, large-scale countercity attack options designed to maximize civilian casualties, or more limited nuclear options against Indian conventional forces in an effort to control escalation?

Nuclear Deterrence and War in Kashmir

A key concern after the 1998 tests was whether the possession of nuclear weapons in both India and Pakistan would encourage Pakistani leaders to believe that they could support limited military operations by Pakistani armed forces or Jihadi fighters in Kashmir with reduced fears of Indian military response against Pakistan itself. The evidence is strong that at least some civilian strategists and military officers in Islamabad did indeed think that the nuclear arsenal was a shield behind which aggressive activities in Kashmir could be supported.[17] In March 1999, for example, Shireen Mazari, the director of a leading government-supported think tank in Islamabad, argued that "with the nuclear deterrence making all-out war between Pakistan and India a receding reality, the opportunity for limited warfare in Kashmir becomes a viable option."[18] Many Pakistani officers also argued soon after the nuclear tests that they believed that Pakistan's nuclear capability increased the ability of the government in Islamabad to provide direct military support for the Kashmiri insurgency.[19] The result of such beliefs has often been called "the stability/instability paradox": strategic stability at the nuclear level provides incentives to use conventional forces because of a perception that there is reduced danger of escalation. Yet as S. Paul Kapur has shown, this phenomenon might be better described in South Asia as "the instability/instability paradox," for the belief in Islamabad that Indian and American leaders fear that the balance is unstable—that is, a conventional conflict could easily escalate to nuclear war—apparently encouraged some Pakistani leaders to plan and initiate offensive military operations into Indian-controlled Kashmir.[20]

How precisely did Pakistan's emerging nuclear capability and doctrine influence its behavior in Kargil? Before the crisis, when he was still chief of army staff, Pervez Musharraf stressed the deterrence role of Pakistani nuclear forces but still maintained that conventional war was possible under the nuclear shadow. Musharraf explicitly told the graduating class at the Pakistan Military Academy in April 1999:

> Our efforts to acquire a viable defensive force both in the conventional and also, by the grace of Allah in the nuclear and missile mode is to guarantee peace and security through potent deterrence. . . . This, however, does not

mean that conventional war has become obsolete. In fact conventional war will still remain the mode of conflict in any future conflagration with our traditional enemy.[21]

It is perhaps noteworthy that Musharraf did not claim that Pakistani nuclear weapons provided a shield behind which the Pakistani military could provide indirect or direct military assistance to the Kashmiri insurgency. Such a belief would be unlikely to be stated publicly even if it was held privately, since the Pakistani government has claimed that the insurgency is purely an indigenous phenomenon and that Islamabad's support is only political, not military, in nature. It therefore may also be more noteworthy that Musharraf acknowledged that nuclear weapons could in principle encourage, rather than inhibit, aggression at lower levels of conflict, albeit in a speech in which he accused Indian leaders of holding such beliefs. According to Brigadier (ret.) A. R. Siddiqi, in April 1999, Musharraf told a group of officers that after the nuclear tests there was a "looming threat of low-level-conflict from India. They (Indians) would want to splinter Pakistan not through direct approach, but through low intensity conflict within Pakistan."[22] Given that this statement was made after Pakistani Northern Infantry Light forces had secretly crossed into Indian-held Kashmir, leading to the Kargil War, Musharraf may well have been "projecting" or "mirror-imaging" his own beliefs onto Indian leaders in New Delhi.

The 1999 Kargil War provides strong evidence supporting the idea, rooted in organization theory, that Pakistani military leaders hold different views than do civilian leaders about the effect of nuclear weapons on the Pakistani-Indian rivalry. First, it is important to note that civilian authorities were not involved in the decision to send Pakistani armed forces, disguised as mujahideen, across the Line of Control into Indian-held Kashmir. The decision was made by a small number of senior Pakistan Army officers, including General Pervez Musharraf, who initially kept the operation secret from senior civilian leaders.[23] Indeed, the initial incursion was kept secret, not only from Prime Minister Sharif but also from the leadership of the Pakistan Air Force, who would later be called on to help defend Pakistani territory and its forces from India's response to the incursion. The result, according to Air Commodore Kaiser Tufail, then Pakistan Air Force director of operations, was that there was "a failure to grasp the wider military and diplomatic ramifications of a limited tactical operation that had the potential of creating major strategic effects."[24] In short, the military officers who believed that nuclear weapons protected Pakistan from a potential Indian reprisal never had their views challenged before launching the Kargil operation. Indeed, according to Owen Bennett Jones, the Pakistan Army leadership failed to inform Prime Minister Nawaz Sharif at a meeting in February 1999 that Pakistani military units were already crossing the Line of Control when they sought and received his permission merely to "increase the heat" in Kashmir:

> Two eyewitnesses at this meeting have claimed that even at this stage (when the military intervention was already well underway) there was no mention of troops crossing the line of control. According to their version, while there was talk of increasing the level of militant activity in Kashmir, the discussion was framed entirely in terms of the insurgency. The army stated its fear that the resistance movement could die out. It argued that if the Lahore process was to bear fruit then the Indians must be made to believe that the pressure in Kashmir would not go away. The army failed to disclose the role of the Northern Light Infantry and did not identify Kargil as a military objective. It is widely agreed, however, that at this meeting the army secured Sharif's agreement to "increase the heat" in Kashmir.[25]

Second, it is important to note that senior military officers continued to hold the belief during the resulting conflict that Pakistan's nuclear capability would deter India from responding by crossing into Pakistani-held territory, a belief that contrasted with that of civilian leaders, who feared that such an Indian attack was likely and would lead to nuclear escalation. For example, at the height of the conflict, Pakistan Army leaders stated that "there is almost a red alert situation," but they nevertheless insisted "there is no chance of the Kargil conflict leading to a full-fledged war between the two sides."[26] This statement leaked to the press apparently reflected what the Pakistan Army was privately advising the government and helps explain why the senior army officers opposed the withdrawal of the Pakistani forces from Indian-held territory. According to then Chief of Army Staff Pervez Musharraf, he briefed the prime minister several times during the war that Pakistan was in an advantageous military position and that India was "in no position to launch an all-out offensive on land, at sea, or in the air."[27] This contrasts sharply, however, with Prime Minister Sharif's statement during the crisis that he was "trying to avoid nuclear war" and his suggestion that he feared "that India was getting ready to launch a full-scale military operation against Pakistan."[28] Sharif later told reporters: "I knew nothing about Kargil until after the soldiers marched over the line of control. Then, when our soldiers were in place, I had to accept that we were at war and of course we understood that everyone was now worried that things could go nuclear very easily."[29]

Third, it should be noted that after the October 1999 coup, the Pakistani military government continued to argue that Nawaz Sharif had lost courage and backed down unnecessarily during the Kargil conflict. The "stab in the back" thesis contends that the Indians would never have attacked Pakistan directly. As Pervez Musharraf wrote in his memoirs, "[T]he military assets committed by the Indians in the Kargil conflict in particular and in Kashmir in general brought about a near parity of forces both in the air and on the ground along the international border. This nearly ruled out the possibility of India's deciding on an all-out war."[30]

Fourth, there is also evidence that the Pakistan Army may have initiated nuclear-alerting operations, without civilian knowledge or involvement, during the Kargil War.[31] Senior Pakistani political authorities did make thinly veiled nuclear threats during the crisis, suggesting that nuclear weapons might be used precisely if Indian forces crossed into Pakistan. Foreign Secretary Shamshad Ahmad, for example, proclaimed in May that Pakistan "will not hesitate to use any weapon in our arsenal to defend our territorial integrity."[32] But there is no evidence that civilians were involved in any operational decisions concerning the alert levels or deployments of nuclear weapons or nuclear-capable missiles during Kargil. Indeed, only after Prime Minister Sharif flew to the United States to meet with President Clinton to find a way to end the crisis did he apparently learn that the Pakistani military had initiated operations that appeared (at least to the U.S. and Indian intelligence agencies) to be preparations for potential nuclear weapons use. As Strobe Talbott wrote:

> [A]dding to the danger was evidence that Sharif neither knew everything his military high command was doing nor had complete control over it. When Clinton asked him if he understood how far along his military was in preparing nuclear armed missiles for possible use in a war against India, Sharif acted as though he was genuinely surprised. Sharif seemed taken aback and said only that India was probably doing the same.[33]

The Indians, also having received intelligence about the Pakistanis' preparation of nuclear-armed missiles, took similar action with their own arsenals. General V. P. Malik, the Indian chief of army staff during Kargil, has con-

firmed both that Indian intelligence picked up signs of missile-alert preparations and that the Indians were concerned enough to respond by alerting
some of their own missile assets:

> There is no doubt that the Pakistani political leaders, including Nawaz Sharif
> and the foreign secretary, Shamshad Ahmad, had been making provocative
> public statements about using nuclear weapons. . . . [We] had no specific
> reports that the Pakistan Army was readying its nuclear arsenal. . . . However,
> in view of intelligence reports about the Tilla Ranges being readied for
> possible launching of missiles and repeated statements being made by their
> political leaders and non-military senior officials, we considered it prudent to
> take some protective measures. Accordingly, some of our missile assets were
> dispersed and relocated.[34]

The Pakistani missile-alerting activity remains shrouded in mystery. Were
the Pakistanis signaling to the United States and India that the crisis was
worsening and might get out of control? Were the Pakistani military taking
defensive actions to reduce the vulnerability of their missile assets, preparing
the nuclear-capable missiles for offensive use, or simply engaging in routine
missile-testing preparations?[35] We do not know. Nevertheless, the mysterious
operations in Pakistan were exceedingly important, for they led to Kargil being South Asia's first confirmed nuclear crisis, and not just a conventional war,
as the Indian military responded to ambiguous Pakistan nuclear activities
with missile-alert and deployment operations of their own.

This interpretation of nuclear doctrine and organizational interests during the 1999 Kargil conflict leads to a more pessimistic prediction about future
crises than is common in the literature. Neil Joeck, for example, has argued
that the Kargil conflict was, borrowing Thomas Schelling's phrase, "a competition in risk-taking" in which the Pakistani government deliberately took
military actions to raise the risk of inadvertent nuclear escalation in order
to achieve its aims in the Kashmir crisis.[36] India and Pakistan were like two
drivers aiming their cars toward each other in a dangerous "game of chicken,"
with the first to swerve losing the contest. That is an insightful metaphor, but
it is important to recognize that a single driver was not in control of the Pakistani automobile in the Kargil game of chicken. Instead, it appears that one
leader was pressing the accelerator, another pushing on the brakes, and both
tugging at the steering wheel. This was hardly a recipe for careful management of nuclear crises in South Asia.

Limited Nuclear Options in Pakistani Doctrine

Pakistani military views on the appropriate uses of nuclear weapons were subsequently outlined in a detailed description of Pakistani nuclear doctrine given by Lieutenant General Khalid Kidwai in late 2001. Kidwai, the head of the Strategic Plans Division, which is responsible for nuclear plans as well as command and control and the physical security of the arsenal, maintained that nuclear weapons would be used only "if the very existence of Pakistan as a state is at stake." He then went on, however, to describe a range of conditions that would be covered by such a doctrine: "Nuclear weapons are aimed solely at India. In case that deterrence fails, they will be used if: a) India attacks Pakistan and conquers a large part of its territory (space threshold); b) India destroys a large part either of its land or air forces (military threshold); c) India proceeds to the economic strangling of Pakistan (economic strangling); and d) India pushes Pakistan into political destabilization or creates a large scale internal subversion in Pakistan (domestic destabilization)."[37] Although the credibility of this final nuclear threat might be considered to be low, it nevertheless demonstrates both that senior Pakistani military planners contemplate nuclear weapons use in contingencies other than a massive Indian conventional attack and that they recognize, at least in theory, that one state's support for "large scale internal subversion" of its neighbor might be encouraged by the presence of nuclear weapons in the region.

The identification of different thresholds for the use of nuclear weapons is an important issue, for it raises the question of what limited options, if any, for the use of nuclear weapons have been created by the Pakistani military. Very little public information is available, however, to determine whether Pakistani military planners have crafted such limited nuclear war options, planning to use nuclear weapons on their own soil in an effort to end the war and reduce the risk of further escalation in the event of an Indian conventional attack on Pakistan. The strategic logic of Pakistan's weaker conventional balance and subsequent first-use doctrine would lead one to predict that limited nuclear options exist both to provide a more credible deterrent threat against Indian conventional operations and to provide less than massive, and some would say suicidal, options to the Pakistani leadership in the event of a major conventional war Pakistan is losing. One small piece of evidence in favor of the limited options argument comes from a 2001 interview with Lieutenant General Kidwai, in which he explicitly maintained that "there are options available in the nuclear response."[38]

That statement by the senior officer in charge of Pakistani nuclear plans and operations is countered, however, by the writings of his former deputy, Brigadier (ret.) Feroz Hassan Khan. Khan has suggested that the Pakistani military would be reluctant to use nuclear weapons in a highly limited manner, such as a demonstration shot, as that option would be seen "as a confirmation of weakness" and would pass the military initiative over to New Delhi.[39] This observation fits more closely with the predictions of both organizational theory and strategic culture, since military officers in general so highly value the principle of the initiative and favor decisive uses of force, and Muslim officers may be particularly culturally sensitive to concerns about weakness and face.

Since no official statement outlining Pakistani nuclear doctrine is available, we do not know whether limited nuclear options exist or whether there are strong proclivities in favor of or against using such options in a crisis or conventional war. Organization theory and the history of American nuclear doctrine, however, suggest that the professional military will resist limited options because they are more likely to favor massive attacks that retain the initiative and minimize the complexity of operational plans and command and control procedures. This logic suggests that even if limited nuclear first-use options do exist in Pakistan's operational plans, Pakistani military leaders, without the counterweight of civilian political authorities, would be more likely to favor larger-scale uses of their nuclear arsenal against a full array of Indian conventional forces, nuclear forces, and command and control targets. Indian government claims that it would respond to any first use of nuclear weapons with a massive retaliation would further encourage Pakistani military proclivities to plan for such major preemptive counterforce nuclear attacks.

It is important here to note that the early exposure of the Pakistan military to U.S. nuclear doctrine from the 1950s and early 1960s may have shaped the way military planners in Rawalpindi perceive first-use doctrines and limited options. Stephen Cohen, for example, has argued: "Present-day Pakistani nuclear planning and doctrine . . . very much resemble American thinking of the mid-1950s with its acceptance of first-use and the tactical use of nuclear weapons against onrushing conventional forces."[40] Unclassified Pakistani military publications do include discussions of scenarios in which Islamabad orders tactical nuclear weapons to be used as warning shots, nuclear tests to be used as a signal of resolve, or a single weapon to be used against invading Indian armored divisions.[41]

If these military publications reflect actual war-planning assumptions, it may be the case that organizational learning from the United States has over-come the Pakistani military's cultural and organizational disposition against limited nuclear options. That could be a positive impact of organizational learning. It is important to note, however, that Pakistani officers' exposure to U.S. military thinking on nuclear use in the 1950s and 1960s could also lead them to prefer large-scale preemptive attacks at the strategic level and predelegation of nuclear-release authority to lower-level commanders in the field. Although U.S. military planners did develop plans to use tactical nuclear weapons first in Western Europe, they also maintained massive preemptive strike options against the Soviet Union and resisted efforts to develop limited nuclear options and a "flexible response" doctrine in the 1960s.[42]

Finally, it is possible that Pakistani military planners focus on massive large-scale first-use nuclear options against Indian cities following an extreme form of the "last-resort" logic suggested by Musharraf in at least some of his public statements. This preference for large-scale attacks, rather than using nuclear weapons in a limited manner to try to create a stalemate termination of a conventional war, is most strongly seen in the May 2002 declaration of a Pakistani cabinet member, Lieutenant General Javid Ashraf Qazi, the former chief of the Inter-Services Intelligence agency (ISI), who declared during the crisis with India that "if Pakistan is being destroyed through conventional means, we will destroy them by using the nuclear option as they say if I am going down the ditch, I will also take my enemy with me."[43] This is the logic of nuclear retribution, not war fighting or war termination.

Influences of Military Biases and Strategic Culture

Even if Pakistan's strategic position dictates the maintenance of some degree of ambiguity in its first-use nuclear doctrine, common professional military biases, and to a lesser degree Pakistan's strategic culture, can be seen to im-pact doctrine in a number of subtle ways. First, there is a widespread shared belief in Pakistan that its development of the bomb represents a proud na-tional achievement and subsequently a tendency to place excessive impor-tance on nuclear weapons as a solution to Pakistani strategic vulnerabilities. At a popular level, this phenomenon is seen in both the veneration given to Pakistani scientists who developed the arsenal and in the placement of mon-uments to the Chagai Mountains test site in prominent locations in major Pakistani cities. At a leadership level, however, the glorification of the nuclear arsenal can be seen in claims by former Islamabad officials that Pakistan's nuclear forces have deterred India from attacking Pakistan in 1984–1985, during the Brasstacks crisis of 1986–1987, in the 1990 crisis over Kashmir, just before the 1998 nuclear tests, during the 1999 Kargil War, and in the 2001–2002 crisis.[44] My point is not that Indian fear of escalation had no influence on New Delhi's behavior but that Pakistani officials often too readily give all the credit to nuclear weapons for preventing a war between India and Pakistan. It is striking, for example, to note how rare it is for Pakistani military officers, even when retired, to downplay the role of Pakistani nuclear threats during past crises with India.

Second, there is strong evidence that Pakistani military leaders suffer from "goal displacement," with nuclear weapons becoming identified with national pride and security to such an extent that official statements confuse ends and means. Senior officials sometimes treat nuclear weapons (euphemistically called "strategic assets") as valued objects to be protected themselves rather than the deterrent that protects the Pakistani people. This kind of goal displacement is seen in then President Musharraf's speech after the September 11, 2001, terrorist attacks.

> The decision we take today can have far-reaching and wide-ranging consequences. The crisis is formidable and unprecedented. If we take wrong decisions in this crisis, it can lead to worst consequences. On the other hand, if we take right decisions, its results will be good. The negative consequences can endanger Pakistan's integrity and solidarity. Our critical concerns, our important concerns can come under threat. When I say critical concerns, I mean *our strategic assets* and the cause of Kashmir. If these come under threat it would be a worse situation for us.[45]

When Musharraf abandoned Pakistan's position supporting the Taliban regime and accepted American overflights and limited uses of bases in Pakistan for the war in Afghanistan, he made a veiled threat, stating that the Pakistan Air Force (though being ambiguous about whether this included nuclear forces) was on alert. He also, however, again argued that Pakistani citizens were ready to defend the nuclear arsenal ("its strategic assets") rather than those strategic assets being ready to defend the Pakistani people:

> If you watch [Indian] television, you will find them dishing out propaganda against Pakistan, day in and day out. I would like to tell India "Lay Off."

Pakistan's armed forces and every Pakistani citizen is ready to offer any sacrifice in order to defend Pakistan and secure its strategic assets. Make no mistake and entertain no misunderstanding. At this very moment our Air Force is at high alert; and they are ready for "do or die" missions. My countrymen! In such a situation, a wrong decision can lead to unbearable losses.[46]

In December 2003, Musharraf again reified the nuclear arsenal, making it the object and not the tool of national security policy, claiming that "there is no pressure whatsoever on me to roll back the nuclear and missile programme, we are not rolling back, there is no question, *these are our national interests and only a traitor would think of rolling back.*"[47]

A third example is Musharraf's February 5, 2004, speech to the Pakistani people in which he once again treated the nuclear arsenal as the vital interest to protect rather than the means to protect the Pakistani people:

We have two national vital interests, our nuclear programme—being a nuclear state and the Kashmir cause is our national vital interests. No leader can go back on these two. There is no compromise on this. Kashmir needs an honourable solution. And there will be no roll back ever. I am a soldier, I have taken oath of defending this country. I have fought wars for defending the country. Besides wars fought skirmishes. I have seen death very closely, not once but six times. We are not one of the cowards. *We will put our lives at stake for these strategic assets.* So we are not those who would roll back and we are not those who deceive the country and the nation just for nothing.[48]

These kinds of statements, in which the weapons themselves are venerated objects of value, should not be dismissed as mere rhetorical flourishes; they reflect a common organizational tendency to place excessive value on means rather than the ends of national policy. The attachment to the arsenal appears to go well beyond the strategic logic of deterrence and stability inside the Pakistani military leadership.

One must be careful, however, when assessing the effects of strategic culture in Pakistan. Stephen Cohen has argued that Pakistani strategic culture has a strong impact on its nuclear doctrine: Koranic passages—such as Allah's statement that "I will instill terror into the hearts of the Unbelievers"—are used by Pakistani military officers to justify supporting Jihadi terrorists in Kashmir and targeting Indian noncombatants with nuclear weapons aimed at urban-industrial areas.[49] I find this particular cultural argument to be unpersuasive.

After all, military officers and political authorities in many non-Islamic countries have also found it convenient to support terrorism when it has been perceived to serve the national security interests of the state, and senior officers in all nuclear weapons states, not just Pakistan, have been able to justify counter-city targeting for the sake of deterrence.

Yet there are more subtle ways in which Islamic beliefs and myths about the "martial races" passed down from the colonial period can interact to shape Pakistani strategic culture and to influence nuclear doctrine today. Islam stresses the power of faith over material strength. President Zia-ul-Haq institutionalized this belief through training in military academies throughout Pakistan; and as Brigadier (ret.) Feroz Khan has noted, "[T]he injunction of faith as a force-multiplier and the belief that superior training and faith will compensate against the otherwise larger and materially superior foe—India—was ingrained."[50] Musharraf's May 2002 injunctions, cited previously, about how the morale and determination of Pakistan's "numerically inferior forces" can "create another chapter full of glory and valour,"[51] can be interpreted as one modern manifestation of this tendency. In his December 2002 speech, Musharraf also stressed that Pakistani military virtues were critical to preventing war: "There is a misconception in the minds of some that this very threat was surmounted owing to someone's help or participation. I want to tell you all today that for facing threats no one comes to anyone's help. It is because of our own strength, morale, 'eman' (faith), determination that we surmounted this threat."[52] Pakistani officials' constant claims that Pakistani nuclear first-use threats are credible—even in response to such potential Indian actions as "economic strangulation" or "political destabilization"—similarly could be a result of this emphasis on determination and faith in military affairs.

Finally, underestimation of the morale and fighting prowess of Indian military forces because they are primarily made up of Hindus has been a constant theme in Pakistani writings about their own military history.[53] General Ayub Khan, to give one prominent example, wrote to his foreign minister and army commander prior to instigating the 1965 war: "As a general rule Hindu morale would not stand more than a couple of hard blows at the right time and place."[54] Leo Rose and Richard Sisson demonstrate that similar cultural blinders influenced Pakistani decision making in the 1971 war with India. Pakistani military planning, they argue, "was bolstered by a firm conviction, held even through the end of the December war, that it was impossible for Pakistan to lose a war to India. . . . The belief was also commonly held that 'Muslims had never been defeated by the Hindus.'"[55] In the middle of the conflict, for example, General A. A. K. Niazii confidently proclaimed that Pakistani soldiers "will take the war onto Indian soil to finally crush the very spirit of nonbelievers through the supreme force of Islam."[56]

I have found no evidence, however, that senior Pakistani political or military leaders have made similar biased statements during the post-1998 nuclear crises with India. It is certainly possible that such cultural discounting continues to exist at lower levels inside the armed forces. But the lack of statements of that sort by current senior Pakistani military officers suggests that at least some cautionary organizational learning has occurred because of their military failures in past wars with India.

THE 2001–2002 CRISIS: RED LINES AND LAST RESORT

During the 2001–2002 crisis between Pakistan and India, both governments were speaking to multiple audiences when making statements about their nuclear arsenals. Officials in Islamabad and Delhi issued multiple threats against their South Asian rival and appealed to domestic audiences through tough rhetoric.[57] At the same time, they sought to reassure the international community (and especially Washington) that they were responsible nuclear powers. This created a severe tension for leaders in Islamabad, especially with respect to nuclear first-use policy. On the one hand, they have, or at least had, an interest in signaling to New Delhi that nuclear use might come earlier in a conflict, to deter any form of limited strike or military retaliation by India in response to terrorist attacks or limited incursions into Kashmir by forces based or believed to be based in Pakistan. On the other hand, the Pakistani government wanted to convince the United States and other international actors that it was a responsible nuclear power and would not use nuclear weapons except as a last resort in extreme self-defense. Civilian leaders in New Delhi, in contrast, attempted to signal that the nuclear first-use threshold was high in order to enhance the credibility of its threat to use conventional forces to attack Jihadi camps in Azad Kashmir or to punish the Pakistani military in a conventional, but limited, war. Individual military officers, however, made threats of massive nuclear retaliation that appeared to move beyond what civilian leaders in India had expected or authorized.

The most dramatic example of a senior Indian military officer making unauthorized statements about nuclear weapons came on January 11, 2002, when

Indian armed forces were mobilizing along the Pakistani border. General S. Padmanabhan, the Indian chief of army staff, told a New Delhi press conference that the morale of Indian mobilized forces was high: "If we have to go to war, jolly good. . . . If we don't, we will still manage."[58] Padmanabhan noted that Pakistani leaders had "stated that they will use nuclear weapons first should the necessity arise," insisting, in an apparent reference to Musharraf, that "if he is man enough, correction mad enough . . . he can use it."[59] When asked, then, how India would respond to Pakistani nuclear use, Padmanabhan replied: "If anyone uses nuclear weapons against India, Indian forces, Indian assets at sea, Indian economic or human interests, the perpetrators of that particular outrage will be punished so severely that their continuation in any fray will be in doubt. . . . Yes, we are ready. Take it from me, we have enough."[60] General Padmanabhan acknowledged that the presence of U.S. military forces inside Pakistan might have "an inhibiting effect" on the Indian armed forces, but then dismissed such constraints in South Asia by concluding that "when two wild bulls fight in the jungle, they carry on regardless."[61]

Government officials quickly told the *New York Times* that Padmanabhan's threats had not been cleared by civilian authorities and the prime minister's office had requested a transcript of the press briefing afterward to find out what had been said.[62] On January 12, Defense Minister George Fernandes issued an unusual written press release stating, "The Government had not been talking of nuclear weapons. I wish everyone gives up this talk of nuclear weapons being brought into play. The use of nuclear weapons is far too serious a matter that it should be bandied about in a cavalier manner."[63]

Later in the crisis, President Musharraf similarly sought to minimize the saber-rattling threats implying that nuclear war might be on the horizon by stating that nuclear use would only be "a last resort" for Pakistan. On April 7, for example, he told the German news magazine *Der Spiegel*:

> For us, the use of nuclear weapons is an utterly last resort. We conduct ourselves responsibly. And I am optimistic and confident enough to believe that we could defend ourselves with conventional forces, even though India, in its attempt to become a great power, buys the most modern weapons. We would consider the nuclear option only if "all Pakistan were in danger of disappearing from the map." In that case: nuclear weapons too.[64]

Musharraf's domestic opponents quickly criticized this statement, arguing that it weakened deterrence against India.[65] Musharraf himself soon took a more aggressive stance when speaking to domestic audiences, especially military officers. In a May 2002 speech filled with "military logic" and strategic-cultural references, for example, he addressed a group of Pakistan Air Force officers:

> Any incursion by the Indian forces across the LoC even by an inch will unleash a storm that will sweep the enemy. . . . Victory comes through offensive strategy and our forces are ready for it if war is thrust on Pakistan by India. . . . Military history is full of examples where numerically inferior forces defeated the larger numbers; and in our own history, the PAF has displayed outstanding performances against IAF which has been a much bigger air force. . . . Seeing the glimmer in the eyes of all pilots and airmen I met, I am fully confident that Insha'Allah (God willing), the PAF will give a befitting response to any adventurism by India and create yet another chapter full of glory and valour in the history.[66]

After the crisis, on December 30, 2002, Musharraf again backed away from the "last-resort" formulation in a speech at a Pakistan Air Force function in Karachi in which he claimed, "We were prepared to take severe action. We have defeated the enemy without going to war."[67] His statement, according to quotations printed in some Pakistani press reports, implied a much lower threshold for Pakistani nuclear response: "In my meetings with various world leaders, I conveyed my personal message to Indian Prime Minister Vajpayee that the moment Indian forces cross the Line of Control and the international border, then they should not expect a conventional war from Pakistan."[68] Another Pakistani paper quoted Musharraf as saying: "[I]f Indian troops moved just a single step across the international border or the Line of Control, then *Inshallah* ('By the Will of God') the Pakistani Army and supporters of Pakistan would surround the Indian Army and it would not be a conventional war."[69]

Indian papers widely interpreted this statement as an oblique nuclear threat, and New Delhi officials protested against what they called "nuclear blackmail."[70] A Pakistani government spokesman stated the next day, however, that Musharraf had been misquoted and that what he had really said was that "[i]f India tries to cross the LOC or international border, Pakistan's conventional forces as well as supporters of Pakistan, whether they be Kashmiri people or people of Pakistan, would engulf and encircle the Indian armed forces."[71] Nevertheless, Indian defense minister George Fernandes called

Musharraf's statement "irresponsible" and added that "we can take a bomb or two or more . . . but when we respond, there will be no Pakistan."[72] Musharraf himself then stepped into the fray, stating that he had been misquoted for "malicious" reasons by the Indian press: "The President stated that he was in fact talking in context of Kashmir and had said that if any one tried to cross the Line of Control (LoC), then there would be guerrilla warfare. He said there was a freedom struggle in the Indian Held Kashmir and if they (India) tried to cross the LoC there were 150,000 retired military personnel in AJK who would have surrounded any invading enemy troops."[73]

It is difficult to avoid the impression that Musharraf wanted two different audiences to hold contrasting perceptions of when Pakistan might resort to nuclear weapons use. He had a diplomatic interest to signal the United States and the international community that he would use nuclear weapons only as a last resort if an Indian conventional attack threatened a complete defeat of Pakistani forces. He also had an interest to signal domestic audiences and the Indian government that he just might authorize nuclear use much earlier in a crisis or conventional conflict. Given the multiple audiences that President Musharraf had when he made doctrinal statements of this sort, and the resulting ambiguity, it is impossible to know which statements most accurately reflect his personal preferences or existing Pakistani proclivities and operational military contingency plans.

It is similarly difficult to avoid the impression that senior Indian civilian leaders wanted to minimize international perceptions that nuclear weapons might be used if there were a war between India and Pakistan over Islamabad's support for terrorist organizations inside India. At the same time, however, Indian military officers, such as Padmanabhan, could not resist going further than authorized when describing nuclear retaliation in a manner that was seen as "cavalier." Domestic politicians also were certainly not reluctant to threaten Pakistan with complete destruction if the crisis escalated to a nuclear war. BJP president Jana Krishamoorthy, for example, stated that if Pakistan used a nuclear weapon, "its existence itself would be wiped off the world map."[74] But Padmanabhan's statement was especially provocative and noteworthy. In short, the central government in New Delhi wanted to keep Indian nuclear weapons in the distant background during the 2002 crisis, but individual actors within the bureaucracy ensured that the shadow of the arsenal was not ignored.

THE EVOLUTION OF INDIAN NUCLEAR DOCTRINE AFTER 2002

In his statement to Parliament on May 27, 1998, explaining his decision to test nuclear weapons, Prime Minister Atal Behari Vajpayee outlined his view of the purpose of India's acquisition of a nuclear arsenal: "Our strengthened capability adds to our sense of responsibility. We do not intend to use these weapons for aggression or for mounting threats against any country; these are weapons of self-defence, to ensure that India is not subjected to nuclear threats or coercion. We do not intend to engage in an arms race."[75] The Vajpayee government proclaimed that India was now a full-fledged nuclear weapons state and maintained that the tests were necessary to protect India's national security, especially against a growing Chinese threat. At the same time, New Delhi officials insisted on a degree of Indian exceptionalism, arguing that Indian nuclear doctrine would be different from doctrines of other nuclear powers. The prime minister soon spelled out the principles behind India's emerging nuclear doctrine in a speech in Parliament in December 1998:

> We have formally announced a policy of No-First-Use and non-use against non-nuclear weapons states. As Hon'ble Members are aware, a policy of no-first-use with a minimum nuclear deterrent, implies deployment of assets in a manner that ensures survivability and capability of an adequate response. We are also not going to enter into an arms race with any Country. Ours will be a minimum credible deterrent, which will safeguard India's security, the security of one-sixth of humanity, now and into the future.[76]

After the nuclear tests, many other Indian officials echoed these themes, emphasizing the continuity of Indian declarations of a no-first-use doctrine, a policy of maintaining only "minimum credible deterrent" forces for retaliation purposes only, and continued Indian commitment to global nuclear disarmament, starting after the other governments' nuclear forces were reduced to the reasonable size of India's minimalist nuclear arsenal.[77] A senior New Delhi official insisted to the press soon after the tests that there is "a defensive orientation for India's nuclear forces and a commitment to avoid a nuclear arms race."[78]

Many scholarly analyses of the emerging Indian nuclear doctrine take such official statements about the continuity of the principles guiding India's "unique" nuclear doctrine at face value. They assume that the statements reflect a unified national view of how best to use nuclear weapons to promote India's national interests. There is, according to these observers, little need to go inside the Indian system to examine who argues what about nuclear weapons and why and little sense of Indian doctrine in transition. Ashley Tellis's 2001 analysis of Indian nuclear policy, for example, argues that the emphasis on no first use is "remarkably pervasive in Indian strategic thought" and the government of India "by all evidence thus far, appears to believe that a global recognition of the country's nuclear capabilities suffices for effective deterrence."[79] Indeed, the personification of the Indian government (and Indian society) as a single rational actor pervades Tellis's analysis, as when he argues that "*India seems satisfied* by the belief that even a ragged nuclear response should deter its adversaries"; or that "*India believes* that sufficiency is ultimately measured by the ability to inflict unacceptable pain on an adversary."[80] Šumit Ganguly and Devon Hagerty similarly argue in their examination of the impact of nuclear weapons in South Asia that "India's evolving nuclear doctrine appears to rest on two pillars": "its pledge never to be the first party in a dispute to resort to the use of nuclear weapons" and a doctrine of "minimum credible deterrence."[81] Even hawkish critics of current Indian nuclear doctrine in New Delhi, such as Bharat Kanard, nonetheless argue that the doctrine adopted by the BJP and Congress governments consistently emphasizes a no-first-use policy and a minimum deterrence posture.[82]

The 2003 Indian Doctrine Shift

This widespread perception of India's nuclear doctrine suggests a degree of continuity and consensus in India's nuclear doctrine since 1998 that is unwarranted. Indeed, a closer look at the evolution of Indian doctrine reveals that it has changed significantly, through contentious debates within the Indian government and between civilian authorities and the official advisory bodies and military organizations that influence doctrinal decisions.[83] Although Indian government officials claimed in January 2003 that there were no major changes in nuclear weapons doctrine, in fact significant shifts in Indian nuclear doctrine were instituted in New Delhi.

In January 2003, the New Delhi government issued its first official statement that outlined in unprecedented detail the principles and goals that would guide Indian operational nuclear doctrine and posture:[84]

    i. Building and maintaining a credible minimum deterrent;

    ii. A posture of "No First Use": nuclear weapons will only be used in retaliation against a nuclear attack on Indian territory or on Indian forces anywhere;

iii. Nuclear retaliation to a first strike will be massive and designed to inflict unacceptable damage;

iv. Nuclear retaliatory attacks can only be authorized by the civilian political leadership through the Nuclear Command Authority;

v. Non-use of nuclear weapons against non-nuclear weapon states;

vi. However, in the event of a major attack against India, or Indian forces anywhere, by biological or chemical weapons, India will retain the option of retaliating with nuclear weapons;

vii. A continuance of strict controls on export of nuclear and missile related materials and technologies, participation in the Fissile Material Cutoff Treaty negotiations, and continued observance of the moratorium on nuclear tests;

viii. Continued commitment to the goal of a nuclear weapon free world, through global, verifiable and non-discriminatory nuclear disarmament.

New Delhi officials later claimed that this official doctrinal statement simply codified long-standing, existing Indian government policy. For example, Defense Minister George Fernandes maintained that "as far as our nuclear doctrine is concerned there is no change. It remains as it was post-1998."[85]

In fact, the January 2003 official statement on Indian nuclear doctrine signaled that five significant shifts in nuclear doctrine were being implemented. First, it enshrined for the first time an official shift away from the traditional interpretation of a minimum deterrent posture to a more flexible doctrine, advocating a "*credible* minimum deterrent." The significance of this change should not be overlooked. A strict minimum deterrent posture—often called a "finite deterrent posture"—calls for building only a limited number of nuclear weapons and targeting them against an adversary's cities. Provided these weapons are invulnerable to an enemy's first strike, there is no need, under this doctrine, to respond to an adversary's arms buildup with any increases in arsenal size of one's own.[86] Prior to the Pokhran tests, many Indian strategic thinkers and Western analysts had advocated and predicted that New Delhi would follow "a third way" in nuclear policy, maintaining only such a minimum deterrent, or even a "recessed deterrent," rather than testing and deploying nuclear weapons and setting arsenal requirements based at least in part on the size of the Pakistani and Chinese nuclear arsenals.[87]

Despite the repeated insistence that the New Delhi government does not intend to enter into an arms race with either Islamabad or Beijing, by 2003 senior Indian officials clearly stated that "credible" deterrent forces must take into account the arsenal size and posture of both of India's nuclear neighbors. Indeed, in May 2003 the Vajpayee government rejected diplomatic overtures by Pakistan to explore a nuclear-free zone in South Asia, noting that "we have to keep in mind developments in other neighboring countries as well": "Pakistan's atomic program is India-specific. But India's nuclear program is not Pakistan-specific."[88] In July 2005, Vajpayee similarly argued that "though we believe in a minimum credible deterrent, the size of the deterrent must be determined from time to time on the basis of our own threat perception. This is a judgment which cannot be surrendered to anyone else."[89] The 2003 doctrinal statement thus codifies the idea that India has nuclear weapons requirements beyond those needed simply to destroy a minimum number of Pakistani or Chinese cities, though it does not specify what alternative targets or alternative requirements might be involved.

Second, in contrast to the 1998 claims that India would follow a strict nuclear no-first-use policy, official and unofficial government statements afterward demonstrate that there was serious internal debate about no first use, leading to a number of conditions having been added to this pledge. For example, the 1999 Indian Draft Nuclear Doctrine, prepared by the newly created National Security Advisory Board (NSAB), recommended a caveat that permitted first use of nuclear weapons against nonnuclear states allied to a nuclear power: "India will not resort to the use or threat of use of nuclear weapons against states which do not possess nuclear weapons, *or are not aligned with nuclear weapons powers*."[90] This subtle alteration of traditional Indian doctrine is a close copy of the U.S. and NATO negative security assurances from the 1980s that were repeatedly given to the nonnuclear weapons state parties to the NPT and that included the same exception clause (the so-called Warsaw Pact exception) to permit targeting the Soviet Union's forces and the Soviet allies' forces and cities in the event of a major war in Europe.[91] The recommended policy change appears to be the result of copying doctrine of the United States and other nuclear weapons powers, rather than the result of direct threats of attack by nonnuclear states on India, since it is very difficult to imagine plausible scenarios in which nonnuclear states near India would go to war against India in conjunction with Pakistan or China (or the other nuclear states—the United States, Russia, Israel, the UK, and France).

The 2003 official doctrine statement kept only the first half of this recommendation (the declaration of "non-use of nuclear weapons against

non-nuclear weapon states"), and the government claimed that this recommendation made official Indian nuclear policy in this regard stricter than
the pledges given by the NPT-"recognized" nuclear states at various NPT review conferences. Indeed, Foreign Minister Jaswant Singh later argued that
India had taken "a conceptual leap by publicly limiting its intentions through
the voluntary declaration of 'no first use,' also 'non use against non-nuclear
states.' This, in fact, is far more than any of the N5 [the five NPT-recognized
nuclear weapons states] have ever promised either to their potential opponents, to friends, or to the global community."[92] This is puzzling. An explicit
promise not to use nuclear weapons against nonnuclear states is redundant
for any government that has already made a no-first-use commitment, and
the Indian government's 2003 declaration is also contradicted immediately
by the subsequent statement that India "retains the right of retaliating with
nuclear weapons" against any state that uses chemical or biological weapons.
Thus, while the "non-use against non-nuclear weapon states" pledge is similar to the U.S. negative security assurances, it also appears to be designed to
advertise India's image as an "exceptional and responsible nuclear power" to
itself and to the United States and other foreign powers.

A third important change in New Delhi's nuclear doctrine in January 2003
was the explicit threat of Indian nuclear first use in response to biological or
chemical weapons use. This was not anticipated or supported by all members
of the first NSAB, whose 1999 recommendations fed into the government decision-making process. For example, K. Subrahmanyam, the NSAB chairman,
called for "a totally uncaveated policy, with no reservation whatsoever about
no-first-use."[93] Jasjit Singh, a member of the NSAB in 1999, similarly argued
that the draft doctrine was a sign of Indian exceptionalism in adopting a strict
no-first-use doctrine, explicitly ruling out threats to counter biological and
chemical weapons:

> *The doctrine does not adopt the conventional wisdom of other nuclear weapon
> states.* To that extent this is not only in contrast to the acknowledged wisdom
> of the main nuclear powers but seeks to chart a new path. . . . Unlike most
> other nuclear weapon states, India's nuclear weapons are *not* meant to deter the
> use and threat of use of conventional weapons, chemical weapons, biological
> weapons or a generalized formulation of protecting national interests any
> time anywhere.[94]

Although the 2003 doctrine claimed to maintain India's no-first-use doctrine, this new clause clearly demonstrated that those advocating a strict interpretation of no first use had lost the internal debate. How can one explain the adoption of this important change in India's official nuclear doctrine?[95] Evidence again suggests that the "innovation" is the result of copying the United States. Indeed, in December 2002, the NSAB—the "engine of isomorphism" that encouraged mimicking U.S. doctrine statements—reportedly recommended a complete abandonment of no first use by the Indian government.[96] Their rationale reportedly focused directly on the perceived need for India to follow in the doctrinal footsteps of the other nuclear weapons states: "India must consider withdrawing from this [NFU] commitment as the other nuclear weapons-states have not accepted this policy."[97] An unidentified member of the NSAB was quoted in the press making a similar argument tying Indian policy to that of the P-5 nuclear powers: "All five nuclear weapon states . . . reserve the right to launch nuclear weapons first. Then why should India not do so?"[98]

It is unclear whether this official movement away from a strict no-first-use doctrine is a sign that further caveats are likely to be added in the future, leading to an abandonment of the no-first-use doctrine altogether. Clearly, there is a significant degree of ad hoc political adjustment in doctrine development in New Delhi rather than a clear central government long-term plan to change doctrine. It is likely, nonetheless, that if such major changes in nuclear doctrine are adopted, the New Delhi government will continue to use the label of "no first use" because of its political benefits. Ganguly and Hagerty maintain that today "India's 'no-first-use' pledge is mainly a rhetorical device aimed at making its peacetime nuclear stance appear unthreatening to its potential adversaries."[99] I agree and would add that continued statements about no first use, even when accompanied by caveats and conditions, also provide at least some reassurance to international allies and to Indian domestic audiences, who might not object to New Delhi's policies regarding its nuclear arsenal provided they believe that India is behaving as a "responsible nuclear power." In short, the no-first-use doctrine has become part of the politics of nuclear legitimacy and responsibility in India.

What is clear is that a number of Indian government officials and military officers agreed with the 2002 National Security Board recommendation to abandon no first use and have privately advocated precisely such a policy shift. Press reports have quoted officials from the Indian Ministry of Defense, for example, claiming that a doctrine of no first use does not constrain India's options during a conflict: "Even a unilateral no first use declaration by India will not take away our fundamental right to defend ourselves by all means at our disposal if our very survival is in jeopardy."[100] It is also noteworthy that an Indian Air Force planning study, *Vision 2020*, reportedly advocated creation of an Indian nuclear "first strike capability" in the future.[101] The resulting uncertainty about the future was well reflected by an Indian foreign ministry official who made this statement to a reporter:

> "No first strike" policy does not mean India will not have a first strike capability. The foundations of the policy of deterrence, of which the Nuclear Air Command will be the key component, is based on having overwhelming superiority over the enemy to launch nuclear strikes. I would say that we (India) are working towards having a first strike capability, but how to exercise this option within the "no first strike" policy will be the subject of political decision-making.[102]

The fourth detail of the 2003 Indian nuclear doctrine that makes it less purely defensive in nature than claimed is its statement that "nuclear weapons will only be used in retaliation against a nuclear attack on Indian territory *or on Indian forces anywhere*." This statement closely followed the 1999 draft nuclear doctrine, with the addition of the word *anywhere* at the end of the sentence, apparently to underscore the possibility that Indian troops could be fighting a conventional war inside Pakistan. Although such a doctrine is still, technically, a no-first-use policy, it conceives of Indian nuclear weapons serving as a shield behind which Indian conventional forces could be engaged in an offensive conventional attack inside Pakistan. The statement is clearly designed to counter the Pakistani threat of using nuclear weapons first inside Pakistan against Indian armored divisions threatening to defeat the Pakistan Army.[103] Yet it is difficult to see how this policy fits with Prime Minister Vajpayee's 1998 claim (cited earlier) that "[w]e do not intend to use these weapons for aggression or for mounting threats against any country."

A final doctrinal debate in New Delhi about changing nuclear doctrine is not represented in the 2003 official statement but is nevertheless worth noting: public discussions of Indian initiation of preventive or preemptive war against Pakistan. In this regard, senior Indian government officials were again clearly influenced by the U.S. government's declaration of the perceived need and legitimacy of what it labeled a preemption doctrine, prior to the American invasion of Iraq in March 2003. Following the U.S. invasion of Iraq, Indian foreign minister Yashwant Sinha claimed that his country reserved the right to use force against Pakistan, stating: "There were three reasons which drove the Anglo-US forces to attack Iraq; possession of weapons of mass destruction, export of terrorism and an absence of democracy all of which exist in Pakistan."[104] Indian defense minister George Fernandes originally endorsed Sinha's argument, stating that "there are enough reasons to launch such strikes against Pakistan," but then backed away, saying that Sinha's comment was "essentially a casual statement and not any policy decision of the government or a considered view."[105] There have been no public discussions of nuclear preemption in India, unlike in the United States, in which the issue was reportedly raised during the Bush administration's internal debates in 2006 about how to prepare for possible military attacks against Iran, leading President Bush to declare that "all options are on the table."[106] Yet it is a noteworthy change in Indian strategic debates that senior Indian politicians could hint—after years of statements about defensive doctrines, no first use, and principles of nonaggression—that an Indian preemptive attack against Pakistan could be justified.

Arms Races and Doctrine

Indian governments, both Congress- and BJP-led coalitions, repeatedly profess their intent to avoid the kind of expansive and expensive arms races that occurred between the United States and the Soviet Union during the Cold War. There is no reason to doubt the sincerity of such statements. Yet the flexibility inherent in the doctrine of "*credible* minimum deterrence," coupled with the new Indian doctrine calling for nuclear attack options in response to chemical or biological weapons use, or in response to a limited nuclear strike by Pakistan on Indian Army formations inside Pakistan, inevitably raises questions about whether the future Indian arsenal will expand significantly to meet the new perceived requirements.

Two related kinds of evidence can be cited that suggest the Indian government faces strong internal pressures to increase the size and diversity of its nuclear arsenal in the future. First, Indian senior scientists and military officers occasionally break the silence that surrounds doctrinal decision making inside the "strategic enclave" in India with calls for new nuclear weapons systems that are needed to implement new doctrinal imperatives. P. K. Iyengar, the former head of the Indian Atomic Energy Commission, for example, called for the development of an Indian neutron bomb in 2000, a weapon that is difficult to justify if India were to maintain a minimum deterrent, no-first-use policy, threatening only massive retaliation against Pakistani cities.[107] Ashley Tellis also notes that "individual components of the Indian Army, Navy, and Air Force have each begun making private representations to the government for their preferred kinds of nuclear weapons on the assumption that such devices ought to be produced to meet various operational needs specific to each service."[108] The shift toward a less strict interpretation of no first use and minimum deterrence provides a doctrinal justification for building a more diverse set and larger arsenal of nuclear weapons.

Second, Indian nuclear scientists and pundits often opposed the proposed U.S.-India nuclear deal in 2006 and 2007, on grounds that the Hyde Act would constrain New Delhi's ability to test nuclear weapons again.[109] Some of this opposition stemmed from concerns about the future reliability of existing Indian nuclear weapons, but much of the Indian opposition cited the need to maintain the option of testing new nuclear weapons if necessary to meet new deterrent requirements in the future. When the Nuclear Suppliers Group (NSG) approved a new policy under which India could receive nuclear technology and uranium from all its members, the restrictions in the Hyde Act became politically irrelevant, since France and Russia could now supply India with nuclear technology and materials in the event of another nuclear test, even if the United States cut off nuclear cooperation. This NSG decision therefore increased the likelihood that India would test nuclear weapons in the future, especially if a BJP-led coalition comes into office. Again, the changes in the 2003 nuclear doctrine, and future potential changes on the horizon, provide further justification for maintaining New Delhi's options regarding nuclear testing of new designs for nuclear weapons and for deploying a larger arsenal in the future.

What is the best explanation for this widespread interest in keeping India's options open with respect to deploying a larger arsenal and testing new nuclear weapons designs in the future? Strategic uncertainty about future force requirements and organizational desire to maximize autonomy are likely to be important to many decision makers in New Delhi. But even on these two issues, I would not ignore the influence of the United States as a role model for Indian strategic thinkers. Raja Menon has noted, for example, that the official adoption of the concept of "a nuclear triad" in Indian nuclear doctrine may not be compatible with nuclear no first use, since Indian Air Force planes are highly vulnerable to any Pakistani large-scale first strike. Instead, Menon argues, "the triad in the USA was the relic of inter-service rivalry" and "the same inter-service rivalry has surfaced in India."[110] With respect to testing, moreover, the NSAB recommended, according to press reports, that India should "resume testing nuclear devices if the US resumes its own nuclear tests."[111] It is highly revealing that for the NSAB the trigger for resumption of nuclear testing was not that China or Pakistan had started to test nuclear weapons—the kind of external threat that realists would focus on—but rather the U.S. resumption of testing.

CONCLUSION: INSIDE NUCLEAR DOCTRINE

Pakistani and Indian nuclear doctrines are both more complex and more malleable than the common portrayals in government statements and scholarly analyses. In Pakistan, the military clearly makes the key decisions on nuclear weapons plans and doctrine on its own, with minimal influence at best from civilians in the government, even when there is a civilian elected government in Islamabad. This was seen most clearly in November 2008, when President Asif Ali Zardari surprised an Indian audience by telling them that Pakistan would institute a nuclear no-first-use policy, essentially reversing traditional Pakistani doctrine. According to press reports, General Ashaq Kiyani, the army chief, immediately called Zardari and told him that Pakistan's nuclear doctrine was "irreversible."[112] Unfortunately, this chapter has also presented arguments and evidence that show how organizational interests and biases influence the Pakistani military's beliefs concerning when and how nuclear weapons should be used against India. Although the evidence is less clear, Pakistani military officers may also hold cultural beliefs about the superiority of Islamic willpower and faith that influence their judgments about coercive bargaining in crises involving nuclear threats. The different branches of the armed services are also likely to have different and often conflicting assessments of deterrence requirements and operational plans in the future, since nuclear policy and plans will impact their services' budgets in peacetime and their importance in any future war with India.

Islamabad officials' statements about nuclear weapons doctrine and specific threats in past crises, however, have clearly been aimed at domestic as well as foreign audiences. This understanding cautions against reading too much into the shifting patterns of such statements. They may represent deliberate signals to diverse audiences and not reflect strategic intentions or core beliefs. Even this brief examination of Pakistani nuclear doctrine, how-ever, suggests that more open and detailed debates about alternative nuclear weapons doctrines in Pakistan might reduce the impact of military biases on decision making in this crucial area. It is quite predictable that Pakistani military officers would develop a nuclear first-use doctrine and contemplate massive response options and preemption, in the absence of civilian policy makers providing a counterweight to military interests and biases. At a mini-mum, therefore, it would be valuable to encourage more civilian expertise on nuclear matters to create a more diverse and detailed debate inside Pakistan about the future roles and missions of nuclear weapons, which would reduce the monopoly of influence that the military has had on doctrinal thinking inside Islamabad and Rawalpindi and could lead to consideration of alterna-tive strategic doctrines.

Shifting government statements about nuclear doctrine in New Delhi and its nuclear signaling in crises have been influenced by debates and di-verse interests of domestic and bureaucratic actors inside India. This chapter has highlighted the changes that were enshrined in the January 2003 Indian nuclear doctrine, but I note in conclusion that these changes in nuclear doc-trine are also subject to further change if new governments come into power in New Delhi or a major shift in the bureaucratic power of the military or nuclear scientists occurs inside India. The evolution of Indian doctrine away from its traditional strict no-first-use policy and minimum deterrent vision has been subtle and is still reversible. But at a minimum, it has opened the door for nuclear weapons to play a larger role in Indian defense policy, with concomitant requirements for a larger nuclear arsenal, in the future.

Some observers in India view these nuclear developments as one more sign of a new "realism" in Indian defense policy.[113] Just before he became foreign minister in the BJP government, for example, Jaswant Singh argued that "whereas India has moved from the totally moralistic to a little more realistic, the rest of the nuclear world has arrived at all of its nuclear conclu-sions entirely realistically."[114] It is deeply ironic, however, that the Indian government has produced a doctrine that is both less defensive in charac-ter and less independent in origin—copying controversial innovations de-veloped in the United States and other nuclear powers—in its effort to be a more "responsible nuclear power" and to add more "realism" to Indian nuclear doctrine.

NOTES

1. The sources of doctrine are discussed in Scott D. Sagan, "The Origins of Military Doctrine and Command and Control Systems," in Peter R. Lavoy, Scott D. Sagan, and James J. Wirtz, eds., *Planning the Unthinkable: How New Powers Will Use Nuclear, Biological, and Chemical Weapons* (Ithaca, NY: Cornell University Press, 2000), 16–46; and Barry R. Posen, *The Sources of Military Doctrine: France, Britain, and Germany Between the World Wars* (Ithaca, NY: Cornell University Press, 1984). Also see Elizabeth Kier, *Imagining War: French and British Doctrine Between the Wars* (Ithaca, NY: Cornell University Press, 1997); Richard K. Betts, *Soldiers, Statesmen, and Cold War Crises*, 2d ed. (New York: Columbia University Press, 1999); and Peter D. Feaver and Christopher Gelpi, *Choosing Your Battles: American Civil-Military Relations and the Use of Force* (Princeton, NJ: Princeton University Press, 2004).

2. See Kenneth N. Waltz, *Theory of International Relations* (New York: Random House, 1979), 127.

3. W. Richard Scott, *Organizations: Rational, Natural, and Open Systems*, 2d ed. (Englewood Cliffs, NJ: Prentice-Hall, 1987), 9, 301–302.

4. "The Cabinet Committee on Security Reviews Operationalization of India's Nuclear Doctrine," New Delhi: Cabinet Committee on Security, January 4, 2003, available at http://meaindia.nic.in/pressrelease/2003/01/04pr01.htm.

5. Alastair Iain Johnston, "Thinking About Strategic Culture," *International Security*, vol. 19, no. 4 (Spring 1995), 46. Also see the essays in Peter J. Katzenstein, ed., *The Culture of National Security: Norms and Identity in World Politics* (New York: Columbia University Press, 1996).

6. On Khomeini, see Scott D. Sagan, "Realist Perspectives on Weapons of Mass Destruction," in Sohail H. Hashmi and Steven P. Lee, eds., *Ethics and Weapons of Mass Destruction: Religious and Secular Perspectives* (New York: Cambridge University Press, 2004), 87; and Sohail H. Hashmi, "Islamic Ethics: An Argument for Nonproliferation," in ibid., 342–345. On Desai, see George Perkovich, *India's Nuclear Bomb* (Berkeley: University of California Press, 1999), 200–201.

7. See Stephen Peter Rosen, *Societies and Military Power: India and Her Armies* (Ithaca, NY: Cornell University Press, 1996); and Kanti P. Bajpai and Amitabh Mattoo, *Securing India: Strategic Thought and Practice* (New Delhi: Manohar Publishers, 1996).

8. Examples of this perspective on military organizations and other government bureaucracies include Dana P. Eyre and Mark C. Suchman, "Status, Norms, and the Proliferation of Conventional Weapons: An Institutional Approach," in Katzenstein, *Culture of National Security*, 79–113; and Martha Finnemore, *National Interests and International Society* (Ithaca, NY: Cornell University Press, 1996).

9. See Walter W. Powell and Paul J. DiMaggio, *The New Institutionalism in Organizational Analysis* (Chicago: University of Chicago Press, 1991); Carol Atkinson,

"Constructivist Implications of Material Power: Military Engagement and the Socialization of States, 1972–2000," *International Studies Quarterly*, vol. 50 (2006), 509–537; and Gili S. Drori, John Meyer, Francisco Ramirez, and Evan Schofer, *Science in the Modern World Polity: Institutionalization and Globalization* (Stanford, CA: Stanford University Press, 2003).

10. On the importance of "process tracing" in such conditions, see Alexander L. George and Andrew Bennett, *Case Studies and Theory Development in the Social Sciences* (Cambridge, MA: MIT Press, 2005).

11. See, for example, Phillip C. Bleek, "Nuclear Posture Review Leaks," *Arms Control Today*, April 2002, available at http://www.armscontrol.org/act/2002_04/npraprilo2.asp; and J. D. Crouch, "Special Briefing on the Nuclear Posture Review," January 22, 2002, available at http://www.defenselink.mil/transcripts/2002/t01092002_to109npr.html.

12. Federation of American Scientists, "Text of Prime Minister Muhammad Nawaz Sharif Statement at a Press Conference on Pakistan Nuclear Tests," May 29, 1998, available at http://www.fas.org/news/pakistan/1998/05/980528-gop-pm.htm.

13. Ibid.

14. Valuable assessments of Pakistani nuclear doctrine include Neil Joeck, "Maintaining Nuclear Stability in South Asia," International Institute for Strategic Studies, Adelphi Paper 312 (Oxford: Oxford University Press, 1997); Peter R. Lavoy, "Pakistan's Nuclear Doctrine," in Rafiq Dossani and Henry S. Rowen, *Prospects for Peace in South Asia* (Stanford, CA: Stanford University Press, 2005), 280–300; Zafar Iqbal Cheema, "Pakistan's Nuclear Use Doctrine and Command and Control," in Lavoy, Sagan, and Wirtz, *Planning the Unthinkable*, 158–181; Rifaat Hussain, "Nuclear Doctrines in South Asia," SASSU Research Report No. 4 (London: South Asian Strategic Stability Unit, 2005); and Zafar Iqbal Cheema, "The Role of Nuclear Weapons in Pakistan's Defense Strategy," *IPRI Journal*, vol. 4, no. 2 (Summer 2004), 59–80.

15. The most authoritative unofficial statements of Pakistani strategic thinking and nuclear weapons prior to 2001 are from Agha Shahi, Zulfikar Ali Khan, and Abdul Sattar, "Securing Nuclear Peace," *News International*, October 5, 1999.

16. See Agha Shahi, "Command and Control of Nuclear Weapons in South Asia," *Strategic Issues* (March 2000), 56. Originally cited in Hussain, "Nuclear Doctrines in South Asia," 12. Also see Michael Ryan Kraig, "The Political and Strategic Imperatives of Nuclear Deterrence in South Asia," *India Review*, vol. 2, no. 1 (January 2003), 37.

17. For alternative arguments, see M. A. Durrani, "Pakistan's Strategic Thinking and the Role of Nuclear Weapons," CMC Occasional Paper (Albuquerque, NM: Sandia National Laboratory, 2004), 31; and Hussain, "Nuclear Doctrines in South Asia."

18. Shireen Mazari, "Kashmir: Looking for Viable Options," *Defence Journal*, vol. 3, no. 2 (February–March 1999), available at http://defencejournal.com/feb-mar99/kashmir-viable.htm.

19. See Lavoy, "Pakistan's Nuclear Doctrine," 288; and Stephen Philip Cohen, *The Pakistan Army* (Berkeley: University of California Press, 1984), 153 (originally cited by Lavoy, ibid.). Also see the excellent analyses in Michael Krepon, "The Stability-Instability Paradox, Misperception, and Escalation-Control in South Asia," in Rafiq Dossani and Henry S. Rowen, *Prospects for Peace in South Asia* (Stanford, CA: Stanford University Press, 2005), 261–279; Sumit Ganguly, "Indo-Pakistani Nuclear Issues and the Stability/Instability Paradox," *Studies in Conflict and Terrorism*, vol. 18, no. 4 (1995), 325–334; and V. R. Raghavan, "Limited War and Nuclear Escalation in South Asia," *Nonproliferation Review*, vol. 8, no. 3 (Fall–Winter 2001), 1–18.

20. See Chapter 5 in this volume.

21. "Pak Defence Strong, Says Army Chief," *Independent*, April 19, 1999, available at LexisNexis *Academic*, http://web.lexis-nexis.com/universe. Also see "Pakistani Leader Outlines Policies at First News Conference," *BBC Monitoring: South Asia— Political*, January 11, 1999, available at LexisNexis *Academic*, http://web.lexis-nexis .com/universe.

22. See "Musharraf's Views Before the Coup: A Collation," *South Asia Analysis Group*, available at http://www.southasiaanalysis.org/%5Cpapers%5Cpaper92.html.

23. General Jamshed Gulzar Kiyani, who served as deputy director of the ISI during the Kargil conflict, later acknowledged that Prime Minister Nawaz Sharif was not fully briefed on the military plans before the operation began. See Praveen Swami, "Pakistan Revisits the Kargil War," *Hindu*, June 21, 2008, available at http://www .hindu.com/2008/06/21/stories/2008062154951000.htm.

24. See Kaiser Tufail, "Kargil Conflict and the Pakistan Air Force," Aeronaut Blog, January 28, 2009, available at http://kaiser-aeronaut.blogspot.com/2009_01_01_ archive.html.

25. Owen Bennett Jones, *Pakistan: Eye of the Storm* (New Haven, CT: Yale University Press, 2002), 102–103.

26. Ihtashamul Haque, "Peace Linked to Kashmir Solution," *Dawn Wire Service*, June 26, 1999.

27. Pervez Musharraf, *In the Line of Fire: A Memoir* (New York: Free Press, 2006), 96.

28. Pamela Constable, "Pakistan Aims to 'Avoid Nuclear War,'" *Washington Post*, July 13, 1999; "U.S. Involvement Essential: PM," *Dawn Wire Service*, July 10, 1999.

29. Adrian Levy and Catherine Scott-Clark, *Deception: Pakistan, the United States, and the Secret Trade in Nuclear Weapons* (New York: Walker, 2007), 288.

30. Musharraf, *In the Line of Fire*, 98.

31. Raj Chengappa, "Pakistan Threatened India with Nuclear Attack During Kargil War: Army Chief," *News Today*, January 12, 2001. Quoted in Tellis, Fair, and Medby, *Limited Conflicts Under the Nuclear Umbrella: India and Pakistani Lessons from the Kargil Crisis* (Santa Monica, CA: RAND, 2001), 56.

32. "Any Weapon Will Be Used, Threatens Pak," *Hindu*, June 1, 1999.

33. Strobe Talbott, "The Day a Nuclear Conflict Was Averted," *Yale Global Online*, September 13, 2004, available at http://yaleglobal.yale.edu/display.article?id=4506.

34. V. P. Malik, *Kargil: From Surprise to Victory* (New Delhi: HarperCollins, 2006), 259–260.

35. In addition, it is possible, as Feroz Hassan Khan argues, that there was no such missile-alert activity at all. See Khan, "Nuclear Signalling, Missiles, and Escalation Control in South Asia," in Michael Krepon, Rodney W. Jones, and Ziad Haider, eds., *Escalation Control and the Nuclear Option in South Asia* (Washington, DC: The Stimson Center, 2004), 86.

36. Neil Joeck, "The Kargil War and Nuclear Deterrence," in Šumit Ganguly and S. Paul Kapur, eds., *Nuclear Proliferation in South Asia: Crisis Behavior and the Bomb* (London: Routledge, 2008), 117–143.

37. *Nuclear Safety, Nuclear Stability and Nuclear Strategy in Pakistan: A Concise Report of a Visit by Landau Network—Centro Volta*, available at http://www.pugwash.org/september11/pakistan-nuclear.htm.

38. Ibid.

39. See the discussion in Michael Krepon, "Limited War, Escalation Control, and the Nuclear Option in South Asia," in Krepon, Jones, and Haider, *Escalation Control*, 156.

40. Stephen Philip Cohen, *The Idea of Pakistan* (Washington, DC: Brookings Institution, 2004), 103.

41. Stephen Philip Cohen, *The Pakistan Army* (Karachi: Oxford University Press, 1998), 177–178.

42. See Scott D. Sagan, *Moving Targets: Nuclear Strategy and National Security* (Princeton, NJ: Princeton University Press, 1989).

43. "Pakistan May Consider Nuclear Options: Minister," *Press Trust of India*, May 22, 2002. As quoted in Rahul Roy-Chaudhury, "Nuclear Doctrine, Declaratory Policy, and Escalation Control," in Krepon, Jones, and Haider, *Escalation Control*, 109.

44. For a detailed discussion of these claims, see Lavoy, " Pakistan's Nuclear Doctrine," 285–287.

45. President Pervez Musharraf, "Address to People of Pakistan," *Presidential Speeches*, September 19, 2001, available at http://web.archive.org/web/20080109040132/http://www.americanrhetoric.com/speeches/pakistanpresident.htm.

46. Ibid.

47. "Nobody Asking Me to Roll Back Nuclear Programme, Compromise on Kashmir Says President Musharraf," Press Releases, December 29, 2003, at President Musharraf's official website, http://www.presidentofpakistan.gov.pk/PRPressReleaseDetail.aspx?nPRPressReleaseId=615&nYear=2003&nMonth=12 (no longer available).

48. "Pakistan President Holds Televised News Conference 5 February," *BBC Mon-*

itoring South Asia, February 9, 2004, available at LexisNexis *Academic*, http://web.lexis
-nexis.com/universe.

49. Cohen, *Idea of Pakistan*, 118–119.

50. Feroz Hassan Khan, "Comparative Strategic Culture: The Case of Pakistan,"
Strategic Insights, vol. 4, no. 10 (October 2005), 4–5.

51. "Musharraf: Pakistan to 'Unleash a Storm' If Indian Forces Cross Line of Control," *News* (Islamabad), May 30, 2002.

52. "Pakistan Successfully Surmounts Internal and External Threats—Musharraf," *Pakistan News Wire*, December 30, 2002, available at LexisNexis *Academic*, http://
web.lexis-nexis.com/universe.

53. See V. R. Raghavan, "Limited War and Nuclear Escalation in South Asia,"
Nonproliferation Review (Fall–Winter 2001), 91; and Michael P. Fischerkeller, "David
Versus Goliath: Cultural Judgments in Asymmetric Wars," *Security Studies*, vol. 7
(Summer 1998), 36.

54. Atlaf Gauhar, *Ayub Khan: Pakistan's First Military Ruler* (Oxford: Oxford University Press, 1996), 216.

55. Richard Sisson and Leo E. Rose, *War and Secession: Pakistan, India, and the
Creation of Bangladesh* (Berkeley: University of California Press, 1990), 223–224.

56. Ibid., 230.

57. A most thorough analysis is in Rahul Roy-Chaudhury, "Nuclear Doctrine,"
101–118.

58. Celia W. Dugger, "Indian General Talks Bluntly of War and a Nuclear Threat,"
New York Times, January 11, 2002.

59. "Army Chief Warns Pak Against N-Strike," Tribune News Service, January 11,
2002, available at http://www.tribuneindia.com/2002/20020112/main1.htm.

60. Ibid.

61. See Rahul Bedi, "India Gives Musharraf Nuclear War Warning," *Daily Telegraph* (London), January 12, 2002.

62. Dugger, "Indian General Talks Bluntly."

63. "Uncalled for Concerns: Fernandes," *Hindu*, January 12, 2002.

64. "Im Notfall auch die Atombombe," *Der Spiegel*, April 7, 2002, 166–170. We
thank Jessica Weeks for this translation.

65. "Benazir's Remarks on Nuclear Weapons Strongly Refuted," *Pakistani Press
International*, April 10, 2002, available at LexisNexis *Academic*, http://web.lexis-nexis
.com/universe.

66. "Musharraf: Pakistan to 'Unleash a Storm' If Indian Forces Cross Line of
Control."

67. "Musharraf Says Pakistan Was Ready to Use Nuclear Weapons," *Japan Economic Newswire*, December 30, 2002, available at LexisNexis *Academic*, http://web
.lexis-nexis.com/universe.

68. "Musharraf Says Message of Unconventional Warfare Conveyed to Vajpayee Stopped War."

69. "Warning Forced India to Pull Back Troops, Says President," *Dawn*, December 31, 2002, as cited in Roy-Chaudhury, "Nuclear Doctrine," 113.

70. B. Muralidhar Reddy, "Musharraf Had Warned of N-War," *Hindu*, December 31, 2002, available at LexisNexis *Academic*, available at http://web.lexis-nexis.com/universe.

71. "Pakistan: Spokesman Elaborates Musharraf Statement," *News* (Islamabad), December 31, 2002, in FBIS-NES-2002-1231.

72. "Indian Defence Minister Warns Pakistan Against Nuclear Rhetoric," *Agence France Presse—English*, January 7, 2003, available at LexisNexis *Academic*, http://web .lexis-nexis.com/universe.

73. Pakistani government press release, "President Musharraf Clarifies Reports Misquoting Him on Nuclear Threat," January 3, 2003, available at http://www.presi dentofpakistan.gov.pk/PRPressReleaseDetail.aspx?nPRPressReleaseId=485&nYear= 2003&nMonth=1.

74. As quoted in M. V. Ramana and Zia Mian, "The Nuclear Confrontation in South Asia," in *SIPRI Yearbook 2003, Disarmament and International Security* (London: Oxford University Press, SPRI, 2003), 208.

75. Shri Atal Bihari Vajpayee, "Suo Motu Statement in Parliament," May 27, 1998, available at http://www.indianembassy.org/pic/pm-parliament.htm.

76. Vajpayee statement to Parliament, December 15, 1998, available at http://www .indianembassy.org/special/cabinet/Primeminister/pm(india-us).htm.

77. For example, see the interview with Foreign Minister Jaswant Singh, "India Not to Engage in Nuclear Arms Race," *Hindu*, November 29, 1999, available at LexisNexis *Academic*, http://web.lexis-nexis.com/universe.

78. "India Committed to Minimum N-Deterrence," *Hindu*, Asia Intelligence Wire, December 7, 1998, available at LexisNexis *Academic*, http://web.lexis-nexis.com/universe.

79. Ashley Tellis, *India's Emerging Nuclear Doctrine: Exemplifying the Lessons of the Nuclear Revolution* (Seattle, WA: National Bureau of Asian Research, 2001), 61, 25. Also see his book-length study, *India's Emerging Nuclear Posture: Between Recessed Deterrent and Ready Arsenal* (Santa Monica, CA: RAND, 2001).

80. Tellis, *India's Emerging Nuclear Doctrine*, 27 (emphasis added), 105 (emphasis added).

81. Šumit Ganguly and Devin T. Hagerty, *Fearful Symmetry: India-Pakistan Crisis in the Shadow of Nuclear Weapons* (Seattle: University of Washington Press, 2005), 196. They maintain, however, that "in the unlikely event that India were to be the victim of a massive conventional assault by China or Pakistan, there can be little doubt that New Delhi's no-first-use pledge would go by the boards." Ibid., 197.

82. Bharat Kanard, *Nuclear Weapons and Indian Security: The Realist Foundations of Strategy* (Delhi: Macmillan India, 2002), 440–441.

83. For alternative views on Indian doctrinal debates, see Harsh V. Pant, "India's Nuclear Doctrine and Command Structure: Implications for India and the World," *Comparative Strategy*, vol. 24, no. 3 (2005), 277–293; Kanti Bajpai, "No First Use in the India-Pakistan Context," from Pugwash Meeting No. 279, "No First Use of Nuclear Weapons," London, November 15–17, 2002, available at http://www.pugwash.org/reports/nw/bajpai .htm#anchor10; and Ramana and Mian, "Nuclear Confrontation in South Asia," 201.

84. Available at Ministry of External Affairs, India, website, http://meaindia.nic .in/pressrelease/2003/01/04pro1.htm.

85. "No Change in 'No First Use of Nuclear Weapons,'" *Press Trust of India*, February 7, 2003, available at LexisNexis *Academic*, http://web.lexis-nexis.com/universe.

86. Useful analyses of minimum deterrence include George H. Quester, "The Continuing Debate on Minimum Deterrence," in T. V. Paul, Richard J. Harknett, and James J. Wirtz, eds., *The Absolute Weapons Revisited* (Ann Arbor: University of Michigan Press, 1998), 167–188; and Rajesh M. Brasrur, *Minimum Deterrence and India's Nuclear Security* (Stanford, CA: Stanford University Press, 2006).

87. See Jasjit Singh, "Prospects for Nuclear Proliferation," in S. Sur, ed., *Nuclear Deterrence: Problems and Prospects for the 1990s* (New York: UNIDR, 1993), 66; and George Perkovich, "A Nuclear Third Way in South Asia," *Foreign Policy*, no. 91 (Summer 1993), 85–104. Also see George Perkovich, *India's Nuclear Bomb* (Berkeley: University of California Press, 1999), 274–275.

88. Harbaksh Singh Nanda and Anwar Iqbal, "India Rejects Pakistan's Offer to Cut Nukes," *United Press International*, May 8, 2003, available at LexisNexis *Academic*, http://web.lexis-nexis.com/universe.

89. "We Share Concern of Nuclear Scientists, Says Vajpayee," *Hindu*, Global News Wire—Asia Africa Intelligence Wire, July 22, 2005, available at LexisNexis *Academic*, http://web.lexis-nexis.com/universe.

90. "Draft Report of the National Security Advisory Board on Indian Nuclear Doctrine," Government of India, New Delhi, August 17, 1999, http://www.indian embassy.org/policy/CTBT/nuclear_doctrine_aug_17_1999.html (emphasis added) (no longer available).

91. See George Bunn and Roland M. Timerbaev, "Security Assurances to Non-Nuclear-Weapon States," *Nonproliferation Review*, vol. 1, no. 1 (Fall 1993), 13.

92. Jaswant Singh, *A Call to Honour: In Service of Emergent India* (New Delhi: Rupa, 2006), 116.

93. K. Subrahmanyam, "Nuclear Tests: What Next?" *IIC Quarterly* (Summer–Monsoon 1998), 57, as quoted in Tellis, *India's Emerging Nuclear Doctrine*, 52.

94. Jasjit Singh, "Indian Draft Nuclear Doctrine: Some Reflections," September 1999, available at http://www.pugwash.org/reports/nw/nw7.htm (emphasis in original).

95. For a critical analysis of U.S. "calculated ambiguity" in nuclear threats and chemical and biological weapons, see Scott D. Sagan, "The Commitment Trap: Why the United States Should Not Use Nuclear Threats to Deter Biological and Chemical Weapons Attacks," *International Security*, vol. 24, no. 4 (Spring 2000), 85–115.

96. Although the *National Security Review* was not released to the public, the Indian press stated that "[t]he last security board—its report was sent to national security advisor Brajesh Mishra on December 20—has recommended not only that India should do away with the no-first-strike commitment but also resume testing nuclear devices if the US resumes its own nuclear tests." See Sujan Dutta, "Rethink on No-First-Use Doctrine," *Telegraph*, January 14, 2003, available at http://www.telegraph india.com/1030114/asp/nation/story_1571767.asp.

97. Praful Bidwai, "Nuclear South Asia: Still on the Edge," *Frontline Magazine*, vol. 20, no. 2 (2003), available at http://www.flonnet.com/fl2002/stories/20030131007211600 .htm.

98. Elizabeth Roche, "India Evaluating, Fine-Tuning Nuclear Doctrine, Experts Say," *Hong Kong Agence France Press*, January 14, 2003, available at http://toolkit.dia log.com/intranet/cgi/present?STYLE=739318018&PRESENT=DB=985,AN=165050958 ,FM=9,SEARCH=MD.GenericSearch.

99. Ganguly and Hagerty, *Fearful Symmetry*, 197.

100. Soumyajit Pattnaik, "India's 'Four-Fold' Nuclear Strategy Noted," *Pioneer*, May 13, 1998, FBIS-TAC-98-133.

101. Mohammed Ahmedullah, "Indian Air Force Advocates 'First Strike Capability,'" *Defense Week*, January 2, 2001.

102. Ibid.

103. Subhash Kapila, "India's New 'Cold Start' War Doctrine Strategically Reviewed," *South Asia Analysis Group Paper No. 991*, April 5, 2004, http://www.saag.org/ papers10/paper991.html (no longer available).

104. "India's Fernandes—'Enough Reasons' to Launch Pre-emptive Strikes on Pakistan," *AFX News Limited*, April 11, 2003, available at LexisNexis *Academic*, http:// web.lexis-nexis.com/universe.

105. "George Tones Down Pre-emptive War Rhetoric," *The Economic Times of India*, Global Newswire, April 15, 2004, available at LexisNexis *Academic*, http://web .lexis-nexis.com/universe.

106. Jennifer Loven, "Bush: 'All Options on the Table' with Iran," *Associated Press Online*, April 19, 2006; Seymour Hersh, "The Iran Plans: Would President Bush Go to War to Stop Tehran from Getting the Bomb?" *New Yorker*, April 17, 2006, 30.

107. P. K. Iyengar, "India Must Test N-Bomb Before Signing CTBT," *Hindu*, May 2, 2000, originally cited in Tellis, *India's Emerging Nuclear Doctrine*, 294n108.

108. Ibid.

109. For examples, see S. Raghotham, "The Case for Nuclear Testing," *Rediff India Abroad*, May 15, 2007, available at http://www.rediff.com/news/2007/may/15guest .htm; and A. Gopalakrishnan, "Amend US Law, or Reject Nuclear Deal," *Rediff India Abroad*, May 14, 2007, available at http://www.rediff.com/news/2007/may/14guest .htm?zcc=rl.

110. Raja Menon, "Nuclear Doctrine in South Asia," in P. R. Chari, Sonika Gupta, and Arpit Rajain, eds., *Nuclear Stability in Southern Asia* (New Delhi: Manohar, 2003), 108.

111. Sujan Dutta, "Rethink on No-First-Use Doctrine."

112. Matthew Rosenberg and Zahid Hussain, "Pakistan's Leader Stirs Fresh Turmoil," *Wall Street Journal*, February 6, 2009, available at http://online.wsj.com/article/ SB123561113179577559.html.

113. See C. Raja Mohan, *Crossing the Rubicon: The Shaping of India's New Foreign Policy* (New York: Palgrave, 2004).

114. Jaswant Singh, *Defending India* (London: Macmillan Press, 1999), 330.

CONTRIBUTORS

ITTY ABRAHAM is Marlene and Morton Meyerson Centennial Chair and associate professor of government and Asian studies at the University of Texas at Austin. His most recent publication is an edited volume of essays, *South Asian Cultures of the Bomb: Atomic Publics and the State in India and Pakistan* (Indiana University Press, 2008).

KANTI BAJPAI is currently teaching international relations and the politics of contemporary India at Oxford University. He was headmaster of the Doon School, India, and professor of international politics at Jawaharlal Nehru University, New Delhi. He has also taught at the Maharaja Sayajirao University of Baroda, Vadodara, India, and has held visiting positions at Wesleyan University, the University of Illinois, the Rajiv Gandhi Foundation, the University of Notre Dame, the Brookings Institution, and the Australian Defence Force Academy. His research interests are security studies, India's foreign policy and national security, and South Asia.

S. PAUL KAPUR is associate professor in the Department of National Security Affairs at the Naval Postgraduate School. Previously, he was on the faculties of the Naval War College and Claremont McKenna College and was a visiting professor at Stanford University's Center for International Security and Cooperation. He also served as a postdoctoral fellow at the University of Chicago, where he received his Ph.D. in political science. His research and teaching interests include nuclear weapons proliferation, deterrence, ethno-religious violence, and the international security environment in South Asia. Kapur is author of *Dangerous Deterrent: Nuclear Weapons Proliferation and Conflict* *in South Asia* (Stanford University Press, 2007). His work has also appeared in journals, such as *International Security, Security Studies, Asian Survey, and Asian Security,* and in several edited volumes.

VIPIN NARANG is a Ph.D. candidate in the Department of Government, Harvard University, focusing on nuclear proliferation in regional powers. He holds a B.S. and M.S. in chemical engineering from Stanford University and an M.Phil. with Distinction in international relations from Balliol College, Oxford University, where he studied on a Marshall Scholarship. Starting in the fall of 2010, he will be an assistant professor in the Department of Political Science at the Massachusetts Institute of Technology.

SCOTT D. SAGAN is a professor of political science at Stanford University and co-director of Stanford's Center for International Security and Cooperation. Sagan has authored a number of books on nuclear weapons and international security, including *Moving Targets: Nuclear Strategy and National Security* (Princeton University Press, 1989) and *The Limits of Safety: Organizations, Accidents, and Nuclear Weapons* (Princeton University Press, 1993), winner of the American Political Science Association's award for Best Book in Science, Technology, and Environmental Studies. He also co-authored *The Spread of Nuclear Weapons: A Debate Renewed* (W. W. Norton, 2002) with Kenneth N. Waltz.

KARTHIKA SASIKUMAR is an Assistant Professor in the Political Science Department at San Jose State University. She has been a Postdoctoral Fellow at the University of British Columbia's Liu Institute for Global Issues, an Associate in the International Security Program at Harvard University's Kennedy School of Government, and a Predoctoral Fellow at the Center for International Security and Cooperation, Stanford University. She completed her M.Phil. at Jawaharlal Nehru University, New Delhi and her Ph.D. at Cornell University. Her research interests are in international relations theory, international regimes in the areas of nuclear weapons and terrorism, and South Asia.

CHRISTOPHER WAY is an associate professor of government at Cornell University. His research and teaching interests include international/comparative political economy, international relations, and nuclear proliferation. Way's current research focuses on the proliferation of weapons of mass destruction and the effectiveness of the nonproliferation regime, topics on which he has published several journal articles and book chapters. He is currently working on a manuscript co-authored with Karthika Sasikumar, "Leaders and Laggards: When and Why Do Countries Sign the NPT?"

INDEX

Abbas, Azhar, 21*n*22
Abdul Kalam, A. P. J., 63*n*43
Abizaid, John, 17
Abraham, Itty, 76
Advani, Lal Kishan, 40, 43, 45, 46, 53, 54, 58, 65*n*73
Afghanistan: Indian Airlines flight hijacked to Kandahar, 47, 48; relations with Pakistan, 83, 190, 237; Soviet intervention in, 49, 95; Taliban regime, 237
agency-structure debate, 59*n*2
Agra summit, 47, 48
Ahmad, Shamshad, 139, 232, 233
Ahmadinejad, Mahmoud, 17–18
Ahmed, Samina, 139
Akash surface-to-air missile, 156, 172
All Parties Hurriyat Conference, 200
AMELIA interpolation software, 102*n*32
anti-ballistic missile defense, 165
Anwar, Tariq, 51
Argentina, 29, 106
Aten, Bettina: *Penn World Table Version 6.1*, 77, 100*n*17
Ayodhya: Ram temple in, 36, 45, 46, 65*nn*73,74
Ayub Khan, Muhammad, 239
Azad, Kirti, 55
Aziz, Sartaj, 155

Babur cruise missile, 173, 179*n*51
Bahujan Samaj Party (BSP), 51
Bajpai, Kanti, 62*n*26
Bajrang Dal, 40, 44
ballistic missiles: circular error probability (CEP) for, 146, 147–48, 177*n*39, 179*n*54; guidance systems for, 147, 148, 162; intermediate-range ballistic missiles (IRBMs), 145, 146, 148; medium-range ballistic missiles (MRBMs), 145, 146, 148; sea-launched ballistic missiles (SLBMs), 145–46, 147, 160, 164. *See also* ballistic missiles, Chinese; ballistic missiles, Indian; ballistic missiles, North Korean; ballistic missiles, Pakistani; ballistic missiles, testing of
ballistic missiles, Chinese, 10, 148, 150, 159, 179*n*58
ballistic missiles, Indian: Agni family, 145, 147, 148, 149, 153, 156, 158, 160, 161, 162–65, 170, 171, 172, 173, 174; Prithvi family, 145–46, 147–48, 149, 153, 158, 160, 162, 163, 164, 170, 171, 172, 173, 174, 177*n*39, 178*nn*40,42, 180*n*66
ballistic missiles, North Korean, 148; No-Dong missiles, 149, 153

India (*continued*)
Industrial Policy Resolution of 1948,
121; vs. Iran, 17–18, 77; Islamabad,
146; military expenditures in, 177n34,
211n50; military leadership in, 13,
76, 220, 221, 225, 226, 240–41, 243,
250, 252, 254; minimum credible
deterrence doctrine in, 12, 13, 219–20,
244, 245, 246–47, 251–53, 254; National
Security Advisory Board (NSAB),
247, 249–50, 253, 262n96; national
strategic culture in, 224, 225, 248;
no-first-use policy of, 13, 16, 220, 221,
223, 225, 244, 245, 246, 247–50, 252,
254, 260n81, 262n96; and NPT, 33,
106, 125, 156–57, 247, 248; Nuclear
Command Authority, 246; nuclear
scientists in, 29, 30–31, 40, 41, 60n5,
63n43, 92, 110, 126, 129n17, 131n60, 141,
252, 254; oppositional nationalism
in, 10, 16–17, 138, 142–43, 144, 158, 159,
160, 161, 163–64, 165–66, 167; Other
Backward Classes (OBCs) in, 46;
vs. other nuclear proliferators, 68,
100n11; policies regarding acquisition
of nuclear weapons, 3, 4–6, 7, 8–9,
19, 27, 28, 35–37, 38–46, 41, 43–44, 57,
58, 59n4, 61n11, 63nn43,45, 64n58,
75–76, 77, 81–82, 83–97, 99n11, 118,
119–28, 131n60, 137, 138, 139, 140–45,
158, 163, 176n30, 212n58, 244; policies
regarding ballistic missile tests,
9–10, 58, 137, 138, 145–48, 150–51, 153,
156–67, 168–74, 180n66, 181nn91,93;
policies regarding future nuclear
testing, 252, 253, 262n96; policies
regarding Kashmir, 44, 47, 48, 57–58,
153, 155, 156, 158, 162, 163, 198–200,
201–3, 209nn31,39, 213n60; policies
regarding use of nuclear weapons,
11, 12, 13, 16, 220, 221, 223, 225–27,
244, 245–51, 252, 254, 260n81, 262n96;
policy of compellence, 198–99;
population of, 77, 78; predictions
regarding, 4, 5–6, 9, 11–12, 14–15, 16–17,
57–59, 138, 167, 168–70, 252; public
statements in, 12, 13, 25, 28, 32–33, 39,

62n29, 69, 110–11, 117, 125, 130n40, 151,
152, 157, 160, 161–62, 164–66, 226–27,
240–41, 242–50, 251–53, 254, 262n96;
relations with China, 5, 6, 10, 28, 31,
32, 33–35, 49, 60n5, 61nn.24,25,27, 74,
78, 83, 84–85, 102n39, 103nn44,47,
105n65, 140, 142, 143, 150, 157, 158, 159,
160, 162, 163, 165, 168, 169, 170–73,
174, 190, 219, 223, 244, 253, 260n81;
relations with France, 58, 110, 252;
relations with Israel, 152, 153, 155–56,
172; relations with Pakistan and
stability/instability paradox, 184–87,
189–90, 191–94, 200–201, 204nn5,7,
205n8, 210n39, 212n56, 229; relations
with Pakistan as enduring rivalry, 31,
73, 74, 79, 80, 83–85, 91, 93, 102nn38,39,
103nn44–46, 105n65; relations with
Russia, 58, 252; relations with Soviet
Union, 27, 31, 49, 95, 103n48; relations
with United States, 5, 11, 13, 29, 31, 32,
33, 43, 48, 59, 62n34, 94–95, 122–23,
131n60, 162, 163, 166, 168, 169, 170,
176n30, 199, 213n64, 240, 241, 252; size
of nuclear arsenal, 246–47, 251–53,
254; Strategic Forces Command, 224;
terrorist attacks on, 4, 5, 12–13, 47, 48,
56, 163, 171, 198–99, 212n54, 216n85,
217n93, 221; uniform civil code issue,
45; uranium resources in, 103n43;
urbanization in, 78; Uttar Pradesh, 51;
West Bengal, 51, 54. *See also* ballistic
missiles, testing of; Bharatiya Janata
Party (BJP); Congress Party; crisis of
2001–2002; domestic politics; Indian
nuclear test in 1974; Indian nuclear
weapons tests in 1998; Kargil War of
1999; Kashmir; prestige motives
India-China crisis of 1986–87, 62n24
Indian airlines flight hijacking, 47, 48
Indian Express, 180n68
Indian nuclear test in 1974, 30, 63n38,
100n11, 124–27, 166, 174n2; as peaceful
nuclear explosion (PNE), 8–9, 25, 106,
117, 126–27, 166, 175, 176n19; vs. tests in
1998, 8–9, 25, 40–41, 43, 46–47, 81, 108,
117, 120, 125–26, 127–28, 139, 176n19

military, 3, 12, 13, 15, 224, 226, 230–32,
253–54, 257*n*23; biases and interests
of Indian military, 220, 226; biases
and interests of Pakistani military, 3,
4, 193–94, 220–21, 224, 226, 234–40,
253–54; goal displacement in, 223,
237–38; Indian military leadership,
13, 76, 220, 221, 225, 226, 240–41, 243,
250, 252, 254; organizational learning
in, 222–23, 225, 235–36, 240; Pakistani
military leadership, 3, 10, 11, 12, 15–16,
21*n*22, 92, 139, 193–94, 197, 202, 203,
214*n*65, 220–21, 224, 226, 229–32,
234–43, 253–54, 257*n*23
Mishra, Brajesh, 5, 38, 40, 41–42, 45, 55,
64*n*58, 141, 262*n*96
Mishra, Dina Nath, 62*n*29
Mitra, Chandan, 55
modernity, 27, 75, 116, 130*n*36
moral hazard, 95
Mubarakmand, Samar, 180*n*70
Mukhatzhanova, Gaukar, 14
Mukherjee, Pranab, 165
Musharraf, Pervez: and Agra summit,
48; on conventional war, 15, 229–30;
during crisis of 2001–2002, 199,
241–43; on doctrine of offensive
defense, 192; on Kargil War, 191,
202, 231, 232; on nuclear deterrence,
229–30, 236, 241–43; on nuclear
weapons as strategic assets, 237–38;
on Pakistani military virtues, 239;
policies regarding ballistic missile
testing, 150, 153, 154, 155–56, 171,
180*nn*66,70; on security for Pakistani
nuclear weapons, 16

Naidu, Chandrababu, 58
Nation, 180*n*68
National Democratic Alliance (NDA),
25–26, 36, 39, 40–41, 48, 52, 58, 67*n*100;
size of, 59*n*1
National Front, 48, 49
nationalism, 27, 37–38, 46, 51, 77. *See also*
Bharatiya Janata Party; oppositional
nationalism
national security interests: alliances

with NWS, 73, 75, 77, 78, 79, 80, 85,
86, 93, 95; enduring rivalries, 31, 73,
74, 79, 80, 83–85, 91, 93, 102*nn*38,39,
103*nn*44–46, 105*n*65; India vs.
Pakistan regarding, 68–70, 83–85,
93, 94–95; influence on nuclear
proliferation policies, 1, 2, 3, 5, 6, 13–
14, 16–17, 26–27, 39, 46, 68–70, 72–73,
74, 75, 77, 79, 80, 83–86, 91, 93, 94–95,
101*n*21, 102*nn*38,39, 103*nn*44–47, 116,
139–40, 143, 144, 147, 168, 169–74,
244; influence on testing of ballistic
missiles, 10, 147, 151–52, 152–57, 159,
160, 161, 162–63, 168, 169–70, 181*n*91,
182*n*95; integration into international
system, 73, 75, 77, 78, 80, 81, 101*n*27,
103*n*42; and MIDs, 73, 74–75, 79;
realist views regarding, 1, 2, 3, 6, 26,
85–86, 116, 140, 143–44, 151–52, 154–55,
156, 176*n*31, 177*n*36, 181*n*91, 219–20,
222–23, 253, 254; relationship to
nuclear doctrine, 222–23
national strategic culture, 224–25, 226,
235–36, 238–39, 238–40, 253
Nayar, Baldev Raj, 98*n*2
NDA. *See* National Democratic Alliance
Nehru, Jawaharlal: attitudes toward
nuclear weapons, 37, 63*n*38; China
and Soviet policy, 49; on Indian
nuclear program, 110–11, 115, 121, 124;
on Indian self-reliance, 110–11, 121,
138, 161, 165, 167
Netherlands, 110
neutron bombs, 252
Niazi, A. A. K., 240
Nitze, Paul, 11
Nixon, Richard, 106
nonproliferation regime: economic
sanctions, 5, 37, 41, 62*n*34, 65*n*72,
96–97, 105*n*71, 106, 123, 125, 139;
nonproliferation as discourse of
control, 7–8, 108–9, 123–28, 128*nn*5,7;
selective enforcement practices of, 69;
technology controls, 96–97, 105*n*68,
108; tightening in 1990s, 86. *See also*
Comprehensive Test Ban Treaty;
Nuclear Non-Proliferation Treaty